THE CONCEPT OF HERESY IN THE MIDDLE AGES

(11th-13th C.)

KATHOLIEKE UNIVERSITEIT LEUVEN
INSTITUUT VOOR MIDDELEEUWSE STUDIES
LEUVEN / LOUVAIN (BELGIUM)

THE CONCEPT OF HERESY
IN THE MIDDLE AGES

(11th-13th C.)

PROCEEDINGS OF

THE INTERNATIONAL CONFERENCE

LOUVAIN MAY 13-16, 1973

EDITED BY

Prof. Dr. W. LOURDAUX and Prof. Dr. D. VERHELST

Members of the Institute of Medieval Studies

LEUVEN
UNIVERSITY PRESS

THE HAGUE
MARTINUS NIJHOFF

1976

ISBN 90 6186 043 1

© 1976 by Leuven University Press/Presses Universitaires de Louvain/
Universitaire Pers Leuven, Krakenstraat 3
B-3000 Leuven / Louvain (Belgium)

D 1976/1869/5

CONTENTS

Preface VII

MOORE R. I., Heresy as Disease 1

LECLERCQ Jean, L'hérésie d'après les écrits de S. Bernard de Clairvaux 12

CLASSEN Peter, Der Häresie-Begriff bei Gerhoch von Reichersberg und in seinem Umkreis 27

HAGENEDER Othmar, Der Häresiebegriff bei den Juristen des 12. und 13. Jahrhunderts 42

WALTHER Helmut G., Häresie und päpstliche Politik : Ketzerbegriff und Ketzergesetzgebung in der Übergangsphase von der De-kretistik zur Dekretalistik 104

ANGELOV Dimiter, Ursprung und Wesen des Bogomilentums . . 144

TRAWKOWSKI Stanisław, Entre l'orthodoxie et l'hérésie : *Vita apostolica* et le problème de la désobéissance 157

CRACCO Giorgio, Pataria : *opus* e *nomen* (tra verità e autorità) . 167

VERBEKE Gerard, Philosophy and Heresy : Some Conflicts be-tween Reason and Faith 172

DUVERNOY Jean, L'acception : 'haereticus' (*iretge*) = 'parfait cathare' en Languedoc au XIIIe siècle 198

D'ALATRI Mariano, 'Eresie' perseguite dall'inquisizione in Italia nel corso del duecento 211

Index nominum propriorum 225

PREFACE

This fourth volume in our series of *Studia*, which focuses on the concept of heresy in the Middle Ages, is the issue of the fourth International Conference held by the Institute of Medieval Studies at Louvain from May 13th to 16th, 1973. Its main purpose is to bring about a better understanding of medieval heresy, which is a very important phenomenon not only in the development of Christianity but also in the social, political and intellectual evolution of Europe during the Middle Ages.

It was not our intention to confine our topic to theological or philosophical reflections on the notion of heresy. Insofar as medieval theologians and philosophers deal formally and explicitly with the concept of heresy, their investigations quite obviously relate to the matter at hand. But the subject to be scrutinized is much broader, for it includes all the aspects and features of the phenomenon as it manifested itself in the framework of medieval society. It is possible to draw valuable conclusions with regard to the concept of heresy on the basis of an analysis of certain social, cultural or political situations closely related to heretical movements or trends, just as it is possible to discover an individual's implicit ideological background in his concrete behaviour. Thus our main concern has been to emphasize the essential features of the heresy phenomenon rather than the history of any particular sect, even though it is impossible to disclose the essential structure of this phenomenon without reference to the historical situation, the origin, the development, and the context of the heretical movements of the Middle Ages.

The decision to study heresy from the 11th to the 13th century of course does not imply that heresy started in the 11th century and that it only lasted until the 13th! Heresy is of all ages; it dates back to the very beginnings of Christianity, and has never completely disappeared. It reflects a permanent conflict, an unavoidable tension within the Christian community. Heresy is not an opposition between the members of the Church and others outside it ; it is not a conflict between believers and unbelievers, between Christians and atheists, or agnosticists. It is a struggle among Christians. Heretics professed to be authentic Christians, but were severely sentenced by Church authorities ; in many cases they strove to be more truly Christian than the others, whose way of life they denounced. Heretics very often endeavoured to disclose and accomplish the authentic and original meaning of the Christian message ; yet they were punished and thrown into jail and even executed. The idea of toleration seems to have been absent, at least when matters of doctrine and the moral behaviour of Christians were involved.

Heresy and orthodoxy are obviously correlative notions. In dealing with the concept of heresy we inevitably become concerned with the idea of orthodoxy. Needless to say, orthodoxy was not so clearly defined at the beginning of Christianity as to make the recognition of all possible deviations a straightforward affair. It was not delineated once and for all, but is rather the result of a progressive, still continuing disclosure. The Christian message is constantly being confronted with the development of science and philosophy; new questions arise and have to be answered. Orthodoxy is repeatedly put to the test, because it has to face new problems. Hence the question : what is the meaning of heresy in the progressive discovery of orthodoxy? Is it not, as Saint Paul implies (I *Cor.* 11.19 : *oportet haereses esse*), one of the ways that lead to the disclosure of the authentic meaning of the Christian message? And if error is one of the paths leading to truth, cannot heresy be a by-way that in the end guides us to a better understanding of revealed truth?

Let us therefore try to elucidate, patiently and carefully, the various aspects of that intricate notion of heresy in the Middle Ages.

* *
*

Our thanks go to all who contributed to the organization of our conference and to the publication of these proceedings. We are especially grateful to the Belgian "Ministerie van Nationale Opvoeding" and "Ministerie van Nederlandse Cultuur", to the Association "Vlaamse Leergangen te Leuven", and to the Rectorate, the Publications Committee, and the Faculty of Philosophy and Letters of our "Katholieke Universiteit te Leuven".

R. I. MOORE

HERESY AS DISEASE

In his account of the *Publicani* who came to England in 1163 William of Newburgh is particularly concerned to emphasise that it was a unique occurrence [1]. Heresy, he said, although it was widespread in other lands, had never appeared in England since the expulsion of the Pelagians, when the island was still called Britain, and thanks to the prompt action of Henry II it did not appear again. Throughout the story he found one metaphor especially appropriate to describe the heresy and his understanding of the problem which it posed :

> tam multi hac peste infecti esse dicuntur... Sane ab hac et ab aliis pestibus haereticis immunis semper exstitit Anglia... nullius unquam ex ea pestis haereticae virus ebullivit : sed nec in eam aliunde, usque ad tempora regis Henrici secundi... Tunc quoque, Deo propitio, pesti, quae jam irrepserat, ita est obviatum...

The *Publicani* came to England *propagandae pestis gratia*, the bishops denounced them *ne virus haereticum latius serperet*, and, triumphantly, *Hujus severitatis pius rigor ... a peste illa ... Angliae regnum purgavit.* The heretics met with little success, but those who did succumb to them *peste ... illa semel hausta ita imbuti, ut ad omnem rigeant disciplinam.*

William is unusual in the consistency with which he sustains his metaphor, but not at all in his use of it. He himself called Eon de l'Etoile a *vir pestifer*, and others described as a *pestis* the heresies of Tanchelm, Henry of Lausanne, Pierre de Bruys, the *Publicani* who were found at Arras and at Rheims, the Cathars at Orvieto in the early 1170's, and at Toulouse in 1178 [2]. In short, and I doubt whether this list is complete,

---

[1] William of Newburgh, *Historia rerum Anglicarum*, edited by Richard Howlett in *Chronicles of the Reigns of Stephen, Henry II., and Richard I.*, Rolls Series (London, 1884-5), I, 131-4.

[2] William of Newburgh, pp. 60-64 ; *Vita Norberti*, edited by Roger Wilmans in MGH, Scriptores, 12 (Hannoverae, 1856), pp. 690-91 ; Hildebert of Lavardin, *Epistolae*, II, 24 in PL, 171, col. 242 ; Peter the Venerable, *Contra Petrobrusianos Hereticos*, edited by James Fearns in Corpus Christianorum, Continuatio Mediaevalis, 10 (Turnholti, 1968), p. 3 ; *Epistolae Alexandri III Papae*, Recueil des Historiens des Gaules et de la France [= Bouquet], 15 (Paris, 1878), p. 790 ; Ralph of Coggeshall, *Chronicon Anglicanum*, edited by Joseph Stevenson, Rolls Series (London, 1875),

the word is used of almost every significant outbreak of heresy in the twelfth century. For its implications we may turn to Isidore of Seville :

> pestilentia est contagium, quod dum unum adprehenderit celeriter ad plures transit [3].

It is generated, he continues, by polluted air-*corrupto aere* -and it infects a man by penetrating the *viscera*. Hence Henry of Lausanne left Le Mans 'to infect other regions with his viper's breath', hence the 'poisonous teaching' which Eckbert of Schönau attributes to Mani, and Cardinal Peter of St. Chrysogonus to the Cathars in Toulouse, of whom Count Raymond V had remarked how ... *in tantum haeresis inviscerata manet* [4]; in the comparatively small body of reports of popular heresy in the twelfth century I have noticed it alleged to 'infect' eight times, and to 'propagate' and 'contaminate' twice each [5]. The image of poison is also commonly used. The teaching of Pierre de Bruys was a *letale venenum* to Peter the Venerable, and heresy was described as a *venenum* or as being *venosus* by the canons of Liège, writing to Lucius II in 1145, by Eckbert of Schönau, King Louis VII, Peter of St. Chrysogonus and John of Orvieto; the source of the poison which the heretics spread was made explicit by Rainerius Sacchoni when he spoke of the *erroris* ... *venenum quod ex ore antiqui serpentis biberunt* [6].

But the *pestis*, or even the *plaga* with which Henry of Clairvaux found the city of Toulouse so infected that from the soles of its feet to the top of its head there was scarcely a healthy piece in it, were general ills. St. Paul pointed the way to a more specific diagnosis when he wrote (II Timothy 2. 17) of the *sermo (qui) ut cancer serpit*, a phrase which is

p. 122 ; *Vita Sancti Petri Parentinii*, edited by Daniel Papebrochius in Acta Sanctorum Maii, V (Antverpiae, 1685), p. 86 ; Henry of Clairvaux, *Epistolae*, in PL, 204, col. 235-40.

[3] Isidore of Seville, *Etymologiae*, edited by Wallace Martin Lindsay (Oxonii, 1911), lib. 4, c. 6, 17.

[4] *Gesta Pontificum Cenomannensium*, Bouquet, 12 (Paris, 1877), p. 554 ; Eckbert, *Contra Catharos Sermones*, 13 in PL, 195, col. 159 ; Peter of St. Chrysogonus, *Epistolae* in PL, 199, col. 1119-24 ; Gervase of Canterbury, *Opera Historica*, edited by William Stubbs, Rolls Series (London, 1879), I, 270.

[5] In addition to the above, the canons of Liège to Lucius II, PL, 179, col. 937-8; *Gesta Synodi Aurelianensis*, Bouquet, 10 (Paris, 1874), p. 536-9 ; Guibert of Nogent, *De vita sua* in PL, 156, col. 952-3; Council of Tours, 1163 in Mansi, *Concilia*, 21, col. 1177 ; Council of Lombers, 1165 in Mansi, 22, col. 168.

[6] *Summa de Catharis*, edited by Antoine Dondaine, *Un traité néo-manichéen du XIIIe siècle : Le Liber de duobus principiis* (Romae, 1939), pp. 64-78 (p. 66).

frequently quoted and interestingly echoed, as for example by the Council of Tours in 1163 :

> in partibus Tolosae damnanda haeresis dudum emersit, quae paulatim more cancri ad vicina loca se diffundens, per Guasconiam et alias provincias quamplurimos jam infecit.

Cancer was, of course, not an internal disease, but one of the terms regularly used for the sores, ulcers, tumours and scabs which were such a common affliction. It is classified by Isidore under the heading *de morbis qui in superficie videntur*, and was so called, he says, from its resemblance to the scaly skin of the crab; it is a wound for which medicine knows no cure except the amputation of the infected member; if it were allowed to live and spread it would bring certain death [7]. Cancer, in fact, was one of the several general terms which collectively, and on the whole indiscriminately, covered diseases which were manifested on the skin, including among the more serious erysipelas, elephantiasis, syphilis and leprosy : Avicenna says that '*lepra* is the cancer of the whole body, cancer the *lepra* of a single member' [8].

Other synonyms are occasionally used in the context of heresy: in his debate with Henry of Lausanne William the Monk, describing the action of original sin, says that it affects everybody *sicut grex totus in agris unius cadit scabie* [9], and Guibert of Nogent explains that Clementius and Everard of Bucy were burned by the people of Soissons *quorum ne propagaretur carcinus*. Raymond of Toulouse, in the letter of 1177, says of that *haec putrida haeresis tabes praevaluit*. The *tabes*, mentioned also in the Life of St. Hugh of Lincoln [10], were leprous sores, and Isidore says that when they become putrid death is inevitable ; one of the ways of treating them was the cauterisation which the canons of Liège recommended to Lucius II against the heretics who had been discovered at Mont-Aimé. It is perhaps in character that Peter the Venerable pre-

---

[7] *Etymologiae*, lib. 4, c. 8, 14; cf. lib. 12, c. 6, 51.

[8] Cited by Charles Creighton, *A History of Epidemics in Britain* (Cambridge, 1891), I, 71.

[9] Edited by Raoul Manselli, 'Il monaco Enrico e la sua eresia', *Bullettino dell' Istituto Storico Italiano per il Medio Evo e Archivio Muratoriano*, 65 (1953), pp. 1-63 (p. 48).

[10] *Magna Vita Sancti Hugonis : The life of St. Hugh of Lincoln*, edited by Decima L. Douie and Hugh Farmer (Cambridge, 1961-62), II, 11-12.

ferred a gentler image of treatment. Although the bishops to whom he wrote had taken action against the heresiarchs, he says :

> supersunt, ut jam dixi, membra letifero adhuc, sicut ipse nuper sensi, veneno infecta,

and he prescribes :

> Ad que curanda Dei est misericordia invocanda et vestra medicinalis diligentia adhibenda.

The first of these phrases, by the way, also shows how the image of disease could be used to explain one of the characteristics of heresy that often puzzled observers, the way in which after a heretic had been disposed of his heresy often survived, and his memory continued to be cherished by his followers. Peter employs the same image again in another illuminating passage :

> Et quia hoc ad lesionem fidei pertinet, sicut publica pestis heretica expellenda, sic occulta languentium passio, si potest fieri, remediis medicinalibus est curanda [11].

Eckbert of Schönau uses the whole complex of images that I have described when he says that the Cathars 'have multiplied in every land, and the church is now greatly endangered by the foul poison which flows against it from every side. Their message spreads like a cancer, runs far and wide like leprosy (*lepra volatilis*) infecting the limbs of Christ as it goes.' There is no doubt that when they used this language our authorities deliberately referred to a familiar and long established allegory. William the Monk made it explicit in defending confession against Henry of Lausanne. He spoke at length of the words of Christ to the cured leper, 'Go shew thyself to the priest and offer for thy cleansing as Moses commanded'. He cited the instructions of Leviticus on the treatment of leprosy, and interpreted the New Testament passage in the orthodox way : *nam nos lepram nichil aliud intelligimus quam diversas maculas peccatorum.* Rhabanus Maurus, writing *De medecina*, had been equally confident. The imbalance of the humours which caused illness, he held, was a manifestation of sin, and diseases could therefore be classified according to the sins of which they were the bodily expression:

> Lepra est doctrina haereticorum falsa atque varia...
> leprosi sunt haeretici Dominum Jhesum Christum blasphemantes [12].

---

[11] *Contra Petrobrusianos*, p. 147.

[12] Rhabanus Maurus, *De Universo* in PL. 111, col. 500-502. Miss Smalley remarks that in the twelfth century theological writers «used the word *leprosy* almost interchangeably with 'sin'»; see Beryl Smalley, *The Becket Conflict and the Schools : A Study of Intellectuals in Politics* (Oxford, 1973), p. 132.

If heresy was leprosy it followed that its secondary characteristics could be likened to those of the disease, and this is reflected both in charges made against heretics and in the language used about them. For example, M. Jonin has shown[13] in his study of the episode in Béroul's *Tristan* where Iseut is handed over to a party of lepers in punishment for her adultery, that the disease was surrounded by sexual associations, and in this area there are two striking analogies with heresy. The horror of Beroul's story depended heavily on the ideas that lepers were exceptionally lecherous, and that the disease was sexually transmitted. Jonin demonstrated that both of these ideas were in fact held and applied in the treatment of lepers. The statutes of leper-houses contain many allegations of their promiscuous inclinations, and of the endeavours of those in authority to restrain them, as for example in the case of Huchon le Gressier who was expelled from the leper house at Amiens for smuggling in a paramour, and readmitted only after promising that he wouldn't do it again. The regular prohibitions of the admission of lepers to brothels are the clearest statement of the belief that the disease was sexually transmitted, and since syphilis was one of the diseases that went under the name of *lepra* this conviction was, of course, well founded in fact.

There is no need to go through the familiar list of heresiarchs, led by Tanchelm and Henry of Lausanne, who were accused not only of spectacularly lecherous behaviour, but of acquiring converts by means of their amorous skills, and there are other reasons for the accusations besides the implied analogy with leprosy. It is however worth noticing that the language of sexual transmission is used of heresy : (Henry)

in remotis partibus virus suae haeresis coepit propagare,

the canons of Liège were concerned *ne virus hoc altius serpat*, and William of Newburgh speaks of the *virus* of heresy four times, using on two of them the verbs *spargere* and *infundere*. *Virus*, says Isidore, *proprie dicitur humor fluens a natura viri*[14], and the image is echoed by Peter the Venerable's reference to the *dogmatis semina* of Pierre de Bruys. Thus when William the Monk speaks of original sin *que de lumbis Adae processit* he thinks of the transmission of spiritual qualities in exactly the same way

[13] Pierre Jonin, *Les personnages féminins dans les romans français de Tristan au XIIe siècle : Etude des influences contemporaines*, Publications de la Faculté des Lettres d'Aix, N.S. 22 (Gap, 1958). I owe this reference to Professor W.H. Lyons.

[14] *Etymologiae*, lib. 9, c. 1, 103.

that William of Conches described the inheritance of physical characteristics : 'every part of the body is created from (the sperm), so that it
is natural that children resemble their parents. From this it follows
that if the father has an incurable infirmity in any part of his body,
the son will have the same infirmity in the same part of his body' [15].

This attempt to retrace some of the associations of the idea of leprosy
in the twelfth century rests on fragile foundations. For the novice at least
it is even more difficult to speak confidently of the reality; this is a subject
of which we need to know more. It is of no great importance for my
purpose that the word *lepra* covered, as I have said, a multitude of conditions, so that *leprosus* was even used in a writ of Henry II to mean
vagabonds and beggars [16]. As for the disease itself, there is plainly
no truth in the old idea that it was introduced into Europe by the
crusaders, and I find myself unconvinced by the common assertion
that its prevalence increased dramatically during the twelfth century.
It was certainly present in Dark Age Europe, the object of legislation
by the Councils of Lyon in 583 and Orléans in 549, Rotharius king of
the Lombards in the seventh century, Pepin the Short in 757 and Charle-
magne in 789, and leprous skeletons from the seventh century have been
found in Britain [17]. Since the impression of a massive increase in the
twelfth century is created largely by the foundation of leper hospitals in
such large numbers it is worth noting the conclusion of Hirsch that
such foundations did not occur in any part of Europe until well after
the disease had become established [18], as well as making the obvious
allowance for the fact that many or even most so-called leper houses
were general hospitals or charitable foundations, and did not cater
exclusively for lepers. More generally, of course, we will think of the
availability of benefactions, and of the social and religious reasons for
the multiplication of institutions of every kind at this time. But the
critical question, both in general and for the implications of the analogy
between leprosy and heresy, is how far the twelfth century saw an
increase in leprosy itself, and how far an increase only in the strength
of the conviction that lepers should be removed from society.

[15] *De philosophia mundi*, LV, 8, PL, 172 (s.n. Honorius Augustodunensis), col. 88.
[16] Cited by Creighton, p. 77 ; he gives no reference.
[17] August Hirsch, *Handbook of Geographical and Historical Pathology*, translated
by Charles Creighton (London, 1885), II, 6-7 ; G. Melvyn Howe, *Man, Environment
and Disease in Britain : A Medical Geography of Britain through the Ages* (Newton
Abbot, 1972), pp. 83-4.
[18] Hirsch, p. 7.

The principle of segregation was enunciated in all the early legislation which I have mentioned, but it is impossible to estimate how effective it was. There are at least some grounds for arguing that in the early part of the twelfth century not all lepers were expected to be segregated, that the segregation of those who were was sometimes only partially effective, and even that the legal disabilities which lepers suffered were not universal. Bracton compared the legal status of the leper to that of the excommunicate ; he could not sue in court, make gifts of land, or inherit, although he was not deprived of his property while he lived [19]. In England this had been true at least since the reign of Stephen, when Brian Fitzcount placed two leprous sons in Abergavenny Priory, and gave lands and tithes for their support because they would not be able to inherit [20]. But about 1123, M. Bienvenu has pointed out, a leper who appears to have been living a normal life made a benefaction of land to St. Aubin at Angers [21]. The *Life* of St. Stephen of Obazine contains a story about two women who lived together in a house at Pléaux, one paralysed and the other a leper, who begged alms for both, and again the context does not suggest that it was a segregated house [22]. Neither of these cases is comparable with the common-place fact that the rule

[19] Frederick Pollock and Frederick William Maitland, *The History of English Law before the Time of Edward I*, second edition (Cambridge, 1968), I, 480.

[20] Rotha Mary Clay, *The Mediaeval Hospitals of England*, The Antiquary's Books (London, 1909), p. 57. A similar case is described by Edmund King, *Peterborough Abbey 1086-1310 : A Study in the Land Market*, Cambridge Studies in Economic History (Cambridge, 1973), pp. 27-8. In 1147 Robert of Torpel, a leper, entered the hospital of St. Leonard, outside Peterborough, and gave Peterborough Abbey two manors 'as his just inheritance, of his own patrimony, to which he had succeeded on the death of his father'. But these manors had been the dowry of Robert's sister, and he had bought them back from her husband, Richard of Reinbuedcurt, for forty marks. Subsequently, when Robert became a leper (*lepra debilitatus*), the honour of Torpel was transferred to his younger brother Roger, but the two manors which Robert had reacquired 'in the king's view and with the king's assent and that of many of the barons of the land (were) to remain to Robert for him to hold and alienate as he please, without restriction'. It would seem, therefore, that the royal court held that Robert's leprosy deprived him of his honour, but not of his acquisitions. In the next reign these two manors were once more controlled by the Torpel family, for no recorded reason (*ibid.* p. 38). We may conjecture either that Stephen's assent 'without restriction' did not mean what it said, or that a later court overruled it.

[21] Jean-Marc Bienvenu, 'Pauvreté, misères et charité en Anjou aux XIe et XIIe siècles', *Le Moyen Age*, 72 (1966), 389-424 (p. 401).

[22] Michel Aubrun, *La vie de saint Etienne d'Obazine*, Publications de l'Institut d'Etudes du Massif Central, 6 (Clermont-Ferrand, 1970), pp. 164-6.

of segregation was often not applied to the very powerful, like the numer-
ous members of royal houses who were alleged, or are known, to have
been leprous. Individual cases apart, many of the followers of Robert of
Arbrissel were lepers while he still wandered from place to place, before
the foundation of Fontevrault. M. Jonin has drawn attention to Guibert
of Nogent's story of how when Thomas of Marle imprisoned a leper 'an
assembly of lepers in the area (*elephantiosorum provincialium coetus*),
heard of it, and besieged the doors of the tyrant, crying out for their
comrade to be returned to them. He threatened that if they did not go
away he would burn them alive. Fleeing in fright, when they had reached
a safe place and had gathered together from every quarter, they called
on God to take vengeance on him ...' Jonin interprets this as a reference
to one of the leper villages to whose existence in large numbers so many
placenames bear witness [23]. These are scattered examples, but since most
of them have been turned up by accident in the pursuit of other researches
they encourage the suspicion that at the beginning of the twelfth century
the leper could and did avoid complete removal from the community.

The English evidence, at least, suggests that attitudes to lepers gra-
dually became more severe. Miss Clay, who thought that 'popular opinion of the contagious nature of the disease developed strongly towards
the close of the twelfth century', pointed to a number of indications that
legal measures to segregate them became more severe in the thirteenth,
among them that the writ for their expulsion, *De leproso amovendo*,
begins to appear in the Curia Regis Rolls about 1220, and that in 1244
the bishop of Exeter agreed to the abolition of the custom, which had
been described as ancient in 1163, of allowing them to move freely
through the streets of the city [24]. This action is reminiscent of that of
the Archbishop of Sens and the bishop of Paris, who in 1201 promul-
gated an ordinance to prevent the contamination of the healthy by
lepers *plus libere quam licite discurrentes* [25].

If the invocation of legal sanctions was becoming more general at
this time we should expect that this followed a period of increasing

---

[23] Guibert, *De vita sua*, PL, 156, col. 944. Among Jonin's examples are Font Mazeau,
Mazeaufroid and Bourg Mesaul, all twelfth century settlements near Dijon. For others
see J.C. Sournia and M. Trevien, 'Essai d'inventaire des léproseries en Bretagne',
Annales de Bretagne, 75 (1968), 317-343 (pp. 328-36) ; and Albert Bourgeois, *Lépreux
et maladreries du Pas-de-Calais*, Mémoires de la Commission départementale des
monuments historiques du Pas-de-Calais, 14, 2 (Arras, 1972).

[24] Clay, pp. 52-4.

[25] Jonin, p. 129.

social pressure, which is perhaps illustrated by the case, cited by M. Bienvenu, of Pierre Manceau, who, towards the end of the century, refused to retire to the company of other lepers, as the law of the church required, and instead obtained the permission of his lord to give himself and his goods to an almonry [26]. It sounds as though his case was similar to that of his predecessor the benefactor of St. Aubin, but that he was under greater pressure to remove himself from society. These thoughts are tentative, and even rash, but it would not be surprising if a society which was experiencing widening extremes of wealth and poverty manifested an increasing desire to protect itself from the spectacle of those most obviously afflicted. Such a view is consistent with the famous decree of the third Lateran Council (1179) *De leprosis*. It is usually presented as an advance in the segregation of lepers, upon which it insists. But it is mainly concerned to point out that the Apostle prescribed that lepers should be respected, and to decree that nobody might withhold from them the separate churches and cemeteries to which they were entitled [27]. If the decree was intended to improve rather than to damage the position of lepers it is possible to regard it as guaranteeing them religious rights which were endangered by growing social hostility.

Do these partial and speculative observations contribute to our understanding of the conception of heresy? I think it is fair to maintain, at least, that the comparison of heresy and disease provided not simply a casual or convenient metaphor, but a comprehensive and systematic model. The references which I have cited appear not as a random collection of images, but as fragments of an intellectual construction which was complete and consistent in itself, as a description of heresy and how it worked, and which conformed also to current beliefs about disease, and particularly about leprosy, as far as I have been able to establish them. It also appears to me that, although the model was of some antiquity [28], and the image continued to be used for a considerable time,

[26] Bienvenu, *Le Moyen Age*, 73 (1967), 5-34 and 189-216 (p. 202-203).

[27] Mansi, *Concilia*, 22, col. 230.

[28] Its use by St. Augustine is particularly to be noted. For example, heretics 'morbidum aliquid pravumque sapiunt' and 'sua pestifera et mortifera dogmata emendare nolunt' (*De civitate Dei*, lib. 18, 51 edited by Bernardus Dombart and Alphonsus Kalb in Corpus Christianorum, Series Latina, 48 (Turnholti, 1955), p. 649). The Manichees aroused a dangerous excitement in their hearers : 'De lethargicis enim phreneticos faciunt : inter quos morbos, cum sit uterque plerumque mortiferus, hoc tamen interest, quod lethargici sine aliena vexatione moriuntur ; phreneticus autem multis sanis, et eis potissimum qui volunt subvenire, metuendus est' (*De utilitate credendi*, PL, 42, col. 92). I must thank Fr. Buytaert for drawing my attention to these passages.

it made a special contribution to the conception of heresy that prevailed in the middle of the twelfth century.

I have not mentioned any of the few texts on eleventh-century heresy. Among them only one, the account by Paul of St. Père of Chartres of the events at Orléans in 1022, makes use of the language of disease. It also includes the famous story of the secret meetings by night, of orgiastic conduct, summoning up the devil and the use of magic powders, which was later used by Guibert of Nogent and became the prototype of countless such allegations against Cathars and witches from the thirteenth century onwards. This story is taken from Justin Martyr, whose text it follows so closely as to suggest that it was directly copied. This chronicler, therefore, seems to be the first to turn directly to the fathers to seek the *auctoritates* which would explain the meaning and nature of the events of which he had been told. To this process also we should attribute his invocation of the images of poison, of disease, and of the *mortiferus nequitiae haustus* of the heretics. [29] In the same way Bishop Gerard of Cambrai in 1025 based his interrogation of the heretical citizens of Arras on St. Paul's prophecy about the last times, and Wazo of Liège turned especially to St. Augustine and Sulpicius Severus to elucidate the history and doctrines of the heretics about whom he was consulted by the bishop of Chalons [30]. It is in the last case that we are most familiar with the process, since it was this search for a framework that would make popular heresy historically and doctrinally comprehensible that created the myth of the medieval manichee whose demolition, at least as far as the eleventh and early twelfth centuries are concerned, has been the subject of so much debate, and such distinguished scholarship, in our own time.

The language of disease, it seems to me, was used in the twelfth century in much the same way as that of manicheeism, except that it was used to describe the nature of heresy itself, rather than its historical or doctrinal antecedents. The various chronicle accounts, and especially the early ones, draw vividly upon it, but do not explicitly invoke sustained analogies. The first to appeal to it more systematically was William the Monk, who was, as Professor Manselli has shown us, a competent theologian, and he was soon followed by Peter the Venerable. Among the chroniclers William of Newburgh is unique in his extended deploy-

---

[29] *Gesta Synodi Aurelianensis*, Bouquet, 10, p. 536.

[30] *Acta Synodi Atrebatensis*, PL, 142, col. 1269-1312, citing St. Paul at col. 1311 ; *Gesta episcoporum Leodiensium*, edited by Rudolph Koepke in MGH, Scriptores,7 (Hannoverae, 1846), 226-8.

ment of the model of disease, and he wrote at the very end of the century. On the other hand, while I have not made a proper exploration of the inquisitorial treatises from this point of view, my impression is that while the authorities of the thirteenth century occasionally used this language, as in the comment of Rainerius cited above, they did not do so in a way which suggests that it figured prominently in their thoughts. I am reminded of how they took for granted the historical descent of the Cathars from the Manichees, but relied for their elucidation of contemporary doctrine and practice on the knowledge which they had at first hand.

The reign of the image of leprosy, therefore, coincided with the period when episodes of popular heresy were frequent enough to be alarming and to require explanation, and before the triumph of the Cathars made available a real structure of doctrine and belief which, once it began to be understood, made it unnecessary to rely on models. My suggestion is that, in its small way, the image helped puzzled observers, and especially those of a more speculative inclination, to create an explanation of the mysterious and alarming events which they saw, or of which they heard rumours. Whether their adoption of this particular explanation, that heresy was to the soul what leprosy was to the body, influenced the debate which took place at the same time about how it ought to be treated, is another question. Yet the parallels between the procedures which were used against the two conditions, and the penalties which were imposed upon them, in the thirteenth century are obvious. It is not too bold to suggest that the conviction of the twelfth century that they were identical did not discourage the contemplation of increasingly severe courses of action against heretics. William the Monk said to Henry of Lausanne, 'You too are a leper, scarred by heresy, excluded from communion by the judgement of the priest according to the law, bare-headed, with ragged clothing, your body covered by an infected and filthy garment; it befits you to shout unceasingly that you are a leper, a heretic and unclean, and must live alone outside the church'. William of Newburgh described how the *Publicani* were branded on their foreheads and driven from the city into the intolerable cold of winter in which they perished. The king commanded that nobody should have contact with them, and that the houses in which they had lived should be carried outside the village and burned [31]. And William is careful to emphasise that the consequence of this treatment was that the *pestis* did not appear in England again.

[31] Assize of Clarendon, c. 21, edited by William Stubbs, *Select Charters and other Illustrations of English Constitutional History*, ninth edition (Oxford, 1913), p. 173.

Jean LECLERCQ

L'HÉRÉSIE
D'APRÈS LES ÉCRITS DE S. BERNARD DE CLAIRVAUX

Pour discerner l'idée que S. Bernard se faisait de l'hérésie, considérons d'abord les cas où il en a parlé d'une façon générale, sans viser des erreurs particulières, puis ceux où il avait en vue des hérétiques déterminés.

I. LES HÉRÉSIES EN GÉNÉRAL

1. L'hérésie parmi les 'tentations' de l'Eglise

Voici d'abord un thème que Bernard a aimé développer dans ses écrits et sa prédication orale, et dont ses disciples et admirateurs se sont emparés ensuite : c'est celui de l'hérésie comme ayant constitué la deuxième des grandes épreuves, ou 'tentations', auxquelles l'Eglise ait été soumise au cours de l'histoire [1]. Il y en eut trois dans le passé, et une quatrième est encore à venir : après les persécutions sanglantes vinrent les hérésies, symbolisées par celle d'Arius ; puis, l'ambition s'introduisit parmi les clercs, et elle y fait encore des ravages ; finalement l'action de l'Antéchrist fera souffrir l'Eglise. L'idée que les hérésies équivalaient à une persécution non sanglante se trouvait déjà dans S. Augustin. Bernard l'a proposée, ainsi que celle des autres tentations, au moyen d'images telles que les chevaux de l'Apocalypse : on retrouvera certains de ces éléments chez Gébouin de Troyes, Anselme de Havelberg, Othon de Freising, Joachim de Fiore, et dans la Glose ordinaire [2].

Pour illustrer cette idée, Bernard a évoqué, en particulier, les quatre périls dont parle le Ps. 90, 5-6 : 'a timore nocturno, a sagitta volante in die, a negotio perambulante in tenebris, ab incursu et daemonio meridiano'. Dès la première édition des sermons sur ce Psaume, il est fait allusion aux *volantes sagittae haereticorum* (In Ps. 'Qui habitat' 6,

---

[1] Des textes ont été indiqués par Yves Marie-Joseph Congar, '*Arriana haeresis* comme désignation du néomanichéisme au XIIe siècle : Contribution à l'histoire d'une typification de l'hérésie au moyen âge', *Revue des sciences philosophiques et théologiques*, 43 (1959), 449-461 (p. 455, n. 4).

[2] Textes indiqués ou cités : Y. Congar, p. 453.

S. Bern. op., IV, p. 412, 17-18). L'idée est reprise dans la troisième édition, avec une précision : savoir qu'à l'origine des 'dogmes divers et pervers que fabriquèrent les hérétiques sortis de l'Eglise', se trouvait une recherche de gloire personnelle (6,7, *ibid.*, p. 409, 23 - 410). Mais aucun nouveau développement n'est donné, car Bernard se contente de renvoyer à ce qu'il a écrit sur ce sujet dans un de ses *Sermons sur le Cantique* (7, *ibid.*, p. 411).

De fait, dans le 33ᵉ d'entre eux, qui fut rédigé vers 1138-1139 [3], après avoir parlé des *philosophorum et haereticorum varia et vana dogmata* (*Sup. Cant.*, 33,8. *S. Bern. op.*, I, p. 239, 21-22), il cite les versets 5 et 6 du Ps. 90 et les commente à propos des 'quatre genres de tentations' : là, on retrouve le jeu de mots sur 'les dogmes divers et pervers', et l'idée que la vaine gloire est l'inspiratrice de ceux-ci (33, 14, p. 243, 23-25). Tel fut le fait de tout hérétique déclaré, *apertus haereticus* (33, 15, p.244, 4-5), qui causa à l'Eglise un 'conflit plus amer' que les persécutions antérieures, mais moins grave que la dépravation des mœurs qui apparut ensuite (33, 16, p. 244, 20-21).

Toute cette symbolique inspira divers 'notaires' de Bernard [4], en particulier celui qui rédigea la parabole *De Aethiopissa* et la longue sentence qui lui sert d'introduction : allusions à l'ennemi qui se transforme en ange de lumière, aux quatre dangers du Ps. 90, en particulier à la *sagitta volans in die, haeresum malitia totam pervolans Ecclesiam in ipsius prosperitate* (*S. Bern. op.*, VI, 2, p. 287, 8-9), et aux quatre chevaux de l'Apocalypse (6,2-8) : 'primus albus, id est lenis et placidus, et qui sedet exit ut vincens vincat, habens coronam laetitiae pro tempore pacis, tenens arcum belli contra haereses, id est sanctae praedicationis instrumentum, per quem emittat sagittas potentis acutas, id est efficaces Sancti Spiritus sententias' (p. 287, 16-19). Et, en effet, à la fin de la parabole, on voit les 'saints docteurs et les confesseurs magnifiques, Ambroise, Hilaire, Augustin' - des copistes ont ajouté Jérôme et Grégoire - 'ainsi que leurs semblables ... réfuter Arius, Pélage, Photin et les hérétiques leurs semblables ... : ainsi l'ennemi de l'épouse du Christ fut-il vaincu

---

[3] Cf. *Recueil d'études sur S. Bernard*, Storia e letteratura, 92, 104, 114 (Roma, 1962-69), I, 230. Dans les notes qui suivront, les titres non précédés de nom d'auteur sont ceux de travaux dans lesquels j'ai traité de sujets qui ne peuvent être ici qu'indiqués. Dans le texte, l'abréviation *S. Bern. op.* renvoie à l'édition critique des *S. Bernardi opera* qui est en cours de publication, 7 vol. parus à Rome de 1957 à 1974.

[4] Cf. 'Etudes sur S. Bernard et le texte de ses écrits', *Analecta Sacri Ordinis Cisterciensis*, 9 (1953), p. 133-136.

en ses persécutions ouvertes et dans les séductions occultes des hérétiques' (p. 294, 12-25).

2. L'hérésie comme obstacle à l'unité de la foi

Outre les textes dans lesquels l'hérésie fait partie d'un développement
plus ou moins long sur les tentations de l'Eglise, elle fait encore l'objet,
dans les grandes œuvres littéraires éditées par Bernard, de mentions
plus ou moins rapides. Elle s'y présente toujours comme une opinion
personnelle que son fauteur préfère à la doctrine commune de l'Eglise,
malgré les avertissements que lui adressent les évêques. Tel est le cas
d'un clerc irlandais : 'praesumpsit dicere in eucharistia esse tantummodo
sacramentum et non rem sacramenti...' On lui demande de se rétracter :
'Suadentibus hoc ipsum episcopis et universo clero, cum non acquies-
ceret, contumaci anathema dicunt, haereticum protestantes' (Vita S.
Malachiae, 57, S. Bern. op., t. III, p. 360, 10-25).

L'hérésie résulte d'une déviation de la sincérité chrétienne, et par là-
même, elle s'oppose à la pureté du sens ecclésial, de la foi : 'ob cavendas
haereticae fraudis decipulas et fidei puritatem ... custodiendam' (Sup.
Cant., 20, 4, t. I, p. 117, 7-9) ; 'ut ab ecclesiastici sensus puritate nulla
veri similitudine, nulla haeretica seu diabolica circumventione aliqua-
tenus devietur' (Sup. Cant., 20, 9, t. I, p. 120, 25-27). L'hérétique est
assimilé à tous ceux qui, d'une façon ou d'une autre, refusent d'adopter
simplement la foi de l'Eglise. Il a en commun avec 'les philosophes' de
se fier aux mots, aux syllogismes, et à son propre jugement, plus qu'à
l'enseignement commun (Sup. Cant., 41, 1, t. II, p. 29; 38, 7, t. II, p. 131,
28; 79, 4, t. II, p. 274, 21). Il est assimilé aux infideles et aux schismatici
(Sup. Cant., 29, 2, t. I, p. 203), à tous ceux qui méritent d'être comparés
à de 'mauvaises pluies qui produisent des épines' (Sup. Cant., 38, 7,
t. II, p. 131, 27-29), ou encore à la nuit : 'Nox est iudaica perfidia, nox
ignorantia paganorum, nox haeretica pravitas, nox etiam catholicorum
carnalis animalisve conversatio. Annon nox, ubi non percipiuntur ea
quae sunt Spiritus Dei? Sed et apud haereticos vel schismaticos, quot
sectae, tot noctes' (Sup. Cant., 75, 10, t. II, p. 253, 3-7).

Les hérétiques représentent donc un grand danger pour l'Eglise.
Quelle attitude celle-ci adopte-t-elle à leur égard? Tout d'abord, alors
qu'elle ne le fait pas pour les excommuniés impénitents, elle prie pour
eux, le Vendredi Saint : 'Ecclesia ... fidenter etiam pro Iudaeis, pro
haereticis, pro gentilibus orat' (De grad. humil., 56, t. III, p. 58, 10-
11). Ensuite, elle s'efforce de les corriger et, si elle n'y parvient pas, de
les empêcher de nuire. Tel est le conseil que S. Bernard donne au pape

Eugène III : 'Dico autem haereticos schismaticosque, nam hi sunt subversi et subversores, canes ad scissionem, vulpes ad fraudem. Erunt, inquam, huiusmodi maxime tuo studio aut corrigendi, ne pereant, aut, ne perimant, coercendi' (*De consid.*, III, 3, t. III, p. 433, 9-11).

Enfin, il est un texte où sont rapidement évoquées les hérésies concernant la Vierge Marie. Se souvenant de l'antienne où la liturgie dit à la Mère de Dieu : 'Tu cunctas haereses sola interemisti', Bernard commente : 'Sola enim contrivit universam haereticam pravitatem. Alius non de substantia carnis suae Christum edidisse dogmatizabat ; alius parvulum non peperisse, sed reperisse sibilabat ; alius vel post partum, viro cognitam basphemabat ; alius, Dei Matrem audire non sustinens, magnum illud nomen Theotocos impiissime suggillabat' (*In Octava Assumptionis*, 4, t. V. p. 265, 4-8).

3. *L'hérésie dans la prédication familière de S. Bernard*

Il est un groupe de textes où le vocabulaire de l'hérésie est relativement fréquent : il s'agit de ces *Sententiae* et de ces *Parabolae* qui sont des résumés ou des 'reportations' de sermons familiers que Bernard prononça mais ne rédigea pas et ne publia pas lui-même. Or, en dépit de ce dernier fait, on y remarque précision et constance quant à deux points déjà mentionnés ci-dessus : la notion d'hérésie et l'attitude à adopter envers celle-ci.

Dans le premier domaine, voici d'abord une sentence où ce que S. Benoît, au premier chapitre de sa Règle, avait dit des quatre espèces de moines, est appliqué - non sans humour - aux membres d'une communauté monastique. L'un de ces groupes est celui des sarabaïtes, auxquels Bernard applique tout le vocabulaire biblique et patristique de l'hérésie : 'Sunt et sarabaitae, qui seipsos amantes (II Tim., 3, 2), quae sua sunt quaerentes (Phil., 2,21) ... sententias novas et privatas sibi adinventiones fingentes, partes et schismata in congregatione faciunt seque invicem et haeresum suarum schismata defendentes, gregem Domini turbare non desinunt' (*Sent.* III, 31, *S. Bern. op.*, t. VI, 2, p. 85, 8-12). Ailleurs encore sont associés les hérésies et les schismes, toutes les formes d'erreur ou de non-adhésion à la foi de l'Eglise : simulacrum et haeresum et schismatum (*Sent.* III, 122, t. VI, 2, p. 230, 12-13) ; haereses et *schismata* (*Par.* 4,4, t. VI, 2, p. 297, 20), haeretici ... Judaei (*Sent.* III, 87, t. VI, 2, p. 128, 14-15). Une variante aux thèmes des tentations de l'Eglise dit également, après avoir parlé des persécutions sanglantes : 'Videns autem rex Babyloniae quod fortitudine praevalere non posset ; immisit haereticos ut fraudulenter, sub specie boni sponsi, eam diriperent et spoliarent. Sed boni confessores qui post apostolos et martyres susceperunt sponsae defensionem, scilicet Hieronymus, Augustinus, Gregorius et ceteri, resistendo haereticis expulerunt eos' (*Sent.* III, 116, t. VI, 2, p. 210, 6-10).

Que fait l'Eglise, en présence de l'hérésie? La sentence qui vient d'être citée réaffirmait le rôle qui fut, jadis, dévolu aux Docteurs. Mais habituellement dans le présent, comme par le passé, les prélats ne doivent pas manquer de vigilance : 'Si vero sit diligens et prudentia careat (praelatus), non habet unde interdum haereticos arceat ...' (*Sent.* III, 112, t. VI, 2, p. 193, 19-20). Il doit savoir faire des reproches sévères : 'duram ad haereticos ... increpationem' (*Sent.* III, 112, t. VI, 2, p. 195, 18-19) et discerner le bien du mal, la foi de l'erreur : 'Sed granum frumenti paleam habet : iactantiae vanitatem vel dogmatis haeretici pravitatem; a qua palea per salubrem discretionem separatum ...' (*Sent.* III, 119, t. VI, 2, p. 217, 16-18).

Si ces textes mineurs méritaient d'être signalés, c'est d'abord parce qu'ils transmettent une conception assez constante et précise de l'hérésie. Mais c'est surtout parce qu'ils sont révélateurs d'une préoccupation que S. Bernard a dû partager avec nombre d'hommes d'Eglise de son temps : l'hérésie n'était pas pour eux de la littérature. Certes, ç'avait été un lieu commun traditionnel, chez les écrivains patristiques et médiévaux, que de dénoncer les hérésies qui avaient marqué si profondément le passé de l'Eglise. Mais il en existait encore, ou, en tout cas, on continuait de les croire menaçantes : elles faisaient partie de la situation contemporaine; on comprend que, spontanément, même en dehors de ses grands écrits publiés, Bernard y ait fait allusion devant ses moines. S'est-il trouvé, de façon concrète, affronté au péril qu'elles constituaient? Ce fut trois fois le cas.

II. Hérésies particulières

1. *La doctrine d'Abélard*

Le premier groupe de textes que l'on puisse dater et dans lesquels Bernard ait employé le vocabulaire de l'hérésie à propos de doctrines bien déterminées est constitué par les lettres dans lesquelles il s'est opposé à Abélard, en 1140. Elles sont au nombre de dix-sept [5] et les

---

[5] *Ep.* 187-190, 192-193, 195-198, 330-336, 338 dans PL, 183. Le texte critique de

notaires de sa chancellerie ont pris une part plus ou moins grande à la rédaction de chacune d'elles; aussi comprend-on que l'on retrouve, en plusieurs d'entre elles, des thèmes semblables, et parfois des formules presque identiques. De l'examen de ce dossier se dégagent les faits suivants.

Tout d'abord, Abélard est désigné comme hérétique soit expressément - ce qui est rare -, soit de façon équivalente, ce qui est plus fréquent. Le premier cas se vérifie par trois fois dans l'*Ep.* 191, qui à vrai dire, est envoyée au pape Innocent II au nom des évêques présents au concile de Sens, et dans l'*Ep.* 331 : *haereticum interius ostendit.* Le second cas est celui où Abélard est assimilé - selon un procédé qui était devenu traditionnel - à des hérétiques déjà condammnés : ' Cum de Trinitate loquitur, sapit Arium; cum de gratia, sapit Pelagium; cum de persona Christi, sapit Nestorium' (*Ep.* 192; expressions similaires dans 330, 331, 332, 336, 338, n. 2). Deux fois, Bernard applique à Abélard des formules de S. Paul où figure le mot d'hérésie : *Haereticum hominem post unam et secundam correptionem devita* (196, n. 1, citant *Tit.*, 3, 10). *Oportet haereses esse* (336, citant *I Cor.*, 11, 19). De plus, Abélard est associé à Arnauld de Brescia comme l'hérésie au schisme, dans 189, n. 5.

Pourquoi mérite-t-il d'être qualifié d'hérétique? Pour deux raisons. La plus fréquemment invoquée réside dans le fait qu'il profère des idées qui sont 'nouvelles' par rapport à l'enseignement reçu de la tradition : *nova proponitur fides* (189, 2) ; *suas novitates catholicorum Patrum doctrinae et fidei praefert* (189,3). Des formules analogues sont dans 192, 190, n. 2, n. 3, 330 : bref, Abélard propage une *nova haeresis* (196, n. 26). Le second motif qui justifie la désignation d'Abélard comme hérétique est son entêtement dans l'erreur; le mot latin qui veut dire 'pertinacité', et qui est employé à ce propos, appartenait au vocabulaire traditionnel selon lequel l'hérésie n'est pas seulement une erreur dans la foi, mais le fait de s'y maintenir alors qu'on a été repris [6] : 'haereticum pro-

ces lettres, préparé pour être imprimé dans le tome VIII des *S. Bernardi opera*, se trouve déjà utilisé dans l'édition donnée, avec traduction italienne, par Albino Babolin, *Bernardo di Chiaravelle : Le lettere contro Pietro Abelardo* (Padova, 1969). Dans l'*Indice dei termini*, qui occupe huit colonnes aux p. 209-212, le mot *haeresis* ne figure pas : sans doute l'auteur a-t-il estimé que la notion qu'il exprime n'est pas, dans cette correspondance, d'une importance primordiale.

[6] Des textes sur la *pertinacia* et l'*obstinata defensio falsitatis* sont cités, par exemple, dans l'art. '*Haereticus*' du *Thesaurus linguae latinae*, VI, 3 (Lipsiae, 1936-1962), col. 2507, 58; 2508, 54-58; 2510, 45. L'idée que ce qui fait l'hérésie n'est pas l'ignorance ou l'erreur, mais l'*obstinata defensio falsitatis*, la contumace, a été largement exposée,

bans non tam in errore quam in pertinacia et defensione erroris' (193);
en effet, Abélard avait déjà été condamné par un concile à Soissons,
en 1121, mais il récidivait : 'succensa fuit una illius haeresis Suessione;
sed iam loco ipsius septem et eo amplius haereses emerserunt' (331).
Bref, Abélard se sépare de l'Eglise, la *Catholica* (190, n. 3), il divise son
'unité', sa 'paix' (334), et il met en péril la foi des simples (336). Il
fait revivre des hérésies que l'on croyait mortes : 'cum eo multorum
haereses, quae dormierant, surrexerunt' (191, n. 1). Il inflige à l'Eglise
une souillure : 'haereticae pravitatis macula' (191, n. 2).

Parmi les thèmes qui servent à développer ces accusations, deux
surtout, qui sont inspirés de la Bible et des Pères, se retrouvent ailleurs,
dans l'œuvre de Bernard, quand il parle des héritiques : l'évocation du
démon qui se transforme en ange de lumière (189, n. 5) et la comparaison
des 'petits renards' (189, n. 3) dont il sera question plus loin à propos
des sermons contre les cathares de Cologne.

En somme, la conception que Bernard se fait de l'hérésie, d'après
ces textes, est hautement traditionnelle. Quant à savoir si elle est appliquée
à Abélard à juste titre, et dans quelle mesure, c'est là une question dont
la réponse revient aux historiens des doctrines.

2. *Les erreurs des cathares*

Il est un groupe d'hérétiques auquel Bernard dut s'opposer durant
les années 1144 et suivantes : il est constitué par ces néo-manichéens,
ou cathares, qui répandaient leurs doctrines en bien des régions, spécia-
lement dans celle de Cologne et dans le midi de l'Europe.

A. *En Rhénanie*

Contre ceux de la vallée du Rhin, il fut incité à écrire par une lettre
que lui envoya le prévôt des Prémontrés de Steinfeld, Evervin : celui-ci
lui dénonçait les erreurs des 'nouveaux hérétiques' et lui demandait
d'intervenir en commentant, dans la série des *Sermones super Cantica*
qu'il publiait alors, le verset 15 du ch. II, *Capite nobis vulpes parvulas,
quae demoliuntur vineas* [7], texte qui, traditionnellement, avait été appliqué
aux hérétiques [8]. De fait, Bernard répondit à cet appel sous la forme des

per exemple, par Facundus d'Hermiane, *Pro defensione trium capitulorum concilii
Chalcedonensis* 1.12, c. 1, PL, 67, 823-833.

[7] *Inter Bernardinas ep.* 483, PL, 182, 692.

[8] Références indiquées dans *Recueil d'études*, I, 292.

deux sermons 65 et 66. Mais, à son habitude, conformément à son souci de composition littéraire harmonieuse, il fit précéder sa réfutation d'une exhortation spirituelle, comme s'il préparait le terrain avant une attaque, ou comme s'il aiguisait son stylet et fourbissait ses armes.

Avant de parler aux hérétiques, il expose ce qu'est la 'vigne' où ils font des dégâts : c'est la conscience, l'esprit, la vie entière de ceux qui tâchent de se conformer à la sagesse de Dieu (*Sup. Cant.* 63, 2, *S. Bern. op.*, II, p. 162, 8-9); c'est toute leur conduite, leur *conversatio* (63, 3, *ib.*, p. 163, 8-9); ce sont les *spirituales viri*, ceux dont toute l'existence est animée par l'Esprit de Dieu (63, 5, *ib.*, p. 164, 7-8); et c'est l'ensemble de ceux qui vivent ainsi, c'est-à-dire l'Eglise, faite de ces églises particulières que le texte du Cantique évoque par le mot *vineae*. Que sont maintenant ces 'petits renards' qui dévastent le champ du Seigneur? (63, 7, *ib.*, p. 166, 3-5). Ces animaux insidieux sont les tentations, qui sont elles-mêmes de diverses sortes (64, 1, *ib*, p. 166, 15-21). Elles viennent de ce que les pensées des hommes sont vaines, ou de ce que Satan se transforme en ange de lumière, pour frapper, en dissimulant ses desseins pervers, ceux qui ont le cœur droit ; et c'est pourquoi elles se font toutes petites, afin d'agir plus efficacement 'en cachette'. Elles exigent donc que l'on soit vigilant, prudent, à cause de la part d'habileté, d'*astutia*, qu'il y a en leur action (64, 6, *ib.*, p. 169). Il faut les dénoncer, les mettre en plein jour, puis s'en emparer, les détruire, avant qu'elles ne grandissent et ne nuisent davantage (64,7, *ib.*, p. 169-170).

Bernard en arrive alors à préciser qu'il va essayer de faire prendre les hérétiques en défaut - et non les mettre en fuite - pour tâcher de les convertir : 'Et si iuxta allegoriam ecclesias vineas, vulpes haereses vel potius haereticos ipsos intelligamus, simplex est sensus, ut haeretici capiantur potius quam effugentur ... Itaque homo de Ecclesia exercitatus et doctus, si cum haeretico homine disputare aggreditur, illo suam intentionem dirigere debet, quatenus ita errantem convincat, ut et convertat' (64,8, *ib.*, p. 170, 11-21). Et la raison pour laquelle il faut ainsi 'vaincre et convaincre l'hérétique, en réfutant l'hérésie' (qui haereticum vicit et convicit, haereses confutavit) est qu'il nuit à l'Eglise en tant qu'être social, communiant dans la vérité et dans l'amour : Bernard emploie ici les expressions *socialius, socialiter, socium, associata est* (64, 9-10, *ib.*, p. 170-171).

De cette introduction à la réfutation des hérétiques de Cologne se dégagent déjà quelques idées. Tout d'abord, l'hérésie est, pour ainsi dire, personnalisée : il s'agit, en réalité, des hommes qui la professent et la répandent, c'est-à-dire des hérétiques. Ensuite, elle comporte un aspect moral : elle n'est pas seulement d'ordre spéculatif; elle trouble et ruine la conduite des fidèles. Et c'est parce qu'elle est d'ordre moral que celui qui la tient, l'hérétique, peut être, non seulement convaincu, mais converti. Enfin, le critère par rapport auquel on doit la juger est la vie 'sociale' de l'Eglise, essentiellement fondée sur cet amour auquel le dernier paragraphe du sermon 64 chante une hymne admirable.

Toutes ces idées sont illustrées dans la réfutation précise et complète des cathares de Cologne qui occupe les sermons 65 et 66. Celle-ci encore est précédée d'une introduction, dans laquelle Bernard montre ce qui distingue les hérétiques nouveaux dont lui a parlé Evervin de ceux de l'antiquité : ceux-là se déclaraient ouvertement, ce qui rendait plus facile de les réfuter 'publiquement' : 'Nam cum Ecclesia semper ab initio sui vulpes habuerit, cito omnes compertae et captae sunt. Confligebat haereticus palam - nam inde haereticus maxime, quod palam vincere cupiebat -, et succumbebat ... non repullubat error publice confutatus' (65, 1,*ib.*, p. 172, 16-24). Or les renards d'aujourd'hui se dissimulent : 'ne apparere quidem volunt, sed serpere'. Ils ont, eux aussi, une intention morale déviée, mais qui n'est plus seulement de chercher leur propre gloire, comme ce fut toujours le cas : 'Omnibus una intentio haereticis semper fuit, captare gloriam de singularitate scientiae' (65, 2, *ib.*, p. 173, 2-3). On sait combien Bernard est sensible à cette recherche de curiosité vaine et de gloriole personnelle, qui s'opposent si profondément à l'idéal qu'il a du chrétien et du moine. Or, cette fois, les hérétiques veulent miner la vie morale du peuple chrétien en se présentant à lui comme les seuls chrétiens authentiques, ce qui est faux : 'longe plus nocet falsus catholicus quam verus haereticus ... Quod signum dabitis, ut palam fiat pessima haeresis haec, docta mentiri non lingua tantum, sed vita?' (65, 4, *ib.*, p. 175, 17-22).

Bernard dénonce d'abord, et réfute, l'erreur par laquelle ils atteignent le plus directement la moralité publique : c'est celle qui prétend que le mariage est mauvais, mais qui, en même temps, autorise toutes les licences sexuelles. Et en conclusion, il résume ce qu'il a essayé de faire : manifester combien est fausse une conception qui se présente comme vraie : 'Cepimus vulpem, quia fraudem percepimus. Manifesti sunt qui latebant falsi catholici, veri depraedatores Catholicae ... qui insidiis pro armis uti cauti sunt'. Avant d'en venir à leurs autres erreurs, Bernard, en conclusion de ce sermon 65, rappelle ce qu'il y a de nouveau en cette 'secte' qui fait des adeptes parmi les gens simples surtout, les femmes de la campagne et les illettrés, 'mulierculis rusticis et idiotis'. Toutes ces erreurs se retrouvent parmi celles des 'hérétiques de l'antiquité'; cependant, elles risquent maintenant de gagner le cœur de chrétiens qui sont de bonne foi, mais peu instruits (65,8, *ib.*, p. 177).

La partie la plus longue de leur réfutation se trouve dans le sermon suivant, qui revêt les proportions d'un traité d'une douzaine de pages : Bernard y parle à nouveau du mariage et de la continence, puis des aliments déclarés impurs, de la matière de l'eucharistie, de la légitimité du baptême des enfants, des ordres, sacrements et ordonnances de l'Eglise. Ne retenons ici que ce qui concerne sa conception de l'hérésie. Dans l'introduction, il rappelle que celle-ci est aggravée par l'hypocrisie : 'Non sufficit haereticos esse, nisi et hypocritae sint ... (66, 1, *ib.*, p.178, 12-13). Comment désigner cette secte? Du nom de quel hérétique antérieur? En effet, bien qu'elles viennent du démon, les hérésies ont toujours eu un initiateur humain. Qu'en est-il dans le cas présent? 'Quae haeresis non ex hominibus habuit proprium haeresiarcham? Manichaei Manem habuere principem ... Quo nomine istos titulove censebis?' (66, 2, *ib.*, p. 179, 15-20). Plus loin, Bernard montrera que l'élément commun à toutes les erreurs en question est, à l'égard de la création qui vient de Dieu, un pessimisme qui relève de la folie manichéenne, *de insania Manichaei* (66, 7, *ib.*, p. 182, 28) : ceci s'applique à une abstention de nourriture qui est associée à une conception fausse : 'haereticos se probantes, non sane quia abstinent, sed quia haeretice abstinent' (66,6 *ib.*, p. 182, 8-9); et il en va de même de l'abstinence sexuelle - 'Haereticus ... horret ... omne quod ex coitu procreatur' (66, 2, *ib.*, p. 182, 18-20) - et des limites apportées à l'efficacité de la rédemption : 'nec contentus erit [Dominus] paucitate haereticorum, qui omnes redemit'(66,9, *ib.*, p. 184, 4).

En conséquence de cette réfutation, que faire? Comment agir? Bernard le dit dans la conclusion de ce sermon. Il ne faut pas tuer ces hérétiques, faisant d'eux des martyrs, selon une tendance - et une tentation - à laquelle le peuple a parfois cédé : 'Itaque irruens in eos populus, novos haereticis suae ipsorum perfidiae martyres dedit'. Et d'ajouter cette formule énergique : 'Approbamus zelum, sed factum non suademus, quia fides suadenda est, non imponenda' (66,12, *ib.*, p. 186, 26-187,1). Il vaudrait mieux, afin que la répression s'opérât dans l'ordre, avoir recours au glaive de celui qui le porte légitimement : 'Quamquam melius procul dubio gladio coercentur, illius videlicet qui non sine causa gladium portat, quam in suum errorem multos traicere permittantur' (66, 12, *ib.*, p. 187, 1-3). Ainsi, en présence d'hérésies de ce genre, deux obligations s'imposent: essayer de convertir les hérétiques, et protéger la foi des chrétiens demeurés fidèles.

Tous ces textes confirment l'interprétation que le P. Congar a donnée, textes à l'appui, de cathares comme ceux auxquels s'opposait S. Bernard: 'Une chose était certaine : c'étaient des hérétiques, et qui attaquaient le christianisme au cœur. Le moyen âge avait une notion à la fois fort claire et très imprécise de l'hérésie: était hérétique tout ce qui contrevenait, avec pertinacité, à l'enseignement ou à la pratique de l'Église; volontiers, on précisait : de l'Eglise romaine. Il y avait aussi une typologie bien arrêtée, non seulement de l'hérétique, mais de l'hérésie, c'est-à-dire de la doctrine contraire à l'enseignement de l'Eglise. D'un côté, l'hérésie était essentiellement *une nouveauté*, mais, d'un autre côté, elle était volontiers présentée et stigmatisée comme une erreur déjà condamnée et réfutée. Un des traits caractéristiques du genre hérésiologique est de chercher à ramener la 'nouveauté' scandaleuse à quelque erreur ancienne et déjà condamnée' [9].

B. *En Languedoc*

Il est un point de la doctrine des cathares sur lequel S. Bernard eut l'occasion de revenir : le fait qu'ils s'opposaient au baptême des petits enfants, réservant aux adultes la réception de ce sacrement. Il s'exprima plusieurs fois sur ce point. Il le fit d'abord vers 1127-1128, en répondant, dans sa lettre 77, à une consultation de Hugues de Saint-Victor sur ce sujet et sur d'autres [10]. Mais en ce long exposé, il n'utilise pas le vocabulaire de l'hérésie, bien qu'il désigne l'adversaire anonyme qu'il réfute au moyen d'expressions qui qualifient son enseignement d'innovation par rapport à la foi reçue - 'novus iste novarum inventor assertionum,

[9] Y. Congar, *Arriana haeresis*, p. 454.
[10] Sur cette lettre et sa date, Damien Van den Eynde, *Essai sur la succession et la date des écrits de Hugues de Saint-Victor*, Spicilegium Pontificii Athenaei Antoniani, 13 (Romae, 1960), p. 132-137 ; et 'Détails biographiques sur Pierre Abélard', *Antonianum*, 38 (1963), 217-223 (p. 222); J.C. Didier, 'La question du baptême des enfants chez S. Bernard et ses contemporains', *Analecta Sacri Ordinis Cisterciensis*, 9 (1953), 191-202 (p. 194); David Edward Luscombe, *The School of Peter Abelard : The Influence of Abelard's Thought in the Early Scholastic Period*, Cambridge Studies in Medieval Life and Thought, n.s. 14 (Cambridge, 1969), p. 26 et p. 184-186. Sur 'le contenu antiabélardien probable' de cette lettre, Piero Zerbi, dans les *Contributi dell'Istituto di Storia Medioevale*, II (Milano, 1972), p. 633, n. 33, a annoncé une étude.

et assertor inventionum' (*Ep.* 77, 7, *S. Bern. op.*, t. VII, p. 189, 14-15),
'plus novitatis curiosus quam studiosus veritatis' (10, *ib.*, p. 192, 29-30)
et de rébellion - 'non fidelis, sed plane rebellis atque contemptor' (8, *ib.*,
p. 192, 1-2).

Puis, dans un sermon pour le Dimanche des Rameaux, Bernard men-
tionne en passant, mais avec précision, l'erreur de tout hérétique opposé
au baptême des enfants : 'etsi murmuret haereticus, parvulos venire
non sinens, parvulorum baptismo detrahens (*In ramis Palmarum*, I, 3,
S. Bern. op., V, p. 44, 15-16). On a pu penser que ce texte fut écrit en
1145 [11], lorsque Bernard luttait contre les Henriciens, ainsi appelés
du nom d'un disciple de Pierre de Bruys contre lequel Pierre le Véné-
rable avait composé un traité et qui faisait des ravages en Languedoc.
Il propageait, entre autres idées, celle-là.

Dans une lettre écrite de Bordeaux, en juin de cette même année,
au comte Ildefonse de Saint-Gilles, conformément au principe qu'il
a énoncé à la fin de son second sermon contre les cathares de Cologne,
Bernard dénonce ce personnage au prince qui est chargé de veiller au
bien de ses sujets en cette partie du midi de la France: cet hérétique agit,
lui aussi, sous des apparences de bon apôtre : 'Henricus haereticus.
Versatur in terra vestra sub vestimentis ovium lupus rapax' (*Ep.* 241,
1, PL. 182, 434 A), et les gens d'Eglise se taisent: 'O infelicissimum
populum! Ad vocem unius haeretici siluerunt in eo omnes propheticae
et apostolicae voces' (2, 434 C). Ici encore, c'est la foi du peuple chrétien
qui préoccupe Bernard. Mais tout ce qu'il demande à Ildefonse est de
bien recevoir le légat envoyé par le Siège apostolique pour s'occuper
de cette affaire, et de l'aider : honorifice suscipere, operam dare' (4,
436 A).

Bernard lui-même fit un long périple en Languedoc, en mai et juin
1145, pour y combattre l'hérésie [12]. Nous n'avons pas le texte des dis-
cours qu'il tint, mais seulement le schéma de ce qu'il dit à Albi: il mit
en garde les fidèles contre les semences mauvaises que l'on avait jetées
en lui - il avait déjà développé ce thème de l'*agricultura Dei* dans les
sermons 63 et 64 *Sur le Cantique* -, puis, 'commençant par le sacrement
de l'autel, point par point, il exposa soigneusement ce que l'hérétique
prêchait et quelle était la vérité de la foi. Et en réponse, tout le peuple
se mit à exprimer son abomination et sa détestation pour l'*haeretica*

---

[11] J.C. Didier, *loc. cit.*

[12] Sur la chronologie et l'itinéraire, cf. l'ouvrage collectif *Bernard de Clairvaux*
(Paris, 1953), p. 601.

pravitas, et à recevoir avec joie la parole de Dieu et la vérité catholique' [13]
De retour à Clairvaux, Bernard adressa aux Toulousains sa lettre 242,
dans laquelle il les félicitait de 'leur zèle et de leur haine envers les hérétiques' (1, PL, 182, 430 B). Il y reprenait la comparaison des renards
qui ont été capturés (436 C). Puis il donnait des consignes concrètes:
'Oboedite episcopo caeterisque praepositis vestris, magistris Ecclesiae...'
(2, 437 A). Qu'on se méfie de tout 'prédicateur étranger ou inconnu,
et de quiconque, sous des apparences de piété, profère des nouveautés:
profanas novitates vocum et sensuum' (3, 437 B).

3. *Gilbert de la Porrée*

La dernière en date des interventions écrites de Bernard contre l'hérésie
se situe peu après le concile de Reims de mars-avril 1148, devant lequel
l'enseignement de Gilbert de la Porrée avait été dénoncé. Là, Bernard
assimile simplement cet évêque de Poitiers à un hérétique; avant de citer
des propositions qu'il fut accusé de proférer, il déclare: 'Recedant a
vobis, carissimi, recedant novelli, non dialectici, sed haeretici...' (*Sup.
Cant.*, 80, 6, *S. Bern. op.*, II, 281, 9-10). 'Sed dicit haereticus ...' (80, 7, *ib.*,
p. 281, 27). A ces doctrines s'opposent le sens catholique - catholicus
refugit sensus (80,6, *ib.*, p. 281, 21-22) - et les écrits de S. Augustin,
marteau des hérétiques: 'Augustinus..., validus malleus haereticorum'
(80, 7, *ib.*, p. 282, 4-5). Enfin, Gilbert de Poitiers est nommé : 'Unde
non immerito nuper in concilio, quod Papa Eugenius Remis celebravit,
tam ipsi quam ceteris episcopis perversa visa est omnino suspecta expositio illa Gilberti episcopi Pictavensis'. Car son 'explication perverse et
obscure' de la Trinité est rejetée par l'Eglise catholique : 'Quod absit,
ut assentiat Catholica' (80, 8, *ib.*, p. 282-283).

En une quarantaine de passages de ses écrits, Bernard a consacré
à l'hérésie de brèves allusions ou, rarement, des mentions plus dévelop-
pées. Ceci est peu, dans une œuvre occupant environ 2200 colonnes

---

[13] Ce résumé du sermon est donné au n. 10 de la lettre de Geoffroy d'Auxerre à
Archenfred, qui figure à la fin du livre VI, dû à Geoffroy d'Auxerre, de la *Vita prima
S. Bernardi*, PL, 185, 414 D - 415 A. Sur cette lettre : Adriaan-Hendrik Bredero,
'Etudes sur la *Vita prima* de S. Bernard', *Analecta Sacri Ordinis Cisterciensis*, 17
(1961), 3-72, 215-260 (p. 237-239).

de la *Patrologie latine* de Migne et 8 volumes de l'édition nouvelle: la proportion n'est même pas de cinq fois par volume. Il n'était certes pas obsédé par ce thème. A ses yeux la cupidité et l'ambition dont tant de clercs étaient la proie constituaient, pour l'Eglise de son temps, des dangers plus graves, comme il l'a dit dans un texte cité plus haut, à propos des tentations de l'Eglise (*Sup. Cant.*, 33, 16, t. I, p. 244, 20-21).

Sur le concept d'hérésie non plus que sur la plupart de ceux qu'il utilise, Bernard ne propose une théorie: il prend ce terme, comme les autres, avec la signification qu'il a dans la tradition dont il dépend, et qui est nourrie de vocabulaire biblique et patristique [14]. Du moins le sens qu'il lui donne est-il conforme à ces sources, et assez précis. Pour lui comme pour S. Paul et les Pères de l'Eglise, l'hérésie comporte toujours un élément d'innovation non garanti par l'autorité de ceux qui ont transmis le dépôt de la doctrine chrétienne, et c'est là ce qui trouble la foi des croyants, surtout dans l'ensemble du peuple. Aussi le critère qui permet de déceler l'hérésie et le moyen qui permet de la réfuter sont-ils constitués par un recours au 'sens catholique': une doctrine est hérétique lorsqu'elle est élément de division, lorsqu'elle sépare ceux qui la 'fabriquent' et ceux qui y adhèrent, de la paix, de l'unanimité fraternelle qui doit régner entre tous les membres du Christ [15].

Le vocabulaire de l'hérésie n'est point très fréquent chez Bernard; il n'est pas associé, par exemple, à celui de la simonie [16], mais réservé à des déviations de caractère doctrinal ayant ou non des conséquences d'ordre moral. L'emploi que Bernard fait de la notion d'hérésie est, d'autre part, constant: sa pensée, sur ce point, ne semble pas avoir évolué.

Il l'applique à l'enseignement des cathares comme le firent tous les

---

[14] Il serait aisé de montrer que, dans les expressions qui ont été citées ici, et dans leurs contextes, tous les termes, ou presque, ont une saveur biblique et patristique; aussi les retrouve-t-on dans les formules rassemblées sous les mots *haeresis* et *haereticus* du *Thesaurus linguae latinae*, VI, 3 (Lipsiae, 1936-62), col. 2501-2511; relevons-y, à titre d'exemples : *perversum dogma, secta, fabricare, perversa, diversa, terror, hypocrisis, philosophia, insania, pravitas, vanitas, profana, adinvenire, falsitas, novitates* etc., et, en opposition, *veritas, catholica,* etc...

[15] Quelques textes sont indiqués par Y. Congar, 'L'ecclésiologie de S. Bernard', *Analecta Sacri Ordinis Cisterciensis*, 9 (1953), 136-190 (p. 158, n. 4)

[16] Par exemple, quand il parle de la simonie dans l'*Ep*. 42, 3, ou y fait allusion, comme dans *Sent*. I, 19, t. VI, 2, p. 13, 12 ; III, 108, *ib.*, p. 180, 6. L'un et l'autre cas sont rares dans son œuvre. Sur le fait que la simonie avait été, avant lui, considérée comme une hérésie, cf. *Simoniaca haeresis, Studi Gregoriani*, 1 (Roma, 1947), p. 523-530.

écrivains du moyen âge, avant lui, de son temps et après lui, et comme S. Augustin l'avait fait au manichéisme. Il y avait là, de fait, un ensemble d'idées étrangères à la tradition commune et dangereuses pour la foi du peuple chrétien.

Dans le cas d'Abélard, et surtout de Gilbert de la Porrée, a-t-il confondu avec une hérésie véritable ce qui n'était peut-être que recherche audacieuse, avec tout ce que celle-ci peut comporter d'innovation et de risque d'erreur, sans mettre la foi en péril? Sa façon de considérer comme hérétiques ces deux théologiens a-t-elle été partagée par ses contemporains et par ceux qui ont jugé ces penseurs dans les générations suivantes? Ce sont là des questions qu'il suffit ici de poser, après avoir tâché de préciser son attitude : celle-ci ne peut être comprise et jugée que par rapport à tout le mouvement des idées au douzième siècle.

Peter CLASSEN

DER HÄRESIE-BEGRIFF BEI GERHOCH VON REICHERSBERG UND IN SEINEM UMKREIS

Nach Abaelard und Bernhard soll nun Gerhoch von Reichersberg erörtert werden: [1] das überrascht wohl manchen. Denn Gerhoch kommt in der Geschichte der Ketzerei normalerweise nicht vor, weder als Ketzer noch als Bekämpfer derselben. Zwar ist er, drei Jahre jünger als Bernhard, Zeitgenosse der Ausbreitung neuer häretischer Bewegungen im zwölften Jahrhundert; aber in seinem bayerisch-österreichischen Umkreis sind diese zu seiner Zeit noch nicht in Erscheinung getreten. *Cathari* ist für ihn ein Wort für Novatianer - gelehrte Reminiszenz [2]. Ich war darum zunächst selbst überrascht, daß man mich um ein Referat über Gerhochs Häresie-Begriff bat. Immerhin wußte ich : Gerhoch hat ein Leben lang um die Reform der Kirche gerungen, und er ist nicht müde geworden, seine Gegner als Häretiker, ihre Lehren als Häresien zu bezeichnen — auf der anderen Seite sah er sich aber auch selbst dem Vorwurf der Ketzerei ausgesetzt.

Im Herbst 1130 fand in Regensburg ein Häresie-Prozeß in Gegenwart des Erzbischofs Konrad von Salzburg und des Bischofs Kuno von

---

[1] Das in Löwen vorgetragene Referat wird hier, nur um die notwendigsten Belege aus den Quellen ergänzt, unverändert vorgelegt.Allgemeine Literatur : Damien Van den Eynde, *L'œuvre littéraire de Géroch de Reichersberg*, Spicilegium Pontificii Athenaei Antoniani, 11 (Romae, 1957); Erich Meuthen, *Kirche und Heilsgeschehen bei Gerhoch von Reichersberg*, Studien und Texte zur Geistesgeschichte des Mittelalters, 6 (Leiden-Köln, 1959); Peter Classen, *Gerhoch von Reichersberg - Eine Biographie : Mit einem Anhang über die Quellen, ihre handschriftliche Überlieferung und ihre Chronologie* (Wiesbaden, 1960) ; A. Lazzarino del Grosso, *Armut und Reichtum im Denken Gerhochs von Reichersberg* (München, 1973). Verzeichnis aller Schriften und ihrer Überlieferung sowie der Editionen bei Classen. Wichtigste Editionen : J.P. Migne, PL, 193 und 194; *Gerhohi praepositi Reichersbergensis libelli selecti,* herausgegeben von Ernst Sackur in MGH, Libelli de Lite Imperatorum et Pontificum saeculis XI. et XII., 3 (Hannoverae, 1897), S. 131-525, im Folgenden zitiert *Lib.* 3; Damianus ac Odulphus Van den Eynde, Angelinus Rijmersdael, *Gerhohus Reichersbergensis : Opera inedita*, Spicilegium Pontificii Athenaei Antoniani, 8-9-10 (Romae, 1955-56), zitiert *Opera inedita*; Nicholas M. Häring, *Gerhoch of Reichersberg : Letter to Pope Hadrian about the Novelties of the Day*, Studies and Texts, 24 (Toronto, 1974), zitiert *Nov.*

[2] Migne, PL, 194, 845 C; *Opera inedita*, II, 67.

Regensburg statt, in den dann anscheinend auch Erzbischof Walther
von Ravenna, der Legat des kurz zuvor gewählten Papstes Innozenz
II., eingriff [3]. Dem Kanoniker Gerhoch, der dem Stift Rottenbuch
angehört hatte, wurde vorgeworfen, er habe die Wirksamkeit der Sakramente sündiger Priester geleugnet; er habe zweitens behauptet, irregu-
läre Priester könnten, sofern sie sich nicht bekehrten, nicht selig werden,
und drittens gesagt, außerhalb der Kirche könne Christi Leib nicht
dargebracht werden. Die Einzelheiten des Prozesses sind nicht ganz
deutlich erkennbar; jedenfalls bestritt Gerhoch entschieden, die Konsekrationsgewalt sündiger Priester in Frage gestellt zu haben, und man
konnte feststellen, der Satz *qui non est castus, non conficit Christi corpus*,
sei häretisch, ohne daß mit diesem Urteil Gerhoch direkt getroffen
wurde. Doch wurde ihm Schweigen befohlen.

Zwei Jahre nach diesem Prozeß berief der Salzburger Erzbischof
den Kanoniker-Reformer Gerhoch zum Propst des Stiftes Reichersberg
am Inn in der Diözese Passau. In diesem Amt verblieb er siebenund-
dreißig Jahre bis zu seinem Tode 1169.

Im Stift Rottenbuch (Diözese Augsburg), dem Zentrum deutscher
Gregorianer in Oberbayern, hatte Gerhoch sich zum Regular-Kanoniker
und radikalen Reformer bekehrt. Seine Radikalität lag nun aber nicht
in der Strenge der asketischen Forderung. An dem Konflikt um die
Augustinus-Regel, der in den 1120er Jahren die Kanoniker bewegte, hat
er sich kaum beteiligt, und später gehörte er zu jenen maßvollen Asketen,
die das Prämonstratensertum für eine monastische Abweichung vom
echten Kanonikertum hielten. Gerhochs Radikalismus liegt vielmehr in der Grundsätzlichkeit der Forderung des apostolischen Lebens
an den gesamten Weltklerus, zunächst und vor allem den Domklerus.
Er selbst, vor dem Eintritt in Rottenbuch, war ein gutsituierter und
angenehm - wenn auch gewiß nicht ausschweifend - lebender Domscho-
laster in Augsburg gewesen, und er hatte sich durch einen Eremiten
zu der Überzeugung bekehren lassen, daß allein die unbedingte Unter-
werfung unter die Regel der *vita communis et apostolica*, unter striktes
Armutsgebot und gemeinsames Leben, sein Seelenheil bewahren könne.
Nun betrachtete er es als seinen Auftrag, seine einstigen Standesgenossen
zu denselben Überzeugungen und Regeln zu bekehren [4].

---

[3] Zum Folgenden Classen, 47-57. Hauptquelle ist der *Dialogus, Lib.* 3, 203-239;
dazu R.B.C. Huygens, 'Le moine Idung et ses deux ouvrages : *Argumentum super
quatuor questionibus* et *Dialogus duorum monachorum*', *Studi Medievali*, Serie terza,
13 (1972), 291-470 (S. 345).

[4] Zur Bekehrungsgeschichte : Classen, 20-30.

Am Anfang von Gerhochs Wirken steht also religiöse Erfahrung und kirchliche Überzeugung; die theoretische - theologische und kanonistische - Begründung folgt hernach [5]. Das Ziel heißt *vita communis et apostolica* für den gesamten Dom-, Pfarr- und Stiftsklerus; zu überwinden sind weltliches Leben, eigener Besitz und private Wohnung der Kleriker, wohlgemerkt aller Weltkleriker. In den Kategorien der Kirchenreform des elften Jahrhunderts und des Kirchenrechtes heißen die Gegner Simonisten und Nikolaiten, und diese sind nach den Dekreten der Reformpäpste Schismatiker und Häretiker.

Betrachten wir die Lehren, die Gerhoch in den Jahren nach seiner Bekehrung um 1124 bis etwa 1132 entwickelt, im Einzelnen. So oft er die Häresie bekämpft und seine Gegner Häretiker nennt, definiert hat er den Begriff nie. Wir müssen also vom Einzelnen ausgehen. Simonie ist Häresie : das hat altkirchliche Lehre festgestellt, und die Päpste von Clemens II. über Nikolaus II., Alexander II., Gregor VII., Urban II. bis zu Paschalis II. haben es genauer bestimmt. Gerhoch wird nicht müde, Papst-Dekrete und Synodal-Canones der Reformzeit zu zitieren und zu interpretieren [6]. Einzelne Canones sind durch ihn am besten überliefert [7]. Neben sie treten echte und vermeintliche, d.h. pseudo-isidorische, Dokumente der Alten Kirche; gern wird auch der Brief Widos (von Arezzo?) gegen die Simonisten zitiert, der unter dem Namen eines Papstes Paschalis verbreitet war [8].

Den Simonie-Begriff faßt Gerhoch weit, indem er sich auf eine Decre-

---

[5] Zuerst in der Schrift *De aedificio Dei*, verfaßt 1128/29, erhalten nur in überarbeiteter Fassung von 1138. Die Edition *Lib.* 3, 136-202 kürzt den Text stark und macht die Zusammenhänge teilweise unverständlich ; die kanonistischen und patristischen Belege sind zwar verifiziert, aber nicht mit abgedruckt. Darum ist die ältere Edition Migne, PL, 194, 1187-1336 (nach Pez) unentbehrlich.

[6] Für die Zitate aus Papstdekreten und Synoden sei nur auf den - nicht immer vollständigen - *Index auctoritatum* in *Lib.* 3,770ff. (Pontifices Romani) verwiesen, dazu die Indices in *Opera inedita*, II.

[7] Der MGH, Leges, IV : Constitutiones, I, Nr. 49, S. 95 edierte Canon Papst Clemens' II. wird von Gerhoch *Lib.* 3,250 und 425 in etwas vollständigerer Form zitiert, als die von den Herausgebern benutzten Handschriften bieten. Über diesen Text vgl. im übrigen Ovidio Capitani, *Immunità vescovili ed ecclesiologia in età 'pregregoriana' e 'gregoriana'* (Spoleto, 1966), 60ff. Ein Auszug aus Akten einer Lateransynode von 1116 scheint am besten bei Gerhoch, *Lib.* 3, 190f., vgl. auch 217, überliefert zu sein.

[8] *Lib.* 3, 249 und 424, vgl. auch 266. Zu dem Brief vgl. Hartmut Hoffmann, 'Ivo von Chartres und die Lösung des Investiturproblems', *Deutsches Archiv*, 15 (1959), 393-440 (395f.) mit weiterer Literatur.

tale Urbans II. stützt, die ihrerseits Vorbilder bei Gregor VII. hat und inhaltlich auf Gregor d. Gr. zurückgeht [9]. Nicht nur Geld, sondern auch das *munus lingue* oder das *munus indebiti obsequii* bewirken Simonie. In Gerhochs Interpretation heißt das: jede unkanonische Verpflichtung, jeder Treueid, jeder materielle Gewinn beim Erwerb eines geistlichen Amtes ist Simonie. Mit Papst Urban II. lehnt Gerhoch die theoretische Trennung von Kirchengut und geistlichem Amt, von *beneficium* und *officium*, ab. Es geht ihm einerseits wie den Reformern des elften Jahrhunderts um die Beseitigung der Laienherrschaft über die Kirche, die jetzt, nach dem Wormser Konkordat, vor allem in Gestalt des *hominium* der Bischöfe auftritt. Aber das ist für ihn noch nicht simonistische Häresie, sondern nur Sakrileg [10]. Die Häresie sieht er vielmehr gerade in den innerkirchlichen Beziehungen, vor allem im Vikarswesen. Die Wahrnehmung der Pflichten eines höheren Geistlichen durch einen anderen gegen persönliche Verpflichtungen oder materielle Vergünstigungen ist die neue und besonders gefährliche Form der Simonie: *conductores* und *conducticii*, wie Gerhoch die Vermieter und Mietlinge des geistlichen Amtes nennt, [11] sind Simonisten, sind Häretiker. Aber auch jeder private Besitz der Kleriker entzieht der Kirche ihr Eigentum, gibt es für das geistliche Amt hin, ist also simonistisch. Die *vita communis et apostolica* der besitzlosen Kanoniker allein kann dies Übel überwinden.

Häretiker sind aber auch die Nikolaiten. Die Synoden der Päpste Nikolaus II. und Alexander II. haben das definiert, und sie haben verboten, die Messen verheirateter oder im Konkubinat lebender Priester zu hören [12]. Auch diese Häresie hat neue Formen entwickelt: mit einem Passus aus dem Apokalypse-Kommentar des Rupert von Deutz - der

---

[9] Urbans II. Brief JL 5743 wird von Gerhoch *Lib.* 3, 178, 212, 250 und öfter zitiert und benutzt, bei Gratian C. 1. 3. 8, vgl. vorher *Register* Gregors VII. VI, 34 (MGH, Epist. 2), Petrus Damiani PL, 145, 464ff.; Gregor d.Gr. PL, 76, 1092.

[10] Kritik am *hominium* zuerst im Erstlingswerk *De aedificio Dei*, *Lib.* 3, 140 ff., vgl. Classen, *Gerhoch*, 41ff. und Peter Classen, 'Das Wormser Konkordat in der deutschen Verfassungsgeschichte' in *Investiturstreit und Reichsverfassung*, herausgegeben von Josef Fleckenstein, Vorträge und Forschungen, 17 (Sigmaringen, 1973), 411-460(bes. 428ff.). Zum Sakrileg-Begriff vgl. *Lib.* 3, 206f. und 250ff.

[11] Dieser Begriff im Mittelpunkt der Polemik gegen innerkirchliche Simonie zuerst im *Dialogus*, *Lib.* 3, 227 und 238, später immer wieder, als Häretiker *Lib.* 3, 244.

[12] *Lib.* 3,215, 217 und öfter. Zur Uminterpretation der Papstdekrete vgl. Giovanni Miccoli, 'Il problema delle ordinazioni simoniache e le sinodi lateranensi del 1060 e 1061', in *Studi Gregoriani*, 5 (Roma, 1956), 33-81 (bes. 75ff.).

zwar nicht autoritatives Gewicht hat, aber die Lehre 'vernünftiger Menschen unserer Zeit' bezeugt, wie Gerhoch meint - wird nachgewiesen, daß nicht nur Ehe und Konkubinat des Priesters, sondern auch *fornicatio* und *vaga luxuria* den Tatbestand des Nikolaitismus erfüllen [13]. Gerhoch beruft sich, wie bemerkt, auf die Päpste. Der tätige Widerspruch gegen die Dekrete der Päpste ist es, der die Vergehen der Simonisten und Nikolaiten zur Häresie macht. Einer der Grundpfeiler für seinen Häretiker-Begriff ist der Satz *hereticum esse constat qui a Romana ecclesia discordat* [14]. Diese schon im Erstlingswerk ausgesprochene Definition kehrt später, z.T. etwas abgewandelt, wieder ; aber Gerhoch gibt niemals eine Quelle, geschweige denn eine verbindliche Autorität an, auf die er zurückgeht. Dabei hat der Satz seine Geschichte. Gregor VII. nennt ihn - in der Fassung *hereticum esse constat qui Romane ecclesie non concordat* - in dem Mandat, mit dem er im Jahre 1180 das Kloster Schaffhausen dem Abt Wilhelm von Hirsau unterstellt und das nicht nur im *Register*, sondern auch im Original erhalten ist [15]. Der Papst führt die Sentenz hier auf den heiligen Ambrosius zurück, bei dem es nicht einmal sinngemäß ähnliche Äußerungen, viel weniger diese prägnante Formulierung gibt [16]. Petrus Damiani hatte den

---

[13] *Lib.* 3, 218f. Doch vermeidet Rupert, die Nikolaiten als Häretiker zu bezeichnen: Das tut erst Gerhoch, freilich im Anschluß an Nikolaus II.

[14] Schon in der Erstlingsschrift : *Lib.* 3, 174, dann in *De simoniacis, Lib.* 3, 244 ; *De fide, Opera inedita*, I, 214.

[15] *Register* VII, 25.

[16] Die Frage, welcher Ambrosius-Text hier benutzt sein könnte, hat zuletzt Walter Berschin, *Bonizo von Sutri : Leben und Werk*, Beiträge zur Geschichte und Quellenkunde des Mittelalters, 2 (Berlin-New York, 1972), 48f. mit Benutzung älterer Hinweise von E. Caspar, C. Erdmann und J.J. Ryan erörtert. Leider ist eine Konfusion dadurch entstanden, daß die verschiedenen Autoren (was Berschin übersieht) verschiedene Ausgaben von Migne, PL, 16 benutzen, die - wie viele Migne-Bände - stark differierende Columnen-Zählung haben. Es geht um zwei Stellen : *Epistola* 11 § 4 in PL, 16 (1845), 946 A = PL, 16 (1866), 986 B und *De excessu fratris sui Satyri* I, 47 in PL, 16 (1845), 1306 AB = PL, 16 (1866), 1362f. Aber keine der beiden Stellen entspricht auch nur von Ferne dem Ambrosius von Gregor zugeschriebenen Gedanken (anders Berschin), den vielmehr zuerst Petrus Damiani prägnant formuliert, worauf schon E. Caspar (zu *Reg. Gregorii VII*, II 55a § 26) hinwies : PL, 144, 241 und PL, 145, 91. Eine ausführliche Analyse der Quellen des Petrus Damiani gibt J. Joseph Ryan, *Saint Peter Damiani and his Canonical Sources : A Preliminary Study in the Antecedents of the Gregorian Reform*, Studies and Texts, 2 (Toronto, 1956), 63ff. und 78ff. Eine plausible Erklärung für die Zuschreibung des Satzes an Ambrosius gibt es bisher nicht und kann ich auch nicht geben.

Satz schärfer gefaßt [17]; im *Dictatus papae* Gregors VII. heißt er : *Quod non catholicus habeatur, qui non concordat Romane ecclesie*, und in den jüngeren *Proprie auctoritates*, juristischer zugespitzt: *Qui decretis sedis apostolice non consenserit, hereticus habendus est* [18]. Bonizo von Sutri im *Liber ad amicum* (1086) [19], Kardinal Otto von Ostia in einem Brief an Bischof Udo von Hildesheim (1085) [20], der Sachse Bernhard in seiner Streitschrift gegen Heinrich IV. (1085) [21] und der Schwabe Bernold [22] zitieren das Wort als Satz des Ambrosius, alle wohl abhängig von Gregors Brief an Wilhelm von Hirsau; bei den letztgenannten ist die von Gerhoch gebrauchte Form zu finden. Wenn dieser aber nie eine Quelle für die Sentenz angibt, so deutet das darauf, daß er keine patristische Autorität für den Satz kannte, mit andern Worten: ihm war bewußt, daß Ambrosius ihn nicht verwendet hatte [22a].

Dabei ist nun freilich für Gerhoch wie für Gregor VII. der Häresie-Begriff austauschbar mit anderen: das Wort des großen Papstes, Ungehorsam gegen den apostolischen Stuhl sei das *peccatum paganitatis*, zitiert Gerhoch gern und verteidigt es mit Nachdruck [23]. So wenig wie bei

---

[17] *Ep.* I 20 in PL, 144, 241 : eos sacri canones haereticos notant qui cum Romana ecclesia non concordant ; *Opusc.* 5 in PL, 145, 91 : qui autem Romanae Ecclesiae privilegium ab ipso summo omnium ecclesiarum capite traditum auferre conatur, hic procul dubio in haeresim labitur, dazu vgl. Ryan a.a.O.

[18] Vgl. Hubert Mordek, 'Proprie auctoritates apostolice sedis : Ein zweiter Dictatus papae Gregors VII.?', *Deutsches Archiv*, 28 (1972), 105-133 (S. 127).

[19] *Bonizonis Episcopi Sutrini Liber ad amicum post editionem Jaffeanam*, herausgegeben von Ernst Dümmler in MGH, Libelli de Lite, 1 (Hannoverae, 1891), S 568-620 (S. 591), vgl. Berschin a.a.O.

[20] *Die Hannoversche Briefsammlung*, herausgegeben von Carl Erdmann in MGH, Die Briefe der deutschen Kaiserzeit, 5, Briefsammlungen der Zeit Heinrichs IV. (Weimar, 1950), S. 1-187 (S. 26).

[21] *Liber canonum contra Heinricum Quartum*, herausgegeben von Friedrich Thaner in MGH, Libelli de Lite, 1, S. 471-516 (S. 480).

[22] Joseph Rupert Geiselmann, *Bernoldus Constantiensis : Sein neuentdecktes Werk über die Eucharistie* (München, 1936), S. 97.

[22a] Gerhoch hat patristische Autoritäten oft kritisch erörtert und z.B. erkannt, daß der später (seit Erasmus) sog. Ambrosiaster nicht mit dem hl. Ambrosius identisch ist, vgl. Classen, *Gerhoch*, 74ff. und öfter, bes. an den im Register 483f. s.vv. historisch-philologische Kritik und Textkritik zitierten Stellen.

[23] Dieser Satz aus Gregors *Epistola extravagans* 32 (*The Epistolae vagantes of Pope Gregory VII*, edited and translated by H.J.E. Cowdrey, Oxford Medieval Texts (Oxford, 1972), S. 32) wird zitiert *Lib.* 3, 215, 216, 220 (alles im Dialog von 1130), später *Lib.* 3, 417f, 245.

Gregor darf man bei Gerhoch juristisch prägnante Begriffsbildung erwarten.

Simonie ist Häresie, Nikolaitismus ist Häresie, Widerspruch zu den Lehren der Römischen Kirche ist Häresie. Diese Sätze hat Gerhoch von den Reformpäpsten übernommen. Indem er nun sowohl den Simonie Begriff wie den Begriff des Nikolaitismus neu und neue Tatbestände umgreifend beschreibt, geraten alle oder nahezu alle Weltkleriker in Gefahr, als Häretiker zu gelten. Das wird zu einer umso kritischeren Frage, als Gerhoch Konsequenzen für die Sakramente zieht. Häretiker und Schismatiker stehen außerhalb der Kirche, sie können daher keine gültigen Sakramente vollziehen. *Extra ecclesiam non est locus veri sacrificii*, heißt der immer wieder zitierte Satz, der Augustin zugeschrieben wird [24]; *non est corpus Christi quod schismaticus conficit*, folgerte schon Papst Pelagius I. in einem Satz, den Gerhoch ebenso oft nennt [25]. Hier muß daran erinnert werden, daß auch noch Hugo von St. Viktor, Petrus Lombardus und andere angesehene Theologen des zwölften Jahrhunderts die Konsekrationsgewalt des von der Kirche getrennten Priesters leugneten; erst später, unter dem Einfluß der Kanonisten wie Simons von Tournai und anderer, wurde der *character indelebilis* des Priesters definiert und schließlich als allgemein gültige Lehre anerkannt [26].

Kritisch wurde Gerhochs Lehre vor allem durch die Behauptung, alle Simonisten und Nikolaiten seien *ipso facto*, ohne besonderen Prozeß und Urteil, durch die Dekrete der Päpste aus der Kirche ausgeschlossen und der Konsekrationsgewalt verlustig gegangen. Wenn dem so war, konnte man fragen, wo es denn noch wahre Sakramente gebe; und der im Prozeß gegen Gerhoch erhobene Vorwurf, er habe die Konsekrationsgewalt der *pravi sacerdotes* geleugnet [27], traf zwar nicht seine Theorie, beschrieb aber ziemlich genau deren praktische Konsequenzen.

Dem augustinischen Einwand, nicht das *pravum factum*, sondern erst die hartnäckige Verteidigung der falschen Lehre begründe den

---

[24] *Lib.* 3,226, 266, 286, 353, 425. Unmittelbare Quelle für Gerhoch ist wohl das Zitat des Satzes in dem angebl. Brief des Papstes Paschalis, d.h. dem Traktat Widos, *Lib.* 1,5 ; der Satz steht im *Liber sententiarum per Prosperum Aquitanicum collectum*, cap. 15 in Migne, PL, 51, 430. Unter Augustins Namen auch bei Gratian C. 1, q. 1, c. 71.

[25] *Lib.* 3,226, 266, 286, 405, 423 nach *Collectio Britannica Pelagius* ep. 22, Jaffé-Ewald 994, Gratian C. 24, q. 1, c. 34. Vgl. auch *Lib.* 3,598f.

[26] Vgl. Artur Michael Landgraf, *Dogmengeschichte der Frühscholastik*, III. 2 (1955), 223-231.

[27] *Lib.* 3, 225.

Häresie-Vorwurf, begegnete Gerhoch mit der Behauptung, dies gelte zwar für alle anderen Häresien, nicht aber für die Simonisten und Nikolaiten: bei diesen liege die Häresie in der Tat selbst [28]. Nur gewisse Einschränkungen für das praktische Leben ließ er gelten: wegen ihrer großen Masse seien die Nikolaiten und Simonisten nicht in gleicher Weise wie Arianer und Sabellianer verurteilt, und man dürfe deshalb mit ihnen leben und persönlich verkehren, aber ihre Sakramente seien gleichwohl ungültig und verboten[29].

Soweit die Lehren, die Gerhoch im Streit gegen die Weltkleriker entwickelt, bevor er als Propst die Verantwortung für ein kleines und entlegenes Stift zu übernehmen hat. Er hat seine Grundpositionen auch als Propst von Reichersberg nicht aufgegeben, aber in Einzelheiten präzisiert und modifiziert — und abgemildert. Der 1135 an Bernhard von Clairvaux gerichtete Traktat gegen die Simonisten wurde überschrieben *Libellus de eo quod princeps mundi huius iam iudicatus sit* [30]. Der Fürt dieser Welt 'ist schon gerichtet' : mit dem Wort des Johannes-Evangeliums (16, 11) wird die These wiederholt, daß *ipso facto* [31] Simonisten und Nikolaiten als Häretiker verurteilt und ihre Sakramente ungültig seien. Neu ist jetzt, daß Gerhoch diese Lehre auf die offenkundigen, *manifesti simoniaci et nicolaite*, einschränkt: die geheimen Sünder bleiben dem Gericht Gottes vorbehalten [32]. Praktisch war es freilich kaum möglich zu sagen, wessen Simonie oder *fornicatio* 'offenkundig' war. Wichtiger ist die genannte Schrift wegen ihrer neuen Distinktionen in der Sakramentenlehre, die die allgemeine Verwerfung der Häretiker-Sakramente ablösen. Jetzt wird zugegeben, daß außerhalb der Kirche *sacramenta integra*, aber *irrita* vollzogen werden können, die einen *effectus passivus* (*quo sacramenta efficiuntur*) haben; aber nur in der Kirche gibt es die *sacramenta rata*, denen der *effectus activus* (*quem sacramenta efficiunt*) zukommt und die das *verum sacrificium* bilden [33]. Schließlich ist einzuräumen, daß bei den an der *creatura rationalis* vollzogenen Sakramenten, Taufe und Ordo, der außerhalb der Kirche fehlende *effectus activus* einem *sacramentum integrum sed irritum* durch

[28] *Lib.* 3,219f.
[29] *Lib.* 3,220.
[30] *Lib.* 3, 239-272; vgl. Van den Eynde, 34-42; Classen, *Gerhoch*, 78-89, 408f. Das Stichwort steht schon *Lib.* 3,214.
[31] Auch dies Stichwort schon im Dialog von 1130, *Lib.* 3, 214.
[32] *Lib.* 3,245, 263 und öfter, vorbereitet im Dialog *Lib.* 3, 220f.
[33] *Lib.* 3, 253-262, vgl. Classen, *Gerhoch*, 84f.; Landgraf, *Dogmengeschichte*, III, 2,240 ff.

eine kirchliche *confirmatio* nachträglich zuteil werden kann [34]. Anders die Eucharistie : außerhalb der Kirche wird nicht das Fleisch des Lammes, sondern die *caro draconis* genossen [35]. Diese für die Sakramentenlehre und die kirchliche Praxis nicht unwichtigen Distinktionen wirken sich aber nicht direkt auf den Häresie-Begriff aus. Für diesen ist aber festzustellen, daß bestimmte Formen des Umgangs mit Kirchengut nun nicht mehr als Simonie, sondern nur noch als Sakrileg bestimmt werden und demnach nicht unter das Häresie-Verdikt fallen [36]. Bernhard von Clairvaux, dem dies alles in einem Traktat vorgetragen wurde, antwortete nicht.

Gerhoch steht, das ergibt sich deutlich aus dem Gesagten, ganz bewußt in der Tradition der gregorianischen Reform. Er kommt aus demselben Kreis wie Paul von Bernried, der Biograph Gregors VII., und wenn es irgendwo im zwölften Jahrhundert noch echte 'Gregorianer' gab, so waren es diese bayerischen Regularkanoniker. Indem sie die Reformgegner rigoros verketzerten, gerieten sie freilich rasch selbst in den Verdacht der Häresie, wie einst die Patarener oder jener Ramihrdus, der zu Gregors VII. Zeit in Cambrai verbrannt wurde, weil er - den päpstlichen Dekreten gemäß - die Messen beweibter Priester verdammte [37]. Nicht nur Manegold von Lautenbach, der frühere Dekan von Gerhochs Profeß-Stift Rottenbuch [38], sondern auch Erlembald von Mailand wurde von den Reichersbergern zu ihren Vorläufern gerechnet: täusche ich mich nicht, so sind diese Regularkanoniker die einzigen Kirchenreformer, die sich so direkt noch um 1150 auf die *Pataria* berufen.

Von ähnlichen Ansätzen ging der Regularkanoniker Arnold von Brescia aus, und er hat in vielen Punkten dasselbe gelehrt und gepredigt wie Gerhoch; vielleicht sind sich beide sogar persönlich begegnet [39]. Der entscheidende Gegensatz zwischen den beiden Reformern, die den Weltklerus angriffen, liegt im Verhältnis zur Römischen Kirche, deren

---

[34] *Lib.* 3,258f., 267; vgl. schon *Dialogus, Lib.* 3,225.- Gerhoch distinguiert zugleich zwischen dem bloßen *sacramentum* und dem *verum sacrificium*, das allein Heil bringt, bes. *Lib.* 3,267.

[35] *Lib.* 3,266.

[36] *Lib.* 3,250ff. bes. über Laien, die Kirchengut gegen *indebitum obsequium* vergeben. Vgl. Classen, *Gerhoch*, 82.

[37] Vgl. *Register* Gregors VII., IV, 20.

[38] *Lib.* 3,232f., vgl. 221, auch Arno von Reichersberg, *Scutum canonicorum*, in PL, 194, 1490-1528 (1499 A).

[39] Classen, *Gerhoch*, 105ff.

Autorität für Gerhoch auch dann noch gültig blieb, als er seit dem Ponti-
fikat Hadrians IV. stärkere Zweifel an der Weisheit des Papstes und
der Richtigkeit seiner Entscheidungen bekam. Über Arnold von Brescia
urteilte Gerhoch später, er habe zwar falsche Lehren verbreitet, doch aus
gutem Eifer, und er verurteilte die Hinrichtung Arnolds, mit dessen Blut
sich die Römer befleckt hätten [40]. Ein Häretiker war Arnold in Gerhochs Augen nicht : deutlich zeigt sich gerade daran, welche Kluft
zwischen Gerhoch und Bernhard von Clairvaux bestand, jenem Bernhard, dem Gerhoch Mangel an Eifer vorgeworfen hatte.

Gegen die Simonisten als Häretiker hatte sich Gerhochs Angriff
zunächst gerichtet. Häresie und Schisma ist nicht dasselbe, das wußte
auch Gerhoch. Aber die Reformer des elften Jahrhunderts, auch die
Päpste, hatten oft genug die Schismatiker als Häretiker gebrandmarkt:
Cadalus und Wibert galten als Häresiarchen - und wer die Simonie
als Häresie betrachtete, hatte doppelten Anlaß für diese Gleichung.
Für Gerhochs wichtigstes Anliegen, die Sakramente, schien es ohnehin
keinen Unterschied zu geben: das Wort *extra ecclesiam non est locus
veri sacrificii* traf die Schismatiker genauso wie die Häretiker; der Satz
non est corpus Christi quod schismaticus conficit [41] bedeutete im Ergebnis
dasselbe. Das hatte seine Konsequenzen im Schisma Anaklets: nach
Gerhoch besaßen dessen Anhänger keine Konsekrationsgewalt, und mit
diesem Argument suchte er - freilich vergeblich - Bernhards Hilfe für
seine Sakramentenlehre zu gewinnen. Zugleich meinte Gerhoch, daß
die häretischen, nämlich simonistischen Weltpriester weithin zu Anaklet
hielten, während seine Freunde von den Regular-Kanonikern den rechten Papst, Innozenz II., unterstützten [42]. Die Gleichung Häretiker =
Simonist = Schismatiker = Weltpriester schien aufzugehen, für Anaklets
Schisma so gut wie für die früheren des Cadalus und des Wibert.

Auch 1159 haben Alexander und Victor sich wechselseitig nicht nur
als Schismatiker, sondern auch als Häretiker angegriffen [43]. Das ist vor
allem für den kanonistisch hoch gebildeten Alexander recht auffallend.
Gerhoch hatte inzwischen, seit dem Tode Eugens III., manche Ent-
täuschung mit Rom erlebt. Die Lehre, die Römische Kirche habe stets

---

[40] *De investigatione Antichristi*, I, 40, *Lib.* 3,347f.

[41] Vgl. oben Anm. 24 und 25.

[42] Der Dialog von 1130 ist als Brief an Innozenz II. gerichtet, vgl. dort bes. *Lib.*
3,236f. Dem *Libellus* von 1135 am Bernhard von Clairvaux liegt derselbe Gedanke
zugrunde.

[43] Als Beispiele seien genannt für Victor IV. JL 14426 bei Rahewin IV 60 S. 299,
für Alexander III. JL 10645.

den rechten Glauben bewahrt, hatte er schließlich unter Hadrian IV,
mit dem Argument gestützt, selbst als Papst Liberius die Ketzer begün-
stigte, habe es in Rom noch einen rechtgläubigen Priester gegeben, der
mithin den 'erwählten Nachfolgern Petri' zuzurechnen sei [44]. Das neue
Schisma beunruhigte ihn tief, weil dieses Mal keine offenkundige Häresie die Ursache war - aber beide Kandidaten der Simonie verdächtig
erschienen. Jetzt schied er scharf: das Schisma spaltet die *unitas*, Häretiker bestreiten die *veritas* [45].

Wir sind damit bereits bei dem späten Gerhoch angelangt, der die
rigorosen Lehren der Frühzeit, ohne das Reformziel preiszugeben, stark
abgemildert, damit aber auch seinen schroffen Häresie-Begriff aufgegeben hat. Noch 1148 schreibt er seinen *Liber contra duas hereses*,
der als Einleitung zu seinem großen Psalmenkommentar dienen soll.
Von den beiden Häresien, die er da bekämpft, ist die eine die Lehre,
auch Schismatiker- und Häretiker-Sakramente seien gültig; die andere
betrifft die Christologie. Von diesem Traktat gibt es eine ungedruckte,
nur ein bis zwei Jahre jüngere Fassung, in dem die bekämpften Lehren
nicht mehr *hereses*, sondern nur noch *assertiones*, Behauptungen, heißen,
und zwar an allen Stellen, wo sie früher Häresien genannt waren. Die
Vokabel ist ausgetauscht, während der Wortlaut sonst unverändert
bleibt [46].

Mit dem zuletzt genannten Traktat haben wir auch Gerhochs christologischen Streit berührt, der ihn seit 1141 über fünfundzwanzig
Jahre lang in immer neuen Anläufen beschäftigt hat. Es begann mit
Angriffen auf die Lehren des kurz zuvor verurteilten Abaelard und seiner auch in Bayern und Österreich auftretenden Schüler ; zugleich
kritisierte Gerhoch die Paulus-Glossen Gilbert Porretas. Später geraten
der Gilbert-Schüler und Schulmeister in Wien, Petrus, sowie der Kano-
nikerpropst Folmar von Triefenstein in den Mittelpunkt der Polemik;
der vornehmste Gegner, mit dem Gerhoch sich mehrmals auseinanderzusetzen hat, ist der Bischof Eberhard II. von Bamberg. Hier können
wir weder die Lehren Gerhochs und seiner Gegner darstellen, noch gar
deren Rechtgläubigkeit prüfen. Es geht um den Häresie-Begriff. Dies
Wort kommt nun in der Polemik oft vor, und doch gewinnen wir aus
dem sehr umfänglichen Stoff wenig für unser Thema. Manchmal werden

---

[44] *Liber de laude fidei*, *Opera inedita*, I, 254, Classen, *Gerhoch*, 190.
[45] *De investigatione Antichristi*, I, 53, *Lib*. 3,359f.
[46] Vgl. Classen, *Gerhoch*, 125f., 416ff. Nur die erste Fassung ist gedruckt : PL,
194, 1161-1184.

die bekämpften Lehren mit denen seit alters verurteilter Häretiker
identifiziert, arianisch, sabellianisch, nestorianisch genannt; ein andermal
werden sie solchen Lehren nur verglichen, ähnlich oder auch schlimmer
als diese geheißen [47]. Oft aber begnügt man sich, von falscher Lehre,
error, perversum dogma oder dergleichen zu sprechen. Wir sahen schon,
daß ein Traktat 'gegen zwei Häresien' in zweiter Auflage 'gegen zwei
Behauptungen' gerichtet wurde. Die Tonart der Polemik schwankt,
nicht selten wird man persönlich; dann kann der Gegner ein Narr, aber
auch ein Vorläufer des Antichrist genannt werden; gelegentlich zieht
man recht unfreundliche Vergleiche aus dem Tierreich - und dann gibt
es auch einmal wieder eine sachlichere und höflichere Tonart [48].

Bei alledem ist deutlich, daß der Vorwurf der Häresie zu den härtesten
gehört, und er wird öfter gegen eine Lehre als gegen eine Person gerichtet. Man droht wohl gelegentlich mit Denuntiation beim Papst oder auch
beim Kaiser - aber es kommt nicht dazu [49]. Sehr auffallend ist aber,
daß in der jahrzehntelangen Polemik Gerhochs gegen Gilbert niemals
auf den Spruch des Reimser Konsistoriums 1148 Bezug genommen
wird, obwohl Gerhoch ihn ganz gewiß kannte [50]. Dieser Spruch war ja
kein Ketzergericht gewesen [51]; immerhin hätte er die Polemik stützen
können. Aber auch die Verurteilung Abaelards durch Papst Innozenz II.
erwähnt Gerhoch eigenartigerweise nie, obwohl er Bernhard anregt, die
Liste der Irrlehren Abaelards noch zu ergänzen [52].

[47] In den 50er Jahren kommt der Häresie-Vorwurf öfter vor als später, doch stets
allgemein gefaßt, etwa *nostri temporis dialectici vel potius heretici, Nov.* 4,30 p. 37,
oder *Iudei et iudaizantes heretici, Nov.* 16, 10 p. 64 und 18,4 p. 73. In der persönlichen
Polemik gegen Gilbert und Petrus von Wien wird dagegen nur indirekt der Häresie-
Vorwurf erhoben. Die Briefe der 60er Jahre sind noch vorsichtiger in dieser Hinsicht.

[48] Besonders drastische Polemik etwa in dem Brief an Petrus von Wien, *Opera
inedita*, I, 357-366 und noch schärfer später gegen Folmar von Triefenstein, vgl. die
folgende Anmerkung - doch auch hier kein direkter Häresie-Vorwurf.

[49] Gerhoch behauptet, Folmar habe ihn beim Kaiser der Häresie bezichtigt :
Pl, 193,530f. Ob das wahr ist, sei dahingestellt. Umgekehrt beschuldigt
Gerhoch Folmar beim Papst, ohne aber direkt von Häresie zu reden : PL, 193,574f.

[50] Die Reimser Sätze gegen Gilbert sind gerade auch in den österreichischen
Bibliotheken öfter überliefert, vgl. Peter Classen, 'Zur Geschichte der Frühscholastik
in Österreich und Bayern', *Mitteilungen des Instituts für Österreichische Geschichts-
forschung*, 67 (1959), 249-277 (bes. 261); Nicolas M. Häring, 'Das sogenannte Glaubensbekenntnis des Reimser Konsistoriums von 1148', *Scholastik*, 40 (1965), 55-90 (bes.
74ff., 86).

[51] Das hat Häring in der eben genannten und anderen Arbeiten mit Recht hervorgehoben.

[52] So in dem von Georg Hüffer, 'Handschriftliche Studien zum Leben des hl. Bernard

Charakteristisch für Gerhoch ist nun aber, wie er stets die dogmatischen mit den Fragen des kirchlichen Lebens verknüpft. Seit der frühesten Auseinandersetzung mit den Weltklerikern schienen die 'Schulen' verdächtig, die die strengen Forderungen des Evangeliums hinweginterpretierten - in denselben Schulen aber wird ein 'regelloses' Leben geführt. So entsteht ein Begriffsgegensatz *scholastice - ecclesiastice*, und dieser wird recht früh auch auf die Formel gebracht *scholae in Francia* einerseits, *ecclesia Romana* andererseits [53]. In den Schulen ohne Regel und Vernunft, *in scholis discolis*, stellen Schüler und Lehrer *questiones indisciplinate* - und das ist der Ursprung irriger Lehren. Zwar lernte Gerhoch in späteren Jahrzehnten, daß es auch unter den Weltklerikern gute und unter den Regularkanonikern schlechte Kirchenmänner gab - aber zu den herbsten Enttäuschungen des 70jährigen zählte es, daß ausgerechnet ein Regularkanoniker-Propst, Folmar von Triefenstein, die schlimmsten christologischen Irrlehren mit den bösartigsten persönlichen Angriffen gegen Gerhoch verband.

Gerhoch war und blieb ein Einzelgänger ohne Einfluß: auch das unterscheidet ihn grundlegend von Bernhard. Aber er ist ein interessantes Symptom, ein Kritiker und Spiegel seiner Zeit. Er zeigt, wie gregorianisches Denken im zwölften Jahrhundert zur Kritik an der Kirche, in der Kirche wird, und dabei der Häresie-Vorwurf gegen die Mehrheit des Klerus und gerade gegen die 'gregorianisch' erscheinenden Bischöfe gerichtet wird - wie aber der Häresie-Vorwurf dann leicht gegen den Urheber gerichtet werden kann.

Gerhoch kennt umfänglichen kanonistischen und patristischen Stoff - ein festes System der Interpretation fehlt ihm ebenso wie ein präziser Begriffs-Apparat, wenn er auch als Philologe und Kritiker Beachtliches leistet. Es wird gut sein, nach Gerhoch auch die Kanonistik zu hören [54].

Zuvor aber noch eine Ergänzung. Ich bin gebeten worden, mit Gerhoch dessen Umkreis zu erörtern. Sein nächster Anhänger, sein Bruder Arno, hat in seinen z.T. noch ungedruckten Werken zwar manchen originellen Gedanken entwickelt; aber zu unserem Thema bringt er, sehe ich recht, nichts Neues [55]. Das wenige, was wir von Gerhochs Gegner

von Clairvaux', *Historisches Jahrbuch*, 6 (1885), 73-91 und 232-270 (268ff.) edierten Brief am Schluß, vgl. Classen, *Gerhoch*, 350.

[53] So schon im Dialog von 1130, *Lib.* 3, 227 und 235, ähnlich später sehr oft.

[54] Dazu die Referate von Othmar Hageneder und Helmut G. Walther, unten in diesem Bande.

[55] Einiges in Arnos *Scutum canonicorum*, PL, 194, 1493-1528. Der *Apologeticus* (herausgegeben von C. Weichert, 1888), bewegt sich auf der Linie wie Gerhochs

Petrus von Wien, vielleicht ein Theologe französischer Herkunft, wissen, enthält zwar manche giftige Ironie und Polemik, aber wiederum nichts für den Häresie-Begriff [56]. Dagegen verdient Otto von Freising hier kurze Erwähnung. Er hat wiederholt Gerhoch kritisiert und Gilbert Porreta gegen Gerhoch in Schutz genommen; doch sind seine Schriften darüber verloren. Bekanntlich hat er aber in seinen *Gesta Friderici imperatoris* den Prozeß gegen Gilbert sehr ausführlich erörtert und zum Anlaß genommen, auch Abaelards letzten Prozeß darzustellen [57]. Liest man diese großen Prozeßberichte, so fällt es auf, daß Otto die gelehrten Theologen niemals *heretici* nennt, auch nicht Abaelard, dem er doch deutlich kritisch gegenübersteht. Nur in den wörtlich wiedergegebenen Aktenstücken, der Klageschrift französischer Bischöfe gegen Abaelard und Papst Innozenz' Urteil gegen diesen, fällt das fatale Wort. Offenbar hat Otto weder Abaelard noch Gilbert als Häretiker betrachtet - was nicht bedeutet, daß er alle ihre Lehren billigte. Dagegen erwähnt er im Zusammenhang mit dem Reimser Konzil von 1148 den damals verurteilten Sonderling Eon von Stella mit der Bemerkung, er habe sich bei den Volksmengen die Ehre eines *hereticus* angemaßt - *quidam pene laicus heretici honorem in vaccis populorum affectans* [58]. Offenbar schien ihm Eon so ernst nun wieder nicht zu nehmen zu sein. Im übrigen kennt Otto in der Chronik selbstverständlich die altkirchlichen Häretiker, und in den geschichtstheologischen Periodisierungen sind sie für ihn wie für andere Theologen vor und nach ihm - darunter auch Gerhoch und Bernhard - Kennzeichen einer bestimmten längst vergangenen Epoche, die auf die der blutigen Verfolger und der Märtyrer folgt.

Zuletzt noch ein Wort über Anselm von Havelberg, Gerhochs Zeitgenossen. Er ist Prämonstratenser, steht dem Kaiserhofe nahe, reist mehr-

dogmatische Schriften um 1163, vgl. Eligius M. Buytaert, 'The *Apologeticus* of Arno of Reichersberg', *Franciscan Studies*, 11, 3/4 (1951), 1-47. Auch das *Hexaemeron*, das noch ungedruckt ist, bietet für unser Thema nichts Wesentliches, vgl. neben Classen, *Gerhoch*, 431-434 künftig die noch ungedruckte Dissertation von Israel Peri (Heidelberg, 1973), die im Jahrbuch des Stiftes Klosterneuburg 1976 erscheinen wird.

[56] Von Petrus' eigenen Schriften ist nur ein Traktat gegen Gerhoch erhalten, herausgegeben von Heinrich Weisweiler, 'Das wiedergefundene Gutachten des Magister Petrus über die Verherrlichung des Gottessohnes gegen Gerhoch von Reichersberg: Ein Beitrag auch zur Wesensbestimmung der Scholastik', *Scholastik*, 13 (1938), 225-246.

[57] *Ottonis et Rahewini Gesta Friderici I. Imperatoris*, herausgegeben von Georg Waitz und Bernhard v. Simson, MGH, Scriptores rerum Germanicarum in usum scholarum, dritte Auflage (Hannoverae-Lipsiae, 1912), S. 67-88.

[58] *Gesta*, I, 56, S. 81.

mals nach Byzanz. In seinem *Anticimenon* berichtet er von den Streit-
gesprächen mit den griechischen Theologen in Konstantinopel 1136 [59].
Diese öffentlichen Disputationen waren von dem ernsten Willen getragen,
einander zu verstehen und zu verständigen. Demgemäß wird von beiden
Seiten der Vorwurf der Häresie sorgfältig vermieden: die abweichenden
Lehren sind noch nicht ohne weiteres Irrlehren, und Anselm schickt den
gut zwölf Jahre nach den Ereignissen niedergeschriebenen Dialogen
ein umfängliches Buch *de uniformitate fidei et multiformitate vivendi* [60]
voraus: der eine Glaube schließt nicht Unterschiede der Lebensform aus.
Das wird an der Vielfalt der Orden des Westens erläutert, und so vorbereitet, kann man auch die Unterschiede zwischen den Kirchen des Ostens
und des Westens verstehen, ohne von Häresie zu sprechen. Nur historisch stellt Anselm fest, daß in der Vergangenheit die Römische Kirche
immer wieder fest gegen alle Häresien gestanden hat, während Konstantinopel ihnen oft unterlag [61]. Das gilt ihm als wesentlicher Beweis für
den besonderen Auftrag und die Autorität der Römischen Kirche. Allein die in der alten Kirche verurteilten Lehren werden hier Häresien
genannt. Von den gegenwärtig strittigen Lehren — insbesondere *filioque*
und Azymen - wird keine als häretisch bezeichnet. Nur ein Vorwurf
bringt die Griechen in den Verdacht der Ketzerei, nämlich daß sie latei-
nische Konvertiten noch einmal taufen. Wiedertaufe ist aber schon
von der alten Kirche als häretisch verurteilt. Indessen machen die Griechen glaubhaft, daß eben dieser Vorwurf zu Unrecht erhoben wird [62].
Anselm wie Otto zeigen eine unverkennbare Vorsicht im Umgang mit
dem Begriff der Häresie, der weder theologisch noch juristisch scharf
definiert ist, eine Vorsicht, zu der Gerhoch sich selbst im Alter nur mit
Mühe durchringen konnte.

---

[59] Migne, PL, 188, 1139-1248. Die wesentliche neuere Literatur ist zusammengestellt
von Johann Wilhelm Braun, 'Studien zur Überlieferung der Werke Anselms von
Havelberg I. : Die Überlieferung des *Anticimenon*', *Deutsches Archiv*, 28 (1972).
133-209 (S.134).

[60] Dies der Titel des ersten Buches des *Anticimenon*.

[61] *Anticimenon*, III, 5f., PL, 188, 1213-1217.

[62] *Anticimenon*, III, 21, PL, 188, 1246f.

Othmar HAGENEDER

DER HÄRESIEBEGRIFF BEI DEN JURISTEN
DES 12. UND 13. JAHRHUNDERTS

Zu den Neuerungen, die das elfte und besonders das zwölfte Jahrhundert im Gefolge der sogenannten Gregorianischen Reform und der
mit ihr parallel laufenden politischen und wirtschaftlichen Wandlungen
hervorbrachten, gehörte der Stand des Juristen. Sein Auftreten hängt
mit einem bildungsgeschichtlichen Ereignis zusammen: das entweder
traditionell überlieferte oder zum Teil wiederentdeckte Recht wurde
nun, vor allem an den sich bildenden Universitäten, mit einer neu
geschaffenen, unterscheidenden und kommentierenden Methode ausgelegt und gelehrt [1]. Für das römische Recht war dafür die Auffindung
der heute in Florenz befindlichen Digestenhandschrift und die kritische
Rekonstruktion eines Textes dieser Quelle, der *littera Bononiensis*, von
entscheidender Bedeutung [2], und in der Entwicklung des Kirchenrechtes
spielten der Camaldulensermönch Joannes Gratianus und seine um
1140 verfaßte sowie rasch verbreitete *Concordia discordantium canonum*
eine ähnliche Rolle. Sie faßte eine Auswahl der durch mehr als 1000
Jahre in den verschiedenen christlichen Ländern und unter diversen
Bedingungen angesammelten Rechtsmaterie zusammen, um das Leben
innerhalb der Kirche zu regeln und ihre Stellung in der mittelalterlichen
Welt festzulegen. Diese traditionell überlieferte Quellenmasse versuchte
Gratian nach der scholastischen Methode des *sic et non* zu gliedern und

---

[1] Vgl. dazu Franz Wieacker, *Privatrechtsgeschichte der Neuzeit*, Jurisprudenz
der Neuzeit, 7, 2. Auflage (Göttingen, 1967), 45ff.; Helmut Coing, 'Die juristische
Fakultät und ihr Lehrprogramm', in *Handbuch der Quellen und Literatur der neueren
europäischen Privatrechtsgeschichte*, 1, *Mittelalter (1100-1500)* : *Die gelehrten Rechte
und die Gesetzgebung*, herausgegeben von Helmut Coing, Veröffentlichung des Max-
Planck-Instituts für europäische Rechtsgeschichte (München, 1973) [=HBPRG],
39ff.; Peter Classen, 'Die hohen Schulen und die Gesellschaft im 12. Jahrhundert',
Archiv für Kulturgeschichte, 48 (1966), 155-180 (bes. 164ff) ; Horst Fuhrmann, 'Das
Reformpapsttum und die Rechtswissenschaft', in *Investiturstreit und Reichsverfassung*,
herausgegeben von Josef Fleckenstein, Vorträge und Forschungen, 17 (Sigmaringen,
1973), 175-203 (bes. 193ff.).

[2] Wieacker, *Privatrechtsgeschichte*, 46ff.; Peter Weimar, 'Die legistische Literatur
der Glossatorenzeit', in HBPRG, 129-260 (158).

ihre Widersprüche durch seine *dicta* auszugleichen, so daß ein innerlich geordnetes Rechtsbuch geschaffen werden sollte [3]. Die besondere kirchenpolitische Situation, wie sie sich um die Mitte des zwölften Jahrhunderts ergab, bildete für dieses Beginnen den geistigen Hintergrund. Der Investiturstreit war zu Ende, der Versuch, die Christenheit unter anderem mit Hilfe der *canones et decreta sanctorum patrum,* also des Rechtes der spätantiken Kirche - so wie man es damals verstand - zu reformieren und aus ihrer Verflechtung mit der Welt der Laien zu lösen, hatte seine Grenzen gefunden. Nun galt es, dieses im Sinne der Reform neu belebte Recht der alten Kirche mit deren innerem Aufbau, wie er sich im frühen und hohen Mittelalter entwickelt und dem ja der Angriff von Seiten der Gregorianer gegolten hatte, in Übereinstimmung zu bringen. Beide Ströme der Rechtsentwicklung mußten nun irgendwie verbunden und einander angeglichen werden. Das war mit ein Zweck des *Decretum Gratiani* und wurde von der Kanonistik als Wissenschaft, die sich jetzt aus der Theologie löste, fortgeführt [4]: die Dekretisten der verschiedenen Schulen begannen, das Dekret mit Glossen und Summen zu versehen, unter denen besonders die Summe des Huguccio von Pisa, das zwischen 1188 und 1190 verfaßte Hauptwerk der Dekretistik, einen besonderen Platz einnimmt [5]. Dieselbe Behandlung erfuhr, besonders an der Universität Bologna, das *Corpus iuris civilis,* das dadurch gleichfalls eine innere Einheit erlangte [6].

Wenn wir nun nach dem Häresiebegriff der Juristen fragen, so ergibt sich aus dem eben Gesagten, daß ihn sowohl die Dekretisten als auch die Glossatoren des römischen Rechts aus der Tradition gewannen; handelte es sich doch meist um alte, vor mehr oder weniger langer Zeit entstandene Texte, über die sie reflektierten. Nur neue Texte, die sie zur Grundlage ihrer Interpretation machen konnten, waren in der Lage, ihrem Denken frische Ansatzpunkte zu liefern. Solche stellten im Bereiche des Kirchenrechtes die päpstlichen Dekretalen dar, die seit dem zwölften Jahrhundert als Urteile, Rechtsgutachten, Delegationsreskripte (*litterae*

---

[3] Alphonsus M. Stickler, *Historia iuris canonici Latini,* I, *Historia Fontium* (Augustae Taurinorum, 1950), 200ff.; Knut Wolfgang Nörr, 'Die Entwicklung des Corpus iuris canonici', in HBPRG, 835-846.

[4] So Stephan G. Kuttner, *Harmony from Dissonance* : *An Interpretation of Medieval Canon Law,* Wimmer Lecture, 10 (Latrobe, 1960), 22ff.

[5] Dargestellt zuletzt von Knut Wolfgang Nörr, 'Die kanonistische Literatur', in HBPRG, 365-383 (370ff.).

[6] Weimar, 168 ff.

revocatoriae) usw. das Recht fortentwickelten; sowie ferner die Akte der konziliaren Gesetzgebung, besonders die Konstitutionen der ökumenischen Konzile [7]. Daß die seit der Mitte des zwölften Jahrhunderts stark auflebenden Häresien der Katharer und Waldenser in diesen Rechtsverfügungen einen Niederschlag fanden, ist zu erwarten. Bald standen sie in den *Quinque antiquae Compilationes* und schließlich im *Liber Extra* Papst Gregors IX. für die Dekretalisten zur Glossierung bereit [8] und bewirkten so eine Erweiterung des kirchenrechtlichen Häresiebegriffs. Er ist daher am besten den großen Glossenapparaten und Summen des dreizehnten Jahrhunderts zu entnehmen, wie zum Beispiel den *Glossae ordinariae* zum *Decretum Gratiani* und zum *Liber Extra*, welche die glossierende Auseinandersetzung der Kanonisten mit diesen Texten zu einem gewissen Abschluß brachten. Für das Dekret hat sie Johannes Teutonicus um 1216 verfaßt und Bartholomäus Brixiensis bald nach 1245 überarbeitet; und was die Dekretalen Gregors IX. betrifft, so widmete sich Bernardus de Botone Parmensis von 1241 bis 1266 derselben Aufgabe [9]. Eine ähnliche Bedeutung besitzen für uns der Glossenapparat Papst Innocenz' IV. (1246-1254), die *Summa in titulos decretalium* des Goffred von Trani, die in den Jahren 1241-1243 entstand, und die *Summa aurea* des Hostiensis (ca. 1250), alle zum *Liber Extra*; handelt es sich bei ihnen doch um reife und gleichsam klassische Zusammenfassungen des damaligen kirchenrechtlichen Denkens [10]. In Bezug auf das römische Recht können der noch in den beiden ersten Jahrzehnten des dreizehnten Jahrhunderts fertiggestellten *Summa in Codicem* des Azo Portius und dazu der ein wenig später entstandenen *Glossa ordinaria* des Accursius zum *Corpus iuris civilis* für unser Problem entscheidende Aussagen entnommen werden [11]. Außerdem mehren sich in der kirchenrechtlichen Argumentation seit dem Ende des zwölften Jahrhunderts die Verweise auf das *ius Romanum*. Meist wurde es bloß suppletorisch verwendet, das heißt dort angeführt, wo eine kanonistische Regel fehlte. Auch diente es zur Interpretation kirchlicher Rechtsnormen. Oft untermauerte man *argumenta* aus kirchlichen Rechtsquellen durch

---

[7] Vgl. dazu Charles Lefèbvre, 'L'âge classique 1140-1378 : Sources et théorie du droit', in *Histoire du droit et des institutions de l'Eglise en Occident*, publiée sous la direction de Gabriel Le Bras, 7 (Paris, 1965), 133ff.

[8] Vgl. Nörr, *Kanonistische Literatur*, 376 ff.

[9] Ebd. 371, 376.

[10] Ebd. 377 f.

[11] Vgl. dazu Weimar, 173f., 180; Wieacker, *Privatrechtsgeschichte*, 63.

gleichgesinnte Zitate, die dem *Corpus iuris civilis* entnommen wurden [12]. Auf all das weist der bekannte Spruch hin: 'Canonista sine legibus nihil, legista sine canonibus parum' [13]. Die Folge war, daß bisweilen das Vorbild der spätantiken Cäsaren eine ausgesprochene Weiterentwicklung der Lehre bewirkte, denn vielfach wurde das römische Kaiserrecht auf die kirchliche Institution des Hl. Stuhles übertragen, wobei man dem Papste Rechte der römischen Imperatoren zuschrieb; ein Prozeß, der sich auf die Entwicklung der Kirche nicht durchwegs positiv ausgewirkt hat [14]. Dieses Phänomen wird uns auch bei der Ausgestaltung des Häresiebegriffes durch die Juristen begegnen.

Was bezeichneten nun die Kanonisten als Häresie? In der ersten Hälfte des dreizehnten Jahrhunderts entstand eine Liste jener Vergehen, deretwegen jemand als Häretiker verurteilt werden konnte. In der *Glossa ordinaria* zum *Liber Extra* lautet sie folgendermaßen [15]:

Zu X.V, 7, 3 ad v. 'haereticum' : haereticus multis modis dicitur:

[1]   Ille dicitur haereticus, qui pervertit sacramenta ecclesie, ut simoniacus, [C.] I q. 1 Eos qui per pecuniam (21) et [C.] 6 q. 1 c. Nos sequentes (19) § Sed licet

[2]   Item ille, qui scindit se ab unitate ecclesiae, [C.] 7 q. 1 Denique (9)

[3]   Item omnis excommunicatus, [C.] 4 q. 1 Quod autem hi (2 fin.)

---

[12] Lefèbvre, 173ff. (bes. 175ff.); Gabriel Le Bras, 'Innocent IV romaniste : Examen de l'Apparatus', in *Studia Gratiana*, 11 (= *Collectanea Stephan Kuttner*, 1), (Bologna, 1967), 305-326 (320 f.); Stephan Kuttner, *Some Considerations on the Role of Secular Law and Institutions in the History of Canon Law*, Scritti di sociologia e politica in onore di Luigi Sturzo, 2 (Bologna, 1953), 354 f. Daraus schöpft Hans Erich Feine, 'Vom Fortleben des römischen Rechts in der Kirche', in *Reich und Kirche : Ausgewählte Abhandlungen zur deutschen und kirchlichen Rechtsgeschichte* (Aalen, 1966), 198 f. Prinzipiell : Coing, Einleitung zum HBPRG, 28.

[13] Friedrich Merzbacher, 'Die Parömie "Legista sine canonibus parum valet, canonista sine legibus nihil"', in *Studia Gratiana*, 13 (= *Collectanea Stephan Kuttner*, 3), (Bologna, 1967), 273-282; Fuhrmann, *Reformpapsttum und Rechtswissenschaft*, 195f. mit Anm. 47.

[14] Vgl. dazu auch die Bemerkungen von Friedrich Kempf im *Archivum Historiae Pontificiae*, 7 (1969), 529 f. und Gabriel Le Bras, 'Le droit Romain au service de la domination pontificale', *Revue historique de droit français et étranger*, 4e série, 27 (1949), 397f.

[15] Der folgenden Wiedergabe liegt der Druck Venetiis, Apud Juntas, 1615 zugrunde, den ich auch im folgenden benütze. Vgl. auch den Abdruck bei Henri Maisonneuve, *Études sur les origines de l'Inquisition*, in *L'Église et l'État au Moyen Age*, 7, 2. Aufl. (1960), 339, Anm. 196. Die Arbeit von C. Pozo, 'La noción de "herejía" en el derecho canónico medieval', *Estudios Eclesiásticos*, 35 (1960) (= Misc. Pérez Goyena?), 235-261 war mir leider nicht zugänglich.

[4] Item qui errat in expositione sacrae scripturae, [C.] 24 q. 3 Heresis
(27)

[5] Item qui confingit novam sectam vel confictam sequitur, [C.] 24
q. 3 Haereticus (28).

[6] Item qui aliter sentit de articulis fidei quam Romana ecclesia,
[C.] 24 q. 1 Haec est fides (14) et c. Quoniam (25)

[7] Vel qui male sentiunt de sacramentis ecclesiae, infra eodem Ad
abolendam, in princ(ipio) (X.V, 7, 9). Tancr(edus).

Die Zusammenstellung wird also hier dem Kanonisten Tancred zugeschrieben. Dasselbe tut Goffred von Trani in seinem Glossenapparat
zum *Liber Extra*, der in der Wiener Handschrift dieses Werkes die Nrr.
1, 2, 4, 5 und 6 der eben wiedergegebenen Liste als Häresiedelikte an-
führt und mit der Sigle T. versieht [16]. In der Tat finden sich nun die
ersten sechs Punkte der oben abgedruckten und der *Glossa ordinaria*
zum *Liber Extra* entnommenen Zusammenstellung in den beiden,
einerseits zwischen 1210 und 1215 und andererseits um 1220 verfaßten
Redaktionen der *Glossa ordinaria* des Tancred zur *Compilatio I*, einer
1190 entstandenen Dekretalensammlung, bei der gleichen Dekretale
(5, 6, 3 = X. V, 7, 3) wieder [17]. Goffred von Trani hat dieselbe Liste
für seine *Summa in titulos decretalium*, deren Entstehung in die Jahre

---

[16] Wien, Nationalbibliothek, CVP 2197, fol. 136 ra. Zu diesem Apparat vgl. zuletzt
Martin Bertram, 'Der Dekretalenapparat des Goffredus Tranensis', *Bulletin of Medieval
Canon Law*, N.S. 1 (1971), 79-83, zur Datierung (1234-1243) ebd. 83. Goffred war
zur Zeit der Abfassung *auditor litterarum contradictarum* an der Kurie : Peter Herde,
*Audientia litterarum contradictarum : Untersuchungen über die päpstlichen Justiz-
briefe und die päpstliche Delegationsgerichtsbarkeit vom 13. bis zum Beginn des 16.
Jahrhunderts*, I, Bibliothek des Deutschen Historischen Instituts in Rom, 31 (Tübingen,
1970), 66.

[17] Admont, Stiftsbibliothek, HS. 22, fol. 71 va zur 1 Comp. 5,6,3 : Sex modis
dicitur hereticus... T. Ebenso Biblioteca Apostolica Vaticana, Borgh. 264, fol. 60
ra; Chis. E VII 207, fol. 74 ra (=1. Rezension) und Graz, Universitätsbibliothek,
HS. 138, fol. 65 ra (= 2. Rezension). Zu diesem Apparat und seinen Handschriften
vgl. Stephan Kuttner, 'Johannes Teutonicus, das vierte Laterankonzil und die Compilatio quarta', in *Miscellanea Giovanni Mercati*, V, Studi e Testi, 125 (Romae, 1946),
608-634 (608, Anm. 2, 624, Anm. 8). Siehe zuletzt Nörr, *Kanonistische Literatur*, 373
und die dort angegebene Literatur. Dem Stiftsbibliothekar und -archivar von Admont, Herrn Univ. Prof. Oberstudienrat DDr. Adalbert Krause, habe ich für die
Liebenswürdigkeit, mit der er mir die hier verwendeten Handschriften zugänglich
machte, herzlich zu danken; ebenso der Universitätsbibliothek Graz und besonders
Frau Oberstaatsbibliothekar Dr. Maria Mairold für die freundliche Beschaffung eines
Mikrofilmes.

1241 bis 1243 gesetzt wird, ein wenig verändert und zum Teil erweitert. Hier heißt es nun [18] :

Haereticus dicitur sex modis:

[1] Haereticus dicitur, qui falsam de fide opinionem vel gignit ut haeresiarcha, sicut Arrius, Sabellius et Macedonius, vel sequitur, vel qui haeresiarcham imitatur, sicut Arriani, Sabelliani et Macedoniani, C. 24 q. 3 c. Haereticus (28) et c. Quid(am) § Sabelliani et § Arriani § Macedoniani (39 § 41-43)

[2] Secundo modo potest haereticus appellari quicunque aliter scripturam intelligit, quam sensus spiritus sancti flagitat, a quo scripta est, licet ab ecclesia non recesserit, ut C. 24 q. 3 c Haeresis (27)

[3] Tertio modo dicitur haereticus, qui a sacramentis ecclesiae et communione fidelium est divisus, ut C. 4 q. 1 c. Quod autem (2)

[4] Quarto modo dicitur haereticus sacramentorum perversor, ut simoniacus, qui emit et vendit sacramenta ecclesiastica, ut C. I q. 7, c. Patet (27)

[5] Quinto modo dicitur haereticus dubius in fide, ut infra eo(dem) titulo) c. 1(X. V, 7, 1). Nam firmiter debemus credere, ut supra de Summa Trini(tate) et fi(de) ca(tholica) Firmiter (X. I, 1, 1), 23 Dist. c. Quando episcopus (D. 24, 5), [C.] 24 q. 1 c. Aperte (36). Unde levi argumento a fide deviare haereticus censetur, ut C(odice) eo(dem) ti(tulo) l(ege) 2 (Codex 1,5,2)

[6] Sexto modo dicitur haereticus, qui Romanae ecclesiae privilegium ab ipso summo ecclesiarum capite traditum auferre conatur, ut Dist. 22 c. 1.

Im wesentlichen handelt es sich auch hier um dieselben Vergehen, wie sie bereits Tancred angeführt hatte, nämlich das Bekenntnis zu einer Irrlehre - sei es, daß man sie verkündet oder ihr bloß folgt-, eine von der römischen Kirche abweichende Schriftauslegung, die Trennung von der kirchlichen Sakramentenspendung und der Gemeinschaft der Gläubigen durch die Exkommunikation, die Simonie, den öffentlich bekundeten Glaubenszweifel sowie jedes auch nur geringfügige Abweichen von der orthodoxen Lehre und schließlich die Leugnung des päpstlichen Jurisdiktionsprimates [19]. Der zuletzt genannte Punkt fehlt allerdings in der Tancred zugeschriebenen Liste, ist aber alt und wurde, wie noch zu

---

[18] *Summa Goffredi de Trano in titulos decretalium* (Venetiis, 1570), fol. 199va/b; vgl. auch Maisonneuve, *Origines de l'Inquisition*, 334f. mit Anm. 183. Über die Entstehungszeit des Werkes vgl. Bertram, 83, Anm. 16.

[19] So auch Maisonneuve, a.a.O., 334f.

zeigen sein wird [20], bereits im zwölften Jahrhundert von Huguccio ausführlich behandelt. Außerdem führt ihn Johannes Teutonicus in seiner *Glossa ordinaria* zum Dekret an, die zwischen 1215 und 1217 entstand sowie um 1245 durch Bartholomäus Brixiensis überarbeitet wurde. Denn auch dieser Apparat enthält eine Liste der häretischen Tatbestände. Sie entspricht der bei Goffred von Trani überlieferten, wenn auch die einzelnen Punkte anders gereiht sind. Nur der letzte Paragraph, eben die Leugnung des Primats der römischen Kirche, findet sich in einer erweiterten Form und schließt in einem angereihten siebten Absatz die Übertretung der Gebote des apostolischen Stuhles an [21]. Wie das gemeint war, wird noch zu zeigen sein.

Mit Ausnahme der von Bernardus de Botone Parmensis in der *Glossa ordinaria* zu X. V, 7, 3 unter dem § 7 angeführten falschen Lehren über das Wesen der Sakramente, einer Neuerung des zwölften Jahrhunderts [22], ist der Häresiebegriff der Kanonisten traditionell; das heißt, er stützt sich auf die im *Decretum Gratiani* gesammelten Quellen. Daher wurden die einzelnen Tatbestände auch schon von den Dekretisten des zwölften

[20] Siehe unten 65 ff.

[21] *Glossa ordinaria* zu C. 24 q. 3 dict. p. c. 25 ad v. 'haeresim' : Vario modo dicitur haereticus :
Vno modo quicumque est dubius in fide, infidelis est, ut ex(tra) de here(ticis) Dubius (X. V, 7, 1)
Secundo dicitur haereticus omnis simoniacus, ut [C.] 1 q. 1 Quisquis (5).
Tertio omnis precisus ab ecclesia, secundum quod excommunicatus dicitur haereticus, ut [C.] 4 q. 1 cap. 2
Quarto modo omnis, qui male interpretatur sacram scripturam, ut infra ea(dem) Haeresis (27)
Quinto modo, qui novam opinionem invenit, ut inf(ra) ea(dem) Haereticus (28)
Sexto modo, qui vult auferre privilegium Romanae ecclesiae, ut 22 d. Omnes (1)
Septimo qui transgreditur praecepta sedis apost(olicae), ut sup(ra) 19 d. Nulli (5).
Dieser Text folgt dem Druck des *Decretum Gratiani* (Venetiis, Apud Juntas, 1615), der die *Glossa ordinaria* selbstverständlich in der Überarbeitung durch Bartholomäus Brixiensis enthält. Die Erstfassung des Johannes Teutonicus ist inhaltlich gleich : vgl. Wien, NB, CVP, 2082, fol. 168 va. Die einzige wichtige Variante findet sich im § 1 : 'in fide, infidelis est, ut' fehlt und 'extra I de her(eticis) dubius' (1 Comp. 5, 6, 1) ist von anderer Hand nachgetragen. Zu dieser Handschrift vgl. Stephan Kuttner, *Repertorium der Kanonistik (1140-1234)* : *Prodromus Corporis glossarum*, Studi e Testi, 71 (Romae, 1937), 98 und Derselbe : 'Bernardus Compostellanus antiquus : A Study in the Glossators of the Canon Law', *Traditio*, 1 (1943), 277-340 (292, Anm. 77). Vgl. auch den Teilabdruck bei Peter Huizing, 'The Earliest Development of Excommunication Latae Sententiae by Gratian and the Earliest Decretists', in *Studia Gratiana*, 3 (Bologna, 1955), 277-230 (284, Anm. 16).

[22] Siehe unten 83.

Jahrhunderts einige Male zusammengestellt, wodurch Modelle entstanden, an die sich die Kanonisten des beginnenden dreizehnten Jahrhunderts halten konnten. Davon mögen die *Summa decretorum* des
Sicard von Cremona (1179-1181) [23], die *Summa decretalium* des Bernardus Balbi von Pavia (1191-1198) [24] und aus dem Anfang des folgenden
Jahrhunderts die *Glossa Palatina* des Laurentius (1212-1214) zum
Dekret [25] sowie die um 1215 entstandene Dekretalensumme des Dama-

---

[23] Zu C. 24 q. 3 : Videndum est, quid sit heresis, unde dicatur, que differentia inter
scisma et heresim. Quot sint genera hereticorum et unde denominentur.

Heresis est dogma perversum fidei Christiane contrarium. Dicitur ab herendo, id
est dubitando, vel ab eligendo vel a greco 'her', quod est virtus. Dicitur enim ab errando.
Heresis est perversio catholicae veritatis. Scisma est perversio catholice pacis.

          In fidei violatione. Hoc proprie
          In contumaci scripture explanatione
Hereticus   In pacis dissensione. Ut scismaticus
          In sacramentorum contaminatione. Ut symoniacus

Wien, NB, CVP, 2166, fol. 53va. Zur HS. vgl. Kuttner, *Repertorium*, 151; Derselbe,
'An Interim Checklist of Manuscripts (II)', *Traditio*, 12 (1956), 560-566 (562); zu Sicard:
Nörr, *Literatur*, 372.

[24] Liber V, titulus VI, De haereticis §1 : Quatuor modis dicitur haereticus. Dicitur
enim haereticus errans a fide, unde sic diffinitur : haereticus est, qui falsam de fide
opinionem gignit vel sequitur; gignit, ut haeresiarcha, ut Arrius, Sabellius; sequitur, ut
qui haeresiarcham imitatur, velut Arriani et Sabelliani, ut C. XXIV qu. 3. Haereticus
est (c. 28). Item dicitur haereticus perversus expositor sacrarum scripturarum, ut C.
XXIV qu. 3 Haeresis (c. 27); dicitur etiam haereticus a sacramentis ecclesiae divisus,
ut est excommunicatus, ut C. IV qu. 1 Quid autem (c. 2); praeterea dicitur haereticus
perversor sacramentorum, sicut ille, qui ecclesiastica vendit vel emit sacramenta, ut
simoniacus ut C. I qu. 1 Quisquis per pecuniam (c. 5) (Ern. Ad. Theod. Laspeyres,
Bernardi Papiensis Faventini episcopi Summa Decretalium (Ratisbonnae, 1860; Nachdruck Graz, 1956), 213, zur Datierung LXI; vgl. auch Nörr, *Literatur*, 374.

[25] Zu C. 24 q. 3 dict. p. c. 25 : Quinque modis dicitur quis hereticus :

Qui levi argumento a fide deviat, C. de hereticis, 1. III (sic, Codex 1, 5, 2), extra
I de hereticis, Dubius (1 Comp. 5, 6, 1)

Qui vendit sacramenta ecclesie, sicut est omnis symoniacus, s(upra) [C.] I q. I
Quisquis per pecuniam (5)

Qui abscidit se ab unitate ecclesie et omnis excommunicatus, s(upra) [C.] III [I]
q. I, Qui (sic!) autem hii (2)

Qui errat in expositione sacre scripture, [C.] XXIIII q. III Heresis (27)

Qui confingit novam sectam vel confictam sequitur aliqua vana gloria, [C.] XXIIII
q. IIII (sic, recte : III) Hereticus (28) Biblioteca Apostolica Vaticana, Palat. lat.,
658, fol. 72 r; Regin. lat. 977, fol. 209 rb; zur Datierung vgl. Alfons M. Stickler,
'Il decretista Laurentius Hispanus', *Studia Gratiana*, 9 (Bologna, 1966), 461-549
(544), zu den HSS., Kuttner, *Repertorium*, 81 ff.

sus [26] als Beispiele genannt werden. Inhaltlich bieten sie gegenüber den späteren Zusammenstellungen des dreizehnten Jahrhunderts nichts neues. Diese wurden schließlich um 1250 vom berühmten Kanonisten Hostiensis nochmals ausgestaltet, wenn auch substantiell keineswegs erweitert. Doch hat er den römisch-rechtlichen Häresiebegriff, wie er inzwischen von den Legisten durch die Interpretation des *Corpus iuris civilis* entwickelt worden war, mit in die Interpretation einbezogen; ein Punkt, über den noch zu handeln sein wird [27].

Der rote Faden, der alle angeführten Häresiearten miteinander verbindet, ist die Trennung von der Kirche auf Grund eines Glaubensirrtums. Daher gelten im weiteren Sinne auch die Juden und Heiden als Häretiker, da sie die von der römischen Kirche gelehrten Glaubensartikel nicht bekennen; wenn auch strikte unter einem Ketzer nur jemand verstanden wurde, der ursprünglich der Kirche angehört und sich wegen eines Irrtums im Glauben von ihr entfernt hatte [28]. Das konnte sich in verschiedener Weise manifestieren, wie die besprochene Liste zeigt. Betrachtet man die in ihr angeführten Tatbestände historisch, so lassen

---

[26] De hereticis : Hereticus est, qui falsam de fide opinionem vel gignit vel sequitur, qui gignit heresiarcha vocatur, ut [C.] XXIIII q. III Hereticus (28). Dicitur etiam large hereticus etiam symoniacus, qui sacramenta pervertit, ut [C.] I q. I Fertur (28). Item excommunicatus, ut [C.] IIII q. I Quod autem (2). Stiftsbibliothek Klosterneuburg, HS. 1048, fol. 41 vb. Zur HS. vgl. Kuttner, *Repertorium*, 394, Derselbe, 'An Interim Checklist of Manuscripts (I)', *Traditio*, 11 (1955), 439-448 (445). Über Damasus und die *Summa titulorum* zur *Compilatio I* vgl. Charles Lefèbvre, Art. 'Damasus', *Dictionnaire de droit canonique*, 4 (Paris, 1949), 1014-1019 (bes. 1016).

[27] *Summa aurea*, Liber V, De hereticis, Neudruck der Ausgabe Lugduni, 1537 (Aalen, 1972), fol. 237r ff. Zu diesem Werk vgl. Nörr, *Literatur*, 378; Über die Allegierung von Texten des römischen Rechts siehe unten 94 f..

[28] So die *Glossa Palatina* des Laurentius (1212-1214) zu C. 24 q. 3 c. 26 : Item nota quod hereticus dicitur quandoque stricte quandoque large : stricte, qui ab initio fuit in ecclesia et ab ea est postea separatus propter heresim, et secundum hoc quilibet est excommunicatus, extra de hereticis Ad abolendam (1 Comp. 5,6,11); large, quicumque sentit aliter de articulis quam ecclesia Romana tenet, et secundum hoc non est omnis excommunicatus, quia non Iudei, non Sarraceni, licet heretici sint, quia utrique sentiunt contra articulos fidei, cum enim numquam tales in ecclesia fuerant, non potuerunt excommunicari (Biblioteca Apostolica Vaticana, Pal. lat. 658, fol. 72rb; mit unwesentlichen, zum Teil fehlerhaften Varianten auch im Regin. lat. 977, fol. 209 ra). Kürzer äußert sich zum Problem die *Glossa ordinaria* zu C. 24 q. 3 dict. p. c. 25 : Item quandoque large dicitur haereticus omnis, qui non tenet articulos fidei, et secundum hoc Iudaei et gentiles sunt haeretici, et secundum hoc non omnis haereticus est excommunicatus. Stricte sumitur haereticus omnis, qui remotus est ab ecclesia, quia errat in fide, et secundum hoc omnis haereticus est excommunicatus, ut extra de here(ticis) Ad abolendam et c. Excommunicamus (X.V, 7, 9.13).

sich mehrere Schichten des Häresiebegriffs erkennen, die seine geschichtliche Entwicklung und Ausgestaltung widerspiegeln.

1) Das älteste Fundament stellen einige Aussagen der Kirchenväter
Hieronymus und Augustinus dar, die im *Decretum Gratiani* Aufnahme
fanden. Nach ihnen galt als Häretiker, wer — auch wenn er Mitglied der
Kirche war — hartnäckig falsche und neu erdachte Glaubenslehren vertrat
und besonders die Hl. Schrift anders interpretierte, als es der vom Hl.
Geist hineingelegte Sinn, der *sensus spiritus sancti*, erforderte [29]. Daraus
folgerten die Kanonisten sinngemäß: Häresie ist ein hartnäckiger Glaubensirrtum sowie die Bildung von Sekten und die Zugehörigkeit zu
diesen [30]. Manche betonten ausdrücklich, daß sich die irrige Schriftauslegung auf die Glaubensartikel beziehen müsse, um als Häresie zu
gelten [31]. Stets wird die Hartnäckigkeit im Irrtum unterstrichen,

[29] C. 24 q. 3 c. 27 : Unde autem heresis dicatur, in eadem epistola Ieronimus diffinit
dicens : Unde dicatur heresis? Heresis grece ab electione dicitur, quod scilicet eam
sibi unusquisque eligat disciplinam, quam putat esse meliorem. Quicumque igitur
aliter scripturam intelligit, quam sensus spiritus sancti flagitat, a quo scripta est,
licet ab ecclesia non recesserit, tamen hereticus appellari potest, et de carnis operibus
est, eligens que peiora sunt.
   Dictum Gratiani : Qui vero proprie dicantur heretici, Augustinus ostendens ait :
C. 24 q. 3 c. 28 : Qui proprie dicantur heretici : Hereticus est, qui alicuius temporalis
commodi et maxime gloriae principatusque sui gratia falsas ac novas oppiniones vel
gignit vel sequitur. Ille autem, qui huiusmodi hominibus credit, est imaginatione quadam veritatis illusus (Ed. Friedberg, I, 997 f.).
[30] Vgl. oben 46 §§ 4,5 und 47 § 1 sowie die *Summa decretalium* des Bernhard Balbi
von Pavia V, 6, 1 : Dicitur enim haereticus errans a fide, unde sic diffinitur : haereticus
est, qui falsam de fide opinionem gignit vel sequitur; gignit, ut haeresiarcha, ut Arrius,
Sabellius; sequitur, ut qui haeresiarcham imitatur, velut Arriani et Sabelliani, ut
C. XXIV q. 3 Haereticus est (c. c. 28). (Ed. Laspeyres, 213; die ganze Stelle vgl. oben
Anm. 24).
[31] Ebd. V, 6, 2 : Hic vero accipitur haereticus in prima significatione, scil(icet)
de eo, qui errat in articulis fidei (Ed. Laspeyres, 213).
   Ähnlich die nach 1202 verfaßte und von Huguccio abhängige Glosse 'Ecce vicit
leo' zu C. 24 q. 3 c. 27 ad v. 'aliter scripturam intelligit': de illis tantum scripturis intellige,
que loquuntur de articulis fidei; qui enim illas male intelligit, est hereticus sive ex
certa scientia sive ab errore, quia in talibus non differt decipere vel post se decipi.
[C.] XVI q. I si cap.(?). In aliis non est... Immo sancti multociens se contradicunt,
ut s(upra) XXVI d. Unius (1) (Stiftsbibliothek St. Florian, HS. XI 605, fol. 96 rb).
Herrn Prof. Dr. Karl Rehberger, dem Stiftsarchivar und -bibliothekar von St. Florian,
danke ich herzlich für die Freundlichkeit, mit der er mir Einsicht in die HS. ermöglichte. Zum Glossenapparat 'Ecce vicit leo' vgl. Nörr, *Literatur*, 372.
   Ein wenig anders formuliert die *Glossa Palatina* des Laurentius Hispanus (1212-
1214) zu C. 24 q. 3 c. 27 ad v. 'aliter scripturam intelligit' : ita quod eius expositio sit

wobei man sich abermals auf einen Brief des Hl. Augustinus, der gleichfalls im Dekret stand, berufen konnte [32]. Spätere Kanonisten sprachen
in einem solchen Falle von einer formellen Häresie, die ein wissentliches
und widerspenstiges Fürwahrhalten des Falschen darstelle, als strafbares
Delikt zu werten sei und zur sogenannten materiellen Häresie, dem
bloßen Irren im Bezug auf die Kirchenlehre, im Gegensatz stehe [33].

Diese Überzeugung vom hartnäckig festgehaltenen Irrtum als Bedin-
gung jeder Häresie kam auch bei der kanonistischen Scheidung zwischen
Häresie und Schisma zur Geltung. Sie geht gleichfalls auf Hieronymus
zurück und wurde durch das *Decretum Gratiani* der Kanonistik bekannt [34].
Uns interessieren hier allein die Folgerungen, welche die Dekretisten
und Dekretalisten aus dem entsprechenden Texte zogen. Ihrer Meinung

contra fidem et religionem christianam, licet alias teneat articulos fidei (Biblioteca
Apostolica Vaticana, Pal. lat. 658, fol. 72 rb, Regin. lat.977, fol. 209 va). Vgl. auch
unten Anm. 35 (*Glossa Palatina*) und 39.

[32] C. 24 q. 3 c. 29 :... Sed qui sentenciam suam, quamvis falsam atque perversam,
nulla pertinaci animositate defendunt..., corrigi parati cum invenerint, nequaquam
sunt inter hereticos deputandi (Ed. Friedberg, I, 998).

Vgl. dazu die Glosse 'Ecce vicit leo' : hic, quod heretici sunt vitandi post ammoni-
tionem et dicitur hereticus, qui errorem suum defendit contumaciter (Stiftsbibliothek
St. Florian, HS. XI 605, fol. 96 rb) sowie die *Glossa ordinaria* ad v. 'pertinaci' : Licet
ergo teneat aliquis ea, quae sunt contra fidem, dummodo paratus sit corrigi, non
est habendus haereticus, ut supra e(adem) q(uaestione) I (nter) schisma, in prin(cipio)
(26?), Haec est (q. 1 c. 14). Im Casus der *Glossa ordinaria* zu diesem *capitulum* heißt
es : Sequentia duo capita plana sunt, in quibus dicitur, quod qui in errorem cadunt
nec volunt corrigi, sunt inter haereticos deputandi. (Vgl. dazu den Text von C. 24
q. 3 c. 31).

Siehe ferner noch die Glosse 'Ecce vicit leo' zu C. 24 q. 3 c. 27 (in Fortsetzung
des in der Anm. 31 wiedergegebenen Textes) : Vel dicatur, quod si quis in sacra scriptura aliam expositionem ex sensu proprio fingat, que aliis expositionibus autenticis
contradicit, quod non debet facere, ut XXXVII dist. Relatum (14), et eam contumaciter defendat contra sacras auctoritates : hereticus reputatur, ar(gumento) infra
e(adem) Dixit (29) (Ebd.).

[33] Nicolaus München, *Das kanonische Gerichtsverfahren und Strafrecht*, 2 (Köln-
Neuß, 1866), 318f., Paul Hinschius, *System des katholischen Kirchenrechts mit besonde-
rer Rücksicht auf Deutschland*, 1 (Berlin, 1869; Nachdruck Graz, 1959), 46 f. mit
Anm. 6. Daher erscheint es mir fraglich, ob auch die C. 24 q. 3 c. 30 auf die Häresie
bezogen werden kann, wie Ludwig Buisson, *Potestas und Caritas : Die päpstliche
Gewalt im Spätmittelalter*, Forschungen zur kirchlichen Rechtsgeschichte und zum
Kirchenrecht, 2 (Köln-Graz, 1958), 182 meint.

[34] C. 24 q. 3 c. 26 : Scismatis et heresis differentia : Inter heresim et scisma hoc
esse arbitror, quod heresis perversum dogma habet, scisma post episcopalem disces-
sionem ab ecclesia pariter separat... Ceterum nullum scisma, nisi heresim aliquam
sibi confingit, ut recte ab ecclesia videatur recessisse (Ed. Friedberg, I, 997).

nach war Häretiker, wer widerspenstig eine falsche Ansicht über den Glauben vertrat, während das Schisma eine offene Trennung von der Gemeinde darstellte. Allerdings sei, so betonten sie, ein Schisma auf die Dauer ohne Häresie nicht möglich, da sich - wie ja auch schon der Kirchenlehrer angedeutet hatte - jede Sekte bald Kirche nenne und eine Häresie erfinde, um ihre Trennung dogmatisch zu rechtfertigen. Daher konnte, so folgerten sie, jedes hartnäckige Verharren in einem Schisma als Häresie angesehen werden. Jeder Häretiker war also als Schismatiker zu bezeichnen, da er sich dogmatisch von der Kirche getrennt hatte; umgekehrt sollte aber nur dann ein Schismatiker als Häretiker gelten, wenn das Schisma lange andauerte [35]. Die Hartnäckigkeit, mit der ein Schismatiker an der Spaltung festhielt, konnte also zur Häresie führen:

---

[35] So schon die Summa '*Elegantius in iure divino*' seu Coloniensis, die um 1169 entstand, in der Pars tertia c. 12 : Quod scismatici heretici dici possint. Porro hereticus est, qui a fidei veritate, scismaticus vero, qui a catholica unitate et pace discedit. Quia tamen nec scissio matris ecclesie sine divisione nec divisio sine scissione agitur, non immerito omnis scismaticus hereticus nominatur (Ed. Gérard Fransen adlaborante Stephano Kuttner, Monumenta Iuris Canonici, Series A : Corpus Glossatorum, Vol. 1 (New York, 1969), 118. Ähnlich Bernardus Balbi von Pavia in seiner *Summa decretalium* V, 7, 1. 3 : Schisma... differt autem ab haeresi, scil(icet) in initio sui ; cum vero iam creverit, incipit dicere congregationem suorum ecclesiam, et ita videtur cadere in haeresim et peccare in illo articulo fidei, scil(icet) : Credo sanctam ecclesiam catholicam, ut C. XXIV q. 3 Inter haeresim (c. 26) (Ed. Laspeyres, 215).

Ein wenig differenzierter ist die *Glossa Palatina* des Laurentius Hispanus zur C. 24 q. 3 c. 26 : Nota quod scisma proprie dicitur cum aliquis, qui erat in ecclesia, recedit ab ea parte, scilicet mente et corpore, male sentiendo de aliquo articulo fidei, non propter alterum tantum puta; vel quia male sentiat (senserat B) et non recedit, quod notat illud 'nisi sibi aliquam' et hoc etiam innuit G(ratianus) i(nfra) e(adem) q(uestione) § ult. in fi(ne) (40?)... Item nota, quod omnis scismaticus hereticus, sed non convertitur, et ita ea est ibi differentia quae inter partem et totum (Biblioteca Apostolica Vaticana, Pal. lat. 658, fol. 72 rb. : A; Regin. lat. 977, fol. 209rb : B. mit einigen weiteren unwesentlichen Varianten).

Siehe außerdem die traditionelle Formulierung in der *Glossa ordinaria* zur C. 24 q. 1 c. 21 ad v. 'sceleratius', c. 31 ad v. 'nil habere' und zur C. 24 q. 3 c. 26 sowie die oben 45 wiedergegebene Liste der Häresiedelikte nach Tancred, § 2.

Abschließend sei noch die *Summa titulorum* des Goffred von Trani zitiert : De schismaticis : Differt schisma ab haeresi, quia haeresis in principio sui habet perversum dogma, quod non habet schisma ; sed in fine confingit aliquam haeresim, ut recte videatur ab ecclesia recessisse, ut dicit Hieronymus [C.] 24 q. 3 c. Inter Heresim (26). Vel est talis differentia inter haeresim et schisma, qualis est inter genus et speciem, quia omnis haereticus est schismaticus, sed non convertitur, nisi schisma duraverit, nam tunc in haeresim incidit, sicut dictum est (Druck Venetiis, 1570, fol. 201 ra).

so formulierten es zumindest die Kanonisten, wobei sie allerdings in einer bis in das vierte Jahrhundert zurückreichenden Tradition standen[36].

Dieser eben dargelegte partristische Häresiebegriff, wie ihn das *Decretum Gratiani* vermittelte, war, wie gezeigt, auf den Abfall vom Glauben konzentriert. Er wurde schon früh auf den Primat Petri und die römische Kirche hin ausgerichtet. Von den entsprechenden Zeugnissen gelangten ein an den Papst Damasus gerichteter Brief des Hl. Hieronymus und ein anderes, für den gleichen Adressaten bestimmtes und dem Kirchenlehrer zugeschriebenes Schriftstück in das Dekret. Ferner stützten sich die Dekretisten auf ein Schreiben Papst Innocenz' I. an den Bischof von Gubbio aus dem Jahre 416 [37]. Hieronymus hatte sich inmitten der Parteiungen der syrischen Kirche, die im antiochenischen Schisma wegen der Besetzung des dortigen Bischofsstuhles entstanden waren, an den Papst gewandt und dabei auf dessen Primat und Lehrautorität berufen. Angeblich erklärte er in dem ihm zugeschriebenen Brief : 'si autem hec nostra confessio apostolatus tui iudicio conprobatur, quicumque me culpare voluerit, se inperitum vel malivolum, vel etiam non catholicum, sed hereticum conprobabit'. Während Johannes Teutonicus in seiner *Glossa ordinaria* zum Dekret daraus die Möglichkeit ableitete, daß jemand schon 'propter solum dictum' für einen Häretiker gehalten werden könne [38], findet sich die gültige Formulierung bei

---

[36] Vgl. zum Beispiel das Quellenverzeichnis zur C. 24 q. 3 c. 7 in der Ed. Friedbergs, I, 997f., Anm. 346.

[37] Hieronymus : C. 24 q. 1 c. 25 und 14 (Ed. Friedberg, I, 970, 975 f.). Das Summarium im *Decretum Gratiani* lautet zum c. 14 : Aliorum ora fides non timet, quam Romana commendat ecclesia. Vgl. dazu Erich Caspar, *Geschichte des Papsttums*, 1 (Tübingen, 1930), 246; Johannes Haller, *Das Papsttum : Idee und Wirklichkeit*, I (Esslingen, 1962), 110f., 518. Zum antiochenischen Schisma vgl. auch Karl Baus-Eugen Ewig, 'Die Reichskirche nach Konstantin dem Großen', in *Handbuch der Kirchengeschichte*, hrsg. von Hubert Jedin, II, 1 (Freiburg-Basel-Wien, 1973), 62f., 68 und Yvon Bodin, *Saint Jérôme et l'Eglise*, Théologie historique, 6 (Paris, 1966), 208ff.

Innocenz I : Dist. 11,11 (Ed. Friedberg, I, 26). Summarium : Ab omnibus servari debet, quod Romana servat ecclesia. Vgl. Caspar, *Papsttum*, 301 f.; Friedrich Heiler, *Altkirchliche Autonomie und päpstlicher Zentralismus* (München, 1941), 210; Baus-Ewig, 265f.

[38] Zu C. 24 q. 1 c. 14 ad v. 'conprobabit' : Item arg(umento), quod propter solum dictum censetur quis haereticus, Joan(nes). Zu 'set hereticum conprobabit' vermerkt der Apparat 'Ecce vicit leo' : quia hereticus est, qui repugnat ecclesie Romane, ut supra proxima XIX dist. Nulli (5) (Stiftsbibliothek St. Florian, HS. XI 605, fol. 93 va). Über die Dist. 19,5 siehe unten 58 mit Anm. 58.

Tancred, Bernhard von Botone und Hostiensis: wer über die Glaubensartikel anders denkt als die römische Kirche, ist ein Häretiker [39].
In dieser, auf solche Art glossierten patristischen Häresievorstellung
spiegeln sich in etwa die Probleme der spätantiken Kirche wider, nämlich der Kampf um die Dogmen über die Natur Christi, die Trinität,
das Verhältnis von freiem Willen und göttlicher Gnade usw [40]. Desgleichen wird in der Verbindung des Häresiebegriffs mit der Vorstellung
von der Rechtgläubigkeit Roms jener starke Ausbau des päpstlichen
Primats, der sich um 400 unter Damasus I. (366-384) und Innocenz
I. (402-417) vollzog, auch im kanonistischen Denken des hohen Mittelalters wirksam [41].

2) Um den so umschriebenen Kern des Häresiebegriffs legt sich nun,
chronologisch gesehen, als erster Ring, wenn man so sagen kann, die
simoniaca haeresis, die Simonie als Häresie. Unter der Simonie verstand
man bekanntlich den Kauf oder Verkauf geistlicher Dinge, besonders
von Weihen und von Ämtern, die mit einer solchen Weihe verbunden
sind. Sie findet sich seit dem vierten Jahrhundert, erhielt jedoch ihre
besondere Bedeutung im frühen Mittelalter, als zahlreiche Eigenkirchen
entstanden und oft durch Laien in der Form einer Investitur an Kleriker
übergeben wurden. Zahlungen, die vom Empfänger dabei zu leisten
waren, sah man als Simonie an. Bekanntlich stellte diese Gewohnheit
einen scharfen Angriffspunkt der gregorianischen Reformer des elften
Jahrhunderts dar [42]. Doch schon vom sechsten Jahrhundert an, das
heißt genauer seit der Synode von Tours im Jahre 567, galt sie als Häresie.
Einmal betrachtete man nämlich den in der Apostelgeschichte 8, 9-20
erwähnten Magier Simon als gnostischen Irrlehrer und damit als ersten
Häretiker überhaupt, und zum anderen wurde den Simonisten vorgeworfen, sie wollten durch den Kauf geistlicher Gaben den Hl. Geist

[39] Siehe oben 46 § 6, 50 Anm. 28 (die *Glossa Palatina*) und die *Summa aurea*
des Hostiensis : Sed stricto modo dicitur hereticus, qui aliter sentit articulis fidei quam
Romana ecclesia, [C.] XXIIII q. I Hec est fides (14) et c. Quoniam (25) (Ed. Lugduni,
1537; Nachdruck Aalen, 1962, fol. 237 rb/va). Über die Glaubensartikel vgl. auch
oben die Anm. 31 (Bernardus Balbi und die Summa 'Ecce vicit leo') sowie die Anm.
35 (*Glossa Palatina*).
[40] Siehe jetzt Baus-Ewig, *Die Reichskirche nach Konstantin dem Großen*, passim.
[41] Hans Erich Feine, *Kirchliche Rechtsgeschichte: Die katholische Kirche*, 4. Aufl.
(Köln-Graz, 1964), 111f.
[42] Vgl. Friedrich Kempf, 'Vom kirchlichen Frühmittelalter zur gregorianischen
Reform', im *Handbuch für Kirchengeschichte*, III, 1 : *Die mittelalterliche Kirche*,
1. Halbband (Freiburg-Basel-Wien, 1966), 316, 391f.

zu ihrem Knechte machen [43]. Das ergab den Tatbestand der Häresie. Allerdings waren die Meinungen darüber nicht einheitlich. Petrus Damiani erblickte im elften Jahrhundert in der Simonie keinen Glaubensabfall, sondern nur ein schweres Vergehen, das er mehr der Bosheit als dem Unglauben zuschrieb [44]. Gratian bezeichnete sie als Häresie, da ihre Anhänger glaubten, den Hl. Geist und seine Gaben kaufen und verkaufen zu können, wodurch sie ihn zu ihrem Sklaven machten. Doch gestand Gratian zu, daß die Simonisten im übrigen den rechten Glauben besäßen und nicht gegen die Glaubensartikel verstießen [45]. In einem seiner *dicta* dehnte er den Tatbestand der Häresie auch auf Geldzahlungen aus, die zum Empfang der mit einem geistlichen Gut verbunden Temporalien geleistet wurden [46]. Auch die Meinungen der Dekretisten über den Häresiecharakter der Simonie waren nicht einheitlich : manche verneinten ihn (Paucapalea, die *Summa Coloniensis*) [47], Rufinus nahm eine differenzierte Haltung ein, [48] während die Mehrzahl (Stephan von Tournai, die *Summa Monacensis*, Simon von Bisignano, Sicard von Cremona und Huguccio von Pisa) in den Simonisten Häretiker sah [49]. Zum oft vorgebrachten Einwand, sie würden ja nicht gegen die Glaubensartikel verstoßen, bemerkte Huguccio, auch der Teufel glaube Vieles [50].

Diesen, auf solche Art erarbeiteten Gedankengängen Gratians und der frühen Dekretisten, folgten sowohl die *Glossa ordinaria* zum Dekret als auch die Dekretalisten. Für alle war der Simonist ein *perversor*

---

[43] Joseph Weitzel, *Begriff und Erscheinungsformen der Simonie bei Gratian und den Dekretisten*, Münchener Theologische Studien, III, Kanonistische Abteilung, 25 (München, 1967), 11ff., 30ff.; Heinrich Flatten, *Der Häresieverdacht im Codex Iuris Canonici*, Kanonistische Studien und Texte, 21 (Amsterdam, 1963), 302ff.

[44] John Gilchrist, '*Simoniaca haeresis* and the Problem of Orders from Leo IX to Gratian', *Proceedings of the Second International Congress of Medieval Canon Law*, Monumenta Iuris Canonici, Series C : Subsidia, Vol. 1 (1965), 216ff., bes. 217.

[45] Weitzel, 36f., 47.

[46] C. 1 q. 3 dict. ante c. 1, vgl. Gilchrist, 215; Weitzel, 43.

[47] Weitzel, 59, 98.

[48] Simonisten, die den Hl. Geist für käuflich halten, stehen seiner Meinung nach außerhalb der Kirche und erkennen möglicherweise gar nicht das Sündhafte ihres Tuns. Innerhalb der Kirche befinden sich dagegen Simonisten, die den Hl. Geist nicht für käuflich halten; sie sind daher auch keine Häretiker (Weitzel, 66). Unklar bleibt die Ansicht der *Summa Parisiensis* (Ebd. 86).

[49] Weitzel 78, 111, 119, 125, 136f.

[50] Ebd. 136 f. Über die Datierung der einzelnen Summen (zwischen 1148 und 1188/90) vgl. Nörr, *Literatur*, 371f.

sacramentorum, der die Gaben des Herren, die Sakramente, kaufen und verkaufen wolle [51]. Aufgrund eines Kanons des Dekrets hielten sie die simonistische Häresie überhaupt für das größte Verbrechen [52], worin sie die Tatsache bestärkte, daß ein gegen die Simonisten erlassenes römisches Kaisergesetz im *Decretum Gratiani* stand. In ihm war die Simonie dem schwersten Vergehen des *ius Romanum*, dem Majestätsverbrechen, gleichgesetzt worden [53]. Daraus folgerte die *Glossa ordinaria* zum Dekret, die Simonie sei ein schlimmeres *crimen* als die Häresie [54]. Desgleichen stellte sie für Innocenz III., der darin einem Kanon aus Gratians *Concordia* folgte, das größte aller Verbrechen dar [55]. Das ist

[51] Vgl. oben 45 § 1 und 47 § 4 und die dort angeführten Stellen aus dem *Decretum Gratiani*. Vgl. ferner die *Summa decretalium* des Bernardus Balbi von Pavia V, 6, 1 : praeterea dicitur haereticus perversor sacramentorum, sicut ille, qui ecclesiastica vendit vel emit sacramenta, ut simoniacus, ut C. I q. 1 Quisquis per pecuniam (c. 5). (Ed. Laspeyres, 213).

[52] C. 1 q. 7 c. 27 : Patet symoniacos, veluti primos et precipuos hereticos, ab omnibus fidelibus respuendos, et si commoniti non resipuerint, ab exteris potestatibus obprimendos. Omnia enim crimina ad conparationem symoniacae heresis quasi pro nichilo reputantur (Ed. Friedberg, I, 437f.). Siehe dazu die *Glossa ordinaria* ad v. 'reputantur' : Hoc dicitur in detestationem criminis et ad terrorem : sicut illud, Omnis peccator, et c. extra de simo(nia) Tanta (X. V, 3, 7). Vel est gravius, quia facilius dicitur hoc crimen committi in Deum quam aliud : quia donum Dei volunt emere pecunia, su(pra) [C.] I q. 1 Eos (21) et ideo gravius dicitur, arg(umento) [C.] 17 q. 4 Sicut (12), [C.] 22 q. 1 Movet (16). Vel ideo hoc dicitur, quia nulla certa poenitentia pro hoc crimine inducitur, nisi quod usque ad mortem aspere poeniteat, sup(ra) ea(dem) qu. 1 Si quis neque (C.I q. 1 c. 115). Ioan(nes).

[53] C. 15 q. 3 c. 4 (es handelt sich um den *Codex Justinianus* 1, 3, 30 [31]) : Lesae maiestatis et publicorum iudiciorum et symoniae accusatio equaliter proponatur. Sane quisquis hanc sanctam et venerandam antistitis sedem pecuniae interventu subisse, aut si quis, ut alterum ordinaret vel eligeret, aliquid accepisse detegitur, ad instar publici criminis et lesae maiestatis accusatione proposita a gradu sacerdotis retrahatur (Ed. Friedberg, I, 752). Vgl. Weitzel, 14. Über das Problem, ob schon Gratian diesen Text in das Dekret aufgenommen hat, vgl. Jacqueline Rambaud 'L'âge classique 1140-1378', *Histoire du Droit et des Institutions de l'Église en Occident*, 7 (Paris, 1965), 126f.

[54] Ad v. 'ad instar' : Item simonia est maius crimen quam haeresis, ut [C.] I q. 1 Eos (21), immo est maius crimen quam aliquod aliud crimen, ut [C.] I q. ult(ima) Patet (27). Über die frühen Dekretisten vgl. Weitzel 26, Anm. 17, 66 mit Anm. 5 (Rufinus), 77 mit Anm. 8 (Stephan von Tournai), 97, Anm. 14 (Summa Coloniensis), 107, Anm. 8 (Johannes Faventinus), 119 mit Anm. 8 (Simon von Bisignano), 125, Anm. 15,16 (Sicard von Cremona).

[55] X. V, 3, 31. 32 : propter immanitatem haeresis simoniacae, ad cuius comparationem cetera crimina quasi pro nihilo reputantur (Ed. Friedberg, II, 761f.). Die Vorlage ist C. 1 q. 7 c. 27 (siehe oben Anm. 52).

auch verständlich, denn der Kauf der Sakramente und der mit ihnen
verbundenen Ämter mußte alle Versuche, die Amtsträger der Kirche
nach Fähigkeit und Lebenswandel auszuwählen, ernstlich gefährden.
Der Bestand dieser Institution war damit von innen her bedroht [56].

3) Wie schon erwähnt : den schärfsten Angriff gegen die Simonie
führte die Reformbewegung Papst Gregors VII. im sogenannten Investiturstreit. Diese Auseinandersetzung mit den Laiengewalten und ihrer
Herrschaft in der Kirche konnte allerdings nur unter der Leitung eines
in seiner Primatsfunktion gestärkten Papsttums zum Erfolge geführt
werden. Das brachte eine dritte Erweiterung des traditionellen patristischen Häresiebegriffes mit sich, die Einbeziehung nämlich der Leugnung
des päpstlichen Jurisdiktionsprimats. Die Wurzeln dafür liegen allerdings zumindest im neunten Jahrhundert. Das *Decretum Gratiani*
enthält einen Text der gefälschten pseudoisidorischen Dekretalen, nach
denen alle, die etwas gegen die *canones* unternehmen, sagen oder einem
wider sie gerichteten Angriff zustimmen, den Hl. Geist beleidigen [57].
In einem Schreiben Papst Gregors IV. von 833, das wohl gleichfalls
aus diesem Fälschungskomplex stammt, heißt es außerdem: wer den
päpstlichen Befehlen nicht gehorchen wolle, ist seines geistlichen oder
bischöflichen Amtes zu entsetzen [58]. Dazu kommen noch zwei weitere

[56] Vgl. Weitzel, 1.

[57] C. 25 q. 1 c. 5 : Violatores canonum voluntarie graviter a sanctis patribus iudi-
cantur et a sancto spiritu (instinctu cuius ac dono dictati sunt) dampnantur, quoniam
blasphemare spiritum sanctum non incongrue videntur, qui contra eosdem sacros
canones non necessitate conpulsi sed libenter, ut premissum est, aliquid aut proterve
agunt aut loqui presumunt aut facere volentibus sponte consentiunt (Ed. Friedberg,
I, 1008). Zur Textüberlieferung vgl. Horst Fuhrmann (siehe Anm. 58) 3 (24/3,
Stuttgart, 1974) 956, Nr. 362.

[58] Dist. 19,5 : Nulli fas est vel velle vel posse transgredi apostolicae sedis precepta
nec nostrae dispositionis ministerium, quod vestram sequi oportet caritatem. Sit
ergo ruinae suae dolore prostratus, quisquis apostolicis voluerit contraire decretis,
nec locum deinceps inter sacerdotes habeat, sed extorris fiat a sancto ministerio,
non de eius iudicio quisquam postea curam habeat, quoniam iam dampnatus a sancta
et apostolica ecclesia sua inobedientia atque presumptione a quoquam esse non dubitatur : quia maioris excommunicationis deiectione est abiciendus, cui sanctae ecclesiae
commissa fuerit disciplina, qui non solum prelatae sanctae ecclesiae iussionibus
parere debuit, sed etiam aliis ne preterirent insinuare. Sitque alienus a divinis et
pontificalibus offitiis, qui noluit preceptis obtemperare apostolicis. (Ed. Friedberg,
I, 61 und MGH, Epistolae, 5, 1899, ed. Karl Hampe, 77, Z. 7-17). Zur Echtheitsfrage
dieses Briefes (JE 2579), der zu den pseudoisidorischen Fälschungen gerechnet wird,
siehe zuletzt Horst Fuhrmann, *Einfluß und Verbreitung der pseudoisidorischen Fälschungen : Von ihrem Auftauchen bis in die neuere Zeit*, 1, Schriften der Monumenta

Texte, und zwar ein Brief Papst Leos IV. von 850 an die bretonischen
Bischöfe, der jedem die Rechtgläubigkeit abspricht (nec catholicam et
apostolicam fidem ... retinere vel credere probatur), der die *canones*
und *regulae decretalium* zurückweist [59]; und der Kanon eines 863 unter
Nikolaus I. gehaltenen römischen Konzils, welcher im Anschluß an
die Absetzung der Erzbischöfe Theutgaud von Trier und Gunthar von
Köln alle Verächter der *mandata, interdicta, sanctiones vel decreta*
des apostolischen Stuhles mit dem Anathem belegt [60].

In diesen Kapiteln ist freilich nirgends von der Häresie die Rede.
Sie konnte allerdings aus dem oft angedrohten Anathem gefolgert
werden, wenn man unter ihm, noch ganz im frühkirchlichen Sinne,
den völligen Ausschluß des Sünders aus der kirchlichen Gemeinschaft
verstehen wollte [61]. Ähnliches ließ sich aus dem zitierten *dictum* Leos
IV. ableiten, das die Zurückweisung der *canones* und Dekretalen mit
einem Mangel an Rechtgläubigkeit gleichsetzte.

In der zweiten Hälfte des elften Jahrhunderts der Zeit, der sogenannten
Gregorianischen Reform, wurden diese Gedanken neu aufgenommen;
konnte sie doch nach den Vorstellungen ihrer Protagonisten nur durch
eine Stärkung der päpstlichen Gewalt innerhalb der Kirche zu einem
Erfolg geführt werden. Daher ist auch diese Epoche durch eine Reihe
von Texten im *Decretum Gratiani* vertreten. Zu ihnen zählt die erwei-

Germaniae Historica 24/1 (Stuttgart, 1972), 161, Anm. 43, 193, Anm. 123; 2 (24/2,
Stuttgart, 1973), 241f., Anm. 13.

[59] Dist. 20,1 (= JE 2599) : ... non convenit aliquos ... sanctorum conciliorum
canones relinquere vel decretalium regulas, que habentur ... apud nos simul cum canonibus ... § 1 : Quam ob causam luculentius et magna voce pronunciare non timeo : quia,
qui illa, que diximus, sanctorum patrum statuta, que apud nos canones pretitulantur
(sive sit episcopus, sive clericus, sive laicus) non indifferenter recipere convincitur, nec catholicam et apostolicam fidem, nec sancta quatuor evangelia utiliter
et efficaciter ad effectum suum retinere vel credere probatur (Ed. Friedberg, I, 65 f.
und MGH, Epistolae, 5 (1899), ed. Adolf v. Hirsch-Gereuth, 595, Z. 22-24, 596,
Z. 1-5). Zum Problem der Zugehörigkeit zu den pseudoisidorischen Fälschungen
vgl. Fuhrmann, 2, 242f. mit Anm. 15.

[60] C. 25 q. 2 c. 18 : Si quis dogmata, mandata, interdicta, sanctiones vel decreta
pro catholica fide vel ecclesiastica disciplina, pro correctione inminentium vel futu-
rorum malorum a sedis apostolicae presule salubriter promulgata contempserit,
anathema sit (Ed. Friedberg, I, 1016 und MGH, Epistolae, 6 (1925), ed. Ernst Perels,
286, Z. 18-22). Zu dem Konzil vgl. Charles Joseph Hefele - H. Leclerq, *Histoire des
Conciles*, IV, 1 (Paris, 1911), 330ff., bes. 334, Nr. 5, Haller, *Papsttum*, II, 86, und zur
kirchengeschichtlichen Wertung der angeführten Stelle auch Ernst Perels, *Papst
Nikolaus I. und Anastasius Bibliothecarius: Ein Beitrag zur Geschichte des Papsttums
im neunten Jahrhundert* (Berlin, 1920), 84.

[61] Siehe dazu unten 81 f.

terte Fassung eines *Capitulum Angilramni*, also ebenfalls ein Stück der pseudoisidorischen Fälschungen. In seiner ursprünglichen, dem neunten Jahrhundert angehörigen Gestalt hatte es die Könige und sonstigen weltlichen Großen, welche die Richtschnur der Kanones verletzten oder solches zuließen, gleichsam als Verletzer des Glaubens mit dem Anathem bedroht. Die in den Sechziger- oder Siebziger-jahren des elften Jahrhunderts entstandene sogenannte *74 Titelsammlung*, die den Reformern viele ihrer rechtlichen Argumente liefern sollte, setzte statt der *canones* die päpstlichen *decreta* in den Text und dehnte die Strafsanktion auf die Bischöfe aus. In dieser Formulierung findet sich das Kapitel auch in der *Collectio canonum* des Anselm von Lucca und schließlich im *Decretum Gratiani* [62].

Die erwähnte Umstilisierung des pseudoisidorischen Kapitels atmet bereits etwas vom Geiste eines Gregor VII. [63], von dem ähnliche Erklärungen überliefert sind. So stellte er 1079 in einem Schreiben an die Gläubigen Deutschlands und Italiens, daß sich gegen Verletzungen des Zölibatsgebotes richtete, die Behauptung auf, daß jeder der Sünde des Heidentums verfalle-auch wenn er sich für einen Christen halte-der sich weigere, dem apostolischen Stuhle zu gehorchen [64]. Was hat man

[62] C. 25 q. 1 c. 11 : Generali decreto constituimus, ut execrandum anathema fiat et veluti prevaricator fidei catholicae semper apud Deum reus existat, quicumque regum seu episcoporum vel potentum deinceps Romanorum pontificum decretorum censuram in quoquam crediderit vel permiserit violandam (Ed. Friedberg, I, 1009f.). Im *Capitulum Angilramni* 20 lautet die entscheidende Stelle : Quicumque regum vel potentum deinceps canonum censuram (Paulus Hinschius, *Decretales Pseudo-Isidorianae et Capitula Angilramni* (Lipsiae 1863, Nachdruck Aalen 1963) 769) und in der *74 Titelsammlung* : regum seu episcoporum vel potentum deinceps Romanorum pontificum (presulum) decretorum censuram (Ed. Johannes Gilchrist, Diuersorum patrum sententie siue Collectio in LXXIV titulos digesta, Monumenta Iuris Canonici, Series B : Corpus Collectionum, Vol. 1 (Città del Vaticano, 1973), 175 § 307, 195f. § 329; vgl. dazu Fuhrmann, *Pseudoisidorische Fälschungen*, II, 456, Anm. 88 und bes. 505f., III 868f., Nr. 190 mit Anm. 519. Die Textänderung ist übrigens schon den Correctores Romani des 16. Jhdts. aufgefallen und wurde von ihnen Anselm von Lucca zugeschrieben. Über die *74 Titelsammlung* vgl. auch Fuhrmann, II 486ff., zur Frage der Datierung Gilchrist *a.a.O.*, XXI ff. und Fuhrmann, 489f.

[63] Vgl. jedoch die einschränkenden Bemerkungen Fuhrmanns, *Pseudoisidorische Fälschungen*, II 506 ff.

[64] Dist. 81,15 : Qui vero huic saluberrimo precepto obedire noluerint (das heißt den Strafverfügungen wider die Verletzungen des Zölibatsgebotes), ydolatriae peccatum incurrent, Samuele teste et B. Gregorio instruente : Peccatum ariolandi est non obedire, et scelus ydolatriae non adquiescere. Peccatum igitur paganitatis incurrit, quisquis, dum Christianum se esse asserit, apostolicae sedi obedire contempnit (Ed. Friedberg, I, 285 und H.E.J. Cowdrey, *The Epistolae vagantes of Pope Gregory VII*, Oxford Medieval Texts (Oxford, 1972), 86, nr. 32).

hier unter der *paganitas* zu verstehen? Der Papst verglich sie mit der *idolatria*, dem Götzendienst; eine Gedankenverbindung, die am Ende der Achtzigerjahre des zwölften Jahrhunderts der Dekretist Huguccio von Pisa wieder aufnahm, als er dieses Heidentum mit Götzendienst, Unglauben und Häresie gleichsetzte. Ebenso verstand die *Glossa ordinaria* zum Dekret unter der *paganitas* eine *infidelitas* [65].

Die Kanonisten dachten dabei zweifellos ganz im Sinne Gregors VII; hatte er doch die Identität von Ungehorsam und Unglauben einem *dictum* Gregors d. Gr., seines Vorbilds, entnommen [66] und im bekannten Privileg für das Kloster Schaffhausen jene Häresie, die auf der Uneinigkeit mit der römischen Kirche beruhte, als *idolatria* bezeichnet [67]. Überhaupt war die Gleichung von Ungehorsam und Götzendienst eine Lieblingsvorstellung des Papstes [68]; und wenn sich dieser 'Götzendienst des Ungehorsams' dauernd gegen den apostolischen Stuhl und seine Anordnungen richtete, so verriet das seiner Ansicht nach eine häretische Einstellung. Der § 26 des *Dictatus papae* umschrieb das mit den Worten

[65] Huguccio zu Dist. 81, 15 ad v. 'peccatum paganitatis' : id est ydolatrie. Unde alibi dicitur infidelis et hereticus, ut di. XXII Omnes (1) (Stiftsbibliothek Admont HS. 7, fol. 106 rb), *Glossa ordinaria* ad v. 'paganitatis' : Id est infidelitatis.

[66] Migne, PL, 76, 765 C : Si enim quasi ariolandi peccatum est repugnare et quasi scelus idolatriae nolle acquiescere, sola est quae fidei meritum possidet, sine qua quisque infidelis esse convincitur, etiamsi fidelis esse videatur. Vgl. dazu L.F.J. Meulenberg, *Der Primat der römischen Kirche im Denken und Handeln Gregors VII.*, Mededelingen van het Nederlands Historisch Instituut te Rome, XXXIII, 2 ('s-Gravenhage, 1965), 44f.

[67] Das Register Gregors VII., Br. VII 24 (Ed. Erich Caspar, MGH, Epistolae selectae, 2 (1923), 504 f.) : Falls einmal der eigentlich zuständige Bischof von Konstanz 'ab apostolica sede discordaverit eique inoboediens fuerit, quod confirmante Samuhele peccatum ariolandi et idolatrie scelus est, dicente quoque Ambrosio : Ereticum esse constat, qui Romane ecclesie non concordat', so können sie die Weihehandlungen von jedem beliebigen, kirchlich gesinnten Bischof erbitten. Vgl. dazu Karl Hofmann, *Der 'Dictatus Papae' Gregors VII. Eine rechtsgeschichtliche Erklärung*, Veröffentlichungen der Sektion für Rechts- und Staatswissenschaft der Görres-Gesellschaft, 63 (Paderborn, 1933), 62 f. ; Meulenberg, 44. Zum angeblichen Ambrosiuszitat und der Verbreitung des zitierten päpstlichen *dictum* vgl. Caspar, *Das Register Gregors VII.*, 504f., Anm. 8 (zu Br. VII 24), J. Joseph Ryan, *Saint Peter Damiani and his Canonical Sources : A Preliminary Study in the Antecedents of the Gregorian Reform*, Pontifical Institute of Mediaeval Studies, Studies and Texts, 2 (Toronto, 1956) 79f.; Walter Berschin, *Bonizo von Sutri : Leben und Werk*, Beiträge zur Geschichte und Quellenkunde des Mittelalters, 2 (Berlin-New York, 1972), 48f., Nr. 15; Fuhrmann, *Reformpapsttum und Rechtswissenschaft*, 187, Anm. 29 und vor allem Hofmann, 63 mit Anm. 23.

[68] Meulenberg, *Primat*, 45f.

'Quod catholicus non habeatur, qui non concordat Romanae ecclesiae' [69], und noch schärfer formulierte der zwischen 1075 und 1085 entstandene sogenannte 'Diktat von Avranches', als dessen möglicher Verfasser neuerdings Gregor VII. selbst hingestellt worden ist, dasselbe mit dem *dictum* : 'Qui decretis sedis apostolicae non consenserit, hereticus habendus est' [70]. In dieser Ansicht, daß die prinzipielle Verneinung der päpstlichen Autorität eine Häresie darstelle [71], traf sich der Papst mit Petrus Damiani, dem Prior von Fonte Avellana und Kardinalbischof von Ostia, einem der bedeutendsten Vertreter der Reformbewegung; ja, dieser kann als der eigentliche Begründer der Doktrin bezeichnet werden.

Im Jahre 1059 versuchte er in seiner Eigenschaft als Kardinallegat zu Mailand einen Aufstand der Pataria, der sich gegen den adeligen und meist verheirateten Stadtklerus richtete, beizulegen. Als man sich dort unter Berufung auf die Sonderstellung der ambrosianischen Kirche seinem Eingreifen widersetzte, zeigte er in einer Rede die Gründe für den Primat des apostolischen Stuhles auf. Ein Teil des Berichtes, den er über diese Vorgänge dem Archidiakon Hildebrand gesandt hatte, fand später im *Decretum Gratiani* Aufnahme und erhielt bei allen kanonistischen Überlegungen, welche die aus dem Ungehorsam resultierende Häresie betrafen, eine Schlüsselstellung. Petrus Damiani führte nämlich unter anderem aus :

> Qui autem Romanae ecclesiae privilegium ab ipso summo omnium ecclesiarum capite traditum auferre conatur, hic procul dubio in heresim labitur, et... est dicendus hereticus. Fidem quippe violat, qui adversus illam agit, que est mater fidei : et illi contumax invenitur, qui eam cunctis ecclesiis pretulisse cognoscitur [72].

[69] Ed. Caspar, 207, Z. 11f.; vgl. Hofmann, *Dictatus Papae*, 62 ff.; Meulenberg, *Primat*, 44f.

[70] Hubert Mordek, 'Proprie auctoritates apostolice sedis : Ein zweiter dictatus papae Gregors VII.?' *Deutsches Archiv*, 28 (1972), 115, Nr. XXVI, 127 § (6). Über die Zeit und den Ort der Entstehung siehe ebd. 113f.; über die etwaige Verfasserschaft des Papstes 120ff. Zur Interpretation des Satzes vgl. ferner Hofmann, *Dictatus Papae*, 64, 66; Meulenberg, *Primat*, 47f.

[71] So Meulenberg, *Primat*, 47 f.

[72] So der Text des *Decretum Gratiani* Dist. 22,1 (Ed. Friedberg, I, 73). Er wird hier irrtümlich, wie auch schon in den Sammlungen der gregorianischen Zeit (Anselm von Lucca, Deusdedit), wohl aus Gründen der höheren Autorität, Papst Nikolaus II. zugeschrieben (Friedberg, I, 73, Anm. 3); vgl. jedoch Migne, PL, 145, 91 CD und MGH, Libelli de Lite, 1 (1891), ed. L.v. Heinemann, 78, Z. 12-17. Über die Mailänder Vorgänge vgl. Haller, *Papsttum*, II, 328f.; Kempf im HKG, III, 1, 420f.; Fridolin

Was er unter dem *Privilegium Romanae ecclesiae* verstand, hatte er vorher dargelegt : während die römische Kirche alle Patriarchate, Metropolitan- und Bischofssitze sowie alle anderen Kirchen eingerichtet hat, wurde sie selbst durch Christus allein begründet, der dem Apostel Petrus auch die Rechte des irdischen und himmlischen Reiches übertrug [73]. Ein Häretiker war, wer das hartnäckig und prinzipiell leugnete : so dachte er wohl und stimmte darin auf jeden Fall mit der Interpretation dieses Textes durch die Dekretisten überein [74]. Auch die für Gregor VII. typische Bezeichnung aller, die mit der römischen Kirche nicht einig sind, als Häretiker, findet sich schon 1062 in einem Schreiben des Petrus Damiani an den Bischof Cadalus von Parma, den Gegenpapst Honorius II. [75]. In derselben Weise hat dann Kardinal Deusdedit in den Indexsätzen zum ersten Buch seiner ca. 1183-1187 entstandenen *Collectio canonum* die beiden Gedankengänge des Petrus Damiani, wohl auch beeinflußt vom § 26 des *Dictatus papae*, wie folgt wiedergegeben : 'Quod haeretici sint, qui Romanae ecclesiae non concordant et qui eius privilegia nituntur auferre' [76]. Das belegte er durch Verweise sowohl auf die Mailänder Rede des Petrus Damiani (I 167), als auch auf je ein Schreiben der Kirchenlehrer Cyprian und Hieronymus, die dem Primat Roms in Glaubensfragen galten. Ungefähr zur gleichen Zeit interpretierte die ganz im Dienste der Reformidee stehende Kanonessammlung des Bischofs Anselm von Lucca, 'die wichtigste unter den Kirchenrechtssammlungen

Dressler, *Petrus Damiani : Leben und Werk*, Studia Anselmiana, 34 (Romae, 1954), 131, 144 ; Ryan, *Saint Peter Damiani*, 59.

[73] Friedberg, I, 73. Zur Übertragung der 'terreni simul et celestis imperii iura' vgl. die Interpretation bei Dressler, *Petrus Damiani*, 97f. Die spätere kanonistische Erklärung siehe bei Friedrich Kempf, *Papsttum und Kaisertum bei Innocenz III. : Die geistigen und rechtlichen Grundlagen seiner Thronstreitpolitk*, Miscellanea Historiae Pontificiae, 19 (Romae, 1954) 206ff.

[74] Diese Interpretation des Textes siehe bei Ryan, *Saint Peter Damiani*, 63ff., § (107) und Meulenberg, *Primat*, 46 f. Zur Wertung innerhalb der Primatslehre des Petrus Damiani vgl. auch Mario Fois, 'I compiti e le prerogative dei Cardinali Vescovi secondo Pier Damiani nel quadro della sua ecclesiologia primaziale', *Archivum Historiae Pontificiae*, 10 (1972), 25-105 (36) und die unten in der Anm. 78 genannten Arbeiten von Pietro Palazzini. Über die dekretistische Interpretation vgl. unten 65ff.

[75] Migne, PL, 144, 241 A : si eos sacri canones haereticos notant, qui cum Romana ecclesia non concordant, qua tu iudicaberis dignus esse sententia... Vgl. dazu Hofmann, *Dictatus Papae*, 66 und Ryan, *Saint Peter Damiani*, 78ff.

[76] Victor Wolf von Glanvell, *Die Kanonessammlung des Kardinals Deusdedit* (Paderborn, 1905), 8. Der Brief des Petrus Damiani steht als I, 167 (136), ebd. 106. Vgl. dazu auch Hofmann, *Dictatus Papae*, 65 und Fuhrmann, *Reformpapsttum und Rechtswissenschaft*, 187 mit Anm. 29.

der gregorianischen Reform', unser Petrus-Damiani-Fragment deutlich
als Manifestation der juridischen Stellung des Papsttums innerhalb
der Kirche, indem sie das *Privilegium Romanae ecclesiae* mit Damianis
eigenen Worten stark in den Vordergrund rückte : 'Quod Romana
ecclesia omnes instituit dignitates ecclesiasticas, ipsam autem verbum
illud fundaverit, per quod creata sunt omnia' [77].

Im Privileg der römischen Kirche, wie es Petrus Damiani und die Kommentatoren seiner Zeit verstanden, fanden also alle damaligen Vorstellungen vom päpstlichen Primat zu einer juridischen Synthese zusammen : der alte Gedanke vom apostolischen Stuhl als dem Hort der
Rechtgläubigkeit, die Strafsanktionen gegen die Verächter päpstlicher
Dekrete und schließlich die Forderungen der Reformbewegung auf
dem Gebiete der Kirchendisziplin. Der Primat erhielt neue Konsequenzen für das tägliche Leben der Kirche und die Begriffe 'katholischer
Glaube', 'römische Kirche' und 'päpstliche Dekrete' wurden mehr und
mehr synonym [78].

Nach der Mitte des zwölften Jahrhunderts standen die Dekretisten vor
der Aufgabe, Inhalt und Reichweite dieser Häresie des Ungehorsams
aufgrund der in das *Decretum Gratiani* aufgenommenen Texte festzulegen. War darunter jede Übertretung eines päpstlichen Gebotes zu
verstehen oder nur die prinzipielle Leugnung des Jurisdiktionsprimats
samt den sich daraus ergebenden Folgen? Gregor VII. und Petrus Da-

---

[77] Fridericus Thaner, *Anselmi episcopi Lucensis Collectio canonum una cum collec-
tione minori*, I (Oeniponti, 1906), 31f., c. I, 61. Es folgt der vollständige Text des Petrus
Damiani, den der angeführte Satz sinngemäß widergibt. Zu Anselm vgl. zuletzt
Fuhrmann, *Pseudoisidorische Fälschungen*, II, 509ff., der zitierte Satz steht auf S. 510.
Vgl. auch Hofmann, *Dictatus Papae*, 65.

[78] Vgl. dazu die Interpretation bei Pietro Palazzini, 'Il diritto strumento di riforma
ecclesiastica in S. Pier Damiani', *Ephemerides iuris canonici*, 11 (1955), 361-408 (372ff)
und Desselben, 'San Pier Damiani, la Riforma e il "Privilegium Romanae Ecclesiae",
L'Osservatore Romano, 104 (1969), Nr. 256 (9. XI), 6; John T. Gilchrist, 'Canon Law
Aspects of the Eleventh Century Gregorian Reform Programme', *The Journal of
Ecclesiastical History*, 13 (1962), 21-38 (26). Zur theologischen Bedeutung des Petrus-
Damiani-Textes vgl. auch Yves M.-J. Congar, 'Der Platz des Papsttums in der Kirchen-
frömmigkeit der Reformer des 11. Jahrhunderts', In *Sentire ecclesiam : Das Bewusst-
sein von der Kirche als gestaltende Kraft der Frömmigkeit*, herausgegeben von Jean
Daniélou und Herbert Vorgrimler (Freiburg-Basel-Wien, 1961), 196-217 (202ff.mit
Anm. 22) und Kurt-Victor Selge, 'Heidelberger Ketzerprozesse in der Frühzeit der
hussitischen Revolution', *Zeitschrift für Kirchengeschichte*, 82 (1971), 176 mit Anm.
18. Die Polemik Fuhrmanns (*Reformpapsttum und Rechtswissenschaft*, 187, Anm.
28) gegen Palazzini trifft nicht den Kern der Sache.

miani dürften höchstwahrscheinlich, wie schon gesagt, letzterer Ansicht gewesen sein. Die Dekretisten machten sich anfänglich über dieses Problem wenig Gedanken und legten unseren Text in einer ziemlich traditionellen Weise aus. So zitierte die Summa *Elegantius in iure diuino seu Coloniensis* um 1169 das Brieffragment Dist. 22,1 im Anschluß an die schon behandelte hieronymianische Definition des Unterschieds von Häresie und Schisma bzw. des Zusammenhangs, der zwischen beiden Delikten besteht [79]. Offenkundig wird unser Text hier gleichfalls im Sinne einer dauernden und darum häretischen Trennung von der Kirche verstanden, die eben auch eine Leugnung des *Privilegium Romanae ecclesiae* als des Ausdrucks des päpstlichen Jurisdiktionsprimats zur Folge haben mußte. Ähnlich umschreibt zehn Jahre später Simon von Bisignano in seiner Summe zum Dekret das der römischen Kirche verliehene Privileg ganz im Sinne des Petrus Damiani als jenes, nach dem sie das Haupt aller anderen Kirchen darstelle [80].

Bis dahin blieb die Interpretation also in einem traditionellen, schon von der gregorianischen Kanonistik vorgezeichneten Rahmen. Das wurde erst um 1188 anders, als sich Huguccio von Pisa in seiner Summe zum Dekret dieses Problems in einer umfassenden Weise annahm und die für die Zukunft verbindliche Interpretation schuf. Sie war von solcher Bedeutung, daß Guido de Baisio um 1300 die entsprechenden Glossen in sein *Rosarium* aufgenommen hat, mit dem er die *Glossa ordinaria* zum Dekret ergänzte. Huguccio, der wohl bedeutendste Dekretist, legte dar : wer leugnet, daß die römische Kirche das Haupt aller Kirchen ist und die Gewalt hat, über diese zu verfügen sowie Gesetze und Dekretalen zu erlassen, wer diese daher aus Ungehorsam und Verachtung nicht befolgt und dazu behauptet sowie öffentlich verkündet, man sei gar nicht verpflichtet ihnen zu gehorchen : der legt durch sein Verhalten nahe, daß er ein Schismatiker und Häretiker ist, und verfällt *ipso iure* den dafür vorgesehenen Strafen, also der Exkommunikation. Entscheidend für den Tatbestand wird allein die Einstellung angesehen. Eine einfache Übertretung der Dekrete des apostolischen Stuhles ohne die Leugnung der Pflicht, sie zu befolgen, stellt nach Huguccio eine Todsünde dar, legt aber noch keine Häresie nahe. Gleich wie bei Simon

[79] Ed. Fransen -Kuttner (vgl. oben Anm. 35), 118f., § 12.
[80] Zu Dist. 22, 1 ad v. 'detrahit' : Illud scilicet, secundum quod ipsa est caput omnium ecclesiarum, nam de aliis privilegiis non est verum (Josef Juncker, 'Die Summa des Simon von Bisignano und seine Glossen', *Zeitschrift der Savigny-Stiftung für Rechtsgeschichte*, 46, Kan. Abt., 15 (1926), 326-500 (400).

besteht auch für ihn das Privileg der römischen Kirche, dessen Leugnung der Häresie nahesteht, im Primat [81]. An einer anderen Stelle seiner

[81] Huguccio zu Dist. 19,5 ad v. 'Nulli' : Canon iste potest intelligi esse date sententie, ad quod faciunt illa verba capituli 'prostratus, dampnatus'. Potest etiam intelligi dande (HS. danda) sentencie, ad quod faciunt illa verba 'fiat' postea 'abiciendus. Si dicant esse date sententie, loquitur de contemptoribus, si dande, de aliis transgressoribus. Sunt enim quidam contumaciter apostolicam sedem esse caput omnium ecclesiarum negantes : dicunt ipsam non posse condere canones vel decreta nec habere auctoritatem condendi ea et statuta ab ea non esse observanda. Isti tales scisma et heresim (HS. heresis) sapiunt et ipso genere delicti tanquam heretici excommunicandi sunt, ut di. XXII c. I et [C.] XXV q. I Violatores (5) et q. II Si quis dogmata (18), et de talibus loquitur iste canon. Sic dicatur esse date sententie. Sunt et alii, qui transgrediuntur decreta apostolice sedis, dicunt tamen et credunt ea esse observanda : tales ipso iure non sunt excommunicati et de talibus loquitur iste canon, si dicatur esse dande sententie. Duobus modis quis (HS. qui) transgreditur decreta apostolice sedis, scilicet aut ipsa reprobando et ex contemptu asserendo ea non esse observanda : hic heresim sapit, et qui hoc facit, ipso iure est excommunicatus; aut non observando, credendo tamen ea esse observanda : hic non sapit heresim, et qui hoc facit, non est ipso (HS. ipsa) iure excommunicatus, licet pec[c]et mortaliter (Stiftsbibliothek Admont, HS. 7, fol. 22 vb).

Derselbe zu Dist. 19,5 ad v. 'noluerit' : id est contempserit iudicando illa non esse observanda nec Romanam ecclesiam habere auctoritatem talia statuendi, et sic loquitur hoc capitulum de publice contemptoribus, ut [C.] XXIIII q. I Ait (35) et ita est date sententie, vel dicatur loqui de aliis transgressoribus et erit(?) dande sententie (Ebd. vol. 23 ra).

Derselbe zu Dist. 20,1 ad v. 'non convincitur recipere indifferenter' : id est indistincte, sine distinctione generaliter, nisi fuit abrogata vel ex causa data vel ex tempore vel ex loco; non enim omnes astringit quelibet constitutio Romane ecclesie. Orientalis enim ecclesia non recipit nec tenetur recipere statuta de continentia clericorum in sacris ordinibus, ut di. XXXI Aliter (14). Et sic loquitur de transgressoribus canonum non reprobando, vel loquitur tantum de contemptoribus canonum, id est de transgressoribus eorum contempnendo et reprobando, qui ipso iure sunt dampnati tamquam heretici, ut di. XVIIII Nulli (5) et di. XXII Omnes (1) et [C.] XXV q. I Violatores (5) et q. II Si quis dogmata (18) et est sensus 'non convincitur indifferenter recipere' : id est non reprobare, non contempnere, dicendo non esse servanda, quamvis ipse ut di. XXII Omnes (1). Sed qui statuta conciliorum et apostolicorum contempnit, contra sedem apostolicam agere non dubitatur (Ebd. fol. 24 va).

Ebd. ad v. 'fidem' : fidem enim violat, qui adversus eam agit, que est mater fidei, ut di. XXII Omnes (1). Sed qui statuta conciliorum et apostolicorum contempnit, contra sedem apostolicam agere non dubitatur (Ebd. fol. 24 va).

Huguccio zu Dist. 22, 1 ad v. 'Romane ecclesie privilegium' : scilicet illud, secundum quod ipsa est caput omnium ecclesiarum, nam de aliis intelligi non potest. Hoc facit ille, qui contumaciter negat Romanam ecclesiam esse caput omnium ecclesiarum et habere auctoritatem disponendi de omnibus ecclesiis vel condendi canones, qui canones ab ea factos tamquam inobediens contempnit et eos non esse observandos asserit

Summe hat er diesen genauer und ganz im Sinne des Petrus Damiani umschrieben : die römische Kirche ist (zeitlich) die erste und allen anderen vorgesetzt, sie richtete alle anderen ein, während sie selbst von Christus allein begründet und den übrigen vorgereiht wurde [82].

Die Thesen Huguccios sollten, wie schon gesagt, für die Zukunft verbindlich bleiben. Vorerst sei aber noch auf eine von ihnen abweichende Meinung hingewiesen, nämlich den Glossenapparat *Ecce vicit leo* aus den ersten Jahren des dreizehnten Jahrhunderts. Mit der Auffassung, sowohl die Leugnung des Primats als auch der Ungehorsam gegenüber den Geboten des apostolischen Stuhles stelten eine Häresie dar, will sich sein Verfasser nicht identifizieren und zitiert sie als die Überzeugung anderer. Am Beispiel der Griechen, die den römischen Primat nicht anerkennen und daher als Häretiker exkommuniziert sein müßten, erklärt sich der kommentierende Dekretist : er glaube das nicht und möchte daher annehmen, daß eine derartige Leugnung keine Häresie sei, sondern nur eine Todsünde zur Folge habe [83]. Ansons-

---

et publice predicat : talis heresim sapit et ipso iure dampnatus censetur hereticus et scismaticus. ut hic et di. XVIIII Nulli (5) et [C.] XXV q. I Violatores (5) et q. II Si quis dogmata (18) (Ebd. fol. 27 vb).

Die entsprechenden Texte siehe oben in den Anm. 58 und 59 sowie 62 zu Anm. 72. Vgl. auch Manuel Rios Fernández, *El Primado del Romano Pontífice en el pensamiento de Huguccio de Pisa decretista*, Compostellanum Sección de Ciencias Eclesiásticas, 8 (1963), 98 mit Anm. 75 und Huizing, *Excommunication latae sententiae*, 290f. Für ein klärendes Gespräch über diese Texte habe ich dem Präfekten der Vatikanischen Bibliothek, Prof. Alphons M. Stickler, herzlich zu danken.

[82] Zu Dist. 21,2 : In hoc capitulo ostenditur, quod ecclesia Romana prima est et prelata omnibus aliis; ipsa enim instituit omnes alias, set ipsa a solo Christo instituta est, et omnibus aliis prelata est, et qui talem prelacionem vult auferre a Romana ecclesia esse hereticus censeatur (John A. Watt, *The Theory of Papal Monarchy in the Thirteenth Century : The Contribution of the Canonists* (New York, 1965), 81, Anm. 19).

[83] Zu dist. 22,1 ad v. 'in heresim labitur' : ergo videtur, quod sit hereticus, qui non habet Romanam ecclesiam pro capite et sic, quod sit excommunicatus ipso iure, quod dixerunt quidam; ar(gumento) supra XIX d. Nulli (5). Quid ergo de Grecis dicetur, qui non habent eam pro capite? Suntne excommunicati ipso iure? Non credo et ideo expono 'in heresim' id est 'in peccatum'; quia peccat talis, sed non est hereticus vel excommunicatus ipso iure (Stiftsbibliothek St. Florian, HS. XI 605, fol. 9 rb). Den entsprechenden Text siehe oben 62.

Ähnlich sagt derselbe Apparat zu Dist. 19,5 ad v. 'prostratus': ergo v (idetur), quod ipse sit ipso iure excommunicatus, et hoc dicunt quidam, quod blasfemat spiritum s(anctum), ut [C.]XXV q.I Violatores (5), ergo est hereticus, sed excommunicatus est hereticus ipso iure, ut [C.] XXIIII q. I Achatius (3). Nos credimus, quod non sit ex-

ten bemüht sich der Apparat, die den Zensuren zu Grunde liegenden Fälle des Ungehorsams auf jene päpstlichen Gebote einzuschränken, welche die Glaubens- und Sittenlehre sowie das Gesamtwohl der Kirche betreffen [84].

Wieder mehr der Linie des Huguccio folgt Alanus Anglicus, ebenfalls ein Vertreter der Bologneser Schule, in seinem Dekretapparat *Ius naturale*, dessen hier verwendete zweite Redaktion um 1202 zu datieren ist. Das *Privilegium Romanae ecclesiae* bildet auch für ihn der Primat, dessen Leugnung in der prinzipiellen Zurückweisung der päpstlichen Dekrete besteht und als eine Häresie im weiteren Sinne des Wortes verstanden wird [85]. Jene, die sich ihrer schuldig machten, waren also

communicatus, sed tamen peccat mortaliter et contra canones fac(it), si tales sint, que ad fidem pertineant vel bonos mores; et expone 'prostratus' id est 'prostrandus', si contumax fuerit (Ebd. fol. 8 ra; den Text der Pariser HS. siehe bei Huizing, *Excommunication latae sententiae*, 291, Anm. 32). Den dazugehörigen Text vgl. oben Anm. 58.

[84] Zu C. 25 q. 1 c. 11 ad v. 'violandis' (sic) : simile scilicet XIX d. Nulli (5). Etiam hoc verum est de illis canonibus, qui sunt de articulis fidei vel qui pertinent ad generalem statum ecclesie et ad bonos mores. Unde dictum est supra XXIII dist. Ecclesiastica (9) (Ebd. fol. 94 vb). Den dazugehörigen Text vgl. oben Anm. 62.

Vgl. ferner zu C. 25 q. 2 c. 18 ad v.

docmata : precepta scilicet, que ad fidem pertinent

mandata : de bonis aliis faciendis

interdictum : de malis vitandis

sanctiones (HS. sacerdotes) : de causis diffiniendis

decreta : de consiliis curis

anathema sit : id est anathematizetur, quia non est canon late sentente, hoc tamen plenius est supra XIX d. De illis (sic, 5) (Ebd. fol. 97 rb). Den dazugehörigen Text vgl. oben Anm. 60. Zum *generalis status ecclesiae* vgl. Brian Tierney, *Foundations of the Conciliar Theory* : The Contribution of the Medieval Canonists from Gratian to the Great Schism, Cambridge Studies in Medieval Life and Thought, 4 (Cambridge, 1955), passim (vgl. Index, 276, Church, and State : status ecclesiae); Derselbe, 'Pope and Council : Some New Decretists' Texts', *Mediaeval Studies*, 19 (1957), 197-218 (201 f., 212, § 12); Gaines Post, *Studies in Medieval Legal Thought* : Public Law and the State 1100-1322 (Princeton, 1964), bes. 264f.; Derselbe, ''Copyists' Errors and the Problem of Papal Dispensations *contra statutum generale Ecclesiae* or *contra statum generalem Ecclesiae* according to the Decretists and Decretalists ca. 1150-1234', *Studia Gratiana*, 9 (Bologna, 1966), 357-405 (359ff., bes. 363f.) und Yves M.-J. Congar, '*Status Ecclesiae*', In *Post Scripta* : Essays on Medieval Law and the Emergence of the European State in Honour of Gaines Post, Studia Gratiana, 15 (Roma, 1972), 1-31 (3 ff. bes. 22ff.).

[85] Zu Dist. 22,1 ad v. 'privilegium' : Illud scilicet, quo cunctis ecclesiis est prelata, de aliis non posset intelligi. Nachtrag (soweit das auf dem Photo zu erkennen ist) : et etiam rursus habetur, quod quelibet ecclesia respectu Romane ecclesie censetur loco metropoliti (HS. proiliti), sicut quelibet civitas respectu Romane civitatis, ff. de v(er-

seiner Meinung nach den Juden und Sarazenen gleichzusetzen. Diese hielten wohl die Glaubensartikel nicht für verbindlich, hatten aber niemals der Kirche angehört [86], so daß die Zwangsmaßnahmen, welche diese zur Rückführung der Ketzer vorsah, auf sie nicht angewendet werden konnten.

Nichts neues bringt dagegen Laurentius Hispanus, als er zwischen 1212 und 1214 die Endredaktion der sogenannten *Glossa Palatina* zum Dekret verfaßt. Auch er setzt das Privileg der römischen Kirche dem Primat gleich [87] und sieht für jede Zurückweisung der päpstlichen Befehle und der *canones*, wenn sie aus einer schismatischen Haltung entsprang, die Exkommunikation vor [88] - so wie seine Vorgänger im Falle der Häresie

borum) sig(nificatione) Eum qui (Dig. 50, 16, 16), C(odice) de servis fugi(tivis) 1(ege)I (6,1,1?) Lau(rentius).

Ebd. ad v. 'in heresim' : large accepto vocabulo

Zu Dist. 19,5 ad v. 'prostratus' :... Respondeo : de illis loquitur canon iste, qui dicunt apostolice sedis decreta non esse servanda, qui ex hoc scismatici et heretici intelliguntur et ipso genere delicti per canonem sunt excommunicati, di. XXII c.I, [C.] XXV q. I Violatores (5), q. II Si quis dogmata (18) et XXX di. Hec scripsimus (16) (Paris, Bibliothèque Nationale, Lat. 15393, fol. 17r, 14 v). Vgl. auch Huizing, *Excommunication latae sententiae*, 292, Anm. 33. Zur 2. Redaktion des Glossenapparats vgl. Alfons M. Stickler,' Alanus Anglicus als Verteidiger des monarchischen Papsttums', *Salesianum*, 21 (1959), 346-406 (bes. 349, 373ff.).

[86] Siehe dazu oben Anm. 28, vgl. auch Anm. 26.

[87] Zu Dist. 22,1 ad v. 'detrahit' : Illud scilicet, quo ipsa est capud omnium ecclesiarum, nam de aliis non videtur verum (Biblioteca Apostolica Vaticana, Pal. lat. 658, fol. 5vb, Regin. 977, fol. 13rb). Dieser Text wurde bereits ediert und interpretiert von Alfons M. Stickler, '*Sacerdotium et regnum* nei Decretisti e primi Decretalisti : Considerazioni metodologiche di ricerca e testi', *Salesianum*, 15 (1953), 575-612 (588) und Derselbe, 'Sacerdozio e Regno nelle nuove ricerche attorno ai secoli XII e XIII nei Decretisti e Decretalisti fino alle decretali di Gregorio IX', In *Sacerdozio e Regno da Gregorio VII a Bonifacio VIII*, Miscellanea Historiae Pontificiae, 18, (Romae, 1954), 1-26 (16). Nach Sticklers Meinung ist unter den anderen Privilegien der römischen Kirche, ebenso wie in der gleichlautenden Stelle des Simon von Bisignano (oben Anm. 80), die Konstantinische Schenkung zu verstehen. Vgl. auch Domenico Maffei, *La donazione di Costantino nei giuristi medievali* (Milano, 1964), 35, 52 f. Die gleiche Interpretation würde selbstverständlich auch für die gleichlautenden Kommentare Huguccios und des Alanus Anglicus (Anm. 81 und 85) gelten. Über Laurentius als den Verfasser der *Glossa Palatina* vgl. Stickler, *Laurentius Hispanus*, 463ff., zur Datierung 544. Die Übereinstimmung von Huguccio und Laurentius bestätigt auch Guido de Baysio in seinem *Rosarium* zu D. 22, 1 ad v. 'privilegium' : illud scilicet, secundum quod ipsa est caput omnium ecclesiarum, nam de aliis non potest intelligi secundum H(ugutionem) et La(urentium).

[88] Zu Dist. 19,5 ad v. 'prostratus' : videtur ergo canon late sentente nec intelligi de omnibus, qui canones transgrediuntur, quia fere iam essemus omnes excommuni-

des Ungehorsams. Gleich wie der Apparat *Ecce vicit leo* und die Summe des Huguccio beschränkt auch Laurentius diesen Ungehorsam auf die Gebote in Glaubens- und Sittenfragen [89].

Huguccio, Alanus und Laurentius haben also den für die Zukunft verbindlichen Begriff der Häresie des Ungehorsams geprägt. Johannes Teutonicus und Goffred von Trani nahmen ihn in ihre Liste von Delikten auf, die ihrer Ansicht nach den Tatbestand der Häresie erfüllten [90]. Dasselbe gilt für Hostiensis. Alle hier aufgezählten Argumente kehren in seiner *Summa aurea* wieder : Häretiker ist, wer der römischen Kirche das ihr vom Haupt der Kirche, also von Christus, übertragene Privileg entwenden will, wer die Gebote des apostolischen Stuhles übertritt, wer die Absicht hat, den päpstlichen Dekretalen entgegen zu handeln und wer sich schließlich weigert sie anzunehmen [91]. Selbstverständlich müssen die in solcher apodiktischer Kürze formulierten Tatbestände immer im Zusammenhang mit den allegierten Quellenstellen verstanden werden und vielleicht auch mit ihrer Interpretation durch die *Glossa ordinaria* zum Dekret. Denn in ihr wird der Widerstand gegen die Gesetze des apostolischen Stuhles abermals auf die prinzipielle Leugnung

cati, cum cotidie contra canones peccemus. Secus tamen de illis, qui per scisma ab ecclesia Romana recedunt, nam (HS. num) eius... potestatem anullat, precepta eius ac canones contempnendo... (Biblioteca Apostolica Vaticana, Pal. lat. 658, fol. 5ra). Vgl. auch Huizing, *Excommunication latae sententiae*, 292, Anm. 33.

[89] Zu C. 25 q. 2 c. 18 (Ebd. Pal. lat. 658 fol. 73 rb, Regin. lat. 977, fol. 213va). Bei Huguccio (z.B. Stiftsbibliothek Admont HS. 7, fol. 332vb zu 'Si quis dogmata') wurde dieser Teil der Summe allerdings von einem Schüler verfaßt : Stephan Kuttner, 'Bernardus Compostellanus Antiquus : A Study in the Glossators of the Canon Law', *Traditio*, 1 (1943), 277-340 (283, Anm. 23) und Derselbe, 'An Interim Checklist of Manuscripts', *Traditio*, 11 (1953), 439-448 (441).

[90] Siehe oben 47 § 6 und Anm. 21 sowie die *Glossa ordinaria* zu C. 25 q. 1 c. 11 (vgl. oben Anm. 62) : Statuit Hadrianus papa in hoc c(apitulo), ut quicumque fecerit vel fieri permiserit contra censuram et decreta apost(olicae) sedis, velut haereticus et catholicae fidei praevaricator anathematizetur.

[91] Liber V, § De hereticis, 1 : Quis dicatur hereticus... Multis tamen modis dicitur hereticus largo sumpto vocabulo ...

Dicitur etiam hereticus, qui privilegium Romane ecclesie ab ipso summo ecclesiarum capite traditum conatur auferre, XXII dist. Omnes (1) ...

Et qui transgreditur precepta sedis apostolice, XIX dist. Nulli (5).

Et qui vult contravenire decre(talibus?) epistolis apostolicis, XIX dist. Nullos (sic, 5).

Et qui eas non recipit, XX dist. de libellis (1), nam pari iure censentur decreta et decretales, XIX dist. in fin(e) (5) et peccatum paganitatis est apostolicis preceptis contravenire, LXXXI di. Si qui sunt presbyteri (15) (Ed. Lugduni, 1537, fol. 237rb).

des Jurisdiktionsprimats zurückgeführt und jede andere, das heißt nicht aus einer solchen Gesinnung erwachsene Übertretung dagegen bloß für sündhaft, jedoch nicht häretisch, erklärt [92].

Ausgenommen von diesem Häresieverdikt ist die griechische Kirche, da sie - jedenfalls nach der Meinung des Johannes Teutonicus - bei der Befolgung ihrer eigenen Gewohnheiten nicht von einer prinzipiellen Widersetzlichkeit gegen die päpstlichen Verfügungen, eben dem *contemptus*, geleitet werde; eine Feststellung, bei welcher der Dekretist allerdings sowohl die griechische Kirche Süditaliens als auch den damals mit Rom unierten Patriarchat von Konstantinopel im Auge gehabt haben dürfte [93].

[92] Zu Dist. 19,5 ad v. 'prostratus' : Hic videtur, quod omnis, qui non obedit statutis Romanae sedis, sit haereticus, et varios modos haeresis notavi [C.] 24 q. 3 § Quia vero (dict. post c. 27) et c. Quidam (39). Sed intelligas,quod hic dicitur, quod qui dicit Romanam ecclesiam non esse caput nec posse condere canones, iste est haereticus, ut 22 distin. c. I et [C.] 25 q. I Violatores (5) et q. 2 Si quis dogmata (18). Sed si quis alias transgreditur eius mandata, non propterea est haereticus, licet peccet, extra de rescriptis, Si quando (X. I,3,5). Jo (hannes). Den entsprechenden Text siehe oben in Anm. 58.

Ebd. zu Dist. 20,1 : ... recurrendum est ad sedem apostolicam, cuius statuta qui non recipit, haereticus esse convincitur.

Vgl. auch noch zu C. 25 q. 1 c. 5 ad v. 'blasphemare' : Immo eo ipso videtur excommunicatus et hereticus, ut 19 d. Nulli (5) et infra ea(dem) c. Generali (11). Die entsprechenden Texte vgl. in den Anm. 59 und 57.

[93] Zu Dist. 20,1 ad v. 'convincitur' : Sed nonne orientalis ecclesia recipit canones? Videtur quod non, ut 31 dist. Aliter (14). Numquid ergo ipsa est haeretica? Sed dico, quod licet ipsa non recipiat istos, tamen non contemnit eos. (Die Autorschaft des Johannes Teutonicus wird bezeugt durch die HS. 101 der Stiftsbibliothek Klosterneuburg, fol. 12rb; vgl. zu ihr Kuttner, *Bernardus Compostellanus antiquus*, 292, Anm. 77). Der von Johannes Teutonicus allegierte Kanon Dist. 31,14 handelt von der Priesterehe, die in der griechischen Kirche erlaubt sei. Tatsächlich wurde sie auch im 13. Jhdt. von den Päpsten für griechische Kleriker gebilligt, so von Innocenz III. in den Br. VI 139 und XIV 99 (Migne, PL, 215, 152 C-153 A; 216, 462 D bzw. X III, 3,6 = Ed. Friedberg, II, 458) sowie im c. 14 des 4. Laterankonzils (=X.III, 1, 13, Ebd. 452). Vgl. auch Theodosius Haluščynskyj, *Acta Innocentii pp. III*, Pontificia Commissio ad redigendum Codicem iuris canonici Orientalis, Fontes, Series III, Vol. II, (1944) 240f., Nr. 40, 408, Nr. 178, 485, Nr. 4). Zur Lage der griechischen Kirche Süditaliens vgl. Peter Herde, 'Das Papsttum und die griechische Kirche in Süditalien vom 11. bis zum 13. Jahrhundert', *Deutsches Archiv*, 26 (1970) 1-46 (bes. 12 und 14), zur Priesterehe ebd. 30ff., ferner Helene Tillmann, *Papst Innocenz III.*, Bonner historische Forschungen, 3 (Bonn, 1954), 218 und Wilhelm de Vries, 'Innocenz III. (1198-1216) und der christliche Osten', *Archivum Historiae Pontificiae*, 3 (1965), 87-126 (115f.). Über das Verhältnis von Schisma und Häresie im Denken Innocenz'III, hinsichtlich der griechischen Kirche vgl. ebd. 104.

4) Im dreizehnten Jahrhundert wurden in der Gesetzgebung der Päpste auch die Modalitäten festgelegt, durch die jemand, der päpstlichen Sentenzen hartnäckigen Widerstand entgegensetzte, als offenkundiger Häretiker verurteilt werden konnte. Für die Bildung dieser Rechtsanschauungen ist zudem ein stetiges Zusammenwirken mit den kanonistischen Schulen maßgebend. Den häufigsten Fall, daß man gegen den päpstlichen Jurisdiktionsprimat verstieß und sich damit der Gefahr der Häresie aussetzte, stellte wohl die Nichtbeachtung einer Exkommunikation dar. Wer sich um diese kirchliche Strafe nicht kümmerte, keine Absolution anstrebte oder gar in seiner Gegenwart Gottesdienst halten ließ, kam in den Verdacht, die dem Apostel Petrus vom Herren übertragene Binde- und Lösegewalt der Kirche zu mißachten. Geschah dies durch längere Zeit, so konnte die Vermutung aufkommen, der Gebannte meine, er habe es gar nicht nötig, die Sentenz zu beachten, da sie ungerecht oder der jeweilige Richter zu ihrer Verhängung nicht befugt sei. Richtete sich ein solches Verhalten gegen den Papst, so wurde davon jenes Privileg betroffen, das der Apostelfürst von Christus erhalten und dessen Verletzung für Petrus Damiani den Tatbestand der Häresie gebildet hatte. Diese Vorstellung dürfte Innocenz III., selbst ein ausgezeichneter Kenner des *ius canonicum* und außerdem durch seine Dekretalen rechtsschöpferisch tätig, dazu veranlaßt haben, 1210 oder 1211 Kaiser Otto IV. - der bereits mit dem Anathem, also der feierlichen Exkommunikation, belegt war und dennoch in seiner Gegenwart Gottesdienst halten ließ - der Verachtung der päpstlichen Schlüsselgewalt zu beschuldigen [94]. Daher kündigte er ihm auch seine Verurteilung als Häretiker an, falls er von diesem Irrtum nicht abstehe, also hartnäckig in seinem Widerstand verharre [95]. Von einem Ketzer-

---

[94] BFW 6112 : post diligentes ammonitiones et dilationes frequentes excommunicavimus et anathematizavimus ex parte Dei omnipotentis, patris et filii et spiritus sancti, auctoritate quoque beatorum Petri et Pauli, apostolorum eius, ac nostra Ottonem dictum imperatorem ...Audivimus autem, quod ipse contra sententiam evangegelicam claves regni celorum contempnit, quas dominus Jeshus Christus beato Petro concessit, ut quodcumque ligaret aut solvetur super terram, esset ligatum vel solutum in celis, faciendo sibi divina officia celebrari, postquam excommunicationis sententiam a nobis prolatam incurrit, quamvis hoc ei veraciter innotuerit per nuncios nostros et suos et etiam per litteras nostras, que fuerunt in eius presentia recitate (Johann Friedrich Böhmer, *Acta imperii selecta* (Oeniponti, 1870; Neudruck Aalen, 1967), 632, Nr. 922).

[95] Porro, nisi a tali et tanto resipuerit errore, nos eum hereticum esse divino iudicio decernemus (Ebd.). Vgl. auch den gleichlautenden Text BFW 6099. Zur Datierung

prozeß Ottos IV. ist allerdings nichts bekannt, doch haben ihn die fürstlichen Wähler Friedrichs II., um ihren Abfall und die Erhebung des Staufers zu rechtfertigen, als Häretiker bezeichnet [96]. Ganz ähnlich drohte 1228 Papst Gregor IX., er würde gegen Kaiser Friedrich II. 'tanquam contra hereticum et clavium ecclesie contemptorem' vorgehen, wenn er noch länger gottesdienstlichen Funktionen beiwohne [97]. Die Mißachtung der Exkommunikationssentenzen legte also den Tatbestand der Häresie nahe [98]. Dazu mag auch das vierte Laterankonzil von 1215 beigetragen haben, daß im Rahmen seiner, der Häretikerbekämpfung gewidmeten Konstitutionen verfügte, daß der Ketzerei verdächtige Personen mit dem Anathem zu belegen sind und, wenn sie ein

dieser Briefe vgl. Anton Haidacher, 'Zur Exkommunikation Ottos IV. durch Papst Innocenz III.', *Römische Historische Mitteilungen*, 4 (1961), 26-36 und Derselbe, 'Zum Zeitpunkt der Exkommunikation Kaiser Ottos IV. durch Papst Innocenz III.', *Römische Historische Mitteilungen*, 11 (1969), 206-209. Dagegen : Helene Tillmann, 'Datierungsfragen zur Geschichte des Kampfes zwischen Papst Innocenz III. und Kaiser Otto IV.', *Historisches Jahrbuch*, 84 (1964), 34-85 (77ff.).

[96] Victor Domeier, *Die Päpste als Richter über die deutschen Könige von der Mitte des 11. bis zum Ausgang des 13. Jahrhunderts: Ein Beitrag zur Geschichte des päpstlichen Einflusses in Deutschland*, Untersuchungen zur deutschen Staats- und Rechtsgeschichte, 53 (Bresslau, 1897; Neudruck Aalen, 1969), 55, Anm. 2. Über die angebliche Absetzung Ottos IV. auf dem 4. Laterankonzil von 1215 vgl. zuletzt Stephan Kuttner und Antonio García y García, 'A New Eyewitness Account of the Fourth Lateran Council', *Traditio*, 20 (1964), 115-178 (162f.).

[97] Ed. Carl Rodenberg, MGH, Epistolae saeculi XIII e regestis Pontificum Romanorum selectae, 1 (1883), 289, Z. 19 Nr. 371.

[98] Ein wenig anders dürfte sich das Problem 1205 gestellt haben, als Innocenz III. Herzog Philipp von Schwaben, den deutschen König, der Verachtung der Schlüsselgewalt, und ihrer Übertragung auf den Apostelfürsten sowie schließlich eines 'error vel haeresis' beschuldigte, da er den exkommunizierten und abgesetzten Bischof Lupold von Worms unterstützte (Br. VIII 84, Migne, PL, 215, 653f.). Sicherlich war dafür auch die Mißachtung der Exkommunikationssentenz maßgebend, doch beklagte sich der Papst vor allem, daß Lupold trotz des päpstlichen Verbots die Wahl zum Erzbischof von Mainz angenommen und ihm Philipp daraufhin die Regalien verliehen habe. Innocenz warf deshalb dem König die Anmaßung des Rechtes der Translation von Bischöfen vor, was er als Angriff auf sein Primatsrecht, diese kraft päpstlicher Dispensgewalt allein zu erlauben, betrachtete (Br. VIII 83, Migne PL, 215, 651f.) Zum Ganzen vgl. Eduard Winkelmann, *Philipp von Schwaben und Otto IV. von Braunschweig*, I, Jahrbücher der deutschen Geschichte (Leipzig, 1873), 191ff., 378ff.; Kempf, *Papsttum und Kaisertum bei Innocenz III.*, 172, und über die Reservation der Bischofstranslationen als Teil des Primatsprivilegs auch Klaus Schatz, 'Papsttum und partikularkirchliche Gewalt bei Innocenz III.', *Archivum Historiae Pontificiae* 8 (1970), 61-111 (108ff.).

Jahr lang diese Strafe verstockt ertragen, als Häretiker verurteilt werden
können [99]. Genauer beschäftigte sich mit diesem Problem Papst Honorius
III. 1217 in einer nach Soissons gerichteten Dekretale. Anlaß war der
Graf von Rethel (Dep. Ardennes), den päpstliche delegierte Richter
wegen seiner Übergriffe gegen das Domkapitel von Laon exkommuniziert
hatten und der bereits zwei Jahre lang, die päpstliche Schlüsselgewalt
verachtend, hartnäckig in diesem Zustand ausharrte, ohne sich um eine
Absolution zu bemühen und die dafür nötige Genugtuung zu leisten.
Obwohl ihn ein solches Verhalten der Häresie verdächtig machte, sollte
der Graf wegen seiner adeligen Abkunft noch geschont und erneut zum
Gehorsam ermahnt werden. Verweigerte er ihn, so blieb die Exkommunikation aufrecht. Dazu verfügte der Papst, das Interdikt zu verhängen
und die Vasallen des Widerspenstigen vom Treueid zu lösen. Wenn er
sich dann noch nicht bessere, müsse er damit rechnen, daß man ihn
für einen Häretiker halte [100].

Bernardus de Botone Parmensis und Hostiensis umschrieben den
Inhalt dieser Texte genauer : nur, wer schon wegen des Verdachtes der
Häresie exkommuniziert ist, kann nach einem Jahr als Ketzer verur-
teilt werden, nicht aber, wenn man die Sentenz auf Grund eines anderen
Verbrechens oder wegen einer sonstigen Widersetzlichkeit gefällt hat[101].

---

[99] c. 3 = X. V, 7, 13 § 2 (Ed. Friedberg, II, 787 f.) : Qui autem inventi fuerint
sola suspicione notabiles, nisi iuxta considerationem suspicionis qualitatemque per-
sonae propriam innocentiam congrua purgatione monstraverint, anathematis gladio
feriantur et usque ad satisfactionem condignam ab omnibus evitentur, ita quod, si
per annum in excommunicatione perstiterint, ex tunc velut haeretici condemnentur.
Zur Interpretation vgl. Flatten, *Häresieverdacht*, 40. Zu den fränkisch-germanischen
und römisch-rechtlichen Wurzeln der einjährigen Frist vgl. Eduard Eichmann, *Acht
und Bann im Reichsrecht des Mittelalters*, Görres-Gesellschaft, Sektion für Rechts-
und Sozialwissenschaft, 6 (Paderborn, 1909), 21ff., 111ff., 114ff.

[100] Potthast, *Regesta Pontificum Romanorum*, 5462 = X.V, 37, 13 (Ed. Friedberg,
II, 884) : ... cum ... comes Registrensis pro multis iniuriis, quas irrogarat eisdem,
per iudices a sede apostolica delegatos excommunicationis vinculo fuerit innodatus,
idem ... per duos annos et amplius in excommunicatione persistens iuri parere pertinaciter renuit, claves ecclesiae in suae salutis dispendium et plurimorum scandalum
contemnendo. Licet igitur huiusmodi pertinacia non careat scrupulo haereticae
pravitatis... Quodsi forsan nec sic tribuat ei vexatio intellectum, poterit non immerito
formidare, ne sua pertinacia eum in haeresis impingat infamiam, quam, cum noluerit,
forte de facili non potuerit evitare. Vgl. Flatten, *Häresieverdacht*, 60 f., 279, Anm. 18.

[101] *Glossa ordinaria* zu X. V, 7, 13 ad v. 'condemnentur':... Nec intelligas, quod
si pro alio crimine seu contumacia steterit per annum in excommunicatione, quod

Es mußte also bereits ein häretisches Verhalten vorliegen, also etwa die Leugnung päpstlicher Primatsrechte, um jemanden wegen der Mißachtung von Exkommunikationsentenzen als Häretiker zu verurteilen. Doch bestand auch die Möglichkeit, allein aus der durch längere Zeit hindurch aufrecht erhaltenen Verachtung des Kirchenbanns auf eine häretische Einstellung zu schließen, denn der Exkommunizierte verwarf ja *de facto* die Binde- und Lösegewalt der Kirche. Hostiensis scheint so gedacht zu haben [102]. Auf jeden Fall legte eine derartige *pertinacia* den Verdacht der Häresie sehr nahe. In diesem Sinne hatte sich schon 1217 Honorius III. ausgesprochen, und auch die Praxis Innocenz'III. und Gregors IX. gegenüber Otto IV. und Friedrich II. folgte dem gleichen Prinzip. Die theologisch-kanonistische Begründung dürfte von Hostiensis stammen: ein solcher Häresieverdacht gründet auf der Vermutung, der ein Jahr lang Gebannte bezweifle die Schlüsselgewalt der Kirche, das heißt in seinem Falle ihr Recht, aus der Gemeinschaft der Gläubigen auszuschließen und wieder in sie aufzunehmen[103].

habendus sit haereticus, sed tantum excommunicatur per suspicionem haeresis. Den dazugehörigen Text vgl. oben Anm. 99.

Ebd. zu X.V ad v. 'haereticae pravitatis': hoc ideo dicit, quia qui propter suspicionem haeresis excommunicatur, si per annum steterit in excommunicatione, postea tamquam haereticus habetur, su(pra) de hereticis, Excommunicamus, § 1 (X. V, 7, 13). Tamen si pro contumacia excommunicetur, sive per annum sive per plures in excommunicatione steterit, non habetur ut haereticus, sed alias contra eum proceditur, ut hic dicit.

Hostiensis, *Summa aurea*, Liber V, De hereticis : Qualiter deprehendatur quis in heresi : § 4a : ... si pro alia causa excommunicatus per annum steterit, non habetur tamen suspectus de heresi, etiam si pro contumacia fuerit lata sententia ... § 4 ab : Ergo sola presumptione vel suspitione quamvis vehementi non tamen probabili de tanto crimine non condemnatur quis, ex quo negat et paratus est ecclesie obedire. Sed ex suspitione et obstinatione et lapsu anni, per quem excommunicatus stetit contemnendo ecclesiam et etiam Petri claves, ut dicit illa infra de pe(nis) c. ult(imo) (X.V. 37, 13) et de exces(sibus) prel(atorum) c. ult(imo) (X.V,31,18). Alias si suspitio habetur quamvis vehemens et paratus sit heresim abiurare et recepta tamen securitate cum iuramento...admittitur... (Ed. Lugduni, 1537, fol. 237vb). Vgl. auch Maisonneuve, *Origines de l'Inquisition*, 343.

[102] Ebd. § 4 b :... ergo si obstinata mente et ex studio dicas ecclesiam sive ecclesiasticos iudices non habere potestatem solvendi et ligandi vel cum eis de fide catholica contra articulos fidei disputaveris, hereticus iudicaris ... Unde potest dici, quod si per talem contemptum per annum in excommunicatione steterit, ex quacunque causa volueris, debeat hereticus iudicari (Ebd. fol. 237 vb/238 ra).

[103] ... dicit Host(iensis), quod pertinacia annalis perseverantiae inducit suspicionem haeresis, primo per decr(etalem) Omnis (X.V,38,12) infra titulo I, quia tunc nec

Gleicher Meinung war jedenfalls Papst Innocenz IV., als er 1245 auf
dem Konzil von Lyon über Kaiser Friedrich II. die Depositionssentenz
verkündete. Als eines seiner Argumente führte er den Häresieverdacht
an, der unter anderem aus der Leugnung der päpstlichen Binde- und
Lösegewalt abgeleitet werden konnte; hatte sich doch der Kaiser trotz
seiner Exkommunikation den Gottesdienst feiern lassen und dazu noch
Gregor IX. als den für die Verhängung des Bannes zuständigen Richter-
wegen dessen offen bekundeter persönlicher Feindschaft ihm gegenüber
und seiner Unwürdigkeit zum päpstlichen Amt - abgelehnt [104].
    Eine solche Argumentation war dem Juristenpapst Innocenz IV.
zweifellos geläufig, dürfte ihm jedoch außerdem noch während des
Konzils durch zwei Flugschriften nahegelegt worden sein, die Kardinal
Rainer von Viterbo, ein erbitterter Gegner jeder Aussöhnung zwischen
Papst und Kaiser, verbreiten ließ. Sie enthielten eine Reihe meist sehr
gehässiger Anklagen, die Innocenz IV. zum Teil fast wörtlich in die
Depositionssentenz übernahm [105]. Auch die Verachtung der Schlüssel-

---

facit nec facere potest, ad quod omnis fidelis tenetur, ut ibi, et sic secundo per id
praesumitur aliter de sacris sentire quam sentiat et doceat ecclesia, de haer(eticis)
Ad abolendam (X. V, 7,9) primo responso, nam qui omnipotentem Deum metuit
et C. XI q. III Qui omnipotentem (95) et qui se ab ecclesia separat nec sanctam communionem recipit, haereticus appellatur, in Aucten(tico) de privil(egiis) do(tis) hae(reticis)
mu(lieribus) no(n) prae(standis) primo responso et § Igitur sacram communionem
(Nov. 109 pr.)... Item praesumitur male sentire de illo arti(culo) 'unam sanctam catholicam ecclesiam', quasi non habeat clavium potestatem, quod si illam habere crederet,
obediret (Joannis Andreae i.c. Bononiensis in quintum Decretalium librum nouella
commentaria, Venetiis, 1581 ; Nachdruck Torino 1963, 122 A) zu X. V, 37, 13 ad v.
'scrupulo'. Vgl. auch Josephus Zeliauskas, *De excommunicatione vitiata apud glossa-*
tores (1140-1350), Institutum historicum iuris canonici : Studia et textus historiae
iuris canonici, 4 (Zürich, 1967), 131 mit Anm. 270 und Flatten, *Häresieverdacht*, 61.
    [104] Vgl unten Anm. 113.
    [105] Ediert bei Eduard Winkelmann, *Acta imperii inedita saeculi XIII et XIV* :
Urkunden und Briefe zur Geschichte des Kaiserreichs und des Königreichs Sizilien,
II (Innsbruck, 1885; Nachdruck Aalen, 1964), 709ff., Nr. 1037 I und II. Zum Autor
vgl. Karl Hampe, 'Über die Flugschriften zum Lyoner Konzil von 1245', *Hist.*
Vierteljahrsschrift, 11 (1908), 297-313 und Elisabeth v. Westenholz, *Kardinal Rainer*
von Viterbo, Heidelberger Abhandlungen zur mittleren und neueren Geschichte,34
(Heidelberg, 1912), 108ff. Über die textliche Beeinflussung der Depositionssentenz
vgl. August Folz, *Kaiser Friedrich II. und Papst Innocenz IV. : Ihr Kampf in den Jahren*
1244 und 1245 (Straßburg, 1905), 53, 121, bes. 93f. Vgl. auch Peter Herde, 'Ein Pamphlet
der päpstlichen Kurie gegen Kaiser Friedrich II. von 1245/46 ('Eger cui lenia')',
Deutsches Archiv, 23 (1967), 468-538 (494 mit Anm. 101-103), wo auch auf die Person des Diktators der Flugschriften nochmals eingegangen wird.

gewalt durch den Staufer findet sich hier, wobei allerdings die theologischen und juridischen Folgerungen schärfer formuliert sind als im päpstlichen Urteil. Dort ist nämlich nur vom Häresieverdacht die Rede, während Rainer oder der eigentliche Verfasser der Flugschriften, der Kaplan Thomas, den Kaiser zu einem offenkundigen Häretiker stempelt [106]. Soweit konnte und wollte sich freilich der Jurist Innocenz IV. nicht vorwagen. Darin mag ihn ein kanonistisches Gutachten bestärkt haben, das ein Bischof am Konzil verfaßte und welches Hostiensis sowohl in seine *Summa aurea* als auch später in den *Apparatus sive Lectura* eingefügt hat, so daß er als Verfasser angesehen werden kann[107]. Dem Autor ging es um die Frage der *idoneitas* des Imperators, die er mit einer Reihe von Vergehen bestritt. Außerdem wurde die päpstliche Absetzungsgewalt behandelt [108] Selbstverständlich kam in diesem Zusammenhang auch die Verachtung der päpstlichen Schlüsselgewalt durch den Staufer zur Sprache. Dabei stützte sich der Gutachter in erster Linie auf den uns schon bekannten Text des Petrus Damiani, fügte aber noch einige weitere Kanones des *Decretum Gratiani* und römische

---

[106] Winkelmann, *Acta*, II, 720, Z. 13-18 : De illo preterea, qui tanto tempore claves contempnit ecclesie, sicut iste, ac ab aliis contempni precipit et predicat contempnendas, scribens per orbem, quod dictus dominus papa G., quia ut fallebat criminosus erat, ipsum excommunicare non potuit, propter quod nisus est sancti Petri privilegium abrogare, super ligandi potestate videlicet ac solvendi, quid iudicent canones, plane patet, cum huiusmodi hominem censeant canonice sanctiones hereticum fieri manifeste. Vgl. auch ebd. 710, Z.1-4 : Vulgavit insuper cesareis litteris, quod non verebatur sententiam, quam in eum papa tulerat criminosus, non metuens, quod decernunt canones, illum in heresim prolabi, qui privilegium Petri ligandi videlicet ac solvendi nititur abnegare. Den entsprechenden Text der Depositionssentenz und die Vorwürfe Friedrichs II. gegen Gregor IX. vgl. unten Anm. 113.

[107] In der *Summa aurea*, Liber I, De electione et electi potestate, im § 10 (Ed. Lugduni, 1537, fol. 18va/b) ; abgedruckt aus der 'Lectura sive Apparatus' bei Hermann Bloch, *Die staufischen Kaiserwahlen und die Entstehung des Kurfürstentums* (Leipzig-Berlin, 1912), 288ff. und - ohne Kenntnis dieser Edition, doch aus mehr Überlieferungen - von J.A. Watt, 'Medieval Deposition Theory : A Neglected Canonist Consultatio from the First Council of Lyons', *Studies in Church History*, 2 (London, 1965), 197-215 (207ff.).

[108] Vgl. dazu Othmar Hageneder.'Das päpstliche Recht der Fürstenabsetzung : seine kanonistische Grundlegung (1150-1250)', *Archivum Historiae Pontificiae*, 1 (1963) 53-95 (85ff., das Gutachten ist 89, Anm. 119 verwendet) und Friedrich Kempf, 'La deposizione di Federico II alla luce della dottrina canonistica, *Archivio della Società romana di Storia patria*, 3a serie, 21 (1968), 1-16. Derselbe, 'Die Absetzung Friedrichs II. im Lichte der Kanonistik', in Probleme um Friedrich II, herausgegeben von Josef Fleckenstein, Vorträge und Forschungen, 16 (Sigmaringen, 1974), 345-360.

Kaisergesetze hinzu, die mit der Schlüsselgewalt als Grundlage des Jurisdiktionsprimats unmittelbar nichts zu tun haben und sich auf den apostolischen Stuhl als dem Hort der Rechtgläubigkeit beziehen[109]. Unter dem *contemptus clavium* erscheint also jegliche Verletzung des päpstlichen Primats subsumiert; wobei unter Anführung der schon besprochenen Dekretale Honorius' III. erklärt wird, daß für einen solchen keine ausdrückliche Meinungsäußerung nötig sei, sondern die Tatsache der ein Jahr hindurch ohne Leistung einer Genugtuung ertragenen Exkommunikation genüge, um einen Häresieverdacht zu begründen[110]. Das stelle außerdem einen Ungehorsam dem Papst gegenüber dar ; so folgerte jedenfalls der Gutachter aus einer in das *Decretum Gratiani* aufgenommenen pseudoisidorischen Dekretale (Dist. 38, 16)[111] und auf Grund des schon erwähnten und in derselben Sammlung erhaltenen Schreibens Gregors VII., das die Verletzer des Zölibatsgebotes betraf (Dist. 81, 15)[112].

Abermals wird hier, der bereits geschilderten kanonistischen Tradition folgend, aus der Verachtung der Exkommunikationssentenzen der Häresieverdacht abgeleitet. Im gleichen Sinne sprach sich Innocenz IV. in seiner Absetzungssentenz aus, wobei er wiederum an das dem Apostel Petrus verliehene Privileg zu lösen und zu binden anschloß[113]. Dieselbe Begründung wiederholte er in seinem Dekretalenkommentar,

---

[109] C. 24 q. 1 c. 14 (vgl. oben 54 mit Anm. 37). 15.19.20; Codex Iustinianus 1,5,8 und 1,1,8 sowie Novelle 131,1.

[110] nam etsi nichil contra potestatem clavium dicere attemptaret, tamen si excommunicatus per annum satisfacere contempneret, talis pertinacia non careret scrupulo heretice pravitatis, infra, de penis, Gravem (X.V, 37, 13). Dazu wird noch bewiesen, daß ein Jahr - und nicht zwei, wie es in der Dekretale heißt - für ein solches Delikt genügten (Bloch, *Kaiserwahlen*, 289; Watt, *Deposition Theory*, 208f.).

[111] Vgl unten Anm. 118.

[112] Vgl. oben Anm. 64.

[113] Ed. Rodenberg 2 (1887), Nr. 124 : ... de heresi quoque non dubiis et levibus sed difficilibus et evidentibus argumentis suspectus habetur (90, Z. 8f.) ... Merito insuper contra eum de heretica pravitate suspicio est exorta, cum postquam excommunicationis sententiam a prefatis I. episcopo Sabinensi et T. cardinali prolatam incurrit et dictus G. papa ipsum anathematis vinculo innodavit, ac post ecclesie Romane cardinalium, prelatorum et clericorum ac aliorum etiam diversis temporibus ad sedem apostolicam venientium captionem claves ecclesie contempserit et contempnat, sibi faciens celebrari vel potius, quantum in eo est, prophanari divina, et constanter asseveravit, ut superius est narratum, se prefati G. pape sententias non vereri (92, Z. 16-23). Dieser *contemptus clavium* war ein wenig vorher folgendermaßen umschrieben worden : Privilegium insuper, quod beato Petro et successoribus eius in ipso tradidit dominus Iesus Christus, videlicet : 'Quodcunque ligaveris super terram, erit ligatum et in celis, et quodcunque solveris super terram, erit solutum et in celis' in quo utique

der ihm die Gelegenheit bot, seine eigene Entscheidung zu glossieren [114].

Rainer von Viterbo war dagegen in seinen Flugschriften anscheinend etwas zu weit gegangen, wenn er wegen einer derartigen Verstocktheit bereits den Vorwurf der offenkundigen Häresie erhob und sich dabei auf die Kanones berief. Doch hatte er diese Behauptung nicht völlig erfunden. Schon Gregor IX. vertrat sie und selbst Hostiensis rechnete durchaus mit einer solchen Folgerung. Meinte er doch ein wenig später in seiner Summa, die ein Jahr hindurch praktizierte Mißachtung der Exkommunikation genüge bereits für eine endgültige Verurteilung als Ketzer; die Kirche vermeide jedoch eine solche aus Gründen der Billigkeit und in Rücksicht auf die menschliche Beschränktheit; aber auch um keine Schismen und *scandala* heraufzubeschwören, die sich aus einer so strengen Anwendung des Rechtes ergeben könnten [115].

Das blieb auch weiterhin die Ansicht der Kirche und wurde am Konzil von Trient wiederholt : wer ein Jahr lang in der Exkommunikation verharrt, gleichgültig, aus welchem Grund er ihr verfiel, zieht sich ein Verfahren wegen Häresieverdachts zu [116].

auctoritas et potestas ecclesie Romane consistit, pro viribus diminuere, vel ipsi ecclesie auferre sategit, scribens se prefati Gregorii sententias non vereri, latam ab eo excommunicationem in ipsum non solum contemptis ecclesie clavibus non servando, verum etiam per se ac officiales suos et illam et alias excommunicationis vel interdicti sententias, quas idem omnino contempsit, cogendo alios non servare (90,Z. 32-40). Friedrichs gegen Gregor IX. gerichtetes Rundschreiben 'Levate in circuitu' von 1239 vgl. in MGH, Const. 2, 1896, ed. Ludwig Weiland, Nr. 215, die entsprechende Stelle 296, Z. 36 - 297, Z. 26.

[114] Innocenz IV. zu 'Ad apostolicae dignitatis' ad v. 'non dubiis' ... item suspectus de heresi, si se non purgaverit, excommunicari debet, et si per annum in excommunicacione steterit, sicut hereticus condempnari debet, i(nfra) de hereti(cis), Excommunicamus § I (X. V, 7, 13 § 1). Item sine ulla dampnacione ipso facto est infamis et alias penas incurrit, i(nfra) de hereti(cis) Excommunicamus § Credentes (X.V. 7, 13 § 5). (Ich benützte den Druck Argentorati, 1478).

[115] Wie oben in der Anm. 103 : Quibus consideratis dicit ipse Ho(stiensis), quod ecclesia de rigore post tantam expectationem et pertinaciam posset illum condemnare de haeresi, sed iuxta maternum affectum aequitatem praeferens et gremium non claudens, humanae fatuitate parcens non sequitur hunc rigorem, sed incedens per viam mediam suspicionem solam attribuit. Et hoc ne videatur dissimulare et peccatorum correctionem negligere. Nam si sine delictu personarum semper illo modo procederet, suscitari possent scismata et scandala, que vitanda sunt, et de renun(ciatione) Nisi § Pro gravi (X. I, 9, 10 § 6). Zu Gregor IX. vgl. Rodenberg 1 Nr. 750, S. 653, Z. 32 : heresim asserit. Vgl. dazu Kurt-Victor Selge, 'Die Ketzerpolitik Friedrichs II.', in *Probleme um Friedrich II.* (Siehe Anm. 108), 309-343 (342 Anm. 86).

[116] Hinschius, *Kirchenrecht*, 5, 665f.; Flatten, *Häresieverdacht*, 61. Zu der im Falle der Verachtung der Schlüsselgewalt geübten Rechtspraxis vgl. Eichmann, *Acht und Bann*, 111ff.

5) Dem eben geschilderten Konzept von Häresie und Häresieverdacht lag also, wie auch den anderen besprochenen Delikten, die *contumacia* oder *pertinacia*, eine hartnäckige Ablehnung kirchlicher Lehren, Gebote und Zensuren zugrunde.

Dieses gedankliche Prinzip hatte schon die Dekretisten des zwölften Jahrhunderts zu Überzeugung gebracht, ein dauerndes Verharren in einem schweren und allgemein bekannten Vergehen, wie zum Beispiel der Simonie, dem Konkubinat oder dem Ehebruch, stelle bereits eine Häresie dar. Dazu veranlaßte sie das Bemühen, einen Grund zu finden, kraft dessen ein verbrecherischer Papst angeklagt und verurteilt werden könne. Die Rechtstradition sah das nur im Falle der Häresie vor, und daher mußte eine solche bewiesen werden. Man sah sie als gegeben an, wenn der Papst durch ein offenbares und hartnäckiges sündhaftes Verhalten für die Kirche ein *scandalum* bildete [117]. In diesem Zusammenhang beriefen sich die Dekretisten auf den schon ausführlich behandelten Text Gregors VII. über das *peccatum paganitatis*, das er dem Ungehorsam gegenüber dem apostolischen Stuhle gleichgestellt hatte, und zogen ferner eine pseudo-isidorische Dekretale heran, die gleichfalls im *Decretum Gratiani* stand und welche sich in ähnlichem Sinne interpretieren ließ [118]. Beide Quellenstellen gaben allerdings die Vorstellungen eines anderen, noch kaum juridisch unterscheidenden Zeitalters wieder und konnten höchstens als Beweise für die auf der Leugnung des

[117] Huguccio zu Dist. 40,6 ad v. 'nisi deprehendatur a fide devius' : Preterea contumacia est crimen ydolatrie et quasi heresis, ut di. LXXXI Si quis (sic) presbyteri (15), unde et contumax dicitur infidelis, ut di. XXXVIII Nullus (16); Johannes Teutonicus zu Dist. 40, 6 ad v. 'a fide devius' : Nam contumacia dicitur haeresis, ut 81 dist. Si qui presbyteri (15) et contumax dicitur infidelis, ut 38 dist. Nullus (16); ediert bei Tierney, *Foundations of the Conciliar Theory*, 249, 251. Vgl. ebd. 59ff. und Buisson, *Potestas und Caritas*, 182ff. Buisson führt die durch die *contumacia* begründete Häresie auf Tit. 3,10 zurück (182f.), was aber zweifellos eine Fehlinterpretation der Schriftstelle darstellt : der zu Ermahnende und Zurückzuweisende ist dort bereits ein Häretiker und wird das nicht erst durch seine Hartnäckigkeit. Vgl. auch Walter Doskocil, *Der Bann in der Urkirche : Eine rechtsgeschichtliche Untersuchung*, Münchener theologische Studien, III, Kanonistische Abteilung, 11 (München, 1958), 87ff.

[118] Dist. 38,16 : Qui enim rebelliter vivit et discere atque bona agere recusat, magis diaboli quam Christi membrum esse ostenditur et potius infidelis quam fidelis monstratur (Ed. Friedberg, I, 144). Über die kanonistische Interpretation des Kanon vgl. zum Beispiel Huguccio ad v. 'infidelis' : id est sine virtute fidei, est tamen fidelis propter sacramentum fidei, quod habet, id est baptismum, simile [C.] VIII q. I Sciendum (10) et [C.] XXIII q. IIII Forte (11) (Stiftsbibliothek Admont, HS. 7, fol. 56 rb). Vgl. ferner die *Glossa ordinaria* ad v. 'ethnicus' : Arg. quod contumax haereticus est iudicandus, 81 dist. c. Si qui (15).

Primats beruhende Häresie gebraucht werden, wie es ja auch 1245 auf dem Konzil von Lyon geschehen ist [119].

Die Verbindung von *contumacia* und Häresie, wie sie die Glossen zur Dist. 40,6 herstellen, bildet daher eher einen Seitentrieb in der kanonistischen Spekulation über den Häresiebegriff. An sich war sie für diesen freilich von zentraler Bedeutung, doch wurde sie im dreizehnten Jahrhundert, wie schon gezeigt worden ist, durch die Dekretalengesetzgebung der Päpste auf Grund anderer Voraussetzungen weiterentwikkelt [120].

6) Aus der Frühzeit der Kirche stammt noch ein anderer Häresiebegriff, den die Kanonisten übernahmen und weiter fortbildeten, nämlich die Bezeichnung der Exkommunizierten als Häretiker [121]. Dabei bezog man sich auf die C. 4 q. 1 c. 2, einen Brief Papst Nikolaus' I. an den oströmischen Kaiser Michael aus dem Jahre 865. In ihm wird ein Kanon des ersten Konzils von Konstantinopel (381) zitiert, nach dem jeder Exkommunizierte, der von den Sakramenten ausgeschlossen und damit von der Kirche getrennt ist, als Häretiker zu betrachten sei. Der Papst wollte dadurch beweisen, daß der Patriarch Ignatios von Konstantinopel nicht dem Urteil der von ihm abgesetzten und mit dem Anathem belegten Bischöfe unterworfen werden könne, da es Häretikern nicht zustehe, ihre Bischöfe anzuklagen [122] Im Konzilstext folgte das Anathem der Ausstoßung aus der Kirche; es konnte jedoch auch schon für sich nach der Rechtsauffassung des vierten Jahrhunderts als vollständiger Ausschluß von der Kirchengemeinschaft gewertet werden [123]. Wegen dieser

[119] Vgl. oben 78.

[120] Siehe oben 72ff.

[121] Vgl. die von Tancred und Goffred von Trani zusammengestellten Listen der einzelnen Häresiedelikte oben 45 und 47, jeweils §3.

[122] C. 4 q. 1 c. 2 : Heretici probantur, qui scismate vel excommunicatione ab ecclesia sunt separati : Nikolaus I., das Konzil von Konstantinopel zitierend : Hereticos autem (inquiunt)... dicimus tam eos, qui olim ab ecclesia proiecti sunt, quam qui post hec a nobis anathematizati sunt (Ed. Friedberg, I, 537 und MGH, Epistolae 6, 1925, ed. Ernst Perels, 462, Z. 7f.). Den Konzilstext vgl. in *Conciliorum Oecumenicorum Decreta*, ed. Bologna, 1962, 29, Z. 36-39, wo statt 'proiecti' 'abdicati' steht. Zum Brief des Papstes an den Kaiser vgl. Haller, *Papsttum*, II, 105f.; Hans-Georg Beck, 'Die byzantinische Kirche im Zeitalter des photianischen Schismas', *Handbuch der Kirchengeschichte* III, 1 (Freiburg i. B., 1966), 203 und Perels, *Nikolaus I. und Anastasius Bibliotecarius*, 153ff., 307.

[123] Hinschius, *Kirchenrecht*, 4, 694f., 699 mit Anm. 1 und 2, 701ff., bes. 708 mit Anm. 1, 738f.; Jean Gaudemet, 'Note sur les formes anciennes de l'excommunication', *Revue des sciences religieuses*, 23 (1949), 64-77 (bes. 67f., 69f., 73f., 75 mit Anm. 3,77).

Trennung nannte man die davon Betroffenen Häretiker [124]. Der gleichen
Meinung gab das *Decretum Gratiani* im Summarium zum zitierten
Kanon Ausdruck : 'Heretici probantur, qui scismate vel excommunicatione ab ecclesia sunt separati'. Die Kanonisten folgten ihm darin,
wie zum Beispiel Rufinus, Huguccio, Bernardus Balbi von Pavia und
die *Glossa ordinaria* zum Dekret [125]. Noch um die Mitte des dreizehnten
Jahrhunderts sollte dann Hostiensis diese altchristliche Tradition übernehmen und in seinen Katalog 'Quis dicatur hereticus' einfügen; jedoch
als Beleg zur Stützung eines aus dem römischen Recht genommenen Arguments, wonach Häretiker zu nennen ist, wer kein Glied der Kirche
bildet [126]. Freilich besaß dieser Häresiebegriff während der ganzen
hier behandelten Zeit keinen juridisch-praktischen Gehalt, vielmehr
sollte er auf die tatsächliche Trennung von der Kirche hinweisen, die
jeden traf, der von den Sakramenten und der Gemeinschaft der Gläubigen
ausgeschlossen war [127].

7) Vor der Einbeziehung des eben angesprochenen römisch-rechtlichen Häresiebegriffs möge noch ein weiteres Delikt behandelt werden,
dessen erstmalige Nennung die *Glossa ordinaria* zum *Liber Extra* dem

---

[124] Vgl. W. Maurer, Art. 'Bekenntnis' (VII : Rechtlich) in *Religion in Geschichte und Gegenwart*, I, 3. Aufl. (1957), Sp. 1003-1007 (1003).

[125] Rufinus zur C. 9 q. 1 dict. post c. 3 ad v. 'in numero catholicorum' : ... omnes enim pro sua culpa excommunicati dicuntur non catholici, id est heretici, ut supra Cs. IV (q.I) c. II (Ed. Heinrich Singer, Rufinus von Bologna, *Summa decretorum* (Paderborn, 1902; Nachdruck Aalen, 1963), 299). Die Summe ist zwischen 1157 und 1159 zu datieren.

Bernardus Balbi in seiner *Summa decretalium* V, 6, 1 : dicitur etiam haereticus a sacramentis ecclesiae divisus, ut est excommunicatus, ut C. IV q. 1 Quid autem (c. 2) (Ed. Laspeyres, 213).

Huguccio zu C.4 q. 1 c. 2 ad v. 'Sed nonne hos' : Scilicet excommunicatos ab Ignatio et sunt verba Nicholai, per hoc quod dicitur omnis excommunicatus est hereticus, id est ab unitate vel sacramentis ecclesie separatus (Stiftsbibliothek Admont, HS. 7, fol. 187 ra).

Glossa ordinaria zu demselben ad v. 'ab ecclesia' : s(cilicet) excommunicati. Nota, quod omnis excommunicatus dicitur haereticus, ut inf(ra) [C.] 23 q. 4 Ipsa pietas (24). Vgl. dazu auch Huizing, *Excommunication latae sententiae*, 284 mit Anm. 16.

[126] Vgl. unten 95f.

[127] Vgl. Alfons Gommenginger, Art. 'Kirchenbann', im *Lexikon für Theologie und Kirche*, 6, 2. Aufl. (1961), 197-199 (198); Klaus Mörsdorf, ebd. 222; H(ans) Barion Art. 'Exkommunikation', *Die Religion in Geschichte und Gegenwart* II, 3. Aufl. (1958), 828-829 (828). Zur heutigen Auffassung vgl. Eduard Eichmann - Klaus Mörsdorf, *Lehrbuch des Kirchenrechts auf Grund des Codex Iuris Canonici*, I, 10. Aufl. (Paderborn, 1959), 188; III, 9. Aufl. (Paderborn, 1960), 382f.

Kanonisten Tancred zuschreibt, obwohl es in dessen Glosse zur Compilatio I an der entsprechenden Stelle fehlt [128]. Es handelt sich um die falschen Lehrmeinungen über das Wesen der Sakramente : ein Punkt, der die erste Erweiterung des traditionellen, patristischen Häresiebegriffs, wie er von den Kanonisten übernommen und erläuter worden war, darstellte. Er fußte auf der Dekretale *Ad abolendam* des Konzils von Verona (1184), in dem sich Papst Lucius III. und Kaiser Friedrich I. Barbarossa zum Kampf gegen die Katharer und Waldenser zusammengefunden hatten. Damals wurde die alte Definition der Häresie als einer falschen Schriftauslegung und eines Irrtums im Glauben auf die irrigen, den Lehren der Kirche widersprechenden Ansichten über die Sakramente der Taufe, Buße und Ehe ausgedehnt [129]. Dem schlossen sich sogleich die Dekretisten an: 'quicumque ergo male sentit de sacramentis ecclesie, haereticus est habendus,' so formulierte die *Glossa ordinaria* zum *Liber Extra*, nachdem sie durch die Allegation von zwei Kanones des *Decretum Gratiani* die Verbindlichkeit der Glaubenslehre, wie sie die Kirche bewahrt, vorausgesetzt hatte [130]. Der Anschluß an den patristischen Häresiebegriff wird dadurch ausdrücklich festgehalten.

Es ist klar, daß die Dekretale vor allem auf die Sakramentenlehre der Katharer Bezug nimmt. Diese Sekte, ebenso wie die von ihr beeinflußten Waldenser, lehnte mit verschiedenen Argumenten die Kindertaufe, die Eucharistie und die Ehe sowie ihre teilweise Spendung durch die Priester ab [131], was von nun an offiziell unter die Häresien gerechnet wurde.

[128] Vgl. oben 46 § 7.
[129] 1 Compilatio 5,6,11 = X.V, 7,9 : Universos, qui de sacramento corporis et sanguinis Domini nostri Iesu Christi vel de baptismate seu de peccatorum confessione, matrimonio vel de reliquis ecclesiasticis sacramentis aliter sentire aut docere non metuunt, quam sacrosancta Romana ecclesia praedicat et observat, ... vinculo perpetui anathematis innodamus (Ed. Friedberg, II, 780). Über die religionspolitische Bedeutung des Konzils von Verona vgl. Giovanni de Vergottini, *Studi sulla legislazione imperiale di Federico II in Italia: Le leggi del 1220*, Pubblicazioni straordinarie dell'Academia delle scienze di Bologna, 11 (Milano, 1952), 23f. 53f.
[130] Ad v. 'praedicat et observat' : sim(iliter) [C.] 24 q. 3 Haeresis (27), hoc ergo, quos Romana ecclesia servat et mandat ab aliis observari, generaliter est observandum, 11 dist. Quis nesciat (11 fin.); quicunque ergo male sentit de sacramentis ecclesiae, haereticus est habendus, ut hic patet. Zu C. 24 q. 3 c. 27 und Dist. 11, 11 vgl. oben 51, 54.
[131] Vgl. Arno Borst, *Die Katharer*, Schriften der Monumenta Germaniae Historica, 12(Stuttgart, 1953), 216ff.; Christine Thouzellier, *Catharisme et Valdéisme en Languedoc à la fin du XIIIᵉ siècle*, 2. Aufl. (Louvain-Paris, 1969), 65ff., 88ff.

8) Johannes Teutonicus und Goffred von Trani kennen schließlich
in ihrem Katalog noch ein weiteres Häresiedelikt, das in jenem Tancreds
gleichfalls fehlt : den Glaubenszweifel. Sie berufen sich dafür auf
mehrere Texte. Einmal dient ihnen ein weiterer Passus aus dem schon
zitierten Brief Papst Nikolaus'I. von 865, den er an den Kaiser von
Byzanz gerichtet hatte, als Beleg. Wieder geht es um die Absetzung des
Patriarchen Ignatios, deren Rechtskraft der Papst bestreitet. Um nach-
zuweisen, daß die Bischöfe zu ihr kein Recht besaßen, zitiert er einen
Brief Papst Coelestins I. aus der Zeit des Konzils von Ephesus, in dem
alle von Nestorius und seinen Anhängern vorgenommenen Absetzungen
und Exkommunikationen verschiedener Bischöfe und Kleriker für
ungültig erklärt wurden: denn wer selbst im Glauben schwanke, könne
niemanden absetzen oder entfernen. Umso weniger, erklärte Nikolaus
I., war das den exkommunizierten und häretischen Bischöfen ihrem
Patriarchen gegenüber erlaubt [132]. Das Summarium, welches im *Decretum Gratiani* - wohl schon bald nach seinem Entstehen - dem Kanon
vorgesetzt worden ist, setzte das Schwanken im Glauben bereits der
Häresie gleich [133]; eine Ansicht, der die Kanonisten beipflichteten, wobei
sie sich auf den Brief eines angeblichen Papstes Stephan berufen konnten,
den Bernardus Balbi von Pavia um 1190 in seine Compilatio I aufgenommen hatte. Er stammte aus den pseudo-isidorischen Dekretalen und
enthielt die Bestimmung, daß bei Anklagen gegen Kleriker zuerst die
Glaubwürdigkeit des Anklägers geprüft werden müsse. Könne sie nicht
erwiesen werden, ist er als unglaubwürdig zu betrachten [134]. Im gleichen,

[132] C. 24 q. 1 c. 36 : ... quia neminem deicere vel removere poterat, qui predicans
talia titubabat (Ed. Friedberg, I, 981 und MGH, Epistolae 6 (1925), ed. Ernst Perels,
462, Z. 25ff.

[133] Summarium zur C. 24 q.1 c. 36 : Non habeantur excommunicati qui ab hereticis
excommunicantur. Über den Autor der Summariae vgl. die ausführliche Abhandlung
von Jacqueline Rambaud in : 'L'Age Classique 1140-1378', *Histoire du Droit et des
Institutions de l'Église en Occident*, 7 (1965), 69-77 und zuletzt Adam Vetulani, 'Les
sommaires-rubriques dans le Décret de Gratien', In *Proceedings of the Third International Congress of Medieval Canon Law, Strasbourg 3-6 September 1968*, Monumenta
Iuris Canonici, Series C : Subsidia 4 (1971), 51-57. Dasselbe Summarium besitzt das
capitulum schon in der *Panormia* des Ivo von Chartres V, 135 (Migne, PL, 161, 1244),
doch ist es dort nicht original, sondern wurde wahrscheinlich nachträglich aus dem
Decretum Gratiani übernommen; vgl. Jacqueline Rambaud-Buhot, 'Les Sommaires
de la Panormie et l'édition de Melchior de Vosmédian', *Traditio*, 23 (1967), 534-536
(535f.) und Fuhrmann, *Pseudoisidorische Fälschungen*, III, 776. Zur Überlieferung des
Kapitels vgl. auch Ernst Perels, 'Die Briefe Papst Nikolaus' I.', *Neues Archiv*, 39
(1914), 43-153 (128).

[134] 1 Comp. 5,6,1 = X.V,7,1 : Dubius in fide, infidelis est. Nec eis omnino creden-

prozeßrechtlichen Sinnzusammenhang steht die Dekretale im *Decretum* des Burchard von Worms und bei Ivo von Chartres [135]. Erst die Compilatio I setzte sie in den Titulus 'De hereticis' [136] wodurch sich die Bedeutung von *fides* änderte : aus 'Glaubwürdigkeit' wurde 'Glaube'. In diesem Sinne verstanden den Text auch die Dekretalisten, als sie die Sammlung kommentierten. Für sie war *dubius in fide*, wer die Glaubensartikel nicht fest bezeugte [137]. Tancred nahm dann in seiner *Glossa ordinaria* zur Compilatio I, deren erste Rezension zwischen 1210 und 1215 entstand, ein römisches Kaisergesetz zur Hilfe, um diese Interpretation zu stützen [138]. Es handelt sich um den Codex Iustianus 1,5,2, eine Kompilation aus verschiedenen Konstitutionen des Codex Theodosianus. Der hier interessierende Teil stammt aus einem 395 erlassenen Gesetz der Kaiser Arcadius und Honorius und schloß alle, die nur geringfügig vom rechten Glauben abwichen, in den Kreis der Häretiker ein [139]. Diesen Satz griffen in der zweiten Hälfte des zwölften

dum est, qui fidem veritatis ignorant. (Ed. Friedberg, II, 778). Vgl. auch Paulus Hinschius, *Decretales Pseudo-Isidorianae et Capitula Angilramni* (Lipsiae, 1863; Nachdr. Aalen, 1963), 107 § III (Pseudo-Sixti) und 468 Z. 26f. Zur Interpretation vgl. München, *Gerichtsverfahren und Strafrecht*, II, 321f.; Hinschius, *Kirchenrecht*, V, 679, Anm. 7.

[135] Burchard, I, 144 : Migne, PL, 140, 592 C; Anselm von Lucca, III, 55 (Ed. Thaner, 143); Ivo, Decretum V 257 : Migne, PL, 161, 404 A. Über die Sammlungen vgl. Alphonsus M. Stickler, *Historia iuris canonici Latini : Institutiones academicae*, I. *Historia Fontium* (1950), 154ff., 181ff.; zur Übernahme des Kapitels : Fuhrmann, *Pseudoisidorische Fälschungen*, II, 547.

[136] Aemilius Friedberg, *Quinque Compilationes Antiquae* (Lipsiae, 1882; Nachdruck Graz, 1956), 55. Zur Entstehung und Datierung der Sammlung vgl. Fransen, *Les Décrétales*, 23f.

[137] Richardus Anglicus zur 1 Comp. 5,6, 1 ad v. 'Dubius' : nam qui articulos fidei firmiter non crediderint, salvi esse non poterint, ut in Psalmo Quicumque vult in versu extremo et di. XXIII Qui episcopus (2). (Stiftsbibliothek St. Peter in Salzburg, HS. a IX 18, fol. 98 vb). Der Apparat ist um 1196 anzusetzen (Nörr, *Literatur*, 373).

[138] Zur 1 Comp. 5,6,1 ad v. 'in fide' : eciam tenui articulo C(odice) de hereticis, l(ege) ultima in fi(ne) (Codex 1,5,2) et hoc quoad articulos fidei, qui continentur in simbolo, id est in 'Credo in dominum', quibus per fidem adhibenda est credulitas; nam fides est de re non visa, ut de pe(nitentia) di. IIII In domo (11), C(odice) De summa trinitate, l(ege) ult(ima) (Codex 1,1,8), [C.] XXIIII q. III Cum quibus (36). Lau(rentius) (Der Text beruht auf den HSS. der Biblioteca Apostolica Vaticana, Chis. E VII 207, fol. 74 ra. Borgh. 264, fol. 60 ra und der Stiftsbibliothek Admont. HS. 22, fol. 71 rb. Die Varianten sind unwesentlich und wurden daher nicht angegeben).

[139] Codex Iustinianus 1,5,2 : Haereticorum autem vocabulo continentur et latis adversus eos sanctionibus debent succumbere, qui vel levi argumento iudicio catholicae religionis et tramite detecti fuerint deviare (Ed. Paulus Krueger, Berolini, 1895, 51) = Codex Theodosianus 16,5,28 (Ed. Theodor Mommsen, Nachdruck Berlin, 1954, I, 2, 864).

Jahrhunderts die Glossatoren des römischen Rechts auf und verwendeten ihn zur Definition ihres eigenen Häresiebegriffs, den sie um diese Zeit entwickelten. Er ist zum Beispiel in den Summen zum Codex Iustinianus zu finden, die Placentinus in den Siebzigerjahren des zwölften Jahrhunderts zu Montpellier und Azo Portius zwischen 1208 und 1210 - wobei es sich um die zweite Fassung des Werkes handelt - in Bologna verfaßten [140]. Dort dürfte dieser Gedanke dem Laurentius Hispanus bekanntgeworden sein, jenem Kanonisten, dem sowohl Tancred als auch Bernardus de Botone in der *Glossa ordinaria* zum *Liber Extra* die Einfügung des römischen Kaisergesetzes in die Argumentationsreihe zur Dekretale *Dubius* zuschreiben [141]. Er hat auch tatsächlich diesen Schritt vollzogen; allerdings in der zwischen 1212 und 1214 entstandenen *Glossa Palatina* zum *Decretum Gratiani*. Dort stand ja jene Stelle aus dem Briefe Nikolaus' I. bzw. Cölestins I., nach der als Häretiker galt, wer im Glauben schwankte (C. 24 q. 1 c. 36). Huguccio scheint sich in seiner, an dieser Stelle allerdings von Schülerhand verfaßten Dekretsumme dieser Ansicht angeschlossen zu haben; desgleichen Laurentius Hispanus in der *Glossa Palatina*, wobei er neben der Dekretale *Dubius* auch das erwähnte römische Kaisergesetz allegierte [142]. Die damit vollzogene

---

[140] In Codicis domini Iustiniani ... libros IX Summa a Placentino legum interprete ... conscripta (Maguntiae, 1536), 'De Haereticis', pag. 11 : Haeretici sunt, qui vel levi argumento a iudicio vel tramite catholicae religionis detecti fuerint deviare, ut C(odice) eo(dem) ti(tulo) l(ege) Quicumque (1,5,8). Dieses Zitat steht irrtümlich für 1,5,2. *Azonis Summa super Codicem*, Liber I, § De hereticis et Manicheis et Samaritanis : Et quidem hereticus est, qui vel levi argumento a iudicio catholice religionis et tramite detectus fuerit deviare, ut i(nfra) e(odem) l(ege) II in fi(ne) (1,5,2) (*Corpus Glossatorum iuris civilis*, 2, 1966, 6 b). Zu beiden Glossatoren und ihren Summen vgl. Weimar, *Literatur*, 201f.; Hermann Kantorowicz, *Studies in the Glossators of the Roman Law* (Cambridge, 1938; Nachdruck Aalen, 1969), 44, zu Placentinus noch Ch. Lefèbvre: Art. 'Placentin' im *Dictionnaire de Droit Canonique*, VII (1965), 1-10 (2f.).

[141] Oben Anm. 138 und *Glossa ordinaria* zu X. V, 7, 1 ad v. 'in fide' : etiam in tenui articulo, C(odice) de haeret(icis), l(ege) 2 in fi(ne) (1,5,2), sic ex levi offensa revocatur libertus in servitutem, C(odice) de lib(ertis) et eor(um) lib(eris) Si manumissus (6,7, 2)... Laurentius. Der entsprechende Text des Codex Iustinianus 6, 7,2 lautet : Si manumissus ingratus circa patronum suum extiterit et quadam iactantia vel contumacia cervices adversus eum erexerit aut levis offensae contraxerit culpam, a patronis rursus sub imperia dicionemque mittatur (Ed. Krueger, 247).

[142] Huguccio zu C. 24 q. 1 c. 36 : ad v. 'titubabat' : in fide et tamen hereticus erat propria id est Ignotium patriaram (sic!) suum, quem iniuste removerant, cum essent excommunicati (Stiftsbibliothek Admont, HS. 7, fol. 327 rb. Biblioteca Apostolica Vaticana, Vat. lat. 2280, fol. 252 va).
Laurentius zur C. 24 q. 1 c. 36 ad v. 'talia titubabant' : No(ta) titubantem in fide

Einbeziehung des römischen Rechtes in das Delikt des Glaubenszweifels übernahm sodann Tancred; und zwar unter Berufung auf Laurentius, wie die angeführten Siglen bezeugen. Derselben Linie folgten Johannes Teutonicus und Bernardus de Botone in den *Glossae ordinariae* zum Dekret [143] und zum *Liber Extra* [144], ebenso wie Goffred von Trani in seinem Apparat zu den Dekretalen Gregors IX. [145] Nach 1215 kam ein weiteres Argument hinzu, um die Häresie des Glaubenszweifels zu bezeugen, nämlich die erste, dogmatische Konstitution des vierten Laterankonzils, deren Glaubensbekenntnis mit den Worten begann: 'Firmiter credimus et simpliciter confitemur' [146]. Eine solche Betonung des sicheren Glaubensaktes, wie er hier neuerlich verlangt wurde und der sich erstmals 1053 in einem Brief Papst Leos IX. an den Bischof von Antiochia findet, war wohl, wie die ganze Konstitution, als eine Antwort der Kirche auf die theologische Situation um 1200, besonders aber gegenüber den Häresien zu betrachten [147]. Dasselbe gilt wahrschein-

hereticum sicut falsi a) assertorem dici, s(upra) [C.]IIII q. III In testibus (q. 2 et 3, c. 3 § 1); nam et hereticorum vocabulo continentur, qui levi etiam argumento a fide deviant, C(odice) de here(ticis), Omnes in fine (1,5,2)
a) In A auf Rasur, in B. : fas sit. Biblioteca Apostolica Vaticana, Pal. lat. 658, fol. 71 rb (A), Regin. lat. 977, fol. 206 ra(B). Laurentius nahm die Geringfügigkeit des Glaubensirrtums auch in seine Liste der Häresiedelikte auf und verwies dabei auf den Codex Iustinianus, vgl. oben Anm. 25.

[143] Zur C. 24 q. 1 c. 36 ad v. 'titubabat' : No(ta) titubantem in fide esse haereticum : sicut falsi assertor dicitur haereticus, ut supra [C.] 4 q. 3 In testibus (q.2 et 3, c. 3 §1), ext(ra) de Her(eticis) Dubius (X. V, 7,1), nam et hereticorum vocabulo continetur, qui levi etiam argumento a fide deviat, C(odice) de haere(ticis), Omnes, in fin(e) (1,5,2)... Joan(nes).

[144] Zu X.V,7,1 ad v. 'Dubius' : de fide enim nullus debet dubitare, sed firmiter credere articulos fidei, supra de summa trinitate capitulo primo in princip(io) (X.I,1,1); aliter salvus esse non poterit, ut in Psalm(o) Quicumque vult, et 24 distinct. Quando episcopus (5) et [C] 24 questio(ne) I Aperte (36); nullus enim titubare debet in fide, ut ibi dicitur. Bernardus.

[145] Zu X.V,7,1 ad v. 'Dubius' : firmiter enim credere debemus, ut s(upra) de sum-(ma) trinitate et fide ca(tholica), Firmiter (X. I, 1,1) XXIIII (HS. XXIII) di. Quando episcopus (5), [C.] XXIIII q. 1 Aperte (36) et in Psalmo Quicumque vult salvus esse. Nam levi argumento a fide devians hereticus censetur, ut C(odice) e(odem) t(itulo) l(ege) II (1,5,2). Est autem fides de re non visa, ut de pe(nitentia) di. IIII In domo (11) et ar(gumento) de con(secratione) di. IIII Venit (71) cetera dic. ut no(ta) s(upra) Firmiter credimus (I,1,1). G(offredus). (Wien,NB, CVP 2197, fol. 136 ra).

[146] *Conciliorum Oecumenicorum Decreta*, 206.

[147] Vgl. Raymond Foreville, 'Latran I, II, III et Latran IV', *Histoire des Conciles Oecuméniques*, 6 (Paris, 1965), 283ff., Migne, PL, 143, 771 C und Antoine Dondaine, 'Aux origines du valdéisme : Une profession de foi de Valdès', *Archivum fratrum Praedicatorum*, 16 (1946), 202.

lich vom ganzen Delikt des Glaubenszweifels: indem man jeden, der eine Lehre der Kirche hartnäckig in Frage stellte und das auch öffentlich bekundete, in gleicher Weise als Häretiker einstufte wie die Schöpfer und Anhänger der Irrlehre selbst, [148] dürfte man geglaubt haben, die rechte Lehre in der Auseinandersetzung mit den Ketzern besonders schützen zu können. Das römische Recht spielte jedenfalls in diesem Zusammenhang seit dem zweiten Jahrzehnt des dreizehnten Jahrhunderts wenn auch keine entscheidende, so doch sicherlich eine stark unterstützende Rolle. 1245 zog es sogar Papst Innocenz IV. heran, als er auf dem Konzil von Lyon Kaiser Friedrich II. absetzte. Nachdem er nämlich eine Reihe von Indizien aufgezählt hatte, die belegen sollten, daß der Kaiser der Häresie verdächtig sei, bezeichnete er diese als überzeugende Argumente; würden doch nach dem römischen Recht schon jene unter die Ketzer gerechnet und mit den für solche vorgesehenen Strafen belegt, denen nur eine geringfügige Abweichung vom Glauben nachgewiesen werden könne [149].

9) Dieser Einbau des *ius Romanum* in die juridische Reflexion über den Häresiebegriff dürfte einen starken Auftrieb erhalten haben, als 1199 Innocenz III. die Dekretale *Vergentis* erließ, die dann seit 1210 in der vom Papst offiziell gebilligten *Compilatio III* allgemein zugänglich war [150]. Sie wurde an den Klerus und das Volk von Viterbo, also Untertanen des Kirchenstaates, gesandt, ihr Inhalt galt jedoch für die gesamte Christenheit. Er bestand aus Strafsanktionen gegen alle, die Häretiker verteidigten, bei sich aufnahmen, begünstigten oder sich um

---

[148] Vgl. dazu München, *Gerichtsverfahren und Strafrecht*, II, 321f.; Hinschius, *Kirchenrecht*, V, 679, Anm. 7. Am deutlichsten umschreibt den Sachverhalt die *Glossa ordinaria* des Accursius zum Codex Iustinianus 1,5,2 ad v. 'levi argumento' : id est erret in illo articulo, qui manifeste debet sciri, quia pertinaciter illud asserit; non autem, si illud dicat causa disputandi... (*Corpus glossatorum iuris civilis*, X (1968), 19 va).

[149] Ed. Rodenberg, 2, Nr. 124 : Nonne igitur hec non levia sed efficatia sunt argumenta de suspitione heresis contra eum? Cum tamen hereticorum vocabulo illos ius civile contineri asserat et latis adversus eos sententiis debere succumbere, qui vel levi argumento a iudicio catholice religionis et tramite detecti fuerint deviare (93, Z. 8-12). Vgl. auch oben 78 mit Anm. 113. Auf die Kaiserkonstitution verweist dann die Glosse, welche der Papst selbst zu seiner Dekretale verfaßte, ad v. 'non dubiis' : cum hereticorum vocabulo contineri debeant et eciam puniri, qui eciam in levi argumento a tramite fidei noscuntur deviare, C(odice) de hereticis, l(ege) I (sic, 1,5,2).

[150] Es handelt sich um den Br. II 1 dieses Papstes : Migne, PL, 214, 537ff. = 3 Comp. 5,4,1 = X.V,7,10 (Ed. Friedberg, II, 782f.). Über die Compilatio III und ihre Empfehlung durch den Papst vgl. Stickler, *Historia iuris Canonici*, 233; Fransen, *Décrétales*, 25, 35.

einen Eintritt in ihre Sekten bewarben [151]. Für sie war die Infamie mit ihren bürgerlichen Folgen vorgesehen, also der Verlust der Fähigkeit, öffentliche Ämter zu bekleiden, vor Gericht als Kläger und Zeuge zu erscheinen, ein Testament zu errichten oder eine Erbschaft anzutreten sowie als Richter, Advokat oder Notar zu fungieren. Dazu kam noch, sowohl im Kirchenstaat als auch in den sonstigen christlichen Reichen, der vollständige Entzug des Vermögens. In ihm sah der Papst wohl ein besonders wirksames Zwangsmittel[152], weshalb es auch auf die Kinder der Häretiker ausgedehnt werden sollte, selbst dann , wenn diese rechtgläubig blieben. Das war neu und nicht zu rechtfertigen, denn auch das römische Recht hatte den Kindern der Ketzer ihr Erbe belassen, wenn sie dem katholischen Glauben folgten und nicht den Irrlehren ihrer Eltern anhingen. Hier zeigte sich also ein Widerspruch in den Auffassungen, den auszugleichen später den Dekretalisten große Mühe bereiten sollte [153]. Innocenz III. wollte die Vermögenskonfiskation wohl deshalb auf die rechtgläubigen Kinder der Häretiker ausdehnen, um diese durch den Gedanken, sie würden durch ihre Haltung ihre Nachkommen der Lebensgrundlage berauben, zu erschrecken [154]. Deshalb griff er auf eine Vorstellung zurück, welche schon die römische, gegen die Manichäer gerichtete Kaisergesetzgebung enthalten hatte, aus der aber noch nicht dieselben harten vermögensrechtlichen Folgerungen gezogen worden waren, wie jetzt von Seiten des Papstes : nämlich den Vergleich der Häresie mit dem Majestätsverbrechen. Erstmals erscheint er 407 in einem Gesetz der Kaiser Arcadius, Honorius und Theodosius II., das die Manichäer und Donatisten betraf, ihre Häresien als *publicum crimen* bezeichnete und über sie die für Majestätsverbrecher vorgesehenen

[151] Auf diese wurden also die ursprünglich bloß für die Häretiker vorgesehenen Strafen ausgedehnt. Erst bei der Redaktion des *Liber Extra* hat man sie unter dem Einfluß der 3. Konstitution des 4. Laterankonzils (=X.V,7,13§5) wiederum auf die offenkundigen Häretiker eingeschränkt; vgl. Othmar Hageneder, 'Studien zur Dekretale 'Vergentis' (X.V,7, 10) : Ein Beitrag zur Häretikergesetzgebung Innocenz' III', ZRG 80, KA 49 (1963), 138-173 (bes. 143 ff.).

[152] ut temporalis saltem poena corripiat quem spiritualis non corrigit disciplina (Ed. Friedberg, II, 783).

[153] Maisonneuve, *Origines de l'Inquisition*, 31, 279ff., 336ff.; Derselbe, 'Le droit romain et la doctrine Inquisitoriale' in *Études d'histoire du droit canonique dédiées à Gabriel Le Bras*, 2 (Paris, 1965), 931-942 (935ff.).

[154] So Goffred von Trani : Credo, quod Innocentius in poena filiorum consideravit parentes, an parentes intelliguntur puniri poenis filiorum... (Ed. Maguntiae, 1536, fol. 200 rb und Maisonneuve, *Origines de l'Inquisition*, 337 mit Anm. 191 ; Derselbe, *Droit romain*, 938 mit Anm. 35).

Strafen verhängte. Allerdings nicht mit aller Strenge, denn sie konnten
noch bis zum zweiten Grad der Verwandtschaft beerbt werden; was
man, wie noch zu zeigen sein wird, den Majestätsverbrechern selbst
nicht zugestanden hat [155]. Dieselbe Möglichkeit einer Gunstgewährung
läßt auch um 1175 Placentinus in seiner Summe zum Codex Justinianus
offen : die rechtgläubigen Söhne und anderen Verwandten der Häretiker dürfen entweder erben oder auch nicht - 'tamquam in maiestatis
crimine' [156]. Innocenz III. wollte in diesem Punkte augenscheinlich
klare Verhältnisse schaffen und gegen die Ketzer der italienischen Städte

[155] Codex Iustinianus 1,5,4 : Manichaeos seu Manichaeas vel Donatistas meritis-
sima severitate persequimur. Huic itaque hominum generi nihil ex moribus, nihil
ex legibus sit commune cum ceteris. Ac primum volumus esse publicum crimen,
quia quod in religione divina comittitur, in omnium fertur iniuriam. Quos bonorum
etiam publicatione persequimur : quae tamen cedere iubemus proximis quibusque
personis, ita ut ascendentium vel descendentium vel venientium ex latere cognatorum
usque ad secundum gradum velut in successionibus ordo servetur. Quibus ita demum
ad capiendas facultates esse ius patimur, si non et ipsi pari conscientia polluuntur...
Nam si in criminibus maiestatis licet memoriam accusare defuncti, non immerito
et hic debet subire iudicium. (Ed. Krueger, 51) Daher wird jedes Testament eines
Manichäers für ungültig erklärt : hoc quoque casu eadem illa circa gradus superius
comprehensos condicione servata. Vgl. Maisonneuve, *Origines de l'Inquisition*, 34,
über den Vermögensverlust der Majestätsverbrecher ebd. 33 und unten 91. Über
den Anwendungsbereich des Gesetzes vgl. Jean Gaudemet, 'L'Église dans l'Empire
romain (IVe-Ve siècles)', *Histoire du Droit et des Institutions de l'Église en Occident*,
III (Paris, 1959), 612 mit Anm. 7 und Ernst Ludwig Grasmück, *Coercitio : Staat und
Kirche im Donatistenstreit*, Bonner Historische Forschungen, 22 (Bonn, 1964), 209,
Anm. 249 : das Gesetz galt für die Manichäer und Priscillianisten.
[156] Placentinus (wie oben Anm. 140) in offenkundiger Anlehnung an den Codex
Iustinianus 1,5,4 : Haereticorum alii maximam haeresim praedicant, alii sapiunt levio-
rem. Maiores haeritici (sic!) sunt Manichaei, Arriani, Eutichiani, Samaritani,
Ophitae, Donatistae, Priscillianistae. His omnibus legitimus actus interdictus
est, omnis legitima conversatio adempta, his nihil ex moribus, nihil
ex legibus est commune cum caeteris, horum bona publicantur. Hi non a parente
nec a parentibus aliquid quocumque titulo percipere poterunt, non in alium conferre :
forte in filios catholicos aliosve homines orthodoxos. Ergo horum bona aut filii
catholici et consimiles cognati habebunt, aut forte minime tamquam in maiestatis
crimine (Ed. Maguntiae, 1536, 11). Vgl. Maisonneuve, *Origines de l'Inquisition*,
63. Siehe auch die *Summa super Codicem* des Azo: hi (die Häretiker)... nec in ultima
voluntate aliquid alicui relinquere possunt etiam filiis, quia omnino tamquam crimine
lesae maiestatis tenentur : et ideo in bona eorum succedit fiscus, nisi filios habeant
fideles, licet Pla(centinus) etiam in filios fideles dixerit eos non posse testari, lex tamen
infra eo(dem) l(ege) Manichaeos (1,5,4) dicit contra... Omnes ergo heretici testari
possunt in filios fideles non in infideles...(Ed. Torino, 1966, 6). Vgl. Maisonneuve,
Origines de l'Inquisition, 64 f., Anm. 191, 192).

die schwersten Vermögenssanktionen, welche auch alle Nachkommen einschlossen, verhängen. Dazu griff er auf römische Kaiserkonstitutionen zurück, die direkt den Majestätsverbrechern gegolten hatten. Besonders bot sich dafür das Gesetz *Quisquis* der Imperatoren Honorius und Arcadius aus dem Jahre 397 an. Es sah für alle, die Verschwörungen eingingen bzw. die Ermordung des Kaisers, eines seiner Ratgeber oder eines Senators planten, die Todesstrafe wegen Majestätsverbrechens und die Konfiskation des Vermögens vor. Schwere Strafen trafen zur Abschreckung auch die Söhne, darunter der Verlust jeglichen Erbrechts, sei es von Seiten der Eltern und Verwandten oder auch Fremden gegenüber. Der Infamie verfielen ferner alle, die es wagten, für solche Majestätsverbrecher oder ihre Söhne beim Kaiser einzutreten [157].

Das Gesetz fand auch in das *Decretum Gratiani* Eingang, wo ihm allerdings eine andere Bestimmung zugedacht war als im *Corpus iuris civilis*. Es enthielt nämlich noch die Verfügung, daß belohnt werde oder zumindest straffrei ausgehe, wer eine solche Verschwörung rechtzeitig verrate [158]. Gratian verwendete diese Stelle, um im Rahmen der 'Quaestio' die Frage zu beantworten, ob Personen, die in ein Verbrechen verstrickt oder mit der Infamie behaftet sind, zur Anklage eines anderen Verbrechens zugelassen werden können. Aus der Kaiserkonstitution zog er nun den Schluß, dem Mitglied einer Verschwörung sei es rechtlich erlaubt, jemanden wegen eines Majestätsverbrechens anzuklagen[159].

---

[157] Codex Iustinianus 9,8,5 (Ed. Krueger, 373 f.), vgl. Maisonneuve, *Origines de l'Inquisition*, 33 ; Hageneder, *Dekretale Vergentis*, 144 f.

[158] C. 6 q. 1 c. 22 : Si quis cum militibus vel privatis, barbaris etiam, scelestam inierit factionem aut factionis ipsius susceperit sacramentum vel dederit, de nece etiam virorum illustrium, qui consiliis et consistorio nostro intersunt, senatorum etiam (nam et ipsi pars nostri corporis sunt) vel cuiuslibet postremo, qui nobis militat, cogitaverit... ipse quidem, utpote maiestatis reus, gladio feriatur, bonis eius omnibus fisco nostro addictis. Filii vero eius, quibus vitam imperatoria specialiter lenitate concedimus, (paterno enim deberent perire supplicio, in quibus paterni, hoc est hereditarii, criminis exempla metuuntur) a successione omnium proximorum habeantur alieni, testamentis extraneorum nichil capiant, sint perpetuo egentes et pauperes, infamia eos semper paterna comitetur... sint postremo tales, ut his perpetua egestate sordentibus et sit mors solatium et vita supplicium. Denique iubemus etiam notabiles esse... sine venia, qui pro talibus umquam apud nos intervenire temptaverint (Ed. Friedberg, I, 560).

[159] Dict. post. c. 21 : ...exemplo... laesae maiestatis..., ad cuius accusationem ... socius initae factionis admittitur... (Ebd.). Zur Interpretation vgl. Vito Piergiovanni, 'La lesa maestà nella canonistica fino ad Uguccione', in *Materiali per una storia della cultura giuridica*, raccolti da Giovanni Tarello, 2 (1972), 61 f.

Ganz gleich, was der Magister beabsichtigte : das Gesetz stand nun einmal im Dekret und Innocenz III. konnte es für seine Zwecke verwenden. Allerdings mußte er dafür noch die gedankliche Verbindung zwischen dem römischen Majestätsverbrechen, das sich wider das Wohl des *populus Romanus* richtete und später besonders auf die Bedrohung der kaiserlichen Person und des Lebens seiner höchsten Beamten bezogen wurde, und der Häresie herstellen. Er tat dies durch die kühne Frage, ob denn nicht jene, die durch ihren Glaubensirrtum Jesus Christus beleidigen, von Christus, dem Haupt der Kirche, durch geistliche Strafen getrennt und ihrer weltlichen Güter beraubt werden sollen, so wie es die staatlichen Gesetze für die zum Tode verurteilten Majestätsverbrecher und deren Söhne vorsehen : wiege es doch weit schwerer, die ewige Majestät zu beleidigen als die zeitliche [160]. Diese *conclusio* dürfte der Papst abermals dem *ius Romanum* entnommen haben, und zwar der Novelle 77 des Kaisers Justinian, durch welche die Gotteslästerung unter das bürgerliche Strafgesetz gestellt und streng geahndet wurde. In ihrem Beginn heißt es : wenn schon Lästerungen der Menschen nicht ungestraft bleiben, um wieviel mehr hat, wer Gott beleidigt, mit den schwersten Sanktionen zu rechnen [161]. Daß Innocenz III. diesen Satz im Sinne hatte, ist wahrscheinlich; jedenfalls verweist Hostiensis im

---

[160] X.V,7,10 : Cum enim secundum legitimas sanctiones reis lese maiestatis punitis capite bona confiscentur ipsorum, eorum filiis vita solummodo ex misericordia conservata : quanto magis, qui aberrantes in fide Deum Dei filium Iesum Christum offendunt, a capite nostro, quod est Christus, ecclesiastica debent districtione precidi et bonis temporalibus spoliari, cum longe sit gravius eternam quam temporalem ledere maiestatem? (Ed. Friedberg, II, 783; hier ist der Text nach dem Registrum Vaticanum 4, fol. 147 r wiedergegeben). Zum Majestätsverbrechen vgl. Dig. 48, 4,1 : Maiestatis autem crimen illud est, quod adversus populum Romanum vel adversus securitatem eius committitur... (Ed. Theodor Mommsen, Berolini, 1893, 793), Placentinus : Ad legem Iuliam maiestatis, Tit. VIII(Ed. Maguntiae, 1536, 426) und Piergiovanni, *Lesa maestà*, 57 mit Anm. 3. Die Gleichstellung von Häresie und Majestätsverbrechen geht allerdings auf das Dekret C.6 q. 1 dict. post c. 21 zurück, wurde jedoch von Gratian und den Dekretisten nur auf die Fähigkeit zur Anklage der beiden Vergehen bezogen; vgl. Ebd. 60ff., Stephan Kuttner, *Kanonistische Schuldlehre von Gratian bis auf die Dekretalen Gregors IX.*, Studi e Testi, 64 (1935), 55 Anm. 2 und Peter Landau, *Die Entstehung des kanonischen Infamiebegriffs von Gratian bis zur Glossa ordinaria*, Forschungen zur kirchlichen Rechtsgeschichte und zum Kirchenrecht, 5 (Köln-Graz, 1966), 102.

[161] Nov. 77,1 : Si enim contra homines factae blasphemiae impunitae non reliquuntur, multo magis, qui ipsum deum blasphemat, dignus est supplicia sustinere (Ed. Schoell - Kroll, 382, Z. 16-19). Zur Gotteslästerung vgl. Theodor Mommsen, *Römisches Strafrecht* (Leipzig, 1899; Nachdruck Graz, 1955), 598.

Zusammenhang mit der Dekretale *Vergentis* auf ihn [162]. Eine kirchen-rechtliche Tradition, die ähnliches besagt, gibt dagegen schon 1216-1220 Tancred in seiner Glosse zur *Compilatio III* beim entsprechenden Passus der Dekretale an, indem er unter anderem die C. 17 q. 4 c. 12 des *Decretum Gratiani* zitiert, bzw. die in ihr enthaltene Stelle : 'maius peccatum est, quod in Deo committitur, quam quod in homine' [163]. Sei es, wie es sei : Innocenz III. wird wohl gar keine Vorlage gebraucht haben, der Schluß lag ja nahe. Auf jeden Fall hat aber der kanonistische Häresiebegriff eine neue römisch-rechtliche Akzentuierung erhalten.

Der vom Papst gewiesenen Richtung folgten die Dekretalisten. Dazu mag beigetragen haben, daß für den Codex Iustinianus seit 1208/10 die Summe des Azo, 'eines der erfolgreichsten Hauptwerke der euro-päischen Jurisprudenz', [164] vorlag. Jedenfalls übernahmen seit der Mitte des dreizehnten Jahrhunderts die Kanonisten jene Bestimmung der Kaiserkonstitution *Manichaeos* (Codex 1, 5, 4), wonach die Häresie ein *publicum crimen* darstellt, da allen zum Schaden gereicht, was gegen die göttliche Religion unternommen wird. So steht es in der *Glossa ordinaria* zum *Liber Extra* und bei Hostiensis [165]. Das römische *crimen*

---

[162] *Summa aurea*, Liber V, § De hereticis, 8 : non ergo debemus dimittere inultum opprobrium illius, qui probra nostra delevit, ut supra de iude(is) in nonnullis, § Illud (X.V,6,15), quia longe gravius est divinam quam temporalem offendere maiestatem, ut infra e(odem) Vergentis (X.V,7,10) et in Aut(entico) ut non luxu(rietur) contra naturam col. VI (Nov. 77,1) et dicitur infra de maledi(cis) (Ed. Lugduni, 1537, fol. 238 rb).

[163] Vgl. Biblioteca Apostolica Vaticana, Vat. lat. 1377, pag. 234 b, Borgh. 264, fol. 213 ra : zu 5, 4, 1 ad v. 'gravius'. Vgl. auch die *Glossa ordinaria* zum *Liber Extra* unten Anm. 165.

[164] Wieacker, *Privatrechtsgeschichte*, 63.

[165] *Glossa ordinaria* zu X.V,7,10 ad v. 'longe sit gravius' : [C.] 17 q. 4 Sicut qui ecclesiam (12) et [C.] 23 q. 5 Si apud (24) et quod in religionem divinam committitur, in omnium fertur iniuriam et publicum crimen committitur, C(odice) eod(em) tit(ulo) Manichaeos (1,5,4), unde gravius est.Hostiensis, *Summa aurea*, Liber V, § De hereticis, 8 : hereticus omnes offendit : quod enim in religionem divinam committitur, in omnium fertur iniuriam, et ideo publicum crimen dicitur, ut C(odice) e(odem) tit(ulo) Mani-cheos (1,5,4) (Ed. Lugduni, 1537, fol. 238 rb). In den Glossen des Vincentius Hispanus, Laurentius Hispanus, Johannes Teutonicus und Tancred zur 3 Comp. 5,4,1 (Vergentis) ist noch kein Hinweis auf das *publicum crimen* enthalten. Maisonneuve, *Origines de l'Inquisition*, 85 f. mit Anm. 304 glaubt allerdings, schon Huguccio habe in seiner Glosse zur C. 23 q. 4 c. 3 den Häretiker mit einem Dieb öffentlichen Gutes verglichen, was indirekt wohl eine Gleichsetzung von Häresie und *crimen publicum* bedeuten würde. Nun ist bei Huguccio, ebenso wie in der zugrundeliegenden Augustinusstelle nicht von Häretikern, sondern von *sacrilegi* die Rede, und Gratian hat sie woh'

publicum war eine Rechtsverletzung, ein Vergehen gewesen, das durch einen Strafprozeß vor dem Schwurgericht geahndet werden sollte, wobei es jedermann, nicht nur dem Geschädigten, freistand, die Anklage zu erheben. Die römischen Kaiser sahen also in der Abweichung vom wahren Glauben einen direkten Angriff auf den Staat, was für die Häretiker die entsprechenden Rechtsnachteile zur Folge hatte [166].

Das hängt auf das engste mit der spätantiken Religionspolitik zusammen, die im gemeinsamen Glauben aller Reichsangehörigen eine Stütze für die Einheit des Imperiums erblickte [167]. Die Kanonisten übertrugen die Vorstellung vom *crimen publicum* nun auf die Christenheit; und zwar auf Grund der Bemerkung Innocenz' III., daß die Häresie eine (Majestäts-)Beleidigung Gottes darstelle. Das *Corpus Christi mysticum*, dessen Haupt der Herr ist, scheint hier, wie es Otto Gierke formuliert hat, als Staat aufgefaßt und konstruiert worden zu sein [168]; ein Faktum, aus dem wohl zu erklären ist, daß seit Hostiensis auch die anderen Bestandteile des Häresiebegriffs der Glossatoren des römischen Rechts von der Kanonistik rezipiert wurden. Da ist einmal der Trennungscharakter des Häresiedelikts : wer nicht Glied der heiligen katholischen Kirche ist und wer nicht an die Lehre der ersten vier Konzile glaubt, der ist ein Häretiker ; so sagt es mit Verweisen auf den Codex und die Novellen

nur deshalb in die von der Verfolgung der Häretiker handelnde Causa versetzt, um aus ihr zu argumentieren, daß - wie es im später eingefügten Summarium heißt - 'pro pace ecclesiae mali sunt tollerandi'.

[166] Codex Iustinianus 9,9,29 (30) pr. : Quamvis adulterii crimen inter publica referatur, quorum delatio in commune omnibus sine aliqua legis interpretatione conceditur... (Ed. Krueger, 376). Vgl. auch Hitzig in Pauly-Wissowa, RE, 8 (1901),1713f. (Crimen publicum), 8/2 (1913) 1380 (Heterodoxia) und Gaudemet, *L'Église dans l'Empire romain*, 614.

[167] Rudolf Lorenz, 'Das vierte bis sechste Jahrhundert', in *Die Kirche in ihrer Geschichte* : *Ein Handbuch*, I (Göttingen, 1970), 36ff.; Mommsen, *Strafrecht*, 597; Baus im HKG,II,1 (1973) 84, 92.

[168] Otto v. Gierke, *Das deutsche Genossenschaftsrecht*, 3 (Nachdruck Darmstadt, 1954), 540. Vgl. auch Ernst Kantorowicz, *Kaiser Friedrich der Zweite*. Ergänzungsband (1931, Nachdruck Düsseldorf-München, 1964), 110. Über den hochmittelalterlichen Begriff des Corpus mysticum und seine (vermeintlichen?) Wandlungen vgl. Ernst H. Kantorowicz, *The King's Two Bodies*: *A Study in Mediaeval Political Theology* (Princeton, 1957), 194ff. und Friedrich Kempf, 'Untersuchungen über das Einwirken der Theologie auf die Staatslehre des Mittelalters', *Römische Quartalschrift*, 54 (1959), 210ff. Walter Ullmann, 'The significance of Innocent III's decretal *Vergentis*', In *Études Le Bras*, 2 (1965), 729ff. versucht, die Dekretale in sein System vom hierokratischen Papsttum einzubauen.

Kaiser Justinians Azo in seiner Summe (1208/10) [169]. Dieselbe Ansicht wiederholt die *Glossa ordinaria* des Accursius zum Codex, die aber auch, was die einzelnen Häresiedelikte betrifft, bereits auf den *Liber Extra* verweist [170]. Zumindest seit Hostiensis mündet nun die römisch-rechtliche Tradition über dieses Problem in die Gedankenarbeit der Kanonisten ein. Denn er übernahm den Häresiebegriff Azos, also vor allem die Negation der kirchlichen Mitgliedschaft und deren Untermauerung durch die philologische Herleitung des Wortes 'Häresie' von 'Teilung' oder 'Scheidung'. Als Beleg dafür zitierte er allerdings auch die C. 4 q. 1 c. 2 des Dekrets, also das Schreiben Papst Nikolaus' I. an den oströmischen Kaiser, in dem dieser einen Passus des ersten Konzils von Konstantinopel (381) über die Identität von Anathem und Häresie angeführt hatte [171]. So verband er die frühchristliche Vorstellung, der

[169] Videndum ergo, quis sit hereticus et unde dicatur : Es folgt der oben in Anm. 140 wiedergegebene Text, und dann : Vel qui non est membrum sancte catholice ecclesie vel qui est diversarum heresum, ut in Auten(tico) de privil(egiis) do(tis) col. VIII (Nov. 119 pr.), vel qui non credit secundum quod predicant sancta IIII concilia, ut infra e(odem) l(ege) Quicunque (1,5,8) et dicitur ab hercisco, id est divido. Inde in di(gesto?) fami(liae) here(sciscundae) (Dig. 10,2), id est hereditatis dividende. Inde et heremita quasi divisus ab aliis et ita heresis dicitur divisio, id est separatio a catholica fide (Ed. Torino, 1966, 6). Die entscheidende Stelle der Nov. 109 pr. lautet : quibus (i.e. den Häretikern) coniungimus et connumeramus...omnes, qui non sunt membrum sanctae dei catholicae et apostolicae ecclesiae... Igitur sacram communionem in catholica ecclesia non percipientes ab eius deo amabilibus sacerdotibus haereticos iuste vocamus : nam licet nomen Christianorum sibimet imposuerint a vera tamen Christianorum se et fide et communione separant dei iudicio semet ipsos subdi cognoscentes (Ed. Schoell-Kroll, 517, Z. 24f., 518, Z. 1-3, 8-14).

[170] Zum Codex Iustinianus 1,5,2 ad v. 'levi argumento' : vel dicitur hereticus, qui non est membrum sancte ecclesie vel qui sunt diversarum heresum, ut in Au(tenti)c(o) de privilegio dotis col. VIII (Nov. 109 pr.), vel qui non credunt quattuor concilia ut i(nfra) eo(dem) Quicumque (1,5,8) et in Au(tenti)c(o) ut cum de appel(latione) co(gnoscitur) § Generaliter col. VIII (Nov. 115,3,14) et aliis multis modis potest dici hereticus, ut no(ta) extra de hereticis c. ult(imum) (X.V,7, 15?) (*Corpus glossatorum iuris civilis*, X (1968), fol. 19 va). Die Glosse des Accursius dürfte wohl noch vor der Mitte des 13. Jhdts. entstanden sein : Wieacker, *Privatrechtsgeschichte*, 63; Weimar, *Literatur*, 174.

[171] *Summa aurea*, Liber V, § De hereticis, 1 : Quis dicatur hereticus : ... nam qui non est membrum ecclesie hereticus iudicatur in Aut(entico) de privi(legiis) doti(s) hereti(cis) muli(eribus) non prestan(dis) post prin(cipium) ibi et ad hoc omnes, qui non sunt membrum sancte et apostolice ecclesie et c(etera) col. VIII (Nov. 119 pr.) et probatur [C.] IIII q. 1 c. II...Dicitur autem hereticus ab herciscor, hercisceris, id est divido, dividis, inde fami(lie) erci(scunde) (Dig.10,2), id est iudicium substantie dividende. Inde et eremita quasi divisus ab aliis : ita et heresis dicitur divisio, id est separatio a fide catholica secundum Azo(nem) (Ed. Lugduni, 1537, fol. 237 r/v). Zur C.4 q.1 c. 2 vgl. oben Anm. 122.

durch diese Kirchenstrafe von der Gemeinschaft der Gläubigen Getrennte sei eben auf Grund dieses Status ein Häretiker, mit dem Häresieindiz des spätrömischen Reiches. Als solches ist außerdem die Forderung zu werten, der Rechtgläubige müsse an die Entscheidungen der vier ersten christlichen Konzile, also von Nicaea, Konstantinopel I, Ephesus und Chalcedon glauben [172]. Wenn auch seit dem vierten Jahrhundert, als das Christentum eine Staatsreligion geworden war, das Anathem nicht mehr den völligen Verlust der Kirchenmitgliedschaft bedeutete und die Trennung nur mehr theologisch verstanden wurde [173], so mag dennoch die Verbindung dieser Vorstellung mit Prinzipien der römischen Gesetzgebung zu einer Verhärtung der kirchlichen Einstellung gegenüber den Häresien beigetragen haben. Immerhin ging dieser gedankliche Prozeß mit dem Ausbau der Ketzerinquisition und der Einführung der Todesstrafe für die Häretiker sowie der Folter in den Inquisitionsprozeß -letzteres erfolgte bekanntlich 1252 durch die Dekretale *Ad exstirpanda* Innocenz' IV - Hand in Hand [174].

Diese allgemeine Entwicklung macht es auch verständlich, daß der Vergleich von Häresie und Majestätsverbrechen nicht nur in der Gedankentradition der Glossatoren und Kanonisten erhalten blieb [175], sondern auch in das Recht eines der sich am stärksten zu einem modernen Herrschaftsgebilde entwickelnden Staaten, nämlich der normannisch-staufischen Monarchie Siziliens, Eingang fand. Schon 1220 war unter päpstlichem Einfluß die Dekretale *Vergentis* in den Krönungsgesetzen Kaiser

[172] Vgl. oben in den Anm. 169 und 170 den Text Azos und die Glosse des Accursius. Vgl. auch die Novellen 131,1 und 115,3,14 (Ed. Schoell-Kroll, 654 und 541) sowie Maisonneuve, *Origines de l'Inquisition*, 279.

[173] Hinschius, *Kirchenrecht*, IV, 749; Feine, *Kirchliche Rechtsgeschichte*, 122f.; Hans Barion in *Die Religion in Geschichte und Gegenwart*, II, 3. Aufl. (1958), 829. Vgl. auch oben Anm. 123.

[174] Zum letzteren vgl. Maisonneuve, *Origines de l'Inquisition*, 312, zum Ganzen Hans Wolter im *Handbuch für Kirchengeschichte*, III, 2 : *Die mittelalterliche Kirche*, 2. Halbband (Freiburg-Basel-Wien, 1968), 268ff.

[175] *Glossa ordinaria* des Accursius zum Codex Iustinianus 1,5,4 ad v. 'debet subire' : est ergo simile crimen hereseos crimini lese maiestatis, ut utrumque possit post mortem accusari ut hic et i(nfra). Gulielmus Duranti, *Speculum iuris* (Venetiis, 1577), Pars III et IIII, 489 : Ceterum cum crimen laesae maiestatis in quibusdam conveniat cum haeresi, ut extra eod(em titulo) Vergentis (X. V,7,10) et C(odice) eodem Manicheos (1,5,4) et ideo hic formemus... (ein Anklagelibell wegen Majestätsverbrechen). Das *Speculum iuris* (*iudiciale*) des Gulielmus Duranti entstand in der ersten Redaktion zwischen 1271 und 1276, in der zweiten zwischen 1289 und 1291. Vgl. zuletzt Knut Wolfgang Nörr, 'Die Literatur zum gemeinen Zivilprozeß', HBPRG, I, 394.

Friedrichs II. rezipiert worden; und zwar gemeinsam mit dem Vergleich von Häresie und Majestätsverbrechen [176]. Elf Jahre später erscheint in den Konstitutionen von Melfi, dem berühmten *Liber Augustalis*, der uns schon bekannte römischrechtliche Häresiebegriff von neuem : das Delikt wird unter die *publica crimina* gerechnet und als Beleidigung der göttlichen Majestät schlimmer gewertet als ein etwa gegen Friedrich II. selbst gerichtetes *crimen laesae maiestatis*. Schon bei einem leichten Verdacht (*levis suspicionis argumento*) sollte eine Untersuchung eingeleitet werden [177]. Wiederum ist es die *Glossa ordinaria* - Marinus de Caramanico verfaßte sie noch vor 1282 -, welche dazu teilweise dieselben Belege aufzählt, wie sie die Dekretale *Vergentis* enthielt [178]. Auch diese

---

[176] Vergottini, *Legislazione imperiale di Federico II in Italia*, 110f.; Hageneder, *Dekretale Vergentis*, 150f.; Selge, *Ketzerpolitik Friedrichs II.* (siehe Anm. 115), 319.

[177] Lib. I. Tit. I : De hereticis et Patarenis : ... statuimus in primis, ut crimen hereseos et damnate secte cuiuslibet, quocumque censeantur nomine sectatores, prout veteribus legibus est indictum, inter publica crimina numeretur. Immo crimine lese maiestatis nostre debet ab omnibus horribilius iudicari, quod in divine maiestatis iniuriam dignoscitur attentatum, quamquam in iudicii potestate alter alterum non excedat. Nam sicuti perduellionis crimen personas adimit damnatorum et bona et damnat post obitum etiam memoriam defunctorum, sic et in predicto crimine, quo Patareni notantur, per omnia volumus observarii ... inquisitione notatos, etsi levis suspicionis argumento tangantur, a viris ecclesiasticis et prelatis examinari iubemus (J.L.A. Huillard-Bréholles, *Historia diplomatica Friderici secundi*, IV, 1 (Paris, 1854), 6f.). Vgl. auch die Neuedition von Hermann Conrad (†), Thea von der Lieck-Buyken und Wolfgang Wagner, *Die Konstitutionen Friedrichs II. von Hohenstaufen für sein Königreich Sizilien*, Studien und Quellen zur Welt Kaiser Friedrichs II., 3 (Wien, 1973), 6 Z. 28-35, 8 Z. 1-3. Zu den Konstitutionen von Melfi vgl. jetzt Armin Wolf, 'Die Gesetzgebung der entstehenden Territorialstaaten', HBPRG, I, 698ff.

[178] Ad v. 'imo crimine' Bene dicit : imo. Nam divina gratia debet legibus praevalere, ut in Auth(entico) de mona(chis) § Hinc autem colla(tione) I (Nov. 5,2), cum etiam longe gravius sit aeternam quam temporalem offendere maiestatem, ut C(odice) eo(dem) Gazaros (Novelle Friedrichs II. nach 1,5,19) et extra eod(em) c. Vergentis (X.V,7,10)...

Ad v. 'divinae maiestatis iniuriam' : quod enim in divinam religionem comittitur, in omnium infertur iniuriam, ut in praeallegat(a) le(ge) Manichaeos (1,5,4) § 1. Auch hier wird also die Häresie als eine gegen Gott gerichtete Majestätsbeleidigung verstanden und nicht als ein wider den weltlichen Herrscher verübtes *crimen maiestatis*, wie Kantorowicz, *Ergänzungsband*, 110 interpretiert, indem er im Text der Konstitutionen *crimen* statt *crimine* lesen will. Vgl auch Christoph Ulrich Schminck, *Crimen laesae maiestatis : Das politische Strafrecht Siziliens nach den Assisen von Ariano (1140) und den Konstitutionen von Melfi (1231)*, Untersuchungen zur deutschen Staats- und Rechtsgeschichte, NF 14 (1970), 88 und Selge, *Ketzerpolitik Friedrichs II.*, 324ff., 333f.

selbst wird zitiert. Eine starke Betonung liegt in diesem Zusammenhang auf dem *crimen publicum* : alle haben das Recht, wegen Häresie Anklage zu erheben; auch solche, denen das sonst nicht zugebilligt wird, wie Sklaven und Frauen. Ferner sollen die erschwerenden Förmlichkeiten des Akkusationsprozesses wegfallen, wie das Anklagelibell und die Verpflichtung, im Falle des Mißlingens eines Beweises dieselbe Strafe auf sich zu nehmen, die den Beschuldigten getroffen hätte [179].

Damit war die Inquisition in das weltliche Staatsrecht inkorporiert. Die Ketzergesetzgebung des spätantiken Zwangsstaates triumphierte sowohl in der Kirche als auch im weltlichen Herrschaftsbereich. Bekanntlich hat dann 1233 Friedrich II. sizilische Rebellen als Häretiker bezeichnet und unter dieser Beschuldigung hinrichten lassen [180].

10) Das war freilich eine willkürliche Übertragung des Häresiebegriffs. Doch auch innerhalb der Kirche ist dazu eine Parallele feststellbar, denn die sich ständig mehrenden und verfeinernden Bestimmungen über die Ketzerverfolgung bringen auch dort eine Erweiterung des entsprechenden Begriffs mit sich. So bestimmte bereits 1215 das vierte Laterankonzil, daß ein der Häresie Verdächtiger, der sich weigere, vor dem Inquisitionsgericht den ihm zur Rechtfertigung auferlegten Reinigungseid zu leisten, für einen Ketzer gehalten werden solle. Allerdings mußte diese Ablehnung des Eides aus der Überzeugung entspringen, daß ein solcher prinzipiell unerlaubt sei [181]. Das war eine den Katharern

---

[179] Ad v. 'divinae maiestatis iniuriam' : Et cunctis veluti in publico crimine est licentia accusandi, ut C(odice) de pag(anis) l(ege) ulti(ma) (1,11,10?), C(odice) de epis(copis) et cler(icis) Si quanquam (1,3,30[31]). Quinimmo in hoc omnes admittuntur ad deferendum etiam qui alias non admitterentur, ut servi et mulieres, et sine libello, sine inscriptione et solemnitate accusationis, ut C(odice) de apost(atis) l(ege) Apostatarum (1,7,4) in princ(ipio), tanquam videlicet quilibet in hoc suam iniuriam prosequatur, ut no(ta) in Auth(entico) Quomodo opor(teat) epis(copos) ad ordi (nationem) dedu(ci) § Licentiam (Nov. 6, Epilogus), in gl(ossa) ord(inaria), forte etiam servus etc. (Constitutiones regni utriusque Siciliae, glossis ordinariis commentariisque excellentiss. I.V.D. Domini Andreae de Ysernia ac D. Bartholomei Capuani atque nonnullorum cum (!) veterum, tum recentiorum I.C. lucubrationibus illustratae et maxime studio et opera prestantissimi iurisconsulti D. Gabrielis Saraynae, Veronensis... (Venetiis, 1580), 7. Über die Glosse und ihre Verfasser vgl. Norbert Horn, 'Die legistische Literatur der Kommentatoren und der Ausbreitung des gelehrten Rechts', HBPRG, I, 269, 358, 362; Wolf, *Gesetzgebung*, 701.

[180] Eduard Winkelmann, *Kaiser Friedrich II*, Jahrbücher der deutschen Geschichte, 2 (Leipzig, 1897; Nachdruck Darmstadt, 1963), 414, 446; Kantorowicz, *Kaiser Friedrich II*, 1, 257, vgl. auch 243, *Ergänzungsband*, 111; Selge, *Ketzerpolitik Friedrichs II.*, 336f.

[181] Const. 3 = X.V,7,13 § 7 : Si qui vero ex eis iuramenti religionem obstinatione damnabili respuentes iurare forte noluerint, ex hoc ipso tanquam haeretici reputentur

eigene Vorstellung, so daß eine derartige Weigerung als Geständnis der Häresie gewertet werden konnte [182].

Bald darnach rechnete Papst Gregor IX. auch die *Credentes* der Häretiker zu diesen. Dabei handelte es sich um jenen Personenkreis, der einer Irrlehre innerlich anhing, das auch irgendwie bekundete, doch sie im einzelnen formell nicht vertrat. Die *Credentes* galten als eine Art von Adepten der Häresie, welche sich um die Aufnahme bewarben und daher einen niedrigeren Grad innehatten als die *Perfecti* [183]. Eng verwandt waren ihnen, schon gemäß der Dekretale *Vergentis* von 1199, die *fautores, defensores* und *receptatores* der Ketzer, also alle, die sie irgendwie begünstigten und verteidigten oder ihnen sonstwie Vorschub leisteten und somit in einer, wenn auch nur sehr lockeren Beziehung zu den Häretikern standen [184]. Sie galten als der Häresie verdächtig, und die *defensores* hielt man bisweilen für verdammenswerter als die Ketzer selbst [185]. Insgesamt sollten sie erst nach einem Jahr vergeblicher Exkommunikation dem Ketzerurteil unterliegen [186]. Schließlich unter-

(Ed. Friedberg, II, 789). Daß es sich hier um den Reinigungseid handelt, sagt die *Glossa ordinaria* ad v. 'iurare' : per iuramentum debet quis purgare conscientiam suam de heresi... Vgl. dazu Hinschius, *Kirchenrecht*, V, 352f., 472 § h, 486 mit Anm. 7.

[182] Vgl. die *Glossa ordinaria* a.a.O. : ...unde si iurare non vult, pro condempnato debet haberi, sicut qui de calumnia iurare non vult, actor cadit a causa et reus pro condemnato habetur... Zur Verwerfung des Eides vgl. Borst, *Katharer*, 185f.

[183] Gregor IX. in X.V,7,15 § 1 : credentes autem eorum erroribus similiter haereticos iudicamus. (Ed. Friedberg, II, 789). Vgl. auch Hostiensis, *Summa aurea*, Liber V, § De hereticis 1 : Sed et his (i.e. hereticis) credentes hodie per dominum Gregorium coniunguntur, ut infra eo(dem) Excommunicamus II § ult(imus) (X.V,1,15 § 1). (Ed. Lugduni, 1537, fol. 237 va). Zu den Credentes vgl. Vergottini, *Legislazione imperiale di Federico II in Italia*, 26; Flatten, *Häresieverdacht*, 186; Borst, *Katharer*, 203.

[184] Flatten, *Häresieverdacht*, 187; Hinschius, *Kirchenrecht*, I, 47.

[185] Vgl. die *Glossa ordinaria* zu X.V, 40, 26 ad v. 'defendunt' : Et isti defensores hereticorum sunt excommunicati, supra de haeret(icis) Excommunicamus § Credentes (X.V,7,13 § 5), et tales damnabiliores sunt quam ipsi heretici, [C] 24, quaest. tertia, Qui aliorum (32). Et est hoc arg. C(odice) de his qui latron(es) occu(ltaverint) l(ege) 1&2 (9,39, 1.2).

[186] Vgl. zum Beispiel das *Speculum iuris* des Gulielmus Duranti, Pars III et IIII : Eodem etiam modo concipitur contra credentes et receptatores, qui et haeretici reputantur, si excommunicationem propter hoc in se latam per annum sustinuerint, ext(ra) eo(dem) c. pe(nultimo) in fi(ne) (X.V,7,15 § 1) et c. Excommunicamus infra § Credentes (X.V,7,13 § 5), qui § est C(odice) eo(dem) Auth(entico) Credentes (Nach 1,5, 19) et C(odice) de his, qui latro(nes) occul(taverint) l(ege) 1& 2 (9, 39, 1.2), et cum aliquis credens vel receptator ab initio recusatur, tunc peti potest, quod excommunicetur (Ed. Venetiis, 1577, 489 b).

warf noch Papst Bonifaz VIII. alle getauften Juden, die wieder zu ihrem Glauben zurückkehrten, den Häresiestrafen [187].

Auf diese Weise wurden seit dem dreizehnten Jahrhundert der Häresiebegriff und zugleich der Umfang des Häresieverdachtes ständig erweitert. Das mag auch, wie Heinrich Flatten meint, durch eine gewisse Gesetzmäßigkeit der Bürokratie mitbedingt gewesen sein : die Inquisitionstribunale besaßen die Tendenz, ihre Kompetenzen zu mehren, so daß bald alle Delikte, die sie an sich zogen und die ursprünglich mit Häresie kaum etwas zu tun hatten, zumindest mit einem Häresieverdacht in Verbindung gebracht wurden [188].

11) Welche Rolle spielte nun die Kanonistik für die Entwicklung des Häresiebegriffs? Man muß wohl zwei gedankliche Schichten unterscheiden. Da ist einmal die traditionelle, zum Teil aus der Spätantike und dem frühen Mittelalter stammende Vorstellung : ein hartnäckiger Irrtum in jener Glaubenslehre, der auch der apostolische Stuhl anhängt, die dauernde Trennung von der Kirche durch ein Schisma und die Simonie sind häretisch. Dazu kommt im Zeitalter der gregorianischen Reform der Angriff auf den päpstlichen Primat. In diesen Häresiedelikten spiegeln sich drei große Probleme der Kirche aus dem ersten Jahrtausend ihres Bestehens wider: die christologischen Kämpfe der Spätantike, die starke Bindung an den kulturell-staatlichen Bereich und seine Institutionen seit Konstantin, und schließlich der Versuch, sich daraus unter der Führung eines monarchisch gestärkten Papsttums zu befreien.

Diesen Häresiebegriff überlieferte das *Decretum Gratiani*; er wurde von den Kanonisten durchdacht, indem sie ihn, auch durch die Verweise auf andere Rechtstexte, genauer umschrieben und damit in seinem Umfang festlegten. Im Rahmen dieser Gedankenarbeit hat man auch verschiedene Delikte, die noch in der ersten Jahrhunderthälfte unter dem Eindruck der gregorianischen Reform bisweilen als Häresie galten, ausgesondert, wie die als *simoniaca haeresis* angesehene Laieninvestitur und die Übertretung der priesterlichen Zölibatsgesetze [189].

---

[187] VI° V, 2,13 : erit tanquam contra haereticos... procedendum (Ed. Friedberg, II, 1075). Vgl. dazu die bald nach 1300 entstandene *Glossa ordinaria* des Johannes Andreae : No(ta) principalem effectum huius c(apituli), quod Christiani transeuntes ad ritum Iudaeorum sunt haeretici censendi et tanquam haeretici sunt puniendi.

[188] Flatten, *Häresieverdacht*, 66. Vgl. auch die Liste bei Hinschius, *Kirchenrecht*, V, 472f.

[189] Laieninvestitur : MGH, Libelli de lite, 2 (1892), 564, Z. 27-37, 565, Z. 11, 23ff. (Bruno von Segni), 590, Z. 21 f., 603, Z. 3-6, 604, Z. 26ff. (Placidus von Nonantula), 682, Z. 24f. 685, Z. 29f. (=simoniaca haeresis), 690, Z. 13ff., und 697, Z. 47ff. (Gottfried

Zum anderen, und dabei handelt es sich meines Erachtens um die zweite gedankliche Schicht, wurde der Häresiebegriff durch die Hinzufügung neuer Tatbestände und die Erweiterung der alten angereichert. So taucht im *Summarium* zur C. 24 q. 1 c. 36 erstmals der Glaubenszweifel als Häresie auf, was später auch durch Texte aus Pseudoisidor und dem römischen Recht belegt wird [190]. Das Konzil von Verona erweitert 1184 den Glaubensirrtum auf die Lehren der Katharer und Waldenser vom Wesen der Sakramente [191]. Wiederum aus dem *ius Romanum* stammen die Begriffe des Majestätsverbrechens und des *crimen publicum*, denen man seit Innocenz III. die Häresie gleichsetzte, um die römischen Kaisergesetze gegen ihre Anhänger mit voller Härte anwenden zu können [192]. Ebenso wurde die von der frühchristlichen Vorstellung über die Folgen des Anathems hergeleitete Identität von Exkommunikation und Häresie durch die Rezeption der Ketzergesetzgebung spätantiker Imperatoren unterbaut [193]. Diese ganze Steigerung, Erweiterung und Verhärtung war, zumindest seit der zweiten Hälfte des zwölften Jahrhunderts, zweifellos durch die Abwehr der sich ständig ausbreitenden und die Kirche bedrohenden Häresien mitbedingt. Es hatte sich eine defensive Situation herausgebildet, welche vielleicht Huguccio veranlaßte, zu Ende der Achtzigerjahre des Jahrhunderts in seiner Summe zum Dekret jene Häresie, die von Petrus Damiani in der Verletzung des *Privilegium Romanae ecclesiae* gesehen worden war, näher zu erläutern und damit erst rechtswirksam zu machen. Sie wurde von ihm und seinen Nachfolgern der hartnäckigen Nichtbefolgung der *canones* und päpstlichen Dekretalen, die auf eine prinzipielle Leugnung

---

von Vendôme), Migne, PL, 163, 466 A (Konzil von Vienne 1112). Kritisch äussert sich dazu Ivo von Chartres, MGH, Libelli de lite, 2, 653, Z. 21ff. Zu Bruno von Segni vgl. auch Gérard Fransen, 'Réflexions sur l'étude des collections canoniques à l'occasion de l'édition d'une lettre de Bruno de Segni', *Studi Gregoriani*, 9 (1972), 530f. Vgl. außerdem Gilchrist, *Simoniaca haeresis* (s. oben Anm. 44), 215, Anm. 25 und Peter R.Mc. Keon, 'The Lateran Council of 1112, the Heresy of Lay Investiture and the Excommunication of Henry V', *Medievalia et Humanistica*, 17 (1966), 3-12 (bes. 5f., 7, 11). Nikolaiten (d.s. die Übertreter des Zölibatsgebotes) als Häretiker : MGH, Libelli de lite, 3 (1897), 756 s.v. Nicolaita.

Vgl. auch Berschin, *Bonizo von Sutri*, 110 : die Häresie ist im Gegenpapst Clemens III. verkörpert. Zum Ganzen vgl. ferner Herbert Grundmann, 'Ketzergeschichte des Mittelalters', In *Die Kirche in ihrer Geschichte : Ein Handbuch*, II, 1 (1967), G 13ff.

[190] Siehe oben 84ff.
[191] Siehe oben 82ff.
[192] Siehe oben 88ff.
[193] Siehe oben 81f., 94ff.

des Gesetzgebungsrechtes schließen lasse, gleichgesetzt [194]. Die praktischen Konsequenzen haben daraus Innocenz III., der Schüler Huguccios, und die späteren Päpste gezogen. Für sie begründete besonders
ein lang andauernder Widerstand gegen Exkommunikationssentenzen
den Verdacht der Häresie, der im Lauf der Zeit zum Ketzerurteil führen
konnte [195].

In diesem Zusammenhang ist auch die Bestimmung des Konzils
von Vienne (1311) zu sehen, nach der als Häretiker verurteilt werden
sollte, wer behauptete, Wucher sei keine Sünde : dieses Vergehen galt
zumindest seit dem dritten Laterankonzil von 1179 als *crimen* und *peccatum* [196], so daß man durch eine derartige Meinungskundgebung das
Gesetzgebungsrecht der Kirche prinzipiell in Zweifel zog.

Diese Ausgestaltung eines auf die Leugnung des päpstlichen Jurisdiktionsprimats begründeten Häresiebegriffs war wohl der bedeutendste
Beitrag, den die Kanonistik während ihrer klassischen Periode, also
zwischen 1150 und 1300, zu dessen endgültiger Fixierung leistete.

Aber die Kanonistik war ambivalent ; ihre Spekulationen steigerten
nicht nur die päpstliche Gewalt in der Kirche, sie konnten auch zu
ihrer Beschränkung beitragen. So stellten die *Glossa Palatina* des Laurentius und die *Glossa ordinaria* des Johannes Teutonicus übereinstim-
mend fest, daß es dem Papst nicht erlaubt sei, vom *status generalis*,

---

[194] Siehe oben 72ff.

[195] Diese Häresie der Leugnung des Jurisdiktionsprimats, die sich besonders im
hartnäckigen Widerstand gegen päpstliche Verfügungen und Zensuren äußerte, ist
wohl auch der Grund für jenen weiteren Häresiebegriff, der 'nicht bloß die Leugnung
einer formellen Offenbarungswahrheit, sondern jede ernste Gefährdung des Glaubens-
lebens und jeden hartnäckigen Widerstand gegen die kirchliche Disziplin' umgreift
und den Albert Lang für das Spätmittelalter und auch noch das Konzil von Trient
feststellt : 'Der Bedeutungswandel der Begriffe 'fides' und 'haeresis' und die dogmatische Wertung der Konzilsentscheidungen von Vienne und Trient', *Münchener
Theologische Zeitschrift*, 4 (1953), 133-146 (135, 137, 140, 144ff.). Vgl. auch Flatten,
Häresieverdacht, 53. Was die Kanonisten betrifft, kann man allerdings kaum sagen,
daß 'aus den Ausdrücken 'veritas fidei catholicae' und 'haereticus' *allein*... durchaus
noch nicht auf den Glaubenscharakter der Definition im Sinne der *fides divina* ge-
schlossen werden(kann)' (Ebd. 139, ähnlich 141, 145, 146), da ja, wie gezeigt, ihrer
Meinung nach hinter dem hartnäckigen Widerstand gegen die Glaubensdisziplin
eine Leugnung des Primates und seiner Rechte stand.

[196] c. 29 : Sane quisquis in illum errorem inciderit ut pertinaciter affirmare praesu-
mat, exercere usuras non esse peccatum, decernimus eum velut haereticum puniendum
(COD, 1962, 360f. = Clem. 5,5 un. § 2, Ed. Friedberg, II, 1184). Vgl. dazu 3. Lat.
Konzil c. 25 : crimen usurarum, bzw. si in hoc peccato decesserint (COD, 1962, 199,
Z. 21, 25 = X.V,19,3, Ed. Friedberg, II, 812).

besonders aber den Glaubensartikeln, zu dispensieren ; auch nicht mit Zustimmung der gesamten Kirche. In einem solchen Falle würden alle Gläubigen zu Häretikern [197].

---

[197] Die entsprechenden Texte siehe bei Post, *'Copyists' Errors* (siehe oben Anm. 84), 374f., 380f., 392f., 395. Der Text der *Glossa Palatina* lautet : hinc colligunt quidam, quod dominus papa non potest contra generalem statum ecclesie dispensare, et hoc indubitabile quidem est circa articulos fidei. Etiam si tota ecclesia consentiret, non posset; immo omnes essent heretici, ar(gumento) XV di. Sicut sancti (2) (Ebd. 374, 395).

Helmut G. WALTHER

HÄRESIE UND PÄPSTLICHE POLITIK :
KETZERBEGRIFF UND KETZERGESETZGEBUNG
IN DER ÜBERGANGSPHASE
VON DER DEKRETISTIK ZUR DEKRETALISTIK

Voller Freude glaubt Paul von St. Père in Chartres berichten zu können, daß die Irrlehre der 1022 in Orléans gefaßten Ketzer, die sich leider schon längere Zeit in den Provinzen Frankreichs verbreitet habe, durch das Verdienst des Ritters Arefast völlig unterdrückt werden konnte [1]. Raoul Glaber stimmt in seinem Bericht über die Ketzerei von Orléans in das Lob des tatkräftigen Zupackens ein, da es doch die Folge gehabt habe, daß der katholische Glaube nun wieder überall klarer hervorleuchte [2]. Beide Autoren verhehlen damit nicht ihre Sorge, daß die Ketzerei sich jahrelang unbemerkt verbreiten konnte [3].

In der Tat ist diese jahrelange Verborgenheit bei gleichzeitiger Ausbreitung nicht der Regelfall für mittelalterliche Ketzereien bis ins zwölfte Jahrhundert. In einer noch fast ausschließlich agrarisch struk-

---

[1] Paul v. Chartres, *Vetus Agano*, VI, 3 in Migne, PL, 155, 263 = *Gesta Synodi Aurelianensis*, Recueil des historiens de la France (=Bouquet), 10, 536 : Rursum quoque duxi dignum memoriae tradendum de praefato viro, scilicet Arefasto, quomodo in Aureliana urbe divina ope, suique ingenii salubri acumine, haereticam pravitatem latenter pullulantem, jamjamque per Gallicarum provincias nefandi erroris venena exitialia propinantem, non solum deprehenderit, sed etiam omnino compresserit.

[2] Raoul Glaber, *Les cinq livres de ses histoires*, éd. Maurice Prou, Collection de textes pour servir à l'étude et à l'enseignement de l'histoire, 1 (Paris, 1886), III, 8 : Preterea venerabilis catholice fidei cultus, exstirpata insanientium pessimorum vesania, ubique terrarum clarior emicuit (81).

[3] Durch Ademar v. Chabannes (*Historiarum Libri tres* III, 59) wissen wir, daß im Zusammenhang mit der Ketzerverfolgung die Leiche des bereits vor drei Jahren verstorbenen Kantors Theodat von Orléans verbrannt wurde (MGH, Scriptores, 4,143). Zur Ketzerei von Orléans : Ilarino da Milano, 'Le eresie popolari del secolo XI nell' Europa occidentale', *Studi Gregoriani*, 2 (1947), 43-89 (hier 52-60) ; Jeffrey Burton Russell, *Dissent and Reform in the Early Middle Ages*, Publications of the Center for Medieval and Renaissance Studies, 1 (Berkeley-Los Angeles, 1965), 27-35 ; Herbert Grundmann, *Ketzergeschichte des Mittelalters* in *Die Kirche in ihrer Geschichte*, 2,G 1, 2. Auflage (Göttingen, 1967), 8ff.

turierten Umwelt, konnten sich Ketzereien nur der rudimentären Kommunikationswege jener Zeit bedienen und waren somit als vornehmlich isolierte Erscheinungen relativ leicht durch die lokalen geistlichen und weltlichen Institutionen zu kontrollieren [4]. Der Umstand, daß im Fall der Ketzer von Orléans von König Robert II. erstmals die Verbrennung als Strafe für Ketzerei praktiziert wurde, mag also - jenseits der persönlichen, religiösen wie rachsüchtigen Motive beim Herrscherpaar [5] - auch auf die Empörung über die lange verborgene Wirksamkeit der Ketzergruppe - und dann auch noch in Kanonikerkreisen - zurückzuführen sein.

Die Kirchenreformbewegung veränderte jedoch die Beziehungen zwischen Volksreligiosität und kirchlichen Instanzen. Im Verhalten Gregors VII., der sich auf die städtische Volksbewegung Mailands stützte, um kirchenpolitische Ziele zu erreichen, deuten sich neue Kommunikationsformen an. Gerade an der Geschichte der Pataria wurden auch die Beziehungen zwischen Volksreligiosität und Reformpartei untersucht [6]. Aber das leidenschaftliche Klima in den Auseinandersetzungen erleichterte es, den Gegner als *haereticus* oder *haeresiarcha* abzuqualifizieren. Wenn man wie H. Grundmann urteilt, daß 'die Selbstkritik und Reinigung der Kirche ... der Ketzerei zunächst den Wind aus den Segeln (nahm)'[7], so darf man nicht vergessen, wie sehr der bislang als patristisches Erbe mitgeführte Ketzerbegriff in intoleranter Atmosphäre eine Ausweitung ins rein Plakative und auch Willkürliche

---

[4] Zu diesem Problem vgl. Arno Borst, 'La transmission de l'hérésie au Moyen Age', in *Hérésies et sociétés dans l'Europe préindustrielle, 11e-18e siècles : Communications et débats du colloque de Royaumont* présentés par Jacques Le Goff, Civilisations et sociétés, 10 (Paris-La Haye, 1968), 272-277.

[5] Bericht Pauls v. Chartres ; dazu Russell, *Dissent*, 31f.

[6] Cinzio Violante, *La società milanese nell' età precommunale*, Pubblicazioni dell'Istituto Italiano per gli studi storici, 4 (Bari, 1953) ; Ders., *La Pataria Milanese e la riforma ecclesiastica*, I, *Le premesse (1045-1057)*, Studi Storici dell' Istituto Storico Italiano per il Medio Evo, 11-13 (Roma, 1955); Giovanni Miccoli, 'Per la storia della pataria milanese', *Bullettino dell'Istituto Storico Italiano per il Medio Evo e Archivio Muratoriano*, 70 (1958), 43-123; Ernst Werner, *Pauperes Christi : Studien zu sozial-religiösen Bewegungen im Zeitalter des Reformpapsttums* (Leipzig, 1956), 111-164; Hagen Keller, 'Pataria und Stadtverfassung, Stadtgemeinde und Reform : Mailand im "Investiturstreit", in *Investiturstreit und Reichsverfassung*, herausgegeben von Josef Fleckenstein, Vorträge und Forschungen, 17 (Sigmaringen, 1973), 321-350.

[7] Grundmann, *Ketzergeschichte*, 11.

erfuhr [8]. Die Behandlung des Ramirdus von Cambrai [9] und das weitere Schicksal der Pataria bekommen unter diesem Gesichtspunkt exemplarischen Stellenwert.

Nicht übersehen werden dürfen aber vor allem die Veränderungen des zwölften Jahrhunderts in den Häresien selbst. Allen aus reformerischen Ansätzen stammenden Häresien ist gemeinsam, daß man Kritik an der Lebensweise von unwürdigen Klerikern übte, ihnen die Sakramentalgewalt bestritt und diese Ablehnung schließlich auf die Autorität der gesamten Kirche ausdehnte und dogmatisch verfestigte. Nicht die Kirche in ihrer Dogmatik stand im Mittelpunkt der Kritik, sondern das konkrete Verhalten der Geistlichkeit, die Frage nach der rechten Lebensform [10]. Wie sehr dieses persönliche Verhalten die Religiosität jener Zeit prägte, wie sehr die Frage nach der richtigen *vita evangelica* und *apostolica* zum Problem wurde, hat Pater Chenu gezeigt [11]. Aber seit der Mitte des zwölften Jahrhunderts ging es in den religiösen Bewegungen weniger um ein eremitisch geprägtes Wanderpredigertum, sondern um die Suche nach neuen Formen von religiöser Gemeinschaft [12]. Dem religiösen Impetus der Laien, ebenfalls den Weg der *vita apostolica* in ihnen gemäßer Form einer *vita communis* zu beschreiten, zeigte sich nicht nur die traditionelle Mönchstheologie nicht gewachsen [13], sondern auch die lokalen kirchlichen Institutionen erwiesen sich von ihren sozialen

---

[8] Eine kurze Begriffsgeschichte bei Arno Borst, Artikel 'Häresie', in *Historisches Wörterbuch der Philosophie*, 3 (Basel-Darmstadt, 1974), col. 999-1001. Zur Bedeutung der Patristik für den mittelalterlichen Häresiebegriff : Herbert Grundmann, '*Oportet et haereses esse* : Das Problem der Ketzerei im Spiegel der mittelalterlichen Bibelexegese', *Archiv für Kulturgeschichte*, 45 (1963), 129-164.

[9] *Chronicon Sancti Andreae Castri Cameracensis*, MGH, Scriptores, 7, 540; Brief Gregors VII. an Gottfried von Paris, *Reg. Greg. VII*, hg. von Erich Caspar in MGH, Epistolae selectae, II, 1, 328; Russell, *Dissent*, 43f.

[10] Grundmann, *Oportet*, 159; Russell, *Dissent*, 6ff.

[11] Marie-Dominique Chenu, 'Moines, clercs, laïcs : Au carrefour de la vie évangélique', *La théologie au XIIe siècle*, Etudes de philosophie médiévale, 45, zweite Auflage (Paris, 1966), 225-251.

[12] Herbert Grundmann, *Religiöse Bewegungen im Mittelalter*, dritte Auflage (Darmstadt, 1970), 13-50 und 487-513 ; Raoul Manselli, *Studi sulle eresie del secolo XII*, Studi storici dell' Istituto Storico Italiano per il Medio Evo, 5 (Roma, 1953); Ders., 'Grundzüge der religiösen Geschichte Italiens im 12. Jahrhundert', in *Beiträge zur Geschichte Italiens im 12. Jahrhundert*, Vorträge und Forschungen, Sonderbd. 9 (Sigmaringen, 1971), 5-35.

[13] M.D. Chenu, 'Le réveil évangélique', in *La théologie*, 252-273.

und organisatorischen Strukturen her als unfähig, diesen religiösen Bewegungen pastoral gerecht zu werden.

I

Als Waldes 1179 während des dritten Laterankonzils in Rom erschien, um den nötigen Dispens für die Erlaubnis zur Predigt einzuholen, zeigte sich Papst Alexander III. gerührt, umarmte Waldes und stimmte der Bildung einer neuen Gemeinschaft gemäß den evangelischen Räten auf der Grundlage der freiwilligen Armut zu : In der strittigen Sache selbst blieb der Papst jedoch hart. Entsprechend den kanonischen Vorschriften verweigerte er Waldes den generellen Dispens [14].

Im Sommer 1210 gelang es Franz von Assisi, mit Vermittlung seines Bischofs Guido bis zu Papst Innocenz III. vorzudringen. Franz hatte es abgelehnt, eine der herkömmlichen mönchischen Lebensformen zu wählen. Um den Vorschriften zu genügen, erhielt er die Tonsur und durfte predigen. Im übrigen vertröstete ihn aber Innocenz auf später : Wenn die Zahl seiner Anhänger gewachsen sei, möge er doch wiederkommen [15].

[14] Für die Vorgänge von 1179/80 (Lateranum II, Glaubensbekenntnis und Propositum des Waldes) nun am besten Kurt-Victor Selge, *Die ersten Waldenser : Mit Edition des Liber Antiheresis des Durandus von Osca*, Arbeiten zur Kirchengeschichte, 37 (Berlin, 1967), I, 19-35. Ob Waldes auf dem Konzil tatsächlich 'Missio und Dispens ... grundsätzlich erhalten hat', die 'genaue Entscheidung auf die lokale Ebene abgeschoben' wurde (S. 23) und 1180 in Lyon die Entscheidung über die Predigt vertagt wurde (S. 34), kann wohl mit letzter Sicherheit nicht geklärt werden. Die Wandlungen während des 12. Jhs in den Anschauungen über die *vita apostolica* sprechen aber dafür, daß das Recht zur Predigt in der Tat der kritische Punkt bei der Bildung neuer religiöser Gemeinschaften wurde. Dies wurde während des Kongresses in Löwen auch besonders von Prof. Trawkowski herausgestellt. Mit Selge ist die Übereinstimmung des Verfahrens von 1179, wie es die beiden Hauptquellen (*Chronicon Laudunense* u. Moneta von Cremona) schildern, mit den kanonischen Vorschriften zu betonen. Notwendigkeit des Dispenses, c. 19 C. 16 q. 1 : 'specialiter statuentes, ut preter Domini sacerdotes nullus audeat predicare, sive monachus sive laicus ille sit, qui cuiuslibet sententiae nomine se glorietur'; c. 29 Di. 23 : 'Laicus autem presentibus clericis (nisi ipsis rogantibus) docere non audeat' - *Chron. Laud.* :' inhibens eidem (sc. dem Waldes), ne vel ipse aut socii sui predicationis officium presumerent, nisi rogantibus sacerdotibus' (MGH, Scriptores, 26, 449).

[15] Kurt-Victor Selge, 'Franz von Assisi und die römische Kurie', *Zeitschrift für Theologie und Kirche*, 67 (1970), 129-161; Kaspar Elm, 'Franziskus und Dominikus : Wirkungen und Antriebskräfte zweier Ordensstifter', *Saeculum*, 23 (1972), 127-147; vgl. die Kongressakten : *San Francesco nella ricerca storica degli ultimi ottanta anni,*

108   H.G. WALTHER

Beide Päpste konnten in den Bittstellern wohl nicht die künftige Entwicklung und Bedeutung von deren religiösen Gemeinschaften erkennen. Aber die Art der Behandlung von Waldes und Franz ist nicht nur für die beiden Papstpersönlichkeiten bezeichnend sondern zugleich für die Institution, die sie vertraten: In jenen dreissig Jahren zwischen den beiden Ereignissen formierte sich die kirchliche Ketzerpolitik. Das Lateranum III faßte die ersten gesamtkirchlichen Ketzerbeschlüsse des Hochmittelalters ; 1210 war der Albigenserkrieg in vollem Gange. Die Haltung der beiden Päpste weist somit auf kontinuierliche Grenzen, innerhalb derer sich in der zweiten Hälfte des zwölften Jahrhunderts die Auseinandersetzung der Institution Kirche mit religiösen Bewegungen vollziehen mußte.

Wie bereits betont, hatte sich seit den Zeiten des Reformpapsttums die Situation gewandelt : Damals benutzte man Laienbewegungen, um Reformziele gegenüber unwilligen Geistlichen durchzusetzen. Noch das Lateranum II von 1139 forderte die Laien auf, nicht die Messe offensichtlich unzüchtiger Priester anzuhören [16]. In der Folgezeit rückten spirituelle und organisatorische Probleme der (Kleriker-) Kirche ins Zentrum der Diskussion, während die religiösen Bedürfnisse der Laienwelt vernachlässigt, zumindest nicht als bedeutsam betrachtet wurden. Das Sonderbewußtsein der Kleriker und Mönche drückte sich einerseits im Streben nach Spiritualisierung der Ekklesiologie aus - was praktisch eine Verkürzung des Kirchenbegriffs der *universitas fidelium* bedeutete - und andererseits in einer Intellektualisierung im theologischen und kirchenrechtlichen Bereich. Die neuen Orden des frühen zwölften Jahrhunderts waren wesentlich mehr an den Idealen einer auf den einzelnen abgestellten Frömmigkeitshaltung orientiert, als daß man sie zu den sich allenthalben rührenden Bedürfnissen nach neuen Formen von Gemeinsamkeit rechnen dürfte [17].

Convegni del centro di studi sulla spiritualità medievale, 10 (Todi, 1971). Spekulationen über eine nachdrückliche Unterstützung bzw. sogar freiwillige Förderung der frühen Gemeinschaft des Franziskus durch Innocenz III. finden keinerlei Stütze in den zeitgenössischen Quellen. Die Beschlüsse des Lateranum IV gegen die Gründung neuer Orden (s. dazu u. S. 20f.) können diese Einschätzung nur bestätigen.

[16] Conc. Lat. II, c.7 (*Conciliorum Oecumenicorum Decreta* = COD, Basel, 1962, 174) nach c. 5 des Reimser Konzils von 1131. - Wie sehr Gregor VII. auch jenseits Oberitaliens die Laien zu aktivem Widerstand gegen simonistische und nikolaitistische Priester aufforderte, braucht hier nicht im einzelnen dargelegt werden; vgl. nur den Brief an Gräfin Adela v. Flandern (Reg. IV, 10, ed. Caspar I, 309).

[17] Chenu, *Moines* u. *Le réveil*, pass.

Wo immer diese Bedürfnisse sich in lokal verdichteter Form als Bewegungen Bahn brachen, erwiesen sich die kirchlichen Instanzen zumeist nicht mehr als fähig, der Herausforderung Herr zu werden. Während Zisterzienser durchaus die geistige Führung bei den adeligen Kreuzzugsunternehmungen übernehmen konnten oder Bernhard von Clairvaux (1145) die selbst aus individuellen Frömmigkeitsidealen hervorgegangene Bewegung Heinrichs (v. Lausanne) in Südfrankreich zumindest äußerlich erfolgreich bekämpfen konnte, entsprachen die pastoralen Abwehrmaßnahmen dieses Ordens gegen die neuen ketzerischen Gemeinschaften des Midi nicht den in sie gesetzten Hoffnungen[18].

Die Katharer, die als erste Häretikergruppe überlokale Gegeninstitutionen schufen, wurden auch als erste von konzentrierten Abwehrmaßnahmen getroffen, die das übliche lokale Maß überschritten. Die kirchenrechtliche Diskussion hatte den von der päpstlichen Politik zu Beginn des Jahrhunderts erzielten Ausgleich mit den weltlichen Gewalten systematisch verarbeitet. Nun versuchte das Papsttum, die neu gewonnene Eintracht von geistlicher und weltlicher *potestas* im Abwehrkampf gegen die Ketzer zu nutzen[19]. Griff man zu leichtfertig zur Gewalt? Gab es nicht geeignetere Mittel? Von der Theologie waren sie freilich wohl kaum zu erwarten. Ohne Zweifel stellt die Entwicklung der Theologie im zwölften Jahrhundert von der monastischen Bibelexegese zur *doctrina sacra* eine intellektuelle Leistung hohen Grades dar[20].

[18] Mit James Fearns ('Peter von Bruis und die religiöse Bewegung des 12. Jahrhunderts', *Archiv für Kulturgeschichte*, 48 (1966), 311-335) muß für die Petrobrusianer bei all ihrer Betonung des persönlichen Glaubens und der freien Verantwortlichkeit des einzelnen (S. 319f.) eine Abgrenzung von den übrigen religiösen Bewegungen des frühen zwölften Jhs angenommen werden. Direkt wirkte diese Ketzergruppe über die Heinricianer weiter, indirekt mit ihrer radikalen Ablehnung der Kirche vorbereitend auf den großen bogumilischen Missionserfolg im Midi seit der Jahrhundertmitte. R. Manselli, *Studi*, 73ff.; Fearns, *Peter*, 347f.

[19] Hierher gehören die Beschlüsse des Lateranum II, die nahezu wörtlich die Bestimmungen der Synode von Toulouse (1119) wiederholen (Toulouse : Mansi, *Concilia*, 21, 226f.; Lat. II. c. 23 : COD, 178), der Synoden von Montpellier (1162) und Tours (1163) (Mansi, *Concilia*, 21, 1159 u. 1177f.), die sich besonders der Hilfe der weltlichen Fürsten zu versichern suchen. H. Grundmann, *Religiöse Bewegungen*, S. 50ff.; Arno Borst, *Die Katharer*, Schriften der Monumenta Germaniae Historica, 12 (Stuttgart, 1953), 89-108 (Frühgeschichte der Katharer); Raoul Manselli, *La eresia del Male* (Napoli, 1963).

[20] Joseph De Ghellinck, *Le mouvement théologique du XIIᵉ siècle : La préparation lointaine avant et autour de Pierre Lombard, ses rapports avec les initiatives des canonistes*, Museum Lessianum, Section historique, 10, 2 Aufl. (Bruges, 1948, reprint 1969) ; Beryl Smalley, *The Study of the Bible in the Middle Ages*, Notre Dame Press, 39 (Notre Dame, 1964).

Aber dem religiösen Bedürfnissen der Laien war mit spiritueller oder
dialektischer Bibelexegese nicht gedient. Ein religiöser Laie verstand die
Bibel wörtlich, ließ sich die wichtigsten Stellen in die Volkssprache über-
setzen, um sie verwirklichen zu können, und mußte sich dann von gebildeten Leuten wie dem Hofkleriker Walter Map wegen seines primitiven
Bibelverständnisses verhöhnen lassen [21].

Zwar gab es in der Theologie des zwölften Jahrhunderts durchaus
eine pastoral ausgerichtete Strömung, die nach Pater Chenu von den
Viktorinern bis zu Alain de Lille, Petrus Comestor und Petrus Cantor
reichte [22]. Damit ist aber nicht der Zweifel ausgeräumt, ob die Predigten
dieser theologischen Richtung den laikalen Bedürfnissen nach Bibel-
erklärung entsprachen, wie Chenu folgert [23], zumal er im übrigen den
Theologen des zwölften Jahrhunderts abspricht, ein neues Gleichge-
wicht in der Exegese gefunden zu haben. Es wird gelegentlich noch auf
das Verhältnis der Theologie zu den religiösen Bewegungen zurückzukom-
men sein ; aber bereits aus dem hier angesprochenen unterschiedlichen
Verhältnis zur Heiligen Schrift als Kanon für eine *vita evangelica* zeigt
sich eine Diskrepanz, die von der praktischen Haltung der kirchlichen
Institutionen wohl noch eher verstärkt als kompensiert wurde. Die
Tendenz, die Kirche als juristische Gemeinschaft zu sehen, die vom
Klerus nach festliegenden Normen geleitet wird, rückte den Aspekt
der *potestas* in den Vordergrund, unter dem das Verhältnis zu nonkon-
formistischen religiösen Gruppen gesehen wurde.

Gab es aber seit frühchristlichen Zeiten nicht stets den Ruf nach Toleranz, die Forderung, daß das Christentum sich durch *caritas* auszu-
zeichnen habe? Wie dieses Gegen- und Nebeneinander von *potestas*
und *caritas* seit jeher eine bedeutende Rolle im Christentum spielte,
so war auch noch die Haltung der Kirche zu den religiösen Bewegungen
und Ketzern des zwölften Jahrhunderts durch eine Auseinandersetzung
über das Verhältnis zwischen beiden Prinzipien geprägt [24].

[21] Walter Map, *De nugis curialium*, I, 31. Abdruck bei James Fearns (Hg) *Ketzer
und Ketzerbekämpfung im Hochmittelalter*, Historische Texte : Mittelalter, 8
(Göttingen, 1968), S. 38f.

[22] Chenu, *Le réveil*, 256ff. - Chenu verweist auf die Bezeichnung der Predigt als
der höchsten Vollkommenheitsstufe bei Alanus ab Insulis, *Summa de arte praedica-
toria* und die Graduierung *lectio, disputatio, predicatio* bei Petrus Cantor.

[23] Chenu, *Le réveil*, 260. - Grundmann, *Oportet*, 162f. urteilt negativ.

[24] L. Buisson stellte beide Begriffe 1958 leitmotivartig über seine Untersuchung
zur päpstlichen Gewalt im Spätmittelalter (*Potestas und Caritas : Die päpstliche
Gewalt im Spätmittelalter*, Forschungen zur kirchlichen Rechtsgeschichte und zum
Kirchenrecht, 2 (Köln-Graz, 1958). Dieser Studie verdankt die hier unternommene
Untersuchung viele Anregungen.

II

Gratians um 1140 fertiggestellte *Concordia discordantium canonum* mag zunächst nur wie eine Anhäufung disparaten Materials aus 1000 Jahren Kirchengeschichte anmuten. Eingehendere Analysen zeigten aber deutlich, wie sehr Gratians Sammlung in der politischen Wirklichkeit ihrer Zeit steht. Es ist das Verdienst St. Chodorows, jüngst geklärt zu haben, daß Gratian die Probleme aufnahm, die sich der Partei der Reformer um Haimerich während des Schismas von 1130 stellten, und Lösungsvorschläge erarbeitete [25]. Dem Weg der mystisch-theologischen Ekklesiologie, die den Dualismus zwischen der überirdischen und der irdischen Kirche nicht praktisch löste, stellte Gratian die Betonung der institutionell verankerten irdischen Kirche entgegen, einer konkret faßbaren *congregatio fidelium* [26]. Die Bedeutung der Lösung Gratians liegt in ihrer Trennung der geistlichen und irdischen Naturen der Kirche, um zu einer klaren Legitimationsbasis für die 'Regierungsgewalt' des Klerus zu gelangen. Hierbei kommt den vier *Causae haereticorum* (C. 23 - 26) ein besonderer Rang zu. Denn Gratians Bemühungen um klare juristische Normen bei der Leitung der irdischen Kirche müßten ohne Erfolg bleiben, wenn ihnen nicht eine Ekklesiologie mit genauer Abgrenzung des Kreises der Mitglieder der irdischen Gemeinschaft zugrunde läge. Deshalb wurde für Gratian das Problem der Häresie zum Teil des Verhältnisses der Kirche zur Gewalt überhaupt, so daß angesichts dieser juristischen Aufgabenstellung für ihn keine inhaltliche Auseinandersetzung mit Ketzereien von Interesse sein konnte. Trotzdem zeigt die Position von Gratian in seiner Lehre von der Begründung der Kirchenmitgliedschaft durch das Sakrament der Kinder-taufe und durch den Glauben ihn inmitten der dogmatischen Ausein-

[25] Stanley Chodorow, *Christian Political Theory and Church Politics in the Mid-Twelfth Century : The Ecclesiology of the Gratian's Decretum*, Center for Medieval and Renaissance Studies (Berkeley-Los Angeles-London, 1972). Zum Schisma von 1130 vgl. Franz Josef Schmale, *Studien zum Schisma des Jahres 1130*, Forschungen zur kirchlichen Rechtsgeschichte und zum Kirchenrecht, 3 (Köln-Graz, 1961); Friedrich Kempf, 'Kanonistik und kuriale Politik im 12. Jahrhundert', *Arch. Histor. Pontificiae*, 1 (1963), 11-52.

[26] Der Vorstellung vom spirituellen Fortschritt von der Kirche des Alten Testamentes zu der des Neuen bei Bernhard und Hugo v. St. Viktor stellt Gratian die institutionelle Wandlung von der Synagoge zur Ecclesia entgegen : dict. a. c. 1 Di. 2.- Vgl. dazu Johannes Beumer, 'Ekklesiologische Probleme der Frühscholastik', *Scholastik*, 27 (1952), 183-209; Chodorow, *Christian*, p. 71ff.

andersetzungen seiner Zeit mit Ketzerlehren über das Verhältnis von Taufe und Glauben [27]. Für Gratian konstituiert der Glauben die *communitas ecclesiae*, so daß sich die Legitimation der Gewalt des Prälaten aus der Notwendigkeit der Reinhaltung des Glaubens und damit der Unversehrtheit der Gemeinschaft ergibt. Die besondere Gewalt des Stuhles Petri erschließt sich dann daraus, daß dort der Glaube stets rein bewahrt wird [28].

Der Häresiebegriff in Gratians Sammlung stammt aus patristischen Quellen, vor allem aus den Werken Augustins [29]. Nach Meinung dieses Kirchenvaters macht den Häretiker die Erfindung neuer Lehren und deren Befolgung aus eigennützigen Beweggründen aus [30]. Hieronymus' Meinung - von Gratian zuvor zitiert - differenziert : Häresie ist die Wahl einer Lebensweise (*disciplina*), die dem Wählenden subjektiv als die richtigere erscheint, objektiv gesehen aber als falsch bezeichnet werden muß [31]. Weder Augustin noch Hieronymus zweifeln somit daran, daß es ein objektives Kriterium für Häresie gibt : das Abweichen von jener Schriftauslegung, die der Hl. Geist fordere [32]. Zwei weitere Problempunkte ergaben sich daraus und beschäftigten die Häresiediskussion der Kanonisten : die Frage nach der Instanz, die die richtige Bibelaus-

---

[27] dict. p. c. 16 C. 23 q 4 erkennt der Kirche nur eine Verfügungsgewalt über diejenigen zu, 'qui sunt nostri iuris'. - Möglicherweise ist die dogmatische Diskussion des 12. Jahrhunderts um die Kindertaufe gerade von den Lehrer der Petrobrusianer und Ketzer angeregt worden. Die polemische Literatur greift auch diesen Dissenspunkt auf. Zur Rolle der Taufe in der Theologie der Frühscholastik bietet Chodorow, *Christian*, 76-86 eine gute Zusammenfassung. - Die Synode von Toulouse (1119) und c. 23 des Lateranum II (1139) wenden sich ausdrücklich gegen diejenigen, die die Kindertaufe ablehnen.

[28] cc. 5 - 17 C. 24 q. 1.

[29] Von den 253 Canones der Quaestionen 23 und 24 stammen 87 von Augustin (Vgl. d. Statistik bei H. Maisonneuve, *Études sur les origines de l'Inquisition*, in *l'Église et l'État au Moyen Age*, 7,2. Aufl. (Paris, 1960), 67.

[30] c. 28 C. 24 q. 3.

[31] c. 27 C. 24. q. 3.

[32] Im frühen 12. Jahrhundert kann deshalb die *Glossa ordinaria* die wohl in der Exegetenschule von Laon entstand, im Hochgefühl erreichten wissenschaftlichen Niveaus einen durch Exegese objektiv zu konstituierenen Sinn der Hl. Schrift voraussetzen und als Ketzer daher denjenigen ansehen, der diesen bewußt verfälscht. ad Tit. 3, 10 : Haereticus est, qui per verba legis legem impugnat; proprium enim sensum astruit ex verbis legis, ut pravitatem mentis suae legis auctoritate confirmet, qui vitandi sunt, quia frequenter correcti exercitatiores essent ad malum (Migne, PL, 114, co. 538).

legung in der Kirche sichert [33], und die nach dem einzuschlagenden Verfahren gegen Abweichler von der richtigen Auslegung, die sich nicht überzeugen lassen.

Die erste Frage rückt das Häresieproblem mitten in die ekklesiologische Diskussion der Dekretisten. B. Tierney konnte zeigen, daß die Dekretisten die Formulierungen einiger Canones, daß die *sedes apostolica* bzw. die heilige römische Kirche die Reinheit des katholischen Glaubens immer bewahren werde (c. 11 u. 14 C. 24 q. 1), keineswegs auf ein *magisterium* des Papstes allein bezogen, sondern dem Universalkonzil in Glaubensfragen die oberste Entscheidungsgewalt vorbehielten [34].

Anders war das Problem bei bereits verurteilten Häresien gelagert. Den Zeitgenossen des Frühmittelalters ging die Erfahrung großer häretischer Bewegungen ab, so daß man die Namen der Häresien der Spätantike, deren Irrtümer der Häresienkatalog Isidors von Sevilla verzeichnete [35], wiederholte. Für Abwehrmaßnahmen waren bei all diesen Ketzereien keine neuen Glaubensentscheidungen notwendig. Aber es bestand natürlich die Gefahr-und man verfiel ihr auch-, daß man religiöse Bewegungen einfach mit den alten Namen belegte, ohne den Versuch zu machen, sich mit ihrem eigentlichen Anliegen auseinanderzusetzen. Diese Geisteshaltung findet sich bis ins zwölfte Jahrhundert bei Theologen wie Kircheninstitutionen. Die noch lange die moderne Forschung verwirrende, weil Kontinuität vorspiegelnde Bezeichnung von Ketzergruppen des elften und zwölften Jahrhunderts als *manichaei*, gibt uns weniger Aufschluß über die Wirklichkeit dieser Gruppen als über die Unwilligkeit der gebildeten Geistlichkeit sich mit neuartigen Erscheinungen auseinanderzusetzen. Der allegorische Topos von den Füchsen des Samson (Judic. 15,4f.), die zwar verschiedene Köpfe hätten aber doch am Schwanze zusammengebunden seien - d.h. die als rein äußerlich zu wertende Unterschiedlichkeit der Ketzereien bei ihrer entscheidenden Gemeinsamkeit der Kirchenfeindlichkeit - verrät

[33] Es ist somit kaum verwunderlich, daß im 12. Jh. der Text der Hl. Schrift ins Zentrum der neuen Impulse zu einer *vita evangelica* rückte, und für Theologie und religiöse Bewegungen gleichermaßen das Problem der richtigen Exegese zum entscheidenden Punkt ihres Anliegens wurde.

[34] Brian Tierney, *Foundations of the Conciliar Theory : The Contribution of the Medieval Canonists from Gratian to the Great Schism*, Cambridge Studies in Medieval Life and Thought, NS. 4 (Cambridge, 1955), 47-67. - Zu Gratians Haltung in dieser Frage, die noch nichts vom Problembewusstsein in der späteren Dekretistik verrät, Chodorow, *Christian*, 183-186.

[35] c. 39 C. 24 q. 3.

genau diese Einstellung und leitet noch den Ketzerkanon des Lateranum IV ein [36]. Erst seit der Zeit Papst Alexanders III. benutzt man in der Kirche neue Namen für die neuen Ketzereien.

Ein Augustinzitat dient Gratian als Weisung für das Verhalten gegenüber Ketzern, die zwar vielleicht subjektiv unschuldig, im objektiven Sinne aber häretisch sind : Man darf denjenigen als Ketzer behandeln, der nach zweimaliger Ermahnung nicht auf den richtigen Weg zurückkehrt. Denn diese Starrheit und Unbeugsamkeit im Irrtum (*pertinacia, contumacia*) macht das Wesen der Ketzerei aus [37]. Freilich war damit noch nicht geklärt, zu welchen Maßnahmen die Kirche gegen solche offenbar gewordenen Ketzer berechtigt war.

Gratian widmet sich diesem Problem in der Quaestio 4 der Causa 23 ausführlich. Der Gedankengang der acht Teile dieser Quaestio rückt durch ständig weitere Differenzierung in den Anwendungsfällen von der zunächst als Grundprinzip vorgetragenen Toleranz immer deutlicher ab, so daß eine tolerante Haltung am Ende beinahe als Ausnahmefall erscheint [38].

Nicht zu übersehen ist dabei freilich, daß Gratian vor dem Problem stand, widersprüchliche Äußerungen Augustins über die Ketzerbehandlung in Einklang zu bringen, die sich historisch aus der Wandlung der Ansichten des nordafrikanischen Kirchenvaters erklären. Gegen die donatistische Sekte hatte sich Augustin zur Befürwortung staatlicher Gewaltanwendung entschlossen. Fast 700 Jahre später bezog Anselm von Lucca im Streit um die Kirchenreform Augustins Deutung des *compelle intrare* aus Lucas 14,23 auf die Simonisten und die Anhänger des als Haeresiarchen bezeichneten Gegenpapstes Wibert von Ravenna und nahm sie auch in seine Canones-Sammlung auf. Von dort übernahm sie wohl Gratian [39].

---

[36] Zur Geschichte dieses Topos für die mittelalterliche Ketzerauffassung Grundmann, *Oportet*, 140ff.; Borst, *Häresie*, 1000.

[37] cc. 29,30,31 C. 24 q. 3.

[38] dict. a.c.1 C. 23 q. 4 : Quod autem vindicta inferenda non sit, multis modis probatur. Mali enim tollerandi sunt, non abiciendi; increpatione feriendi, non corporaliter expellendi.

[39] Augustinus an Vincentius Donatista (ep. 93 in CSEL, 34, 2, 445ff.), an Donatus (ep. 173 in CSEL, 44, 640ff.). Anselm v. Lucca, *Liber contra Wibertum*, hg. von Ernst Bernheim in MGH, Libelli de Lite, I, 517-528 (522f.); *Collectio canonum*, XII, 54, 57. Gratian, cc. 37, 38 C. 3 q. 4. Dazu Carl Erdmann, *Die Entstehung des Kreuzzugsgedankens*, Forschungen zur Kirchen- und Geistesgeschichte, 6, Nachdr. (Darmstadt, 1965), 223-229; Alfons M. Stickler, 'Il potere coattivo materiale della

Er leitet die Augustin-Canones über die Behandlung der Donatisten mit einer Rechtfertigung körperlicher Strafen für Ketzer ein [40]. Welchen Umfang diese Strafen annehmen sollen, wird in diesem Zusammenhang nicht erörtert. Die Frage der Todesstrafe ist aber Gegenstand der folgenden Quaestio. Da Gratian mehrmals äußere und innere Störenfriede gleichsetzt, kann man vielleicht den Analogieschluß wagen, daß der Magister auch bei Ketzern die Todesstrafe für erlaubt hält [41]. Gegen eine Enteignung von Ketzern hat Gratian nichts einzuwenden und belegt dies mit Augustin-Canones, die wiederum der antidonatistischen Phase des Kirchenvaters entnommen sind [42]. Mag diese Maßnahme auf den ersten Blick als rein weltliche Strafe erscheinen, so rechtfertigt sie sich im Argumentationszusammenhang bei Gratian geistlich : Sie stellt die Konsequenz aus der Forderung Augustins dar, daß sich die Christen von den Ketzern vollkommen zurückzuziehen hätten (c. 4 u. 9 C. 23 q. 4).

Für die Konfiskation und die körperlichen Strafen benötigt die Kirche die Hilfe des weltlichen Armes : Enteignet werden muß nach weltlichem Gesetz, und körperliche Strafen sind ebenfalls eine Aufgabe der weltlichen Gewalt, da sich die Geistlichkeit nicht mit Blut beflecken darf. Damit ist einer der problematischsten Punkte für die Folgezeit erreicht; denn Gratian und die Dekretisten machten sich gerade zur Aufgabe, die Wirkungsbereiche beider Gewalten sorgfältig gegeneinander abzugrenzen, während das Häresieproblem die Verwobenheit beider Gewalten verdeutlicht [43]. In der christlichen Gemeinschaft hat die weltliche Gewalt

chiesa nella riforma Gregoriana secondo Anselmo di Lucca', *Studi Gregoriani*, 2 (1947), 235-285; Grundmann, *Oportet*, 142-144; J. Ziese, *Historische Beweisführung in Streitschriften des Investiturstreites* (München, 1972), 47f, (Zum *Liber contra Wibertum*). Zu Augustins Kontroverse mit den Donatisten Ernst Ludwig Grasmück, *Coercitio* : *Staat und Kirche im Donatistenstreit*, Bonner historische Forschungen, 22 (Bonn, 1964).

[40] dict. a.c. 37 C. 23 q. 4 : Porro illud Ieronimi, quo ecclesia negatur aliquem persequi, non ita intelligendum est, ut generaliter ecclesia nullum persequatur, sed quod nullum iniuste persequatur. Non enim omnis persecutio culpabilis est, sed rationabiliter hereticos persequimur, sicut et Christus corporaliter persecutus est eos, quos de templo expulit.

[41] cc. 45, 47 C. 23 q. 5; in einem dictum bemerkt Gratian eigens, daß diejenigen, die aus Glaubenseifer Exkommunizierte töten, nicht gegen das 5. Gebot verstoßen ; 'patet quod malo non solum flagellari sed etiam interfici licet (dic. p.c. 48 C. 23 q.5)'. 42 C. 23 q. 7 pass.

[43] Chodorow sieht wohl zurecht die Intention Gratians darin, die Kirche als juristische Gemeinschaft unter weitestgehender Ausschaltung des weltlichen Rechtes zu begründen, um beide Sphären trennen zu können (*Christian*, 54-63). - Zu den Lehren

ihre Legitimation und Funktion in dem Schutz des Glaubens und der
Gläubigen und der Sicherung des Friedens : Ketzerei ist dagegen eine
Störung des Friedens, da sie wie eine ansteckende Krankheit alle übrigen
Gläubigen gefährden kann. Deswegen ist das Vorgehen gegen die Ketzer
einerseits der Sorge um Kranke, andererseits der präventiven Maßnahme
der Amputation kranker Glieder vergleichbar [44]. Gratian sieht in Augustins Toleranzforderung eine Präponderanz geistlicher Maßnahmen, um
eine *correctio* - notfalls auch unter dem Druck der Exkommunikation -
zu erreichen. Wer aber durch *pertinacia* bewiesen hat, daß er nicht in
die Gemeinschaft zurückkehren will, darf auch mit weltlichen Mitteln
bekämpft werden, da er sich eines *crimen* an der christlichen Weltordnung
schuldig gemacht hat. Vom weltlichen Arm kann erwartet werden,
daß er seine Gewalt gegen die *perturbantes ecclesiae pacis* einsetzt [45].

Gratian weiß sehr wohl zwischen den Ungläubigen außerhalb der
christianitas, die nicht mit Gewalt zum christlichen Glauben gebracht
werden dürfen, zu unterscheiden und den Ketzern : letztere sind seit
ihrer Taufe Christen [46] ; die Kirche hat daher die Pflicht, sie um ihres

der Dekretistik über die Beziehungen der beiden Gewalten sind die zahlreichen Einzel-
studien A.M. Sticklers heranzuziehen, die hier nicht einzeln aufgeführt werden sollen.
Eine Zusammenfassung von Sticklers Ergebnissen bietet Friedrich Kempf, *Papsttum
und Kaisertum bei Innocenz III. : Die geistigen und rechtlichen Grundlagen seiner Thron-
streitpolitik*, Miscellanea Historiae Pontificiae, 19 (Roma, 1954), S. 194-231 und
Derselbe, 'Kanonistik und kuriale Politik im 12. Jahrhundert', *Archivum Historiae
Pontificiae*, 1 (1963), 11-52 (26-50).

[44] dict. a.c. 26 C. 23 q. 4 : Ecce, quod crimina sunt punienda, quando salva pace
ecclesiae feriri possunt : in quo tamen discretio adhibenda est. Aliquando enim delin-
quentium multitudo diu per patienciam ad penitenciam est expectanda : aliquando
in paucis est punienda, ut eorum exemplo ceteri terreantur, et ad penitenciam provo-
centur. Hinc, cum discipuli celesti igni Samaritanos vellent consumere, prohibiti
sunt, et Samaritani ad penitenciam sunt expectati, ut Christo predicante convertentur
ad fidem, — dazu c. 25 C. 23 q. 4; c. 18 C. 24 q. 9 (medizinische Vergleiche). Auf dem
Löwener Kongreß untersuchte Dr. Moore in einem Beitrag die mittelalterliche Einstellung zur Häresie als Krankheit s.o. S. 1-11.

[45] dicta a. cc. 24, 26 C. 23 q. 5 : 'Ipsis autem principibus et potestatibus fidem et
reverentiam servari oportet, quam qui non exhibuerit apud Deum premia invenire
non poterit. ... Preterea, sicut principibus et potestatibus fidem et reverentiam exhibere
cogimur, ita secularium dignitatum amministratoribus defendarum ecclesiarum necessitas incumbit. Quod si facere contempserint, a communione sunt repellendi'. - Mit
dem Problem beschäftigen sich speziell die Canones 18 bis 45 dieser Quaestio.

[46] S.o. S. 111 f. Vgl. auch Gratians Meinung zu Judenbekehrungen dict. p. c. 4 Di. 45 :
Iudei non sunt cogendi ad fidem, quam tamen si inviti susceperint, cogendi sunt retinere.
Unde in Tolletano Concilio IV. statutum est : Sicut non sunt Iudei ad fidem cogendi
ita nec conversis ab ea recedere permittitur.... Vgl. die dicta p. cc. 16,17 C. 23 q. 4.

Seelenheiles willen zum rechten Glauben zurückzuführen, wofür Strafen als wirksame Druckmittel angesehen werden können [47].

Aus Gratians Canones-Sammlung ist nicht ein völlig klares Bild für die Behandlung von Ketzern zu gewinnen : Nehmen sich die ersten Augustin-Canones der Quaestio 4 der Causa 23 fast wie 'ein kleiner Traktat über christliche Toleranz' aus [48], so legt Gratian im folgenden den Nachdruck auf das Recht und die Pflicht zur Ketzerbekämpfung und-bekehrung. Nach fruchtloser Ermahnung sollen geistliche Strafen zur Umkehr zwingen, bei weiterer Hartnäckigkeit folgen weltliche Strafen, die bis zu Enteignung und Todesstrafe reichen können. Prozessuale Einzelheiten sind in den Canones der Sammlung nicht enthalten.

Gratians Ketzerbegriff stützt auf dem Fundament, daß die Richtigkeit der Glaubenssätze durch das höchste Lehramt der Kirche objektiv überprüfbar ist. Die Divergenzen in den ihm vorliegenden Ketzer-Canones versuchte der Magister aufzulösen, indem er seine Methode der dialektischen Kasuistik anwandte [49]. Freilich führte dies in den Einzelfällen oft dazu, daß von der prinzipiellen Toleranz des gedanklichen Ausgangspunktes nur noch wenig übrig blieb : Gemäß ihrem allgemeinen Anliegen, Normen für das Handeln des Prälaten zur Sicherung der Integrität der Kirche festzulegen, liegt der Akzent der Rechtssammlung Gratians eindeutig auf den Möglichkeiten, Zwang auszuüben. Eine klare Entscheidung für die Zukunft war damit aber nicht getroffen. Die Mehrdeutigkeit in den Beziehungen der Canones untereinander erlaubte noch immer unterschiedliche Deutungen : Toleranz wie Repres-

---

[47] dict. p.c.4 C. 23 q. 6 : Si bonum, ad quod mali coguntur, semper inviti tollerarent, et numquam voluntari servirent, inutiliter ad illud cogerentur. Sed quia humanae naturae est et ea, que in dissuetudinem ducuntur, abhorrere, et consueta magis diligere flagellis tribulationum cohibendi sunt mali a malo, et provocando ad bonum, ut, dum timore penae malum in dissuetudinem ducitur, abhorreatur, bonum vero ex consuetudine dulcescat. Vgl. die ähnliche Einstellung in dict. a.c. 26 C. 23 q. 4 (o. Anm. 44).

[48] Piero Barbaini, 'Tolleranza e Intolleranza nel "Decreto", nei "Decretisti" e nelle loro Fonti', *La Scuola Cattolica*, 96 (1968), 228-260 und 334-354 (hier 258).

[49] Zu Gratians Methode vgl. St. Kuttner, 'The Father of the Science of Canon Law', *The Jurist*, 1 (1941), 2-19 ; Alphons Van Hove, 'Quae Gratianus contulerit methodo scientiae canonicae', *Apollinaris*, 21 (1948), 12-24; A.M. Stickler, *Historia Iuris Canonici Latini institutiones academiae*, I, *Historia fontium*, Editiones Pontificii Athenaei Salesiani (Augustae Taurinorum, 1950), 208ff.; M. Rambaud, 'L'Age classique 1140-1378', in *Histoire du droit et des institutions de l'Eglise en Occident*, 7 (Paris, 1965), 66-69.

sionsmaßnahmen waren gleichermaßen durch Canones gedeckt, im Falle Augustins sogar durch solche des gleichen Autors.

<h1 style="text-align:center">III</h1>

Der Bologneser Magister Roland Bandinelli, der spätere Papst Alexander III., richtete sein Interesse bei der Glossierung der *Causae haereticorum* (*Stroma* vor 1148) bereits deutlich auf die Rechtfertigung von Zwangsmaßnahmen. Der Toleranzaspekt kehrt nur in einer merkwürdigen Brechung wieder : Die Strafen würden nicht Böses mit Bösem vergelten, sondern stammten aus dem *amor correctionis* : '*Causa vero correctionis et iustitiae malos interficere Deo vere est ministrare*' [50]. Roland legt Nachdruck auf die doppelte Motivation dieser Strafen, den Abschreckungseffekt und die Drohwirkung (*causa correctionis*) und den Schutz der Unschuldigen (*causa iustitiae*). Ketzer dürften gegen ihren Willen zum Glauben zurückgebracht werden, auch wenn der Glaube eigentlich eine Willensentscheidung voraussetze : '*licet bonum, quod est tantum coactionis et non voluntatis Deo minime placeat, sunt tamen mali ad bonum cogendi, ut quod primo fuerat necessitas, fiat quoque liberae voluntatis*' [51].

Als Theologe betonte Roland gleichermaßen die Bedeutung des Glaubens als Voraussetzung für die Erlösung [52]. Das Problem des Glaubens

---

[50] *Die Summa Magistri Rolandi*, herausg. von Friedrich Thaner (Innsbruck, 1874), ad C. 23 q. 5, p. 93.

[51] ad C. 23 q. 5 : Ad quod notandum, quod aliud est vindictam zelo propriae ultionis inferre atque aliud amore correctionis et afflictum liberationis. Zelo propriae ultionis vindictam irrogare non licet, sicut ex superiorum decretorum serie manifeste coniicitur. Verum et [est!] ut delinquens corrigatur atque innocens liberetur, vindicta est irroganda. Capitula igitur, quae vindictae illationem prohibent, secundum primam interpretationem accipimus; quod vero iubent, prout secundo loco expositum est, intelligantur (91). - Der doppelte Zweck der Strafe ist gut Gratianisch. Vgl. dessen dictum a.c. 26 C. 23 q. 4 (o. Anm. 44).

[52] Die Sentenzen Rolands nachmals Papstes Alexander III. hg. v. Ambrosius M. Gietl (Freiburg i.Br., 1891, Repr. 1969) : Tria sunt in quibus humane salutis summa consistit, fides scilicet, sacramentum et caritas. ... Quod vero sine fide et sacramento nullus possit salvari, probatur auctoritate qua dicitur : 'euntes baptizate omnes gentes' etc. [Matth. 28, 19], et statim subponit : 'qui crediderit et baptizatus fuerit, salvabitur, qui vero non crediderit, condemnabitur' etc. [Mark. 16,16] (p. 1). - Ein direkter Einfluß von Ketzerlehren auf die Akzentsetzung der Sentenzen könnte nur postuliert werden. Bei einer Datierung auf 1150 - 1153 (so Herausgeber Gietl S. XVIf. der Einleitung gehört die Rolandsche Sentenzensammlung in die Nähe der in Auseinandersetzung mit Ketzerlehren gemachten theologischen Äußerungen etwa Bernhards

war in der zeitgenössischen Kontroverstheologie mit dem der Taufe verknüpft, so daß es auch bei Gratian seinen Niederschlag gefunden hatte [53]. Bereits die Ketzer von Lüttich und Arras in den 20er Jahren des elften Jahrhunderts hatten die Notwendigkeit der Taufe angezweifelt ; bei den Häretikern des zwölften Jahrhunderts war diese Lehre weit verbreitet [54]. Die Polemiken Bernhards und seiner Zeigenossen gegen die Ketzergruppen richteten ihr besonderes Augenmerk auf die Taufe [55]. Es war wohl Hugo von St. Viktor, der mit seinem Kommentar zu Marcus 16, 16 zuerst das Verhältnis von Taufe und Glauben in die theologische Diskussion einbrachte und auch Roland anregte, sich in seinen Sentenzen mit dem Problem auseinanderzusetzen. Daß dieser in seiner *Stroma* die zwangsweise Bekehrung der einmal Getauften zum rechten Glauben für zulässig erachtet kann wohl als verbreitete Anschauung in der Bologneser Dekretistik der Zeit angesehen werden. Gratian nimmt zum Zwang die gleiche Haltung ein, die die willentliche Zustimmung des einzelnen beim Empfang der Sakramente vernachlässigt [56].

Gratian hatte die Simonie als besondere Form der Häresie an anderer Stelle in seiner Sammlung behandelt (Causa I). Er zitierte Gregor d. Gr., der die *simoniaca haeresis* sogar als schlimmste aller Häresien angesehen hatte [57]. Roland setzt zwar die Häresie eines Geistlichen und

v. Clairvaux (Brief 241 von 1145, Migne, PL, 182, 434-436), und Peters des Ehrwürdigen von Cluny (*Contra Petrobrusianos hereticos*, hg. von James Fearns, Corpus Christianorum, Continuatio Mediaevalis, 10 (Turnholti, 1968), c. 78f., S. 48f.). Marcel Pacaut diskutiert in seiner monographischen Untersuchung über Alexander III. mögliche Beziehungen zu den religiösen Bewegungen des 12. Jhs nicht ; zu Übernahmen aus Gratians Dekret in Alexanders Dekretalen vgl. M. Pacaut, *Alexandre III : Étude sur la conception du pouvoir pontifical dans sa pensée et dans son oeuvre* (Paris, 1956), 311-318. Stärker verweist Marshall Whithed Baldwin (*Alexander III and the Twelfth Century* (Glen Rock-New York, 1968), 7ff. u. 199ff.) auf Beziehungen zwischen den theologischen Sentenzen und der *Stroma* einerseits und der späteren Politik des Papstes andererseits.

[53] s.o. S. 111 f.

[54] Russell, *Dissent*, 23f (Lüttich/Arras); 66ff. (Tanchelm u. d. anderen Ketzereien des frühen 12. Jhs) jeweils mit Lit.. Vgl. a. Grundmann, *Ketzergeschichte*, 18ff.

[55] Chodorow, *Christian*, 76ff. - S.o. Anm. 52.

[56] d.p.c. 4. Di. 45 (s.o. A. 46). Der darauf folgende Canon 5 stammt vom 4. Toletanum 633 und führt aus : ut fidem, quam vi vel necessitate susceperint, tenere cogantur ne nomen Domini blasphemetur, et fides, quam susceperunt, vilis ac contemptibilis, habeatur.

[57] c. 21 C. 1 q. 1 : Tollerabilior enim est Macedonii et eorum sancti spiritus impugnatorum inpia haeresis. - In dieser Einschätzung folgen Gregor I. aus dem Kreis

Simonie in Parallele, spricht letztere aber stets nur als *peccatum* oder *crimen* an. Er vermeidet so den Extremismus der Kirchenreformer des elften Jahrhunderts [58], macht sich vielmehr die gemäßigte Einschätzung der Mehrheit aller Autoren seit Leo IX. zueigen, die J. Gilchrist nachwies [59] : Gratian stimmt mit Anselm von Lucca, Ivo von Chartres und Bernold von Konstanz weitgehend in der Beurteilung simonistischer und häretischer Ordinationen als gültig überein [60].

Simonie galt in der Zeit der Kirchenreform des elften Jahrhunderts als eines der abscheulichsten Verbrechen eines Geistlichen. Während Gregor VII. auch die Laien aufgefordert hatte, den Gehorsam gegenüber simonistischen und als häretisch bezeichneten Priestern zu verweigern und unwürdige am Vollzug der Sakramente zu hindern [61],

der Kirchenreformer des 11. Jhs vor allem Petrus Damiani und Humbert v. Silvacandida. Dazu Jean Leclercq, 'Simoniaca haeresis', *Studi Gregoriani*, 1 (1947), 523-530 (hier 526f.). - Zum Platz der Simonie im Ordnungsgefüge von Gratians Sammlung Joseph Weitzel, *Begriff und Erscheinungsformen der Simonie bei Gratian und den Dekretisten*, Münchener theologische Studien, 3. Abt. Bd. 25 (München, 1967), 23ff.

[58] Vgl. dafür Petrus Damiani, *De sacramentis* : Simoniacam haeresim, primam omnium haereseorum... Quapropter omnes huius nefandae hereseos peste corruptos hereticos esse indubitanter asserimus (Migne, PL, 145, 523); Humbert, *Adversus simoniacos*, I, 3 : 'Si autem, credunt manifeste heretici sunt' (MGH, Ldl, I, 107). - Für weitere Belege s. J. Leclercq, *Simoniaca haeresis*, 527.

[59] J. Gilchrist, "Simoniaca haeresis' and the Problem of Orders from Leo IX to Gratian', *Proceedings of the Second Congress of Medieval Canon Law* (Città del Vaticano, 1965) 209-235. Zu Roland vgl. jetzt mit der Arbeit Weitzels, die seine Ergebnisse bestätigt.

[60] dict. p. Di. 101 : Nunc ad symoniacorum ordinationes transeamus, et ut facile liqueat, quid super haec heresi sanctorum patrum decrevit auctoritas; vgl. a. dict. a.c. 24 C. 1 q. 7. *haeresis* meint in diesen Zusammenhängen bei Gratian immer *simoniaca haeresis*; zu Gratian : Weitzel, *Begriff*, 36ff. - Roland spricht bei Simonie von *peccatum* und *crimen*, nicht von Häresie. Gratian folgt er in der Betonung der Gültigkeit von Ordinationen durch ketzerische u. simonistische Bischöfe, wenn die Form der Weihe gewahrt ist (ad C. 1 q. 7).

[61] Reg. I,80, ed. Caspar I, 114 (April 1074, An Klerus und Volk von Le Puy) : Gregors Aufforderung an alle, unzüchtige Priester (in crimine fornicationis) zu meiden und an der Amtsausübung zu hindern (nullus vestrum eorum audire praesumat officium, quia benedictione eorum vertitur in maledictionem et oratio in peccatum). Über Ivos *Panormia* fand der Brief Aufnahme in Gratians Sammlung (c. 15 Di. 81). Für die *Glossa ordinaria* des Johannes Teutonicus zum Dekret dient dieser Canon als Beweis für die Richtigkeit der Gleichsetzung von *contumacia* und *haeresis* (ad c. 6 Di. 40 s.v. '*a fide devius*', Augustae Taurinorum 1620, col. 195). - Vgl. F. Lotta, *La Continenza dei Chierici nel Pensiero Canonistico Classico da Graziano a Gregorio IX* (Milano, 1971).

legte die kirchliche Hierarchie im zwölften Jahrhundert wesentlich stärkeren Nachdruck auf den Amtscharakter des Geistlichen, um der in Laienschichten aber auch in Klerikerkreisen verbreiteten Auffassung von der Unwirksamkeit der Sakramente unwürdiger Priester entgegenzutreten. Die jene Auffassung teilenden Ketzereien des frühen zwölften Jahrhunderts, in denen noch die alte Reformmentalität wirkte, wurden bereits erwähnt [62]. Das von Waldes verlangte Glaubensbekenntnis (Lyon, 1180) richtete sich gerade gegen solche Lehren, und noch im Testament des Franziskus aus dem frühen dreizehnten Jahrhundert spiegeln sich diese alten Vorbehalte, so daß Franziskus ausdrücklich auf die Trennung von Amt und Person beim Geistlichen hinweist [63].

Innerhalb der Bologneser Schule gab es in der Frage wohl keine einheitliche Meinung. Rufinus vermeidet in seiner etwa zehn Jahre nach Rolands *Stroma* beendeten Summe (1157-59) wie Roland die direkte Bezeichnung als Häresie, nennt vielmehr die Simonie ganz in gregorianischem Ton das höchste Verbrechen eines Klerikers, das deswegen auch im Strafmaß dem Majestätsverbrechen des weltlichen Bereiches gleichgestellt sei [64]. Die *Glossa ordinaria* des Johannes Teutonicus griff diese Meinung auf und lehrte : '*simonia est maius crimen*' [65].

Als Papst Alexander III. sah sich Roland Bandinelli bald direkt mit der Ketzerfrage konfrontiert. Könnte sein Interesse bei der Interpretation der Ketzer-Canones des Dekrets in ihm einen harten Kirchenpolitiker vermuten lassen, so zeigt das praktische Verhalten des Papstes

---

[62] S.o. S.106.

[63] Glaubensbekenntnis des Waldes : 'Sacramenta quoque, que in ea celebrantur, inestimabili atque invisibili virtute spiritus sancti cooperante, licet a peccatore sacerdote ministrentur, dum ecclesia eum recipit, nullomodo reprobamus, neque ecclesiasticis officiis vel benedictionibus ab eo celebratis detraimus...Approbamus ergo baptismum infancium...' (Antoine Dondaine, 'Aux origines du Valdéisme, une profession de foi de Valdès', *Archivum Fratrum Praedicatorum*, 16 (1946), 191-235 (232); zur Datierung Selge, *Erste Waldenser*, I, 26-35; Vgl. a. c. 3 des Testaments des Franziskus : 'fidem in sacerdotibus ... et nolo in ipsis considerare peccatum, quia Filium Dei discerno in ipsis', = Kajetan Esser O.F.M., *Das Testament des Hl. Franziskus v. Assisi* (Munster, 1949), S. 101. Vgl. a. Esser, ibid., S. 146ff. (Kommentar)!

[64] Rufinus, *Summa Decretorum*, herausg. v. Heinrich Singer (Paderborn, 1902), C. 1 dict. Grat. '*Quidam habens filium*' : Et sciendum est quoniam, sicut in constitutione legis forensis precipuum crimen lese majestatis, sic inter omnia crimina ecclesiastica maxima est symonia et temporis prioritate et sui perversitate (197). Gratian hatte mit c. 4 C. 15 q. 3 eine Analogie zwischen Simonie und Majestätsverbrechen nur bei der Zulassung des Personenkreises zum Verfahren gesehen. Zu weiteren Abweichungen Rufins von der Lehre Gratians Weitzel, *Begriff*, 66. - *Stroma* Rolandi, ed. Thaner ad C. 24 q. 1 : 'Item crimen haereseos crimine simoniae minus non est' (99).

[65] ad c. 4 C. 15 q. 3 s.v. '*ad instar*' (Augustae Taurinorum, 1620), 1076).

zumindest gegenüber religiösen Randgruppen tolerante Züge : 1162
wurde (von beschuldigten flandrischen Bürgern) zum ersten Mal in
Ketzerangelegenheiten direkt an den Papst appelliert. Alexander III.
schrieb darauf an Erzbischof Heinrich v. Reims, den Bruder des französischen Königs, daß es besser sei, die Schuldigen freizusprechen
als Unschuldige zu verurteilen [66] - ein Satz, der an die Toleranzforderung zu Beginn der Quaestio 4 der Causa 23 des Dekrets erinnert.

Andererseits schlug Alexander III. nur fünf Monate später auf der
Synode von Tours (Mai 1163) scharfe Töne gegen die Katharer Süd-
frankreichs an [67]. Er stellt ihnen geistliche und weltliche Strafen in Aus-
sicht : Für die Ketzer selbst und ihre Förderer ist das Anathem als Ab-
schreckungsmittel gedacht. Auch sollen die Ketzer völlig aus der Gemeinschaft der Christen ausgeschlossen und damit auch ökonomisch getroffen
werden : Ihre Enteignung durch die Fürsten wird gefordert. Dieser
Strafenkatalog entsprach genau den Vorstellungen des Dekretisten
Roland, der in seiner *Stroma* breit das Recht zur Konfiskation des
Besitzes von Ketzern erörtert hatte [68]. Rolands Hinweis auf das Vorbild
der christlichen Kaiser bei der Enteignung von Ketzern sollte noch nach-
haltige Folgen in der dekretistischen Ketzerlehre wie der päpstlichen
Ketzerpolitik haben.

Wo die Häresie noch nicht verhärtet war und sogar - wie mittlerweile
im Falle der Katharer [69] - zu eigenen Institutionen geführt hatte, war
Alexander III. anscheinend zu Flexibilität bereit. Bei den Maßnahmen
gegen Häretiker sollte im übrigen ein Bereich nicht vergessen werden,

[66] Scire debet tue discretionis prudentia, quia autius et minus malum est nocentes
et condemnandos absolvere quam vitam innocentium severitate ecclesiastica condemnare, et melius viros ecclesiasticos plus etiam quam deceat esse remissos quam in
corrigendis vitiis supra modum existere et apparere severos. (Migne, PL, 206, 187). -
c. 10 C. 23 q. 4 : Nam facta nocentium, que innocentibus demonstrari vel ab innocentibus credi non possunt, non inquinant quemquam, si propter innocentes etiam
cognita sustinentur.
[67] c. 4, Mansi, XXI, 1177-1178 = Comp. I c. 10 V. 6.
[68] *Stroma* Rolandi ad C. 23 q. 7 (ed. Thaner 95f.). - spätantikes Vorbild der Ketzer-
enteignung : ad c. 1 C. 23 q. 7. Iure autem humano haereticos nichil vere possidere
probatur. Imperatorum siquidem iure statutum est, ut quicumque a catholica unitate
inventus fuerit deviare, suarum rerum debeat omnimodam praescriptionem perferre.
In jenem Canon bezieht sich Augustinus auf Cod. Theod. XVI, 5. 43.
[69] Vgl. dazu Antoine Dondaine, 'Les actes du concile albigeois de Saint-Félix de
Caraman : Essai de critique d'authenticité d'un document médiéval' in *Miscellanea
Giovanni Mercati*, 5, Studi e Testi, 125 (Città del Vaticano, 1946), 324-355; Borst,
Katharer, 97-99.

an den man in diesem Zusammenhang im ersten Augenblick vielleicht nicht denken würde. Die Sexualfeindlichkeit vieler bogumilisch beeinflußter Ketzergruppen und besonders der Katharer hatten die in der zeitgenössischen Theologie ohnehin nicht besonders hoch angesehene Institution der Ehe weiter in Mißkredit gebracht. Sowohl Rolands *Stroma* wie seine Sentenzen räumen dem Eherecht einen ungewöhnlich breiten Raum ein [70]. Auch in der Dekretalengesetzgebung Alexanders III. nimmt das Eherecht beinahe einen bevorzugten Platz ein [71]. Sollte man aus diesem Interesse Rolands/Alexanders nicht zumindest auf eine Nebenabsicht schließen dürfen, der Propaganda der Ketzer gegen die Ehe entgegenzutreten? [72]

Für die Katharer selbst sah Alexander weitere Strafverschärfungen vor [73]. Wohl unter dem Eindruck des Berichtes über die Legationsreise Heinrichs von Albano und auf dessen Betreiben und das der Bischöfe wurden die Bestimmungen des Canon 27 des dritten Laterankonzils formuliert, der zusammen mit dem Canon 4 der Synode von Tours als erste päpstliche Ketzergesetze später in der Compilatio I rezipiert wurden [74]. Alexanders *amor correctionis* artikulierte sich im Drang, die Schuldigen aus der christlichen Gemeinschaft auszuschließen [75].

Welche Spannweite der Häresiebegriff um diese Zeit besaß und sich keineswegs auf religiöse Bewegungen konzentrierte, zeigt Canon 2 des Lateranum III : Die Gegenpäpste Alexanders werden als *haeresiarchae*

---

[70] Dieser Umstand wird von den beiden Herausgebern Thaner und Gietl betont. Vgl. a. Baldwin, *Alexander III*, 210.

[71] Zur Entwicklung des Eherechts im 12. Jh. jüngst G. Fransen, 'La formation du lien matrimonial au Moyen-Age', *Revue de droit canonique*, 21 (1971), 108-126.

[72] Ich bin Prof. Duggan (London) dankbar, daß er diesen Punkt in der Diskussion nach dem Vortrag unterstützte.

[73] In Rufins Apparat-Summe zum Dekret (ca. 1157-59) wurde zum ersten Mal in der kanonistischen Diskussion die Waffengewalt eines militärischen Vorgehens gegen Ketzergruppen befürwortet, um damit die Ketzer zum Glauben zurückzubringen, ad dict. Grat. a. C. 23 q. 1 : quomodo haeretici, ut ad fidem catholicam redeant, armis etiam compellendi sunt (ed. Singer, 403), ad C. 23 q. 6 : mali non sunt cogendi ad bonum, quod nunquam elegerunt, sed conpellendi sunt redire ad bonum, quod reliquerunt (411).

[74] COD, 200 (c. 27); Comp. I cc. 6, 7 V. 6. Zur Benutzung und Aufnahme des Ketzerkanons des Lateranum III vor der Comp. I in Dekretalensammlungen G. Vergottini, *Studi sulla Legislazione Imperiale di Federico II in Italia : Le Legge del 1220* (Milano, 1952), 179-209. - Zu c. 10 V. 6 (Tours) s.o. Anm. 67.

[75] S.o. Anm. 51. - Vgl. a. Roland ad C. 23 q. 5 (*potestas gladii*, ed. Thaner 93); ad C. 24 q. 3 (*excommunicatio*, 102f.).

bezeichnet [76]. Diese enge Beziehung zwischen Schisma und Häresie war der Dekretistik vertraut. Gratian hatte einen Hieronymus-Canon aufgenommen, nach dem Häresie und Schisma zwar zunächst zu scheiden seien ; aber jedem Schisma wohne die Tendenz zur Häresie inne, da es sich zur Aufrechterhaltung der Trennung ein eigenen Dogma schaffe[77a]. Rufinus legte in seiner Summe den Nachdruck auf die Dauer eines Schismas, da man Häresie gerade aufgrund von *pertinacia* und *contumacia* als gegeben ansah [77b].

IV

In der Zeit nach 1180 war für Rom auch im Falle der Waldenser die Toleranzschwelle überschritten. Das Glaubensbekenntnis des Waldes hatte nur eine Verpflichtung auf die einzeln aufgeführten Sakramente enthalten. Falls es eine Predigterlaubnis für die Waldenser gegeben haben sollte, so waren die sicherlich engen Predigtrichtlinien nicht eingehalten worden [78]. Dem lokalen Klerus waren die 'Armen von Lyon' seit jeher unbequem gewesen. 1184 schritt Lucius III. zur offiziellen Verurteilung im Rahmen eines umfassenderen Ketzergesetzes [79]. Zumindest seit ihrer Aufnahme in die Compilatio I (1188-92) wurde diese Dekretale *'Ad abolendam'* zum Kern des Ketzerrechts.

Besondere Beachtung verdient die Einzelaufzählung am Beginn, die einen kleinen Katalog der Ketzereien des zwölften Jahrhunderts bildet : Zusammen mit den der offenen Häresie schuldigen Katharern, Patarinern, Passaginern, Josephinern und Arnaldisten werden diejenigen genannt *'qui se humiliatos vel pauperes de Lugduno falso nomine mentiuntur'*, also diejenigen, die sich fälschlich Humiliaten und Arme von Lyon nennen. Eigens werden außerdem noch diejenigen genannt, die sich

[76] COD, 187.

[77a] c. 26 C. 24 q. 3.

[77b] Rufinus, *Summa* ad c. 26C. 24 q. 3. (ed. Singer, 421). - Vgl. a. ad c.6 Di. 40 s.v. 'a nemine est iudicandus' : scisma autem quamvis heresis proprie non sit, tamen sine comite heresi non permaneat (ed. Singer, 96).

[78] Selge, *Erste Waldenser* I, 26ff., 251ff.

[79] Mansi, *Concilia*, 22, 476ff.; Comp. I c. 11 V. 6 = c. 9 X V. 7. - Die genauen Umstände, unter denen es zu diesem Ketzergesetz kam (das weltliche Gegenstück ist uns nicht erhalten), sind nicht bekannt. Offensichtlich ist nur, daß das neue Einvernehmen zwischen Papsttum und Kaisertum die Voraussetzung für den Erlaß der Dekretale auf dem Kongreß (Synode?) von Verona 1184 war. Zu diesem De Vergottini, *Studi*, 23-25; Maisonneuve, *Études*, 151-155.

das Predigtrecht anmaßen oder von der Sakramentenlehre der römischen Kirche abweichen [80].

Nun hat K.-V. Selge mit Recht darauf verwiesen, daß die in der Dekretale genannten Ketzernamen besonders auf oberitalienische Verhältnisse passen [81]. Der Kongreß von Verona umfaßte sicherlich nur eine Synode für die Länder des Imperiums [82]. Ob Lucius III. mit '*Ad abolendam*' zunächst an mehr als an eine regional begrenzte Gültigkeit dachte, wissen wir nicht. Im Jahr darauf machte der Papst die Dekretale zur Grundlage seines Vorgehens gegen die Katharer in Rimini. Die Bestimmung der Verhängung der Infamie gegen alle *fautores haereticorum* könnte sehr wohl für die Verhältnisse der oberitalienischen Städte gedacht sein, von denen wir in jener Zeit in Zusammenhang mit größeren Aktivitäten der Katharer [83], Humiliaten und Waldenser hören [84a]. Bereits vor der Aufnahme in die Compilatio I wissen wir auch von einer weitergehenden Verbreitung durch den Papst selbst : Im März 1185 erhielt Bischof Peter von Arras eine besondere Ausfertigung von '*Ad abolendam*' mit Zusätzen [84b]

Andererseits sind uns Nachrichten von Auseinandersetzungen zwischen der Waldensergemeinschaft und der kirchlichen Hierarchie um das Predigtrecht im (zum Reich gehörigen) Lyon für die Zeit nach 1180 überliefert [85]. Bereits die Synode von Toulouse von 1111 hatte Ketzer

---

[80] Imprimis ergo Catharos et Patarinos et eos, qui se Humiliatos vel Pauperes de Lugduno falso nomine mentiuntur, Passaginos, Iosephinos, Arnaldistas perpetuo decernimus anathemati subiacere. Et quoniam nonnulli, sub specie pietatis virtutem eius, iuxta quod ait Apostolus, denegantes, auctoritatem sibi vendicant praedicandi : cum idem Apostolus dicat : quomodo praedicant nisi mittantur ? omnes qui vel prohibiti, vel non missi, praeter auctoritatem ab apostolica sede vel ab episcopo loci susceptam, publice vel privatim praedicare praesumpserint, et universos, qui de sacramento corporis et sanguinis Domini nostri Jesu Christi, vel de baptismate, seu de peccatorum confessione, matrimonio vel reliquis ecclesiasticis sacramentis aliter sentire aut docere non metuunt, quam sacrosancta Romana ecclesia praedicat et observat...

[81] *Texte zur Inquisition*, herausgegeben von Kurt-Victor Selge, Texte zur Kirchen- und Theologiegeschichte, 4 (Gütersloh, 1967), 26 Anm. 94. Zu den Ketzernamen vgl. Borst, *Katharer*, 264ff.

[82] De Vergottini, *Studi*, 23f.

[83] Borst, *Katharer*, 99f.

[84a] Selge, *Erste Waldenser* I, 284ff.

[84b] Grundmann, *Religiöse Bewegungen*, 67 Anm. 119.

[85] Selge, *Erste Waldenser* I, 253-259. -Um 1182/83 ist es nach Selge zu einer Exkommunikation der Pauperes de Lugduno in Lyon gekommen.

als *'religionis species simulantes'* genannt, was 1139 vom Lateranum III wiederholt wurde. Teil dieser *simulatio* war die Anmaßung des Predigt-amtes, wie Bernhard von Clairvaux unter Bezug auf Röm. 10,15 fest-stellte [86]. Die fehlende *missio canonica* wird auch in *'Ad abolendam'* neben dem Abweichen von der Sakramentenlehre als Kriterium der Ketzerei hervorgehoben [87]. Hier wird ein klarer Trennungsstrich gezogen, der die Mehrdeutigkeiten des Propositums von Waldes aus dem Jahre 1180 ausschloß.

Aber die Dekretale gibt auch Aufschluß über eine andere Verengung, die aus der allgemeinen Stärkung der römischen Kurie resultierte : Es wird speziell die Sakramentenlehre der r ö m i s c h e n Kirche zum Häresiekriterium erhoben. Bezeichnenderweise hat Lucius III. aus seiner Vorlage in Gratians Sammlung die dort genannten weiteren Kriterien der Rechtgläubigkeit weggelassen : die Lehre der übrigen Apostel (neben Petrus) und die der Väter [88]. *'Ad abolendam'* schränkte mit ihren Bestimmungen den Divergenzspielraum erneut ein, verbaute aber nicht notwendige Differenzierungen, die erst die Rekonziliation von Rand-gruppen unter Innocenz III. ermöglichten.

V

Die Dekretsumme Huguccios von Pisa (zwischen 1190 und 1210 erarbeitet) stellt ohne Zweifel den Höhepunkt der Bologneser Schule der Dekretistik dar. Leider ist diese Summe gerade bei der Behandlung der *Causae haereticorum* nicht fertiggestellt [89]. Gleichwohl ist auch ohne

[86] Bernhard, Ep. 242 : ut nullum extraneum sive ignotum praedicatorem recipiatis, nisi qui missus a summo seu a vestro permissus pontifice praedicaverit. 'Quomodo', inquit, 'praedicabunt nisi mittantur' (Migne, PL, 182, col. 437).

[87] Et quoniam nonnulli, sub specie pietatis virtutem eius, iuxta quod ait Apostolus denegantes, auctoritatem sibi vendicant praedicandi : cum idem Apostulus dicat : 'quomodo praedicabunt nisi mittantur'? - S. o. Anm. 80.

[88] c. 15 C. 24 q. 1 : Rogamus vos, fratres dilectissimi, ut non aliud doceatis neque sentiatis, quam quod a B. Petro apostolo et reliquis apostolis et Patribus accepistis. - Zur Formulierung von *'Ad abolendam'* s.o. Anm. 80.

[89] St. Kuttner, *Repertorium der Kanonistik, (1140-1234)* : *Prodromus corporis glossarum*, I, Studi e Testi, 71 (Città del Vaticano, 1937, Reprint 1972), p. 158f.; Luigi Prosdocimi, 'La "Summa Decretorum" di Uguccione da Pisa : Studi prelimi-nari per una edizione critica', *Studia Gratiana*, 3 (1955), 349-374; G. Le Bras, 'Notes pour l'histoire du droit canon', *Revue de droit canonique*, 5 (1955), 131-146 (138); A.M. Stickler, 'Problemi di ricerca e di edizione per Uguccione da Pisa e nella decre-tistica classica', (Congrès de Droit Canonique Médiéval, Louvain et Bruxelles, 1958), *Bibliothèque de la RHE*, 33 (1959), 111-128; Maisonneuve, *Études*, 83-88.

diese fehlenden Teile zu erkennen, daß Huguccio Anhänger einer flexiblen Ketzerbehandlung ist. Ihm geht es vor allem um die Relation von Zweck und Mittel. Die *animadversio debita*, wie sie '*Ad abolendam*' forderte, muß nach seiner Meinung einen Besserungszweck erfüllen. Nur bei offenkundigen Verbrechen dürfe massiv gestraft werden. Huguccio greift dafür auf die Formulierung Rolands vom *amor correctionis* zurück [90]. Er verweist nachdrücklich auf Augustins Forderung nach geistiger Trennung von den Ketzern, die der Kirchenvater als positives Gegenbild zum Verhalten der Ketzer gezeichnet habe, die körperliche Strafen befürworteten [91].

Es bestehe zwar die Pflicht zur Ketzerbekehrung, aber man solle diese doch durch geistliche Strafen zu erreichen suchen. Auch Huguccio schließt jedoch nach dem Vorbild seiner kanonischen Vorlagen weltliche Strafen nicht aus : Schließlich gleiche ein Ketzer einem Dieb auf geistlichem Gebiet. Er begehe somit ein *crimen publicum*, wobei Huguccio die einschlägigen Bestimmungen der Digesten zur Bestimmung des Strafmaßes heranzieht. Die Gleichsetzung der Ketzerei mit einem an öffentlichem Eigentum begangenen Diebstahl zeigt, mit wie wenig Nachsicht Ketzer auch bei einem so zur Differenzierung geneigten Kirchenmann wie Huguccio in letzter Konsequenz rechnen konnten. Augustin hatte zwar in Huguccios Vorlage darauf verwiesen, daß ein Sakrileg eigentlich strenger zu bestrafen sei als ein Diebstahl an öffentlichem Gute, zugleich aber im Gegenzug Toleranz über diese Straflogik gestellt. Wenn die Existenz des Diebes Judas in der Apostelschar einen Sinn habe, dann denjenigen, daß Christus seiner Kirche habe lehren wollen, die Bösen in ihren Reihen zu ertragen.

---

[90] Huguccio, *Summa decretorum* ad dict. Grat. a.c. 1 C. 23 q. 3 s.v. '*Quod vero*' : Dummodo fiat zelo ultionis, sed correctionis amore, sed iusticie, ut et a malis facultas deliquendi adiuvatur et bonis facultas libere consulendi Ecclesie cum rei publicae ministraretur (Vat. lat. 2280, fo. 244 va). - ad dict. Grat. a. c. 1 C. 23 q. 4 '*Quod autem vindicta*' : vindicta quandoque infertur ex odio et zelo ultionis et non iusticie, quandoque infertur amore correctionis et afflictorum liberationis. Primo modo non est inferenda ... Super manifestis vero criminibus vindicta est inferenda, quo casu intelliguntur que vindicte hoc percipiunt. Est inferenda dico nisi quando multitudine in scelere est et nisi quando ille qui committit sociam habet multitudinem (Vat. lat. 2280, fo 245ra). - Vgl. dazu auch Maisonneuve, *Études*, 84f.

[91] Huguccio, *Summa* ad c. 4 C. 23 q. 4 s.v. '*Ecce*' : Unde dicunt malos non esse tollerandos sed corporaliter ab eis recedendum esse. Sed econtra Augustinus... dicit quod recedere a malis est societatem eorum saltem in animo improbare, exire de eis est corripere et redarguere; non tangere est non consentire (Vat. lat. 2280 fo. 245rb).

Huguccios Summe konzentriert sich dagegen auf den Passus der Ange-
messenheit einer höheren Strafe für einen geistlichen als für einen weltlichen
Dieb [92]. Schon die weltlichen Strafen für das weltliche Vergehen des
peculatus schlossen einst - wie Huguccio selbst referiert - die Todesstrafe durch Verbrennen oder Ertränken ein, heute aber die Deportation
und Enteignung [93a]. Er stimmt damit implizit dem von den Bestimmungen
des Lateranum III und des Kongresses von Verona beschrittenen Weg
des Ausschlusses der Ketzer aus allen Gemeinschaften und der Konfiskation zu. Vor der Todesstrafe schreckt er aber zurück. Denn auch
in dem Glossenapparat, der sich in manchen Handschriften anstelle
der fehlenden Teile der Causae 23 bis 26 befindet, zu denen mit Quaestio
5 der Causa 23 gerade der Teil über die Todesstrafe gehört, hält körperliche Strafen, besonders die Todesstrafe, im allgemeinen nicht für
angemessen [93b]. Wie Luigi Prosdocimi wahrscheinlich machen konnte,
handelt es sich bei diesem Glossenapparat um eigene Aufzeichnungen
Huguccios oder aber um eine Schülerreportatio von Huguccios Lehr-
veranstaltung [94]. Als letzte Konsequenz schließt somst Huguccio bei
hartnäckigen Ketzern - hierfür ist ihm der Fall Arnolds von Brescia
exemplarisch - eine Hinrichtung nicht aus [95].

---

[92] *Summa* ad c. 3 C. 23 q. 4 s.v. *'iudicandus'* : ille dicitur fur qui furatur rem privati
[am?] et iste similiter qui rem publicam, etsi hic magis puniatur quam ille, quanto
fortius sacrilegus debet dici fur et est magis puniendus, cum res ecclesie et sic dei
furetur (Vat. lat. 2280, fo. 245rb).- vgl. auch s. vv. *'peculatus'* u. *,non undecumque'*
(ibid.).

[93a] ibid. s.v. *'iudicatur'* : pena peculatus aqua et igni interdiccio in qua hodie successit
deportatio et omnium bonorum amissio. His tamen, qui tempore administrationis
crimen peculatus et ff. ad legem Iuliam peculatus etc. de crimine peculatus, lege I
[= Dig. 48. 13, 1 (und 3)] (Vat. lat. 2280, fo. 245rb).

[93b] Vgl. Maisonneuve, *Études*, 87f. mit Quellennachweisen. - Datierung auf 1185
bis 1187 (also vor Fertigstellung der *Summa* Huguccios) und Nachweis der Handschriften mit diesem Glossenapparat bei Kuttner, *Repertorium*, 158. Ich habe die Hs.
StB. Bamb. Msc. can. 41 in Mikroverfilmung eingesehen.

[94] Prosdocimi, *La "Summa Decretorum".* (s.o. Anm. 89). Zustimmend Le Bras,
Notes, 138.

[95] *Summa* ac c. 41 C. 23 q. 4 s.v. *'Et certe longe'* : quod pro sola heresi non sunt
morte puniendi, ut in C. ne san. baptis. 1. II [= Cod. Just. I. 6, 2] contra sup. c. quando
[= c. 39 C. 23 q. 4]. Solve ut hic prius : quando enim sunt incorrigibiles, ultimo supplicio feruntur, aliter non, ut de Arnaldo Brixiensi factum est (Vat. lat. 2280, fo. 248va).
Dieses Zitat stammt aus dem Glossenapparat ('Frühform' der Summe). Für weitere
Glossen dieses Apparates s. Maisonneuve, *Études*, 87f. nach der Hs. Paris Bibl. nat.
Ms. lat. 15397.

Bereits Roland Bandinelli hatte als Kanonist sein Interesse an der kaiserlich-römischen Ketzergesetzgebung bekundet und diese für die Praxis nutzbar gemacht, indem er als Papst in seiner Ketzergesetzgebung die kaiserlichen Bestrafungsarten zum Vorbild nahm. Der Tendenz, bei der Ketzerbehandlung immer stärker den weltlichen Arm zuhilfezunehmen, gab Lucius' III. Dekretale 'Ad abolendam' voll nach. Huguccios romanistische Bildung ließ ihn noch stärker Parallelen und Vorbilder des römischen Rechts heranziehen [96]. Bei aller Betonung differenzierender Gesichtspunkte bei der Strafzumessung band sich die Häresiediskussion der Dekretistik damit immer mehr an den Leitgedanken eines Abschreckungs- und Sühnestrafrechts, in dem der amor correctionis verloren ging. Die Ketzerpolitik des Huguccio-Schülers Innocenz III. sollte dennoch auch von diesem amor correctionis geprägt sein, den Huguccio als kanonistischer Magister in Bologna betonte, wie die 'Frühform' der Summe zeigt.

VI

Bis zum Regierungsantritt Innocenz' III. hatten die getroffenen Abwehrmaßnahmen gegen Ketzer wenig Erfolg zu verzeichnen. Die Lage im Midi schien für geistliche Maßnahmen beinahe aussichtslos : Wie sollte die Isolierung der Ketzer von den Christen praktisch durchgeführt werden, wenn die Ketzer dort in der Majorität waren? Der größte Teil des dortigen Episkopats zeigte sich seiner Aufgabe nicht gewachsen. Die Aufrufe der Konzilien an die Bischöfe zu verstärkter Ketzerbekämpfung waren also vergeblich. Damit war aber auch der für ein erfolgreiches Wirken der päpstlichen Legaten notwendige institutionelle Rückhalt nicht gegeben. Die Kleriker der Kirche des Midi waren für die von ihnen verlangte geistige und moralische Auseinandersetzung kaum geeignet [97]. Nicht viel besser war die Lage der vom Papst gesandten Zisterzienser. Sie kamen nicht mit der Mentalität der Bevöl-

---

[96] Unter diesem Gesichtspunkt der zunehmenden Inanspruchnahme der weltlichen Gewalt bei der Ketzerbekämpfung scheint mir Huguccios Behandlung von c.3 C23 q.4, wo er einen Ketzer in Analogie zu einem Dieb geistlichen Eigentums setzt, durchaus verständlich. Man braucht also nicht wie Maisonneuve Überlegungen zu Erwägungen Huguccios über den privaten Charakter von Ketzereien (Études, 86 u. 304) anzustellen.

[97] Marie-Humbert Vicaire, O.P., Geschichte des Hl. Dominikus, I (Freiburg i. Br., 1962), 93-108; vgl. dazu den Überblick über die Ermahnungen und Absetzungen von Bischöfen im Midi um die Wende des 13. Jhs bei Maisonneuve, Études, 186-193.

kerung zurecht, die jahrzehntelang von der weltfeindlichen Lehre der Katharer und den religiösen Ansprüchen der Waldenser beeinflußt worden war, da ihrem Orden eine andere Spiritualität und Lebensform zugrundelag [98].

Der Klerus des Midi zeigte sich bereits von der Forderung nach einer *vita apostolica*, die sich auf ein wörtliches Verständnis der Evangelientexte stützen wollte, verstört. Die päpstliche Politik seit Alexander III. setzte die Toleranzschranke jenseits der lokalen Querelen an : Nicht die Frage der Armut wurde zum Dissenzpunkt erklärt, sondern bestimmte Folgerungen aus dem Ideal der *vita apostolica*, die die kuriale Ekklesiologie nicht billigen konnte, weil jede zu weit gehende Spiritualisierung des Kirchenbegriffs die Kirche als sichtbare, juristische Körperschaft, die vom Klerus aufgrund seiner Sonderstellung geleitet wurde, infrage stellen mußte. Für ein Predigtrecht von Laien war in einem solchen Kirchenbild kein Platz.

Von Herbert Grundmann stammt die These, daß Innocenz III. 'eine grundsätzliche Abkehr von der Politik seiner Vorgänger' vollzogen habe. Seine Politik sei 'der klaren Einsicht in die Aufgaben der Kirche angesichts der religiösen Bewegung dieser Zeit' entsprungen [99]. Ein solches Urteil rückt Innocenz wohl zu sehr von seinen Vorgängern ab. Gesteht doch Grundmann selbst zu, daß man bei Innocenz nicht 'eine religiöse Wandlung der kirchlichen Leitung' konstatieren könne. Man wird stattdessen auf der Suche nach einer für das gesamte Verhalten des Papstes verbindlichen Grundlage bald auf feste ekklesiologische Überzeugungen stoßen. Bei allen Rückschlägen, die Innocenz im politischen Kräftespiel hinnehmen mußte [100], kehren doch stets zwei Punkte in den Handlungsbegründungen des Papstes wieder : daß die Kirche

---

[98] Die Wahl für das päpstliche Legatenamt und für neue Bischöfe fiel nicht zufällig auf Zisterzienser. Bis zur Missionsreise Bischof Diegos von Osma (1206) - z.T. auch sicher bis zur Zurückgewinnung der Katholischen Armen - versprach sich Innocenz - letzlich vergeblich - Erfolg von einer Missionstätigkeit des Ordens, dessen geistiger Führer Bernhard von Clairvaux bereits einmal jenes Gebiet - wenn auch nur scheinbar - erfolgreich missioniert hatte. Voller Stolz hatte doch Bernhard 1245 nach seiner Predigtreise durchs Midi an die Herren von Toulouse geschrieben : deprehensi sunt lupi, qui venientes ad vos in vestimentis ovium, devorabant plebem vestram sicut escam panis... (Ep. 242, Migne, PL, 182, 436).

[99] Grundmann, *Religiöse Bewegungen*, 71. Ähnlich das Urteil in Ders., *Ketzergeschichte*, 35.

[100] Dazu Helene Tillmann, *Papst Innocenz III.*, Bonner Historische Forschungen, 3 (Bonn, 1954).

als *corpus mysticum Christi* einer festen irdischen Organisationsform bedürfe, die den Klerikern aufgrund ihrer Funktion einen Vorrang einräumte, und daß dem Papst die Führung der gesamten *christianitas* zukomme ; [101] zum anderen, daß diese feste Kirchenstruktur nicht ohne das Äquivalent der *caritas* auskomme, woraus die verstärkte Zuwendung Innocenz' zur Pastoraltheologie entsprang [102].

Es gibt dabei bei Innocenz keine Spannungen zwischen dem Kanonisten, der die Maßnahmen gegen Orvieto [103] und den Albigenserkrieg verantworten müßte, und dem Theologen, dem die Politik der Wiedergewinnung gefährdeter Randgruppen und die Förderung neuer Armuts-Gemeinschaften gutzuschreiben sei ; hatte doch das *Decretum Gratiani* gerade am Beispiel der Ketzerfrage beide Aspekte - *caritas* und *potestas* - betont. Die Aufforderung Alexanders III. an Heinrich von Reims, besser die Schuldigen zu schonen als die Unschuldigen zu verurteilen, findet bei Innocenz ihre Entsprechung in den Briefen an den Bischof von Verona zugunsten der Humiliaten (1199)[104] und an den Episkopat von Narbonne zugunsten der Katholischen Armen (1209) [105].

[101] Kempf, *Papsttum und Kaisertum*, bes. 280ff; Tillmann, *Papst Innocenz*, 15ff. 220ff.; demnächst auch H.G. Walther, *Imperiales Königtum, Konziliarismus und Volkssouveränität : Studien zu den Grenzen des mittelalterlichen Souveränitätsgedankens* (München, 1975). - Vgl. a. L. Buisson, *Potestas und Caritas*, 69ff.

[102] Die Beziehungen zum Kreis um Petrus Cantor sind jetzt dargestellt in John W. Baldwin, *Masters, Princes, and Merchants : The Social Views of Peter the Chanter and His Circle* (Princeton, 1970), I, 317f.; Tillmann, *Papst Innocenz*, 240.

[103] Zu Orvieto jetzt am besten M. Maccarone, 'Studi su Innocenzo III', *Italia Sacra*, 17 (Padova, 1972), c. 1 : Orvieto e la predicazione della crociata, 3-163. Die Kreuzzugsidee Innocenz' will neuerdings Helmut Roscher, *Papst Innocenz III. und die Kreuzzüge*, Forschungen zur Kirchen- und Dogmengeschichte (Göttingen, 1969), bes. 260ff. aus der 'Vorstellung vom Papst als Leiter der Christenheit' (239) abgeleitet sehen, Ähnlich schon Tillmann, *Papst Innocenz*, 220. Damit ist leider noch wenig über die Umsetzung dieser Vorstellung in die konkreten Motivationen für bestimmte Entscheidungen in den einzelnen Kreuzzugsunternehmen ausgesagt. Vgl. nun auch Elizabeth Kennan, 'Innocent III and the First Political Crusade : A Comment on the Limitations of Papal Power', *Traditio*, 27 (1971), 231-249.

[104] Ep. 2, 228 : Prudens agricola vinitor que discretus salubre debet remedium invenire... Similiter etiam, licet *ad abolendam hereticam pravitatem* invigilare debeat sollicitudo pastoris, sollicite tamen debet attendere, ne vel damnet innoxios vel nocentes absolvat.... Quia vero non est nostre intentionis innoxios cum nocentibus condemnare...; et si nihil senserint quod sapiat hereticam pravitatem, eos catholicos esse denunties et predicta setentia non teneri (Migne, PL, 214, 788f.). Die Hervorhebung ist von mir. - Die Bezugnahme auf '*Ad abolendam*' erfolgte sicherlich nicht zufällig. Während Lucius III. zur Ausrottung der verschiedenen Ketzereien den *vigor ecclesias-*

Die dem Kanonisten geläufige Forderung nach *distinctio* wird von Innocenz zur Maxime bei der Behandlung der verschiedenen religiösen Randgruppen erhoben [106] und auch zur Richtschnur im Falle der Waldenser von Metz (1199) gemacht [107]. Freilich fand dann nicht der Brief an den Bischof von Metz mit seinem Insistieren auf genauer Untersuchung Aufnahme in die von Innocenz 1210 offiziell promulgierte Sammlung von Dekretalen seiner ersten 12 Pontifikatsjahre, sondern die Compilatio III enthält den Brief an Volk und Klerus von Metz (*Cum ex iniuncto*). Hier werden wesentlich nachdrücklicher die juristisch-ekklesiologischen Grenzen gegenüber religiösen Ansprüchen der Laien hervorgekehrt. Wie '*Ad abolendam*' lehnt '*Cum ex iniuncto*' eine *missio praedicandi* für Laien ab und verteidigt die Geschlossenheit des Klerikerordo auch bei unwürdigen Vertretern aus seinen Reihen [108].

ticus und die *imperialis fortitudo* ansprach, distanziert sich Innocenz hier von solchem vehementen Vorgehen, das auch der Klerus von Verona angewandt hatte, und fordert stattdessen vor allem den Einsatz der *sollicitudo pastoris*.

[105] Ep. 12, 68 : Sic enim erroneos ab heretica pravitate intendimus revocare, ut velimus fideles in catholica veritate fovere, cum tolerabilius sit perversos in sua perversitate perire quam iustos a sua iustitia declinare (Migne, PL, 216, 74). - Zur Deutung dieses Briefes Grundmann, *Religiöse Bewegungen*, 113ff.

[106] Ep. 2, 228 : archipresbyter tam contra Humiliatos quam universos hereticos sine distinctione, quam posueramus in litteris nostris, excommunicationis sententiam promulgavit (Migne, PL, 214, 778).

[107] Brief vom 11. Juli 1299 : Sicut ecclesiarum prelatis incumbit ad capiendas vulpes parvulas, que demoliri vineam domini moliuntur, prudenter et diligenter intendere, sic est eis precavendum, ne ante messem zizania colligantur, ne forsan quod absit cum eis etiam triticum evellatur. Sane sicut non debet heretica pravitas tolerari, sic enervari non debet religiosa simplicitas, ne vel patientia nostra hereticis audaciam subministret, vel simplices impatientia multa confundat, ut nobis diruptis convertantur in arcum perversum et in hereticos de simplicibus commutentur... Inquiratis etiam sollicite veritatem, ... ut super his et aliis quae necessaria sunt ad indagandam plenius veritatem per litteras vestras sufficienter intructi quid statui debeat melius intelligere valeamus (Migne, PL, 214, 698f.).

[108] Brief vom 12. Juli 1299 (Comp. III c. 3 V. 4 = c. 12 X V. 7) : pro universorum salute nos oportet esse sollicitos, ut et malos retrahamus a vitiis, et bonos in virtutibus foveamus. Tunc autem opus est discretione maiore, cum vitia sub specie virtutum occulte subintrant... Licet autem desiderium intelligendi divinas scripturas, et secundum eas studium adhortandi, reprehendum non sit, sed potius commendandum : in eo tamen apparent quidam laici [qui] officium praedicationis Christi sibi usurpant... Tanta est enim divinae scripturae profunditas, ut non solum simplices et litterati, sed etiam prudentes et docti non plene sufficiant ad ipsius intelligentiam indagandam... Sicut enim multa sunt membra corporis, omnia vero membra non eundem actum habent, ita multi sunt ordines in ecclesia, sed non omnes idem habent officium. Cum

In den Zusammenhang der Bemühungen um Differenzierung gehören die zahlreichen Mahnungen des Papstes an seine Legaten in Südfrankreich zu vorbildlicher Lebensführung [109] die Bemühungen um die Kirchenreform, die schließlich in die Bestimmungen des Lateranum IV mündeten [110], und vor allem die Institutionalisierung der neuen Gemeinschaften des Durandus von Osca, von Humiliaten, des Bernard Prim und der Bußbruderschaft von Elne [111]. Apostolische Armut ist für Innocenz die geeignete Medizin zur Ketzerbekämpfung [112], weil diese nach Augustinischer Lehre der *caritas* entspringen muß. Mit der von Diego

igitur doctorum ordo sit quasi praecipuus in ecclesia, non debet sibi quisquam indifferenter praedicationis officium usurpare. Nam secundum Apostolum : 'quomodo praedicabunt, nisi mittantur?''... Rursus aliud est, quod praelatus sponte de sua confisus innocentia subditorum se accusationi supponit... et aliud est, quod subditus non tam animo reprehendendi quam detrahendi exsurgit temerarius in praelatum, cum ei potius incumbet necessitas obsequendi. Quodsi forte necessitas postularet, ut sacerdos tanquam inutilis et indignus a curia gregis debeat removeri, agendum est ordinate apud episcopum, ad cuius officium tam institutio quam destitutio sacerdotum noscitur pertinere (Migne, PL, 214, 695). - H. Grundmann kennzeichnete die hier deutlich werdende ekklesiologische Divergenz zwischen Papst und Laienbewegung als den Gegensatz von der 'Idee der apostolichen Nachfolge' und der 'Idee der apostolischen Sukzession im hierarchischen Ordo' (*Religiöse Bewegungen*, 96).

[109] Brief an Arnold-Amalrich v. Citeaux, Peter von Castelnau und Raoul von Fontfroid vom 31. Mai 1204 (Migne, PL, 215, 358f.).

[110] Augustin Fliche, 'Innocent III et la réforme de l'Église', *Revue d'histoire ecclésiastique*, 44 (1949), 87-152; Ders. : 'La réforme de l'Église' in Fliche et Martin, *Histoire de l'Église*, 10, *La chrétienté romaine* (1198-1274) (Paris, 1950), 139-193; Tillmann, *Papst Innocenz*, 152-185 ; Raymonde Foreville, 'Lateran I-IV' in *Geschichte der Ökumenischen Konzilien*, VI (Mainz, 1970), 282ff.; Maccarone, *Studi*, 221-337 (Riforme e innovazioni di Innocenzo III nella vita religiosa).

[111] Grundmann, *Religiöse Bewegungen*, 72-127; Maisonneuve, *Études*, 174-179, 182-186; Selge, *Erste Waldenser*, I, 188-225.

[112] Vgl. den Brief vom 17. Nov. 1206 an Raoul v. Fontfroid : Excursus saeculi tendentis ad exitum incessanter humanae conditionis miseriam tot errorum laqueis irretivit... discretione tuae per apostolica scripta praecipiendo mandamus, quatenus viris probatis, quos ad id videris idoneos exsequendum, qui paupertatem Christi imitando in despecto habitu et ardenti spiritu non pertimescant accedere ad despectos, in remissionem studeas injungere peccatorum, ut ad eosdem haereticos festinantes, per exemplum operis et documentum sermonis eos concedente Domino sic revocent ab errore (Migne, PL, 215, 1024f.) - Die pessimistische Tonart der Beschreibung der Zustände in Südfrankreich entspricht der Tonart der kleinen Schrift Innocenz' aus seiner Kardinalszeit, über den Menschen im Schatten der Sünde, *De miseria humanae conditionis*, auf deren, den Inhalt genau charakterisierenden Titel der Papst wörtlich anspielt. (Lotharii Cardinalis, *De miseria humanae conditionis*, ed. Michele Maccarone, Padova, 1955).

von Osma und Dominikus gefundenen Lebensform der Armut glaubte der Papst, daß der richtige Weg der *caritas* eingeschlagen worden sei.

Doch ist es eben der gleiche Innocenz, der bereits zu Beginn seines zweiten Pontifikatsjahres die Dekretale *'Vergentis'* erläßt, die in bislang unbekannter Schärfe den Strafenkatalog von *'Ad abolendam'* erweitert [113]. Die Dekretisten hatten bislang nicht die spätantiken Ketzergesetze genau herangezogen. Wohl hatte Huguccio Häresie zum *crimen publicum* und *peculatus* erklärt und dabei die Strafbestimmungen der Digesten benutzt [114], aber vor Innocenz III. sah niemand Häresie als *crimen laesae majestatis* an. Freilich hatte Gratian das spätantike Ketzergesetz *'Quis-quis'* von 391, das Simonie als Majestätsverbrechen bestrafte, rezipiert [115]. Der Schritt vom Übergang von der *simoniaca haeresis* zur allgemeinen Häresie lag nicht sehr fern, und die Diskussion der Romanisten über die römischen Ketzergesetze tat das übrige : Gegen Ende des zwölften Jahrhunderts galt den Romanisten die Häresie als Majestätsverbrechen, wobei man sich allerdings nicht einig war, ob Infamie und Konfiskation tatsächlich auch auf die rechtgläubigen Kinder der Ketzer ausgedehnt werden sollten [116].

Innocenz konstruierte eine Analogie zwischen Verbrechen gegen die weltliche und die ewige Majestät und leitete daraus das Anrecht auf Verhängung härtester Strafen im Falle der Ketzerei ab [117]. Es ist O. Hageneders Verdienst herausgearbeitet zu haben, daß der eigentliche Zielpunkt der Dekretale *'Vergentis'* die Begünstiger der Häresie waren [118].

[113] Comp. III c. 1 V. 4 = c. 10 X V. 7.

[114] S.o. S. 127f.

[115] Cod. Just. IX.8,5 = c. 22 C. 6 q. 1.

[116] Maisonneuve, *Études*, 62-65; Othmar Hageneder, 'Studien zur Dekretale "Vergentis" (X: V, 7, 10) : Ein Beitrag zur Häretikergesetzgebung Innocenz' III.', *Zeitschrift der Savigny - Stiftung*, kan. Abt., 49 (1963), 138-173 (hier 144ff.).

[117] Petrus Cantor war mit dieser von ihm klar erkannten Tendenz in der Ketzergesetzgebung nicht einverstanden und wandte sich gegen die Anwendung der Todesstrafe als *animadversio debita*. Sein Ideal war dagegen eine wörtliche Verwirklichung der Augustinischen Forderung nach Trennung von den Ketzern, nun allerdings körperlich und nicht mehr geistig wie noch bei Huguccio verstanden : Er schlug lebenslängliche Einkerkerung vor. Wie sehr gegen Ende des 12. Jhs sich die ganze Mentalität gegenüber der Ketzerei verhärtet hatte, macht Baldwins Studie deutlich : Selbst Robert Courson, der dem engeren Kreis des Petrus Cantor zuzurechnen ist, plädierte offen für Härte. Baldwin, *Masters*, I, 320ff.

[118] Hageneder, *Studien*, 145ff.- Die Deutung Walter Ullmanns, daß hinter dem Rekurrieren auf das römische Recht und der Anwendung von dessen Strafbestimmungen für Majestätsverbrechen die Absicht Innocenz' steht, Kirche und Papst zu

Angesichts der Lage im Languedoc und in Oberitalien - die Dekretale wurde wegen der Zustände in Viterbo erlassen - war den Ketzern nach Meinung des Papstes wohl nur noch auf indirektem Wege beizukommen. Die Begünstiger sollten nicht nur zusammen mit ihren Nachkommen der Infamie anheimfallen, sondern auch ihrer bürgerlichen Existenzgrundlage beraubt werden, indem ihnen die Vererbungsfähigkeit beschnitten wurde. Dabei richtete sich die Dekretale besonders an die Fürsten und übrigen weltlichen Herren unter den *defensores, receptatores et fautores*, denen auf der Grundlage der Bestimmungen ihre Amtsgewalt entzogen werden konnte.

'*Vergentis*' wurde für Innocenz die Grundlage der strafrechtlichen Bekämpfung der Ketzerei. Bereits vor dem Albigenserkrieg fand die Dekretale ihre Verwendung im französischen Midi, und das kriegerische Vorgehen wurde unter Berufung auf die Dekretale eingeleitet [119]. Freilich mußte Innocenz erkennen, daß ihm die politische Entwicklung in diesem Fall aus der Hand glitt. Othmar Hageneders Untersuchungen lassen es einsichtig erscheinen, daß der Papst bereits vor 1215 aufgrund seiner schlechten Erfahrungen mit Denunziationen und Exzessen seine Forderung nach Konfiskation der Güter der Förderer der Häresie stillschweigend zurückstellte, bis der Ketzerkanon '*Excommunicamus*' des vierten Laterankonzils dann offiziell auf eine solche Konfiskation verzichtet. Auch die von Raymund von Penaforte für die Aufnahme in den *Liber extra* Gregors IX. verkürzte Fassung von '*Vergentis*' paßt sich der neuen Rechtslage an [120]. Die Möglichkeit zur Fürstenab-

identifizieren und den Primat des Papstes juristisch abzusichern (734) bzw. den Papst zur wahren irdischen *majestas* zu machen und Ketzerei daher zu einem Angriff auf den Papst (738), trifft kaum die wirklichen Beweggründe für diese Dekretale (The Significance of Innocent III's decretal "Vergentis", in *Etudes d'histoire du droit canonique dédiées à Gabriel Le Bras* (Paris, 1965), 729-741). Ullmann war die Untersuchung Hageneders noch unbekannt. - Allerdings verändert sich unter den Dekretalisten die Akzentsetzung bei der Analyse der Bedeutung von '*Vergentis*'. Dazu weiter unten.

[119] Im Jahr 1200 erhält der Kardinallegat Johannes v. St. Paul '*Vergentis*' zugesandt, um sie im Languedoc anzuwenden (Bouquet, RHF, XIX, 389). Zwischen 1200 u. 1202 erhält sie Emmerich II. v. Ungarn (Migne, PL, 214, 871); dazu Maisonneuve, *Études*, 169f., Hageneder, *Studien*, 152ff. - Hageneder verdanken wir auch eine Analyse der Bedeutung von '*Vergentis*' für den Albigenserkreuzzug (*Studien*, 153-163). Vgl. a. Roscher, *Papst Innocenz*, 214-253.

[120] Hageneder, *Studien*, 150ff.; Ders., 'Das päpstliche Recht der Fürstenabsetzung: seine kanonistische Grundlegung (1150-1250)', *Archivum Historiae Pontificiae*, 1 (1963), 53-95, hier 66ff. - Die Canones des Lateranum IV sind abgedruckt COD, 206-247.

setzung wurde vom Konzilskanon in Verbindung mit den Bestimmungen des weiterhin vollgültigen 'Ad abolendam' als Rechtstitel aufrechter-
halten.

VII

Das Lateranum IV - von Innocenz als Krönung seines Pontifikats
einberufen - systematisierte die bisherigen Bemühungen der päpstlichen
Politik seit 60 Jahren um das Ketzerproblem [121]. Dem Glaubensbekenntnis des ersten Kanon merkt man deutlich die Abwehrstellung zu ketzerischen Lehren an, zumal es in den Bekenntnissen des Waldes und des
Bernard Prim Vorformen besitzt [122]. Der Ketzerkanon (Nr. 3) bezieht
sich direkt auf dieses Glaubensbekenntnis und wollte damit die Ketzerbekämpfung wohl auf sichere dogmatische Grundlagen stellen. Andererseits weist Kanon 13 mit seinem Verbot neuer Ordensgründungen
darauf hin, daß die Phase des Experimentierens nun ein Ende finden
sollte [123]. Ob dieser Kanon völlig den Absichten des Papstes konform
ging oder mehr auf Betreiben des Episkopats zustande kam, der ja in seiner
Mehrheit der Förderung neuer religiöser Gemeinschaften durch Innocenz mit unverhohlenem Mißtrauen gegenübergestanden war, kann man-
gels Quellen nicht entschieden werden.

Die Bestimmungen des Lateranums leiteten die Entwicklung zum
rein strafrechtlich orientierten und aus Gründen der Vorbeugung weiterer
Ausbreitung jeden Verdacht rücksichtslos verfolgenden Ketzerverfahren,
zur Inquisition ein. Für den Ketzer entfiel nun der *amor correctionis*. Die
in der Forschung wiederholt konstatierte Verhärtung der Kircheninin-
stitutionen gegenüber religiösen Laienbewegungen hatte ihre Pa-

---

[121] Zum Konzil zusammenfassend Michele Maccarone, 'Il IV° concilio Latera-
nense', *Divinitas*, 5 (1961), 270-298; Foreville, *Lateran I-IV*, 265-379. - Zur Rolle der
Konzilscanones als Grundlage der Dekretalistik : St. Kuttner, 'Johannes Teutonicus,
das vierte Lateranum und die Compilatio quarta', in *Miscellanea G. Mercato*,
V (Città del Vaticano, 1946), 608-634; Antonio García García, O.F.M., 'El Concilio
IV de Letrán (1215) y sus commentarios', *Traditio*, 14 (1958), 484- 502.

[122] COD, 206.

[123] Selge, *Erste Waldenser*, I, 30ff.; Grundmann, *Religiöse Bewegungen*, 138f.;
R. Foreville, *Lateran I-IV*, 340ff.; Borst, *Katharer*, 119. Zum Vergleich : A. Dondaine,
'Aux origines du Valdéisme : Une profession de foi de Valdès', in AFP, 16 (1946),
198-201. - Vgl. das Urteil Grundmanns, der den Konzilsbeschluß 'als Einspruch und
Abwehr gegen die im Entstehen begriffenen Neubildungen' versteht (*Religiöse
Bewegungen*, 141f.).

rallele in der Haltungsänderung der Kanonistik. Wie Kurie und Kanonistik das Verhältnis zur weltlichen Gewalt mehr und mehr hierokratisch begründeten [124], so spielte der Gedanke der *caritas* in der Auseinandersetzung mit Ketzern kaum noch eine Rolle. Beide Entwicklungen sind direkt miteinander verbunden. Die Kirche schob immer mehr die Verantwortung für die Effektivität der Ketzerbekämpfung an die weltlichen Gewalten ab, die aufgrund der eingenommenen hierokratischen Position bedroht wurden, falls sie den an sie ergangenen Aufforderungen nicht willig nachkamen, was nur dann - wie im Falle Friedrichs II. - geschah, wenn sich damit eigene Vorteile verbanden [125].

Die Behandlung von '*Vergentis*' durch die frühen Dekretalisten ist kennzeichnend für die Entwicklung. Die Glossen der Bologneser Magister zur Compilatio III machen sich sofort die Einordnung der Häresie unter die Majestätsverbrechen zueigen. Nicht ohne weiteres akzeptierte man die Bestimmung über die Enterbung rechtgläubiger Ketzerkinder durch die Konfiskation des elterlichen Vermögens, obwohl die Compilatio III im Unterschied zum *Liber extra* den Volltext der Dekretale enthielt. Ähnlich zurückhaltend war man mit der 1199 verfügten Konfiskation des Vermögens von Ketzerbegünstigern, von der Innocenz selbst bereits vor 1215 wieder abrückte [126].

Dagegen rückte die Möglichkeit zur Fürstendeposition in den Mittelpunkt des Interesses. Dadurch verlor der Ketzerbegriff viel von der Präzision, den er durch die Beziehung auf den Kanon 1 des Lateranum IV hatte erhalten sollen. Johannes Teutonicus leitete in seinen Glossenapparaten zu den Compilationen III und IV (nach 1217) gleichermaßen aus '*Vergentis*' und '*Excommunicamus*' ab, daß der Papst das Recht zur Fürstenabsetzung habe '*non tantum propter heresim, sed propter alias iniquitates*', und setzte beide Dekretalen zu den Dekretalen '*Novit*'

---

[124] Friedrich Kempf, 'Das Problem der Christianitas im 12. u. 13. Jahrhundert', *Historisches Jahrbuch*, 79 (1960), 104-123 ; Ders., *Kanonistik und kuriale Politik*, 30ff.; John Anthony Watt, 'The Theory of Papal Monarchy in the Thirteenth Century : The Contribution of the Canonists', *Traditio*, 20 (1964), 179-317; dazu demnächst auch H.G. Walther, *Imperiales Königtum*, 65-78.

[125] De Vergottini, *Studi*, 69ff., 210ff. - Im übrigen begnügt sich meine Untersuchung mit einem zeitlichen Rahmen, der nur bis kurz hinter das Lateranum IV reichen soll, berücksichtigt also nur die Dekretalenapparate bis ca. 1220 - der Zeitpunkt der Fertigstellung der *Glossa ordinaria* des Tancred zur Comp. III-, nicht aber die Dekretalengesetzgebung Gregors IX. und seinen *Liber extra Decretalium* (1234) als Gegenstände eingehender Analyse.

[126] Hageneder, *Studien*, 169f.

und 'Venerabilem' in Beziehung (Comp. III c. 3 II. 1 = c. 13 X II. 1 bzw. c. 19 I. 6 = c. 34 X 6) [127], in denen Innocenz III. sein Verhältnis zu den weltlichen Gewalten prinzipiell dargelegt hatte. Tancred besiegelte in seiner *Glossa ordinaria* zur Compilatio III (nach 1220) diese Akzentsetzung bei der Deutung der Ketzerkanones. Bernhard von Pavia gab mit seiner Summe zu der von ihm selbst zusammengestellten Compilatio I (1192- 1198) [128] bereits die Richtung an : Häretiker werden durch Exkommunikation, Absetzung, Enteignung und militärische Verfolgung bestraft [129]. In einer Glosse des Alanus (vor 1210), die uns in der *Glossa ordinaria* des Tancred zur Compilatio I (zwischen 1210 und 1215) überliefert ist, ist eine Beziehung zwischen der Teilbestimmung der Bestrafung der Söldnerhorden und der Enteignung ihrer Förderer und dem generellen Recht der Kirche auf Verhängung weltlicher Strafen hergestellt [130].

[127] Johannes Teutonicus ad Comp. III c. 1 V. 4 s.v. *'publicari'* : Quod facere potest papa obtentu peccati supra 'novit' [c. 3 II. 1.] et ita potest papa seculares iudices privare dignitatibus suis non tantum propter heresim sed propter alias iniquitates, ut XV. q. VI 'alius' [=c. 3 C. 15 q. 6]; et ita transtulit dignitatem imperii de loco ad locum, ut supra de electione 'venerabilem' [c. 19 I. 6]' (Frankf. a.M., Ms. Barth. 28 (II), fo. 96ra) - ad Comp. IV c. 2 V. 5 s.v. *'vasallos'* : Sic ergo papa potest omnes iudices sive duces sive comites deponere propter heresim et etiam propter alias iniquitates, ut XV q. VI 'alius': nam et (Qi : etiam) transfert dignitatem de loco ad locum (Qi : de loco dignitatem ad locum), ut extra de elect. 'venerabilem' (Fulda, Msc. D 6, fo. 293vb; Frankfurt Ms. Barth. 28 (II)= Qi, fo. 132f.; vgl. a. Antonius Augustinus, *Antiquae decretalium collectiones,* Parisiis, 1621, 836).

[128] Zur Entstehungsgeschichte der Comp. I Gérard Fransen, 'Les diverses formes de la *Compilatio Prima',* in : *Scrinium Lovaniense : Mélanges historiques Etienne van Cauwenbergh* (Louvain 1961), 235-253. - Speziell zum Schicksal des Ketzerkanons c. 27 des Lateranum III bis zu seiner zweiteiligen Aufnahme in die Comp. I De Vergottini, *Studi,* 179-209.

[129] *Bernardi Papiensis Summa decretalium,* ed. E.A. Th. Laspeyres (Ratisbonae, 1860), V. 6 § 3 : Punitur autem haereticus excommunicatione, depositione, rerum ablatione et militari persecutione, ... depositione ut C. XXIV q. 1 'Qui contra' (c.32) et infra eod. 'Ad abolendam' (c. 11), rerum ablatione, ecclesiasticarum, ut Di. VIII 'Quo iure' (c. 1), rerum suarum, ut infra eod. 'De brabantionibus' (c. 7) 'In partibus' (c. 10); militari persecutione, ut in eisdem cap. et cap. 'Ad abolendam' invenitur.(213f.)

[130] Tancred ad Comp. I c. 7 V. 6 s.v. *'confiscentur'* : hanc penam statuit papa super laicos ratione criminis, quod ecclesiasticum est primo loco; sed pro quilibet crimine, dummodo incorrigibilis sit criminosus, et hanc et alias quascumque penas, sive pecuniarias sive corporales, infligendas statuere potest ecclesia, argumentum LXIII di. 'Adrianus in synodo' [c. 1] et V. q. VI 'delatori' [c. 5]. Infligendas dico saltem per iudices seculares, quoniam omne crimen ex contumacia fit ecclesiasticum, ut II. q.I 'multi'[c. 18]; XXIIII q. III. 'itaque' [c. 20]; XXIII q.V. 'incestuosi'[c. 22] et q. ult. 'si quis membrorum' [c. 31 q. 8]; infra de iudiciis 'novit' 1. III, ala (Bamberg StB Msc. can. 21, fo. 85rb).

Eine Verbindung zwischen Ketzerei, Enteignung, Verbrechen aus *contumacia* und der Dekretale *'Novit'* wird in dem ebenfalls vor 1215 entstandenen Glossenapparat des Vincentius Hispanus zur Compilatio III gezogen [131]. Über die Brücke des *'obtentu peccati'* zu dem *'criminali peccato'* aus *'Novit'* gelangt Vincentius dahin [132]. Johannes Teutonicus leitete gar aus *'Ad abolendam'* und *'Excommunicamus'* ab, daß ein hartnäckiger Widerstand gegen Weisungen der Kirche mit Häresie gleichzusetzen sei. Galt das *'pertinaciter'* ursprünglich nur in Verbindung mit Glaubensabweichungen, so hatte es die dekretalistische Diskussion aufgrund der verschärften Bestimmungen des Ketzerkanons des Lateranum IV aus diesem Zusammenhang gelöst und verallgemeinert. Die 1215 neu eingeführte Bestimmung, daß die *receptatores, defensores et fautores* aber auch die nur *suspicione notabiles* ohne Beweis ihrer Rechtgläubigkeit nach einem Jahr der Infamie verfallen würden, wie die *domini temporales negligentes* nach dieser Frist vom Papst abgesetzt werden könnten, [133] bildet für Johannes Teutonicus die Grundlage für die Lehre, daß *contumacia* und Häresie gleichzusetzen seien [134]. Tancred fügte die Argumente seiner beiden Glossatorenvorgänger zusammen : Der Papst darf *obtentu peccati* den weltlichen Herren Vorschriften machen (soweit Vincentius) und diese wegen Verfehlungen, nicht nur wegen Häresie enteignen und absetzen (Johannes Teutonicus) [135]. Eine Abwägung des rechten Verhältnisses von *caritas* und

---

[131] Der Glossenapparat des Vincentius Hispanus zur Compilatio I (fast gleichzeitig mit dem zur Comp. III anzusetzen) ist vollständig nur in einer Hs. bekannt, die im 2. Weltkrieg schwer beschädigt wurde und nicht mehr zugänglich ist. Leider war es mir nicht möglich, die unvollständige Fassung des Glossenapparates in der Hs. Erlangen 349, fo. 1-72 einzusehen. Zur Handschriftenfrage des App. d. Vinc. Hisp. zur Comp. I : St. Kuttner, 'Notes on Manuscripts : Summae decretorum, Decretal Collections, Vincentius Hispanus, Varia', *Traditio*, 17 (1961), 533-542 (537).

[132] Vincentius Hispanus ad Comp. III c. 1 V. 4. s.v. *'Precipimus'* : Quod facere potest papa obtentu peccati, supra de iudiciis "Novit" (Bamberg StB. Msc. can. 20, fo. 170 ra).

[133] COD, 209f. = Comp. IV c. 2 V. 5 = 13 X V. 7, §§ 2, 3, 5. - Zur Bedeutung der durch den can. 3 des Lat. IV bewirkten Veränderungen Hageneder, *Studien*, 162ff.

[134] Johannes Teutonicus, *Glossa ordinaria* ad c. 6 Di. 40 s.v. *'a fide devius'* : 'Nam contumacia dicitur haeresis' (*Corpus Iuris Canonici* I, Augustae Taurinorum, 1620, 195).

[135] Tancred ad Comp. III c.1 V.4 s.v. *'precipimus'* : Quod facere potest dominus papa obtentu peccati, ut supra de iudiciis II 'novit' i. est Vincentius; et ita potest papa etiam seculares iudices privare dignitatibus suis non tantum propter heresim sed etiam propter alias iniquitates, ut XV q.6 'Alius'. Nam et imperium transfert de loco ad locum, supra de electione 'Venerabilem' i. est Jo(hannes) (Fulda Msc. D.6, fo. 248rb).

potestas, die in der Häresiediskussion des zwölften Jahrhunderts eine so große Rolle gespielt hatte, war nun nicht mehr ein Anliegen der Kanonistik. Als sich Vincentius Hispanus in seinem Apparat zum *Liber Extra* Gregors IX. noch einmal der Diskussion des Häresie - problems zuwandte (nach 1234), stellte er seinen Kommentar ganz unter den Gesichtspunkt der Größe der Strafe [136]. Die *Glossa ordinaria* des Johannes Teutonicus zum *Decretum Gratiani* verdeutlicht, daß man in der Kanonistik nun über Ketzer nur noch im Zusammenhang mit dem Umfang der Enteignungsmaßnahmen oder mit dem Absetzungsrecht des Papstes diskutierte [137].

Der Tendenz zur Entleerung des Häresiebegriffes entsprach auf der anderen Seite die systematische Diskussion der Dekretalisten über den durch *'Vergentis'* und *'Excommunicamus'* als gewichtigen Umstand eingebrachten Häresieverdacht. Gratian hatte Augustins Meinung als

---

[136] Vincentius Hispanus, *Apparatus super Decretales* ad C. 10 X V.7 (*'Vergentis'*) s.v. *'filiorum'* : 'Expresse dicitur hic quod bona haereticorum confiscantur, sive filios habent sive non, nec catholicis filiis hereticorum est aliquid reliquendum, sed dicunt leges (folgen 4 Belege aus Codex und Novellen) ubi dicitur quod bona hereticorum devolvuntur ad cognatos vel agnatos catholicos. Ad hec dixerunt Lau. (rentius Hispanus) et Jo. (hannes Teutonicus) quod hec decretalis corrigit illas et jus illud antiquum trahitur ad istud novum, argumentum ff. de legibus et consuetudine 'non est novum' (Dig. I. 3, 26) et supra de Cog(natione) spi(rituali) c.1 (X IV. 11)' (Paris. Bibl. nat. 3967 fo. 184a, zitiert nach Maisonneuve, *Études,* 281 Anm. 190). Zum Ketzerproblem im Dekretalenapparat des Vincentius ('n'est qu'un commentaire succint du titre 'De Haereticis'') 's. Maisonneuve, 280-282. - Die *Glossa ordinaria* des Bernhard von Parma zum *Liber extra* bringt keine neuen Gedanken; Sie stellt nur die zu den Ketzer-canones bereits von Tancred (für die Comp. I u. III) und Johannes Teutonicus (für die Comp. IV) geschaffenen Standardglossen zusammen und ergänzt z.B. bei *'Vergentis'* um die soeben zitierte Glosse des Vincentius. Druck der *Gl. ord.* in *Corpus Iuris canonici,* II (Augustae Taurinorum, 1621), 1669-1686.

[137] Beispielhaft in der Glosse ad dict. Grat. a. C. 23 q. 7 s.v. *'nunc autem'* : Non solum haeretici, sed omnes hostes licite possent spoliari rebus suis, dummodo bellum sit iustum : et ille qui rem abstulit iure factus est dominus illius rei, supra eadem q.5 'dicat' (c. 25) et supra di. I 'ius naturale' (c.7) et ff. de acquirendo rerum dominio, 'naturale' § ult. (Dig. 41.1,5§7). Haereticis autem licitum est auferri ea, quae habent ...Melius tamen est, quod auctoritate iudicis fiat. ... Si ergo condemnatus est laicus de haeresi, confiscantur bona eius, ut extra de haereticis 'Vergentis' ... et haec vera sunt, etiamsi aliquis haereticus habet filios, vel agnatos, ut extra de eod. 'Vergentis' in fine. ... Licet autem bona sint ablata haereticis, si tamen fuerint reversi ad fidem, priora bona eis ex misericordia restituuntur... Si est melioris conditionis ille, qui revertitur ab haeresi quam qui revertitur ab hostibus. Nam si desertor revertitur sponte ad suos, licet indulgeatur ei vita; tamen in insulam deportatur... (*Corpus Iuris Canonici,* I (Augustae Taurinorum, 1620), 1360f.).

Canon rezipiert, daß man sich damit abfinden müsse, daß es auf der Erde Böse neben den Guten gebe. Alexander III. schrieb übereifrigen Ketzerverfolgern, daß man doch lieber auf die Verfolgung Schuldiger verzichten soll, als wenn man Unschuldige bestrafte; Innocenz forderte zumindest eine peinlich genaue Klärung. Aber in 'Vergentis' hatte er selbst auch denen gedroht 'postquam ab ecclesia fuerint denotati'. Das vierte Laterankonzil behielt in 'Excommunicamus' trotz der schlechten Erfahrung des Papstes im Albigenserkrieg das Verfahren bei, daß unter Verdacht Geratene die Beweislast für seine Unschuld zu tragen habe, bei ungenügender Reinigung vom Verdacht der Exkommunikation anheimfalle und nach Jahresfrist dann als Häretiker betrachtet werde. Die kanonistische Diskussion über jenen Punkt wurde vom Dekretalisten Innocenz IV. (Sinibaldus Fliscus) praktisch genutzt, als er die Absetzungssentenz gegen Kaiser Friedrich II. formulierte. Die theoretische Begründung lieferte er gewissermaßen im Kommentar zur eigenen Dekretale im Rahmen seines großen Kommentars zum *Liber extra* nach [138]. Auch bei seinem Kommentar zu 'Ad abolendam' stand Innocenz IV. ganz im Bann der kurialen kanonistischen Theorie, als er lehrte, daß bei Glaubenszweifeln allein die römische Kirche entscheiden dürfte [139]. Bewegt sich Innocenz damit durchaus in den Bahnen, die Gratian und die Dekretisten betreten hatten, als sie meinten, Häresie sei ein Verstoß gegen die Lehre der römischen Kirche im Glauben - wobei mit *ecclesia Romana* keineswegs nur der Papst allein gemeint war -, so geht Hostiensis noch einen Schritt weiter : Für ihn ist bereits jeder

---

[138] c.2 VI II. 27 (*Ad apostolicae sedis*) = MGH, Leges IV, Constitutiones II, n°400 p. 409ff. : De heresi quoque non dubiis et levibus, sed difficilibus et evidentibus argumentis suspectus habetur ... Merito insuper contra eum (sc. Fridericum) de haeretica pravitate suspitio est exorta, cum postquam excommunicationis sententiam a prefatis Iohannis episcopo Sabinensi et Thomasio cardinalis prolatam incurrit et dictus Gregorius (IX.) papa ipsum anathematis vinculo innodavit. - Dazu Sinibaldus Fliscus, *Commentaria super libros quinque decretalium* ad c. 27 X II. 27 s.v. '*privamus*' (n. 6) (Francofordiae, 1570), fo. 316v. Innocenz IV. reihte die Absetzungsdekretale (wie viele andere), die noch nicht in einer Dekretalensammlung 'offiziell' rezipiert war, als c. 27 unter dem Titel 27 '*De sentia et re iudicata*' des 2. Buches des *Liber extra* ein, um sie zu kommentieren. - Zum Zusammenhang von Absetzungssentenz und Ketzergesetzgebung Hageneder, *Päpstliches Recht*, 24ff.

[139] Sinibaldus Fliscus, *Commentaria* ad c. 9 X V. 7 s.v. '*haereticos*' : id est in haeresim iam damnatam et indubitatam incidentes, alias enim si de articulis fidei dubitatio orietur et dubium esse quis bene vel male diceret, hoc sola Romana ecclesia determinat, 24 q. 1 'quotiens' (c. 12); 17. di. 'multis audientia' (c.5), quod dicit, non proderit eis, si dicant se velle haeresim abiurare (Francofordiae, 1570, fo. 507r).

Verstoß gegen ein Privileg oder ein *praeceptum* des Apostolischen Stuhls unter die Häresien zu rechnen [140].

Diese unverhohlene Dienstbarmachung des Häresiebegriffes für eine Ausweitung der Machtstellung des Papsttums unterscheidet erheblich die Dekretalistik von der Dekretistik. Bei letzterer blieben stets die aus der Konfrontation mit den patristischen Canones rührenden Skrupel spürbar, die an einer exzessiven Auslegung des Rechtes auf Verfolgung von Ketzern hinderten. In der *Glossa ordinaria* des Johannnes Teutonicus ist dieses Problembewußtsein kaum noch greifbar. Die großen Kommentare der Dekretalisten zum 1234 durch Gregor IX. promulgierten *Liber extra* beschränken sich auf die Handhabung päpstlicher Ketzergesetze und auf die Destillation genereller Verfahrensregeln aus ihnen, mehr unter Rückgriff auf die *Glossa ordinaria* als auf das *Decretum Gratiani* direkt. Der in der Forschung des öfteren betonte Verzicht auf Auseinandersetzung mit dem Gedankenreichtum des Dekrets zugunsten der Konzentration auf die Dekretalen, die aus Kanzleien juristisch ausgebildeter Päpste stammten, führte auch im speziellen Fall des Häresieproblems zu einer Vereinseitigung der Kanonistik. Ein wichtiges Bindeglied zwischen Dekretisten und Dekretalisten bildeten die Kanonistenpäpste des ausgehenden zwölften Jahrhunderts. Sind die Dekretisten auf dem Stuhl Petri für die Entwicklung der Häresiediskussion verantwortlich zu machen? Die in den Dekretalen '*Ad abolendam*', '*Vergentis*' und '*Excommunicamus*' feststellbare Verschärfung der Ketzerverfolgung darf nicht ohne den historischen Hintergrund der gesamten päpstlichen Ketzerpolitik gesehen werden. Die spezifische Mentalität, die aus den Dekretalen spricht und die den geistigen Horizont der Häresieauseinandersetzung der Päpste bestimmte, wurde ihrerseits von der Auseinandersetzung mit der Behandlung der Ketzerfrage bei Gratian wesentlich geprägt. So hat wohl die theoretische Bildung der Päpste die Art ihrer Begegnung mit der historischen Wirklichkeit der Ketzerei des zwölften Jahrhunderts entscheidend vorgeformt.

Man mag das in Sympathie für viele religiöse Bewegungen jenes Jahrhunderts bedauern. Aber aus Gratian war zumindest zu lernen, daß kirchliche Gewalt auf zwei Prinzipien, *caritas* und *potestas* beruhen

---

[140] Hostiensis, *Summa aurea* ad X V. 7 '*De haereticis*' no. 1 : 'Multis tamen modis dicitur haereticus largo sumpto vocabulo; dubiis in fide, haereticus dicitur et infidelis... Dicitur etiam haereticus, qui privilegium Romanae ecclesiae ab ipso summo ecclesiarum capite traditum conatur aufferre... et qui transgredit praecepta sedis Apostolicae' (Venetiis, 1574; Reprint Torino, 1963, col. 1529).

sollte. Man kann den Päpsten des ausgehenden zwölften Jahrhunderts nicht absprechen, daß sie auf der Grundlage eines juristischen Kirchenbegriffes den beiden Prinzipien Rechnung zu tragen gewillt waren. Dennoch überwog schließlich in der Konfrontation mit den Ketzereien die *potestas*. Der Erfolg einer rein juristisch ausgerichteten Ekklesiologie und der hierokratischen Doktrin tragen einen großen Teil der Verantwortung dafür. Die Entwicklung war nicht unvermeidlich. Aber wer sich zuviel von rein juristischen Lösungen erhofft, muß wohl meist auf den Geist der *caritas* verzichten. Augustin formulierte diese Erfahrung kaum zufällig in seinem Kommentar zur Bergpredigt, und Gratian bewahrte sie in seiner Kirchenrechtssammlung : '*ubi karitas non est, non potest esse iusticia*' [141].

---

[141] c. 29 C. 24 q. 1.

Dimiter Angelov

URSPRUNG UND WESEN DES BOGOMILENTUMS

Wenn wir die mittelalterlichen Häresien untersuchen, dann verdient zweifelsohne die Lehre der Bogomilen, die wie bekannt Mitte des zehnten Jahrhunderts in Bulgarien erschienen ist und sich im Laufe von fünf Jahrhunderten verbreitete, eine besondere Beachtung. Die Bogomilen-Häresie erweckt mit Recht ein besonderes Interesse, weil sie chronologisch ähnlichen Häresien in Westeuropa vorausgeht (hauptsächlich dem Katharismus in Norditalien und Südfrankreich) und mit ihnen eine enge Verbindung in ideologischer und organisatorischer Hinsicht zeigt. In diesem Sinne steht das Bogomilentum vor den Augen nicht nur der Forscher philosophisch-religiöser Bewegungen in Südosteuropa, sondern auch derjenigen Forscher, die ähnliche Bewegungen in Westeuropa untersuchen. Das ist die eine Seite der Frage. Gleichzeitig ist die Untersuchung des Bogomilentums für uns auch deshalb von großer Bedeutung, weil sie uns erlauben wird, an Hand eines konkreten Beispiels eine der Hauptfragen dieser Konferenz zu stellen und zu versuchen sie bis zu einem gewissen Grade zu lösen. Das ist nämlich die Frage: Was stellt eine Häresie dar, welches ist ihr Wesen, als eine spezifische Erscheinung der mittelalterlichen Epoche? Es handelt sich einerseits darum, den objektiven Inhalt dieses Begriffes zu erläutern und andererseits auch gleichzeitig festzustellen, was die Vertreter der mittelalterlichen theoretischen und theologischen Gedankenwelt, die sich mit den häretischen Bewegungen beschäftigten und das Ziel verfolgten diese zu verleugnen und zu widerlegen, als Häresie betrachteten.

Der Ursprung des Bogomilentums führt uns, wie dies gut bekannt ist, zur Mitte des zehnten Jahrhunderts während der Herrschaft des bulgarischen Königs Peter (927-969). Das ist eine Periode, wo der bulgarische Staat schon seit ziemlich langer Zeit das Christentum angenommen hatte (auf Grund des Beschlusses des Fürsten Boris vom Jahre 865) und es besteht, gleichzeitig mit einer starken weltlichen Macht, auch eine gut aufgebaute und einflußreiche kirchliche Organisation, die nach byzantinischem Beispiel errichtet worden war. Die Mitte des zehnten Jahrhunderts ist eine Periode, wo sich in dem bulgarischen Staat schon eine ziemlich entwickelte feudale Ordnung mit ökonomi-

schen und sozial-rechtlichen Auswirkungen gebildet hatte. Ein bedeu-
tender Teil des Bodens befindet sich in den Händen der weltlichen und
gesitlichen Landsherren (der König, die Bojaren, die hohen geistlichen
Würdenträger, die Äbte der Klöster), deren wirtschaftliche Macht eng
mit ihrem politischen und ideologischen Einfluß verbunden ist. Das
Bauerntum bildete die überwiegende Masse der damaligen Bevölkerung.
Ein Teil der Bauern ist noch frei, während der andere Teil schon in
Abhängigkeit geraten ist. Die Bauern, sowohl die freien, als auch die
abhängigen, waren mit verschiedenartigen Verpflichtungen gegenüber
den Organen der Zentralmacht oder den örtlichen Herrschern belastet.
Wir finden ausführliche Angaben über die Lage der Landbevölkerung
in dem sogenannten *Besedata* (Die Rede) von Präsbyter Kosma,
einem bekannten bulgarischen Geistlichen und Schriftsteller aus der
zweiten Hälfte des zehnten Jahrhunderts.

Parallel mit der sich derart entwickelten gesellschaftlich-politischen
Struktur, entsteht in dem von uns betrachteten Zeitraum des mittelalterlichen Bulgariens ein entsprechendes System von Anschauungen
und Ansichten, welche die Auffassungen der herrschenden Schichten
widerspiegeln und die Kraft einer verpflichtenden Ideologie besitzen.
Diese Anschauungen und Ansichten sind unter der stark ausgedrückten
Einwirkung der kirchlich-religiösen Weltanschauung entstanden, die nach
der Annahme des Christentums in das Bewußtsein der Bevölkerung
eingeführt wurde. Welche sind die charakteristischen Merkmale dieser
Anschauungen? An erster Stelle ist das die religiöse Auffassung, die
gemäß der Bibelerzählung von der Erschaffung des Weltalls, die Welt
als ein vollkommenes Werk Gottes erklärt und sich dem heidnischen
Prinzip des Mehrgöttertums widersetzt. Ein Ausdruck dieser Auffassung
über die Welt ist in einem der bekanntesten Werke des bulgarischen
Schrifttums aus dem Anfang des zehnten Jahrhunderts enthalten und
zwar in dem sogenannten *Schestodnev* (Sechstagebuch) des bulgarischen
Schriftstellers Joan Exarch, der nach dem Beispiel der bekannten *Schestodnevi"* (Sechstagebücher) von Basileios dem Großen, Severian Gavalski
u.a. verfaßt ist, jedoch eine originelle Einleitung enthält, die von dem
bulgarischen Schriftsteller verfaßt ist. Joan Exarch schreibt in dieser
Einleitung mit Begeisterung über die wunderbare Harmonie und Voll-
kommenheit des von Gott erschaffenen Weltalls mit allen seinen Äußerungen. Die monotheistischen und gleichzeitig sehr optimistischen
Anschauungen von der Erschaffung des Weltalls werden auch in einer
Reihe von anderen Werken aus dieser Epoche und insbesondere in den

belehrenden Worten eines anderen berühmten bulgarischen Schriftstellers Kliment von Ochrid (einem Schüler von Kyrillos und Methodios)
durchgeführt.

Eine andere Ansicht, die ebenfalls im Zusammenhang mit der Einführung der christlichen Religion steht, ist die Ansicht, daß die weltliche
Macht, dargestellt vom obersten Herrscher (dem König) und seinen
ersten Dienern (den Bojaren) einen göttlichen Ursprung hat und deshalb als unerschütterlich betrachtet werden muß. 'Der König und die
Bojaren sind vom Gott aufgestellt'... цр҃и и болꙗре бм҃ъ соуть оу҃чинени
sagt ausdrücklich der schon erwähnte bulgarische Schriftsteller (aus der
zweiten Hälfte des zehnten Jahrhunderts) Präsbyter Kosma, Autor des
bekannten polemischen Werkes gegen die Häresie der Bogomilen.
Dieselbe Behauptung finden wir auch in anderen Werken des offiziellen
bulgarischen Schrifttums späterer Zeiten. Diese Auffassung ist in Bulgarien nach byzantinischem Muster angenommen worden, sie widerspiegelt jedoch gleichzeitig auch eine Auffassung, die dem Schoße der
bulgarischen Gesellschaft entsprungen ist und der politischen und sozialen Struktur des bulgarischen Staates im zehnten Jahrhundert entspricht.

Der starke Einfluß der kirchlich-religiösen Weltanschauung zeigt
sich auch im Zusammenhang mit einer anderen sehr wichtigen Frage,
die zu dieser Zeit entstanden ist, und zwar die Frage über 'die Armut'
und 'den Reichtum' und über die materielle und soziale Ungleichheit
innerhalb der bulgarischen Gesellschaft. Es wird hier die Auffassung
vertreten, die wir in einer Reihe von Werken des geistlichen Schrifttums des zehnten Jahrhunderts finden und zwar, daß der Reichtum an
und für sich kein Übel und nicht sündhaft sei und sogar noch etwas
mehr, reich sein bedeutet, daß Du von Gott geliebt wirst und er Dir
deshalb materielle Güter gegeben hat. Das ist eine Auffassung, die dem
Geist der alttestamentlichen Vorstellungen entspricht. Wir lesen z.B. in
einem Sammelwerk aus der Zeit des bulgarischen Zar Simeon (893-927),
daß Abraham reich war, weil er gerecht war und durch den Reichtum
hat ihm Gott sein Wohlwollen gezeigt. Macht, Gold, Silber, Weiden,
Land, Dörfer und Weinreben sind gute Sachen, wenn man sie nicht
mißbraucht - das ist das Leitmotiv eines anderen schriftlichen Werkes
ebenfalls aus dieser Zeit, dessen Verfasser ein gewisser Mönch Peter
ist. 'Der Reichtum ist nicht schlecht für diejenigen, die sich dessen gut
bedienen können', schreibt ein anderer bulgarischer Schriftsteller vom
Ende des neunten Jahrhunderts und dem Anfang des zehnten Jahrhun-

derts, der Bischof Konstantin von Preslav. Durch Behauptungen solcher Art wurde das Ziel verfolgt, die Unzufriedenheit in bestimmten Kreisen der bulgarischen Gesellschaft infolge der großen Vermögensunterschiede zu dämpfen und zu unterstreichen, daß der Widerwille gegen den Reichtum und gegen die Reichen keine Rechtfertigung in den Dogmen der Religion findet.

Es werden ferner interessante Anschauungen in der offiziellen kirchlichen Literatur verbreitet und zwar im Zusammenhang mit einer anderen oft gestellten Frage : weshalb es auf Erden Kummer und Unglück gibt, woher kommen die Sünden, die Laster und die Leiden. Eine interessante Antwort auf diese Frage enthält die belehrende Schrift von Kliment von Ochrid, einer der hervorragendsten bulgarischen Geistlichen vom Anfang des zehnten Jahrhunderts und ein Schüler der Brüder aus Saloniki -Kyrillos und Methodios. Seiner Meinung nach liegt die Ursache der Unglücke, Leiden und Laster in dem Sündenfall von Adam und Eva im Paradies. Die logische Schlußfolgerung dieser Erklärung ist, daß alle negativen Seiten, die das Leben der Menschen begleiten, nicht auf Unvollkommenheiten in der gesellschaftlichen und staatlichen Ordnung zurückzuführen sind, sondern auf einen anfängglichen Sündenfall, für den Gott eine entsprechende Vergeltung festgelegt hat.

Zum Schluß verdienen jene Gedanken eine besondere Beachtung, die in der offiziellen Literatur enthalten sind und den großen Einfluß des kirchlichen Instituts und seiner Vertreter (Metropolite, Bischöfe, Präsbytere usw.) widerspiegeln. Es handelt sich um die andauernd wiederholten Predigten über die Stärke und die unabwendbare Verbindlichkeit der zahlreichen kirchlichen Rituale und religiösen Symbole (Taufe, Kommunion, kirchliche Trauung, Kreuz, heilige Bilder, Reliquien usw.). Die Erfüllung der kirchlichen Rituale und die Erweisung der erforderlichen Achtung für die kirchlichen Symbole wird als Hauptverpflichtung eines jeden Gläubigen erklärt, durch die er seine aufrichtige und tiefe Verbundenheit zum christlichen Glauben unterstreicht und die erwünschte Rettung seiner Seele verdienen wird. Man betonte dabei die entscheidende Rolle des Geistlichen als Vermittler zwischen dem Gläubigen und Gott, als Vollzieher einer bestimmten Funktion zur Verbindung der Menschen mit Gott, ohne dessen Vermittlung und Teilnahme diese Verbindung unmöglich und ungültig sein würde. In den Schriften und Predigten der bulgarischen mittelalterlichen Geistlichen aus dem zehnten Jahrhundert und auch aus den folgenden Jahr-

hunderten, wird dieser Umstand mehrmals betont. Es wird dabei hervorgehoben, daß es nicht notwendig ist, den Geistlichen nach seinen Taten
zu beurteilen, sondern nach dem, was er in seiner Eigenschaft als Voll-
strecker seiner priesterlichen Funktionen tut. Es ist möglich, so vermerkt
der schon erwähnte bulgarische Schriftsteller Präsbyter Kosma, daß
der Priester durch seine Lebensart kein gutes Beispiel gibt, aber er bleibt
ein Diener Gottes und es muß ihm die erforderliche Achtung erwiesen
werden. Ein schlechter Priester ist besser als ein Häretiker.

Aus allem bisher Gesagtem ist ersichtlich, was für ein seinem Charakter
nach vielseitiges System von Ansichten in der bulgarischen Gesellschaft
in der ersten Hälfte und der Mitte des zehnten Jahrhunderts verbreitet
wurde. Das sind Ansichten, in denen die kirchlich-christliche Weltanschauung den Hauptanteil hat, und man spürt die überall durch-
dringende Rolle der religiösen Dogmen und der religiösen Argumen-
tierung. Gleichzeitig aber mit diesen rein religiösen Ansichten, sickern
auch Elemente eines politischen und sozialen Denkens durch, Elemente,
die dazu dienen, die bestehende gesellschaftliche Ordnung zu sanktio-
nieren. Ihrem Charakter nach war also diese Ideologie ein eigenartiger
Komplex von religiösen und weltlichen Anschauungen, die in untrenn-
barer Verbindung miteinander standen.

Unter solchen Umständen taucht die Bogomilenlehre auf, die ihrem
Wesen nach ein Versuch zur Verneinung gerade dieser offiziellen Ideologie
darstellt. Die Bogomilen, deren Hauptprediger ein Priester namens
Bogomil ist, ein Zeitgenosse des bulgarischen Königs Peter I, beginnen
mit der Verwerfung der bereits erwähnten Auffassung von der Voll-
kommenheit des Weltalls als eine Schöpfung des guten Gottes. Im
Geiste des alten Manichäismus und des Paulikianismus vertreten sie
die dualistische Weltanschauung und verkünden als zweite schöpferische
Macht neben Gott den bösen *Satana* (den Teufel), dem sie die Schaffung
der sichtbaren Welt und des Körpers des Menschens zuschreiben.
Diese dualistischen Auffassungen werden ausführlich in ihren kosmo-
genischen Erzählungen dargelegt, von denen eine besondere Aufmerk-
samkeit das sogenannte Evangelium von Johann (oder das Geheim-
buch - *Liber secretus*) verdient. Die dualistische Konzeption der Bogomilen, unabhängig von ihrem nicht originalen Charakter, steht in direkter Verbindung mit den konkreten Verhältnissen im mittelalterlichen
Bulgarien (zehntes Jahrhundert) und widerspiegelt das Bestreben der
unzufriedenen Kreise der bulgarischen Gesellschaft (vornehmlich der
Bauern) die festgelegte politische und soziale Ordnung mit dem Argument zu verneinen, daß die irdische Welt ein Werk der bösen Macht ist.

Indem sie sich an ihren dualistischen Glauben anlehnen, versuchen die Häretiker eine der Hauptthesen der orthodoxen Kirche zu untergraben und zwar die These, daß der König und die Machthaber von Gott eingesetzt sind. Im Gegensatz dazu erheben der Priester Bogomil und seine Anhänger - der Bogomile Basileios, Konstantin Chrisomalas und andere - die Stimme, daß die Könige Diener des Teufels sind und daß alle irdischen Reiche ihm unterstellt sind. Diese häretische Auffassung ist in dem gut bekannten Werk *Panoplia dogmatica* des byzantinischen Theologen Euthymios Zygabenos (Anfang des zwölften Jahrhunderts) klar ausgedrückt. Um ihre Auffassung zu begründen, daß die irdischen Reiche dem Teufel gehören, haben die Bogomilen die bekannte Episode im Evangelium von Mattheus von der Versuchung Christi durch den Teufel, der ihn auf einen hohen Berg hinaufgetragen hat, benutzt. Das neue Testament wird überhaupt sehr oft von den Häretikern zur Begründung ihrer Anschauungen benutzt. Einen sehr interessanten Beweis der feindlichen Stellung der Häretiker gegenüber der staatlichen Macht und ihrem obersten Vertreter, finden wir in dem erwähnten Werk von Präsbyter Kosma '*Beseda* gegen die Bogomilen'. Die Häretiker, so schreibt Kosma, hassen den König und beschimpfen die Vorsteher : 'Sie glauben, daß diejenigen die für den König arbeiten Gott verhaßt sind und verordnen jedem Diener, nicht für seinen Herren zu arbeiten'. Das politische und soziale Element dieser Predigt ist ganz klar. Jedoch ist es hinter einer religiösen Beweisführung versteckt, die im direkten Zusammenhang mit der dualistischen Konzeption der Bogomilen und ihrer Behauptung, daß der Satan der wahre Gebieter der irdischen Welt ist, steht.

Nicht weniger heftig waren die Angriffe der Bogomilen gegenüber der offiziellen Auffassung über den Reichtum. Im Gegensatz zur These, daß 'reich' von Gott beliebt zu sein bedeutet, predigten sie, daß der Reichtum vom 'Mammon', d.h. vom Teufel entstammt, und daß reich und gerecht unvereinbare Eigenschaften sind. Präsbyter Kosma behauptet ebenfalls, daß 'die Bogomilen die reichen Leute beschimpfen'. Ein anderer Kämpfer gegen die bogomilische Häresie, der byzantinische Mönch Euthymios von Akmonia in Kleinasien (erste Hälfte des elften Jahrhunderts) meldet, daß sie predigen 'es sei leichter, daß ein Kamel durch ein Nadelohr durchdringe, als daß ein Reicher ins Paradies Eintritt erlange'. Wir lesen ferner in der *Panoplia dogmatica*, daß eine der Hauptempfehlungen der Bogomilen an ihre Zuhörer war, keinen besitz zu haben (ἀκτημονεῖν). Die Verneinung des 'Reichtums' wurde von einem

Lob der Armut als Haupteigenschaft 'des vollendeten Bogomilen' begleitet, durch die er den bösen Geist besiegen und seine Seele retten wird. Das feindliche Verhältnis der Bogomilen gegen den Reichtum und die reichen Leute hat ohne Zweifel seine Wurzeln in früheren häretischen Lehren und an erster Stelle in dem Manichäismus und der Lehre von Eustathios. Gleichzeitig aber befinden sich die Auffassungen der Bogomilen über diese Frage in direktem Zusammenhang mit den konkreten Zeitverhältnissen und widerspiegeln die Unzufriedenheit, die sich im zehnten Jahrhundert unter jenen Schichten der bulgarischen Gesellschaft verbreitete, die das prächtige und behagliche Leben der Vertreter der weltlichen und geistlichen Aristokratie nicht mit wohlwollendem Auge betrachteten.

Ein großes Interesse rufen zweifellos die Auffassungen der Bogomilen bezüglich der kirchlichen Rituale und Symbole und der Rolle der Geistlichkeit hervor. Auch hier zeigt sich das klar ausgeprägte Bestreben alles das zu verleugnen, welches als offizielle Auffassung angenommen wurde. Im Gegensatz zu den andauernd verbreiteten Predigten, daß der Gläubige eine Reihe von Ritualen befolgen muß, wie z.B. die Kommunion, die Taufe, die kirchliche Trauung, die Beichte usw., daß er das Kreuz, die Ikonen und die Reliquien der Heiligen verehren, den kirchlichen Gottesdienst besuchen und die kirchliche Liturgie anhören muß, treten die Häretiker mit der Behauptung auf, daß die Erfüllung aller dieser Verpflichtungen nicht notwendig ist und mehr sogar, daß die erwähnten Rituale und Sakramente überflüssig sind und nicht zur Rettung der Seele beitragen. Wir finden ausführliche Angaben über diese Auffassungen der Häretiker in dem Werk *Besedata* von Präsbyter Kosma, in der antihäretischen Abhandlung des bereits erwähnten Euthymios von Akmonia, in der *Panoplia Dogmatica* von Euthymios Zygabenos, in der 'Synodik' des bulgarischen Zaren Boril aus dem Jahre 1211, in den Briefen des Patriarchen von Nikäa Germanus der I. (1222-1240) und in anderen antibogomilischen Schriften. Als Hauptargument der Bogomilen diente ihre Grundauffassung, daß die Materie eine Schöpfung und Manifestation der bösen Macht ist und daß in diesem Sinne die verschiedenen Rituale, wie die Kommunion, die Taufe usw., sowie die Verehrung der Ikonen, des Kreuzes, der Reliquien usw., ihrem Wesen nach einen Dienst zu Gunsten des Satans darstellen. Das ist die eine Seite der häretischen Beweisführung, die in einem direkten Zusammenhang mit ihrer dualistischen Weltauffassung steht. Gleichzeitig damit bedienen sich die Bogomilen auch Argumente anderer Art, die eine einfachere und nüchternere Art der Beurteilung zeigen und sich direkt dem für die Erläuterung der kirchlichen Rituale und Symbole charakteristischen religiösen Mystizismus entgegensetzen. Die Häretiker behaupten z.B., daß die Taufe nichts anderes als gewöhnliches Wasser und Öl und die Kommunion ein gewöhnliches Brot und Wein seien. Sie predigen ferner, daß das Kreuz ein gewöhnliches Stück Holz sei und erklären, daß die Reliquien der Heiligen einfach Knochen von Toten seien, ähnlich den Knochen der toten Tiere, sie behaupten weiter, daß die Tempel gewöhnliche Gebäude seien und daß die 'Wunder', die nach dem Evangelium Christus gemacht hat, nur 'Erzählungen' ('Märchen' und 'Fabeln') seien. Der Abgrund zwischen diesen Anschauungen der Häretiker und den Anschauungen der offiziellen Kirche sind so augenscheinlich, daß es überhaupt nicht notwendig ist einen Kommentar darüber zu machen.

Nicht weniger heftig ist das Zerwürfnis zwischen den Bogomilen und der orthodoxen Kirche bezüglich der Rolle der Geistlichkeit. Im Gegensatz zur wohlbekannten und verbreiteten Auffassung, daß 'der Geistliche ein Diener Gottes ist und daß seine Vermittlerrolle zwischen dem Gläubigen und Gott erforderlich ist', behaupten die Bogomilen-Prediger, daß dies nicht notwendig ist und daß der Gläubige auf eigenem Weg, ohne die Einmischung eines speziellen geistlichen Standes, seine Verpflichtungen gegenüber Gott erfüllen und die Rettung seiner Seele erlangen kann. 'Was stellt eigentlich der Priester dar, er ist überhaupt überflüssig', erklärten die Bogomilen in Kleinasien ihren Zuhörern, wie Euthymios von Akmonia in seiner schon erwähnten Schrift gegen die Häresie der Bogomilen berichtet.

Eine Reihe von Zitaten im Zusammenhang mit dem feindlichen Verhältnis der Bogomilen gegenüber der Geistlichkeit sind in der Abhandlung von Präsbyter Kosma *Besedata* (Die Rede gegen die Bogomilen) enthalten. Eines der Hauptargumente, mit denen die Bogomilen ihre Feindseligkeit gegen den geistlichen Stand und besonders gegen den hohen Klerus begründeten und die Notwendigkeit ihrer Tätigkeit verleugnen, war folgendes : die Geistlichen seien von ihren Verpflichtungen abgegangen und stehen nicht auf jener moralischen Höhe, für die sich der Apostel Paulus in seinen Schriften eingesetzt hat. Sie haben dabei seine Worte zitiert : 'Der Bischof muß makellos sein, Mann einer Frau, nüchtern, ehrlich, keusch, gastfreundlich und belehrend, keinen Schaden anrichten, sanft, kein Zänker, nicht goldgierig, sondern ein guter Leiter seines Hauses sein. Wir sehen jedoch nicht, fügten die Bogomilen hinzu, daß ihr solche seid'. Aus dieser Kritik der Häretiker ist klar ersichtlich, daß ihrer Meinung nach kein Unterschied zwischen den Worten und den Taten bestehen darf und daß der Priester nicht einzig und allein wegen seiner Funktionen als Diener Gottes geachtet werden muß, falls seine Lebensart und seine Taten nicht würdig und von Tugend erfüllt sind.

Der beschränkte Charakter des Aufsatzes erlaubt mir nicht auch auf einige andere Anschauungen der Bogomilen einzugehen, wie z.B. ihre Predigt gegen das Blutvergießen und die Kriege, die Ablehnung der kirchlichen Ehe usw. Jedoch ist es auch schon von den bisherigen Darlegungen ziemlich klar, daß die Lehre der Bogomilen ihrem Charakter nach eine völlige Ablehnung des im bulgarischen mittelalterlichen Staat herrschenden System von offiziell angenommenen Thesen und Auffassungen darstellt. Diese offiziellen Thesen und Auffassungen besitzen, wie schon gesagt, einen komplexen Charakter und enthalten, gleichzeitig mit den stark ausgedrückten und vorherrschenden religiösen und theologischen Ansichten auch soziale und politische Elemente (wie z.B. die Idee der von Gott festgesetzten königlichen Macht und das Vorhandensein von Armen und Reichen als eine natürliche Erscheinung, die nicht den religiösen Dogmen entspricht). Einen derartig komplexen Charakter wie die kirchliche Ideologie, besitzt auch die Häresie der Bogomilen, die als Antipode dieser Ideologie im mittelalterlichen Bulgarien auftritt. Auch in der Lehre der Bogomilen spielen religiöse und theologische Konzeptionen eine grundsätzliche und erstrangige Rolle, wie dies aus der Kosmogenie, der Christologie und der Eschatalogie der Häretiker ersichtlich ist, d.h. aus ihren Lehren über die Erschaffung der Welt, die Mission Christi und das jüngste Gericht. Jedoch gleichzeitig mit der religiösen Seite bestehen in den Auffassungen der Bogomilen ganz klar ausgedrückte politische und soziale Elemente (Kritik gegen die Könige und Bojaren, Angriffe gegen die Reichen, feindliche Stellungnahme gegen die Kriege usw.). Kurz gesagt, einer ihrem Charakter nach komplexen Ideologie widersetzt sich eine andere ihrem Inhalt nach ebenfalls komplexe Ideologie. Das ist nämlich die Häresie der Bogomilen.

Wie aus unseren Darlegungen ersichtlich ist, versteht man also in diesem Falle unter Häresie eine religiös-soziale Bewegung, die nicht nur von den offiziellen Dogmen der griechisch-orthodoxen Kirche abweicht, sondern auch von solchen Prinzipien, auf denen die Staatsordnung und die gesellschaftlich-politische Struktur beruht. In diesem

Sinne war die Häresie der Bogomilen im gleichen Grade, sowohl für die Kirche, als auch für die weltliche Macht gefährlich. Es ist deshalb kein Zufall, daß schon von Anfang an erbitterte Verfolgungen gegen ihre Anhänger beginnen. Solche Verfolgungen gab es schon zur Zeit des Königs Peter, als der Priester Bogomil auftrat und sein Wirken begann. Verfolgungen gegen die Bogomilen finden auch während der byzantinischen Herrschaft (11.-12.Jh.) statt, wobei auch einer ihrer Hauptprediger Basileios auf dem Scheiterhaufen verbrannt wurde und zwar während der Regierung des byzantinischen Kaisers Alexeos I. Komnen (im Jahre 1111). Die Bogomilen werden in Bulgarien auch Anfang des dreizehnten Jahrhunderts Verfolgungen unterworfen, nachdem eine spezielle Kirchenversammlung, unter dem Vorsitz von König Boril (1211), in der Hauptstadt Tarnovo einberufen wurde. Auch im nächsten Jarhundert finden Verfolgungen gegen die Häretiker statt. Die heftige Reaktion gegen das Bogomilentum kann dadurch erklärt werden, daß diese Häresie nicht nur eine Abweichung von dem orthodoxen Christentum östlicher Art darstellt, sondern gleichzeitig auch eine Bedrohung für die Vertreter der weltlichen Macht war.

Wenn wir über das Bogomilentum als eine bestimmte Art der 'Häresie' sprechen, so sind wir freilich nicht berechtigt nur auf Grund dieser Lehre den Gesamtbegriff 'Häresie' zu definieren, den wir sehr oft im Mittelalter, sowohl in West-, als auch in Osteuropa begegnen. Das Bogomilentum ist eigentlich nur eine der möglichen Varianten der verschiedenen 'Häresien', ich würde sogar sagen die ihrem Inhalt und ihrer Rolle nach radikalste häretische Bewegung, die sich mit gleicher Stärke, sowohl gegen die kirchliche Institution, als auch gegen die Staatsinstitution richtet. Es gibt jedoch im Mittelalter in Südosteuropa zweifelsohne auch andere Varianten der 'Häresien', die einen beschränkteren Charakter besitzen und nicht den Rahmen der rein religiös-theologischen Konzeptionen und der religiös-theologischen Art des Denkens und Bewertens überschreiten. Als ein Beispiel für solche Häresien können wir die im vierten und fünften Jahrhundert im Bereich des Oströmischen Reiches auftretenden Häresien angeben, in denen, wie bekannt, die Lösung der Streitfragen bezüglich der Natur Christi, des Wesens der Dreifaltigkeit und der Wechselbeziehungen zwischen ihren drei Bestandteilen gestellt wurde. Es handelt sich hier wie bekannt um die Häresien der Arianer, Savelianer, Monophysiten, Nestorianer u.a., die ihrem Wesen nach verschiedene Abweichungen vom Symbol des orthodoxen Glaubens darstellen, das auf der ersten ökumenischen Kirchenversammlung in Nikäa

im Jahre 325 festgesetzt wurde. Es handelt sich um Häresien mit rein
religiös-philosophischer Grundlage, welche die unter der Geistlichkeit
eingedrungenen Meinungsverschiedenheiten widerspiegeln. Wir wissen
jedoch, daß diese Lehren unter bestimmten Umständen den Rahmen
des theoretischen Streites überschreiten konnten und sich als Bewegungen entfalteten, die tiefere Gegensätze, außerhalb der Sphäre des kirchlichen Lebens und der theologischen Kämpfe widerspiegeln. Als Beispiel dafür können wir den Monophysitismus angeben, der sich, wie
das gut bekannt ist, in eine Religion der separatistisch gestimmten
Kreise in der oströmischen Provinz Ägypten verwandelte, die darauf
bestrebt waren sich von der zentralen Macht loszureißen. Das ist sozu-
sagen eine *sekundäre Rolle* bestimmter Häresien, die nicht in direktem
Zusammenhang mit ihrem inneren Wesen steht und die von der Einwirkung anderer Faktoren, vornehmlich sozial-politischer oder ethnischer
Art, bedingt wird.

Wenn wir von der 'sekundären Rolle' der Häresien sprechen, so dürfen
wir nicht auch die Frage der historischen Entwicklung einer jeden Häresie
außer Acht lassen, d.h. wir müssen die Häresie nicht als eine ständige und
unveränderliche Gegebenheit betrachten. Ich möchte hier erneut konkret
auf das Bogomilentum in Bulgarien eingehen. Wie wir schon gesehen
haben, hat diese mittelalterliche bulgarische Häresie eine negative
Einstellung gegenüber der Staatsorganisation und ihren Vertretern
(Könige, Bojaren, zivile und militärische Würdenträger u.a.). Diese
Einstellung der Bogomilen ist besonders stark im Laufe des zehnten
Jahrhunderts ausgedrückt, als ihr Begründer, der Priester Bogomil,
seine Predigten hält. Wie bekannt, fällt jedoch im Jahre 1018 der bulgarische Staat unter der byzantinischen Gewalt und in den bulgarischen
Ländern lassen sich die Vertreter der Administration von Konstantinopel
nieder. Die byzantinische Herrschaft dauert fast 200 Jahre und zwar
bis zum Jahre 1185. Was geschieht während dieser Zeit mit den Bogo-
len in Bulgarien? Aus den Quellenangaben können wir eine sehr interessante Veränderung in den Auffassungen der Häretiker feststellen.
Bei der neuen Lage der Dinge erhalten jetzt ihre Ansichten einen viel
eindeutigeren politischen Charakter und sind scharf gegen Byzanz
gerichtet. Die Bogomilen betrachten jetzt als ihren Hauptfeind den
romäischen Basileus und behaupten, daß die böse Macht - *Satanas* -
sich in der Patriarchenkirche von Konstantinopel niedergelassen und
dort seinen Hauptsitz hat, d.h. im Zentrum des Byzantinischen Reiches
(siehe darüber den entsprechenden Text in der *Panoplia Dogmatica*

von Euthymios Zygalenos). Gleichzeitig, im Unterschied zur ehemaligen ablehnenden Stellung zu den bulgarischen Königen (Simeon,
Peter u.a.) predigen jetzt die Bogomilen, daß in den Grenzen des ehemaligen freien bulgarischen Staates das Leben viel leichter und angeneh-
mer war, daß es damals keine schweren Steuern und Einschränkungen
gab, daß eine Fülle von Lebensmitteln vorhanden war, usw. Diese
Auffassungen der Bogomilen sind in dem bekannten bulgarischen Werk
Apokrifen Letopis (Apokryphe Chronik) aus der Mitte des elften Jahrhunderts enthalten. Wir können folglich daraus ersehen, wie die verän-
derten sozial-politischen Verhältnisse während der byzantinischen Herrschaft eine klar ausgedrückte Widerspiegelung auf das Wesen der
Bogomilen-Häresie ausüben. Ohne seine grundsätzlichen dualistischen
Konzeptionen aufzugeben, wendet das Bogomilentum das dualistische
Prinzip auf eine sehr konkrete Art und Weise an : Diener des Satans
sind jetzt nur die byzantinischen weltlichen und geistlichen Machthaber, während die ehemaligen bulgarischen Herrscher in einem idea-
lisierten Licht dargestellt werden und behauptet wird, daß während ihrer
Herrschaft Ruhe und Wohlsein herrschten. Zweifellos ist dieses Beispiel
sehr bezeichnend. Ich führe dieses Beispiel an, um zu zeigen, daß bei
der wissenschaftlichen Bewertung einer gegebenen Häresie stets ihre
Entwicklung und ihre Rolle in den verschiedenen Perioden und unter
verschiedenen historischen Situationen berücksichtigt werden muß, d.h.
daß man bei einer solchen Schätzung stets den notwendigen Historismus
bei der Untersuchung anwenden muß. Ich glaube, daß dies auch für
die Bewertung anderer mittelalterlicher Häresien und insbesondere für
die Bewertung des Katharismus in Frankreich und Italien gilt.

Wichtigere Quellen

*Euthymii monachi coenobii Peribleptae epistula invectiva contra Phunda-
giagitos sive Bogomilos haereticos*, herausgegeben von Gerhard Ficker
in *Die Phundagiagiten* (Leipzig, 1908). S. 3-86.
Попруженко М.Г., Синодик царя Борила (Български старини VIII)
София 1928 г.
Попруженко М.Г., Козма пресвитер болгарский писател X века
(Български старини XII) София 1936 г.
Иванов Й., Богомилски книги и легенди, София 1925 г.

Zigabenos, *De haeresi Bogomilorim narratio*, herausgegeben von Gerhard
Ficker in *Die Phundagiagiten* (Leipzig, 1908), S : 89-111.

Literatur

Angelov Dimiter, 'Der Bogomilismus auf dem Gebiete des byzantini-
schen Reiches : Ursprung, Wesen und Geschichte', *Jahrbuch der Sofioter
Universität, Hist.- Phil. Fak.*, B. XI IV (1947-48) ; B. XI VI (1949-50)
Ангелов Д., Богомилството в България, София 1969 г. с. 1-562.
Obolensky Dimitri, *The Bogomils : A study in Balkan Neo-manichaism*
(Cambridge, 1948)
Vaillant André und Puech Henri-Charles, *Le traité contre les Bogomiles
du prêtre Cosmos*, Travaux publiés par l'Institut des Etudes Slaves, 21
(Paris, 1948).

Stanisław Trawkowski

ENTRE L'ORTHODOXIE ET L'HÉRÉSIE :
VITA APOSTOLICA ET LE PROBLÈME
DE LA DÉSOBÉISSANCE

Dès les débuts du onzième siècle, les nouveaux ordres et les nouvelles congrégations se multipliaient. Leur accroissement rapide dans les premières dizaines d'années du siècle suivant provoqua l'inquiétude dans les milieux épris de tradition. C'est à eux qu'Anselme de Havelberg adressa les phrases ironiques : 'Beaucoup s'étonnent et se font des problèmes, engendrant scandale pour eux et pour les autres ; ils interrogent en inquisiteurs calomnieux : Pourquoi toutes ces nouveautés dans l'Eglise de Dieu? Pourquoi ces ordres nouveaux? ... Qui ne méprisera une religion chrétienne soumise à tant de variations, changée par tant d'inventions, ballottée par tant de nouvelles lois et par des coutumes presque chaque année innovées?' La polémique concernait les relations entre les ordres, tout d'abord entre les bénédictins et les chanoines réguliers du type nouveau mais la thèse générale d'Anselme cachait un sens plus profond : 'semper est eadem fides credendi, non semper est eadem forma vivendi'. Anselme arrange toute son argumentation pour démontrer 'quomodo Ecclesia Dei sit una in se et secundum se, et quomodo sit multiformis secundum filios suos', ce qui se réalise surtout par la 'mutatio de generatione in generationem' [1].

En fait les mêmes transformations sociales constituaient la base sur laquelle se formaient les nouveaux ordres religieux et les nouveaux groupes hérétiques qui se servaient du mot d'ordre identique, stéréotype : *vita apostolica*. Les rapports entre ces deux sont évidents, néanmoins en faisant l'analyse de ces deux groupes, on se heurte toujours à d'énormes difficultés. Pour ne pas se laisser entraîner à des simplifications, bien que parfois très suggestives dans leur présentation, il faut

---

[1] Anselme de Havelberg, *Liber de una forma credendi et multiformitate vivendi*, dans Migne, PL, 188, col. 1141, 1143, 1160; cf. Georg Schreiber, 'Studien über Anselm von Havelberg. Zur Geistesgeschichte des Hochmittelalters', *Analecta Praemonstratensia*, 18 (1942), p. 5-90.

de temps en temps se rappeler les résultats des recherches historiques qui sont, d'ailleurs, bien connus [2].

L'idéal de la pauvreté volontaire connaissait une nouvelle vague au dixième siècle et fut propagé par la 'Vie de Saint Alexis', copiée dans les couvents en Catalogne et devenue populaire à Rome, où l'abbaye sur l'Aventin dédia son église à ce saint.

Le même idéal fut propagé en Provence par la 'Vie de Saint Gilles'. Ces deux noms - Alexis et Gilles - inventés par les auteurs des légendes, excitaient la curiosité par la nouveauté et l'exotisme. La Vie de Saint Alexis a une grande valeur littéraire ; l'action dramatique qui abonde en péripéties inattendues, encourageait les remaniements, dont la version polonaise du quatorzième siècle occupe une place honorable [3]. Mais ce n'est pas la valeur artistique des légendes qui a influencé le développement du culte de ces deux saints ; c'est avant tout leur idéologie, bien qu'il y ait dissemblance. St. Alexis, homme de Dieu, pratiquait la pauvreté volontaire comme mendiant ; tandis que St. Gilles était ermite, selon la tradition chrétienne, antique et orientale [4].

Au dixième siècle, on avait entrepris dans plusieurs centres de combiner les modes de vie monastique et de vie érémitique. N'y cherchons pas une tentative pour faire revivre l'esprit original de la Règle de St. Benoît, qui était d'avis que la vie cénobitique structurée constitue une prépara-

---

[2] Outre la thèse de Herbert Grundmann, *Religiöse Bewegungen im Mittelalter* : *Untersuchungen über die geschichtlichen Zusammenhänge zwischen der Ketzerei, den Bettelorden und der religiösen Frauenbewegung im 12. und 13. Jht und über die geschichtlichen Grundlagen der deutschen Mystik*, Historische Studien, 267 (Berlin, 1935), réimpression complétée et corrigée avec un suplément : *Neue Beiträge zur Geschichte der religiösen Bewegungen im Mittelalter* (Darmstadt, 1961), on consultera : Marie Dominique Chenu, 'Moines, clercs, laïcs au carrefour de la vie évangélique (XIIe s.)', *Revue d'histoire ecclésiastique*, 49 (1954), p. 59-89 ; Marie-Humbert Vicaire, *L'imitation des apôtres* : *Moines, chanoines, mendiants (IVe-XIIIe siècles)*, (Paris, 1963); Tadeusz Manteuffel, *Narodziny herezji* : *Wyznawcy dobrowolnego ubóstwa w średniowieczu* (Warszawa, 1963), deuxième édition 1964, traductions : *Die Geburt der Ketzerei*, Geist und Gesellschaft (Wien-Frankfort-Zurich, 1965) et *Naissance d'une hérésie* : *Les adeptes de la pauvreté volontaire au moyen âge*, traduit par Anna Posner, Civilisations et sociétés, 6 (Paris-La Haye, 1970); *Hérésies et sociétés dans l'Europe pré-industrielle, 11e-18e siècles* : *Communications et débats du colloque de Royaumont* présentés par Jacques Le Goff (Paris-La Haye, 1968).

[3] Carlo Verdiani, 'Il ritmo polacco su Sant'Alessio (1454)', *Ricerche Slavistiche*, 15 (1967) et 16 (1968).

[4] Aleksander Gieysztor, 'Dobrowolne ubóstwo, ucieczka od świata i średniowieczny kult św. Aleksego' [La pauvreté volontaire, la fuite du monde et le culte de Saint Alexis au moyen âge] dans *Polska w świecie* (Warszawa, 1972), p. 21-40.

tion nécessaire à la *perfectio conversationis*, c'est à dire à la *singularis pugna heremi*. En 1005, Bruno de Querfurt, un des disciples de Romuald, définit le nouvel idéal : 'tota anima nudus sequere Christum'[5], en y soulignant clairement le conseil évangélique de la pauvreté volontaire comme condition de la vie parfaite. Sa formule suggère aussi l'idée de St. Jérome et exprime le sens évangélique en termes identiques : 'nudum Christum nudus sequere'[6]. Au tournant du onzième au douzième siècle cette parole exerça une énorme influence sur les prédicateurs itinérants et sur leurs disciples. Plusieurs auteurs préconisaient alors que ce nouveau courant des dernières années du onzième siècle, n'était en somme que la continuation de la tradition, continuation créatrice il est vrai, mais poussée jusqu'au radicalisme.

Vers la moitié du onzième siècle le mot d'ordre *vita apostolica* fut formulé. Son trait caractéristique était la vie en commun des chanoines. C'est à eux qu'en 1059 et 1063, les synodes de Rome adressèrent l'appel 'ut ad apostolicam, communem scilicet vitam summopere pervenire studeant'. En même temps on suggérait que la communauté des chanoines devait être 'ad instar primitivae Ecclesiae'[7]. Ici on faisait appel à la Règle de St. Isidore de Séville qui recommandait aux moines 'ut aposto-

---

[5] Bruno Querfurtensis, *Vita quinque fratrum eremitarum*, éditée par Jadwiga Karwasińska, Mon. Poloniae Hist., ser. nova, II, t. IV, fasc. 3 (Warszawa, 1973), p. 34: expensa pecunia quam mihi [sc. Ottoni III] mater pro hereditate reliquit, tota anima nudus sequar Christum.

[6] *Ad rusticum monachum*, PL, 22, col. 1085; cf. Karwasińska, p. 34, n. 51.

[7] Outre l'article de Charles Dereine, 'Chanoines : des origines au XIIIᵉ siècle', dans DHGE, 12, col. 353-405 voir du même : 'Vie commune, règle de St. Augustin et chanoines réguliers au XIᵉ siècle', *Revue d'histoire ecclésiastique*, 41 (1946), p. 365-406; 'Le problème de la vie commune chez les canonistes d'Anselme de Lucques à Gratian', dans *Studi Gregoriani*, 3 (Roma, 1948), p. 287-298; *Les chanoines réguliers au diocèse de Liège avant St. Norbert*, Mémoires de l'académie royale de Belgique, Classe des lettres, coll. in 8°, XLVII, 1 (Bruxelles, 1952); 'La prétendue règle de Grégoire VII pour chanoines réguliers', *Revue bénédictine*, 71 (1961), p. 108-118; John Dickinson, *The Origins of the Austin Canons and their Introduction into England*, Publications of the Church Historical Society (London, 1950); Jakob Mois, *Das Stift Rottenbuch in der Kirchenreform des XI.-XII. Jhts.* : *Ein Beitrag zur Ordensgeschichte der Augustiner-Chorherren*, Beiträge zur altbayerischen Kirchengeschichte, 19 (Münich, 1953); *La vita comune del clero nei secoli XI e XII*, Atti della I settimana internazionale di studio, Mendola, settembre 1959, Pubblicazioni della Università Cattolica del Sacro Cuore, serie III, 3 (Milano, 1962); Josef Siegwart, *Die Chorherren- und Chorfrauengemeinschaften in der deutschsprächigen Schweiz vom 6. Jht. bis 1160* : *Mit einem Überblick über die Kanonikerreform des 10. und 11. Jht.*, Studia Friburgensia, N. F. 30 (Freiburg in Sch., 1962).

licam vitam tenentes, sicut in unum constituti esse noscuntur, ita cor habeant unum, nihil sibi proprium vindicantes... sed, iuxta exemplum apostolicum, omnia communia habentes' [8].

Les difficultés initales de la réforme, les obstacles qui ont obligé à suspendre l'action de Grégoire VII, les succès partiels de la réforme, souvent obtenus au prix de compromis, sont des facteurs qui ne pouvaient que provoquer le scepticisme et la frustration. Il en fut de même pour ce qui concerne le contraste entre les idéaux et la réalité. C'est là, semble-t-il, qu'il faut chercher la cause principale pour laquelle certains quittèrent le monde et le monastère pour se réfugier au désert [9]. Le nombre de ces fuites augmentait au dernier quart du siècle et le renom des ermites attirait ceux qui cherchaient la consolation ou la solution à leurs doutes. Certains ermites tendaient consciemment à créer des colonies érémitiques. Ceux qui cherchaient à s'initier à cette vie se groupaient pour la plupart spontanément autour de leur maître et de pareils groupes furent bien souvent à l'origine d'ordres nouveaux. Ainsi l'ermitage de Jean Gualbert, fondé aux environs de Florence vers 1093, a donné naissance à l'ordre de Vallombreuse et celui d'Etienne à Muret est devenu l'ordre de Grandmont. Les disciples d'Eugibald (mort probablement en 1122) fondèrent la congrégation d'Hérival. Ainsi un petit ermitage fut le berceau de la congrégation d'Arrouaise [10].

Certains ermites quittaient leur désert pour s'engager dans l'un ou l'autre apostolat. Ce fut le cas de Pierre d'Amiens, qui quitta son ermi-

---

[8] Isidorus, *Regula monachorum*, PL, 83, col. 870.

[9] *L'eremitismo in occidente nei secoli XI e XII*, Atti della II settimana internazionale di studio, Mendola, 1962, Pubblicazioni della Università Cattolica del Sacro Cuore, serie III, (Milano, 1965); Charles Dereine, 'Odon de Tournai et la crise du cénobitisme au XIe siècle', *Revue du moyen âge latin*, 4 (1948), p. 137-154.

[10] Voir par exemple : Roger Duvernay, 'Citeaux, Vallombreuse et Etienne Harding', *Analecta Sacri Ordinis Cisterciensis*, 8 (1952), p. 379-495; Jean Becquet, article 'Etienne de Muret', dans *Dictionnaire de Spiritualité*, 4 (1961), col. 1504-1514; du même, *Scriptores ordinis Grandimontensis*, Corpus Christianorum, Continuatio Mediaevalis, 8 (Turnholti, 1968); Bernard Bligny, 'Les premiers Chartreux et la pauvreté', *Le moyen âge*, 57 (1951), p. 27-60; du même, *L'église et les ordres religieux dans le royaume de Bourgogne aux XIe et XIIe siècles* (Grenoble, 1960); Ludo Milis, *L'ordre des chanoines réguliers d'Arrouaise : Son histoire et son organisation, de la fondation de l'abbaye-mère (vers 1090) à la fin des chapitres annuels (1471)*, Werken uitgegeven door de faculteit der letteren en wijsbegeerte der Rijksuniversiteit te Gent, 147 en 148 (Brugge, 1969); Ferdinand Pauly, *Springiersbach : Geschichte des Kanonikerstifts und seiner Tochtergründungen im Erzbistum Trier von den Anfängen bis zum Ende des 18. Jhts*, Trierer theologische Studien, 13 (Trier, 1962).

tage pour prêcher la première croisade. Quelques dizaines d'années plus tôt Wery, un moine de Gand, se mit au service de Grégoire VII pour traverser les pays maritimes, prêchant la nécessité de la réforme [11]. Auparavant, à Florence, Jean Gualbert et ses disciples s'efforcèrent de lutter contre le clergé simoniaque et concubinaire, indiscipliné et riche ; autour des moines se forma un mouvement populaire, semblable à la Pataria de Milan [12].

Les moines itinérants de Hirsau qui prêchaient la réforme, étaient traités en vagabonds : 'girovagi sub specie religionis discurentes, maximam ubique seminant discordiam'. La violente critique du clergé indigné souleva contre ces prédicateurs une grande animosité de la part d'une partie considérable de la hiérarchie. Ils furent traités en quasi hérétiques et on leur reprochait en outre qu'ils s'adonnaient à la prédication sans aucune autorisation.

D'autre part, Bernold de Constance fit remarquer qu'on aurait pu donner au moines la permission de faire des sermons en public : 'non nisi ordinati praedicent catholicoque obediant presuli, nisi ab apostolica sede fuerint emancipati' [13].

Robert d'Arbrissel, Bernard de Thiron, Vital de Savigni, Giraud de Sales suivirent les exemples de Hirsau, de St. Jean Gualbert et de St. Romuald. Vu la situation, le nouvel idéal stimulait le zèle pour la prédication itinérante et attirait une foule de fidèles : hommes et femmes appartenant à toutes les classes de la société du douzième siècle, mais surtout des *illiterati* et des *idiotae* qui en constituaient la majorité [14].

[11] Ch. Dereine, *Les chanoines réguliers*, p. 137-169; *Chronicon Affligemense*, dans MGH, Scriptores, 9, p. 407-417; cf. Charles Dereine, 'La spiritualité "apostolique" des premiers fondateurs d'Affligem (1083-1100)', *Revue d'histoire ecclésiastique*, 54 (1959), p. 41-65.

[12] Cinzio Violante, *La pataria milanese e la riforma ecclesiastica*, I : *Le premesse (1045-1057)*, Studi storici dell'Istituto Storico Italiano per il Medio Evo, 11-13 (Roma, 1955); Ernst Werner, *Pauperes Christi : Studien zu sozial-religiosen Bewegungen im Zeitalter des Reformpapsttums* (Leipzig, 1956).

[13] *Libelli Bernaldi presbyteri monachi*, édités par Friedrich Thaner, MGH, Libelli de Lite, 2, p. 1-168 (p. 98); cf. Ernst Werner, 'Bemerkungen zur Hirsauer Bewegung', *Wissenschaftliche Zeitschrift der Universität Leipzig*, 3 (1953), p. 9-17. Cf. Bernold de Constance, *Chronicon*, MGH, Scriptores, 5, p. 453 : His temporibus in regno Teutonicorum communis vita multis in locis floruit, non solum in clericis et monachis religiosissime commanentibus, verum etiam in laicis se et sua ad eandem communem vitam devotissime offerentibus... Quapropter invidia diaboli contra eorumdem fratrum probatissimam conversationem quosdam emulos incitavit, qui eorum vitam malevolo dente corroberent.

[14] Johannes von Walther, *Die ersten Wanderprediger Frankreichs : Studien zur Geschichte des Mönchtums*, 2 vol. (Leipzig, 1903-1906); Jean Leclercq, 'Le poème de

Les sermons de Robert d'Abrissel ont provoqué une profonde indignation dans les rangs de la hiérarchie, à cause de ses attaques contre le clergé indigne devant les 'vulgares turbas et imperitos homines' et l'évêque Marbord a accusé cette manière d'agir : 'Hoc enim non est praedicare, sed detrahere' [15]. Les disciples de Robert agissaient aussi parfois de leur propre initiative, tout en se référant à leur maître. Dans ces circonstances Robert fonda des couvents pour ses disciples et les organisa ensuite en nouveaux ordres; c'était un moyen pour éviter la rupture avec l'Église.

Un autre procédé fut suivi par le moine Henri. Il avait quitté son monastère pour se rendre dans un ermitage ; ensuite, il s'adonna à la prédication, avec la licence d'Ildebert de Laverdin, évêque du Mans, écrivain éminent et partisan de la réforme. La dite licence fut plus tard révoquée à la suite d'un conflit d'Henri avec le clergé ; mais Henri, après avoir quitté Le Mans, n'a pas renoncé à son activité. Lorsqu'on analyse le traité qui le condamne on constate qu'il faut tenir compte des exagérations non seulement possibles, mais inévitables de ses adversaires. Par exemple, Henri ne mit aucunement en doute l'essence des sacrements, mais il interdisait aux prêtres indignes le droit de les administrer [16].

Au temps de Grégoire VII on connaissait toutefois l'existence de la *simoniaca heresis*. Et au synode de Reims en 1131 on a décrété : 'placuit etiam domno apostolico et toti concilio : ne quis audiat missam presbyteri habentis concubinam vel uxorem'. Gerhoh de Reichersberg, comme plusieurs autres d'ailleurs, doutait de la validité des sacrements administrés par des prêtres simoniaques et mariés. Ici et là nous constatons l'inquiétude des âmes : tel Eugibald, un prêtre devenu ermite : 'verumtamen in aliquibus zelum Dei habuit, sed non secundum scientiam. Judicans enim se indignum sacramentis ecclesiae, contra morem ecclesiasticum instituit, in suo loco ecclesiam non construere, non celebrare missam, nusquam communicare, nec cantare psalmodiam iuxta ritum ecclesiae' [17].

Payen Bolotin contre les faux érémites', *Revue bénédictine*, 68 (1958), p. 52-86; cf. E. Werner, *Pauperes*, p. 79sq.

[15] Lettre de Marbord éditée par J. von Walter, *o.c.*, p. 181-189. Ajoutons que l'évêque n'a rien reproché à Robert au point de vue doctrinal.

[16] Raul Manselli, *Studi sulle eresie del secolo XII*, Studi storici dell' Istituto Storico Italiano per il Medio Evo, 5 (Roma, 1953), p. 1-23, 45-67; du même, 'Il monaco Enrico e la sua eresia', *Bullettino dell'Istituto Storico Italiano per il Medio Evo e Archivio Muratoriano*, 65 (1953), p. 1-63.

[17] Charles Louis Hugo, *Sacrae antiquitatis monumenta historica* (Stivagii, 1725), I,

Tant que les discussions ne dépassaient pas le cercle du clergé et des savants, les reproches ne furent pas menaçants. Mais dès que 'eos autem qui religiositatis speciem simulantes', formulaient leur critiques devant le grand public, on les comdamnait. Des prédicateurs, comme Henri, manquaient à l'obéissance envers l'autorité de l'Eglise en prêchant malgré l'interdiction imposée. C'est probablement la raison pour laquelle le problème de l'obéissance constitue le premier point du traité contre Henri. Accusé d'hérésie il est devenu un hérétique.

On pourrait encore citer d'autres exemples, comme l'affaire de Tanchelin, surtout connue grâce aux accusations des intéressés, les chanoines d'Utrecht. Toutefois, vu que l'archevêque de Cologne, ayant examiné Tanchelin, le mit en liberté et que Tanchelin fit appel au pape, les accusations devraient être examinées avec une précaution encore plus grande[18]. Dans les polémiques on abusait excessivement du terme 'hérétique' ; les contemporains s'en plaignaient.

Au synode de Fritzlar Norbert de Gennep fut accusé 'quare praedicationis officium usurpasset et quare religionis habitum praetenderet, cum adhuc de proprio vivens nondum ad religionem accessisset'. Il dut donc renoncer à la propriété privée et demander au pape la licence pour sa prédication. Après un courte période d'activité autonome, il fut obligé à fonder un ermitage où ses convertis pourraient devenir ermites. Norbert déclarait : 'pure evangelica et apostolica vita... vivere'; 'volebat autem saepefactus vir cum fratribus suis ut de laboribus manuum suarum viverant, quod nos (sc. l'évêque de Laon) impossible considerantes, dedimus...'. L'ermitage fut transformé en un monastère de chanoines réguliers, grâce à quoi les prémontrés pouvaient s'adonner à l'activité pastorale.

La similitude du modèle de vie et de l'attitude religieuse entre les membres du nouvel ordre et les disciples de Tanchelin a favorisé le succès des prémontrés à Anvers où on leur attribua l'église de l'Archange Michel.

135; cf. André Galli, 'Les origines du prieuré de Notre-Dame d'Hérival', *Revue Mabillon*, 49 (1959), p. 1-34; Michel Parisse, 'Les chanoines réguliers en Lorraine : Fondations, expansion (XIe-XIIes.)', *Annales de l'Est*, série V, 20 (1968) p. 347-388 (349-350); Jacques Choux, *Recherches sur le diocèse de Toul au temps de la réforme grégorienne : L'épiscopat de Pibon (1069-1107)*, Recueil de documents sur l'histoire de Lorraine, 23 (Nancy, 1952), p. 152-156.

[18] Herbert Grundmann, *Ketzergeschichte des Mittelalters* dans *Die Kirche in ihrer Geschichte : Ein Handbuch*, 2, Lief. G. 1, édité par Kurt Dietrich Schmidt et Ernst Wolf (Göttingen, 1963), p. 16-18. Renseignements bibliographiques récents par H. Grundmann dans *Hérésies et sociétés*.

A Ilbenstadt on interpola au milieu du douzième siècle la bulle de
1139 : 'predicandi per omnem provinciam vel modis omnibus in
vita vel morte salutem animarum operandi licentiam ab archiepiscopo
vobis concessam'. Ces tendances à traiter la *vita apostolica* comme étant
l'activité pastorale et même la prédication itinérante ajoutée à la pauvreté
volontaire, ont été réfutées dans les milieux monastiques par l'auteur
du *Dialogus inter cluniacensem monachum et cistersiensem* [19].

Au tournant du troisième au quatrième quart du douzième siècle,
l'affaire de la prédication des laïques occupait de nouveau les esprits.
Les groupes des *humiliati* existant en Lombardie dès la moitié du siècle,
voulaient participer à la lutte contre les hérésies et à la réforme de l'Eglise.
Le même but fut poursuivi par Valdès et ses adeptes - *pauperes spiritu* -.
L'initiative Lyonnaise n'a pas réussi, bien que rien ne suggère que l'in-
succès ait été causé par des erreurs dogmatiques, comme le suppose
Etienne de Bourbon, d'ailleurs bien informé sur les débuts de l'activité
de Valdès. L'interdiction de l'archevêque de s'adonner à la prédication,
était sans doute la révocation de la licence qui fut donnée à Valdès et
à ses *pauperes*. 'Magister eorum, usurpans Petri officium, sicut ipse
respondit principibus sacerdotum, ait : Obedire oportet magis Deo,
quam hominibus qui preceperat apostolis : Predicate evangelium omni
creature' [20]. C'est l'argumentation dont Henri s'est servi lorsqu'il se
défendait contre le reproche de désobéissance.

[19] Charles Dereine, 'Les origines de Prémontré', *Revue d'histoire ecclésiastique*
42 (1947), p. 352-378; du même, 'Le premier ordo de Prémontré', *Revue bénédictine*,
58 (1948), p. 84-92; Georg Schreiber, 'Praemonstratenserkultur des 12. Jhts.', *Analecta Praemonstratensia*, 16 (1940), p. 41-107 et 17 (1941), p. 5-33 ; François Petit,
La spiritualité des prémontrés aux XIIᵉ et XIIIᵉ siècles, Etudes de théologie et d'histoire
de la spiritualité, 10 (Paris, 1947); I.J. Van de Westelaken, 'Premonstratenser wetge-
ving : 1120-65', *Analecta Praemonstratensia*, 38 (1962), p. 7-42; Stanisław Trawkowski,
Między herezją a ortodoksją : Rola społeczna premonstratensów w XII w. | Res. :
Entre l'hérésie et l'orthodoxie : Le rôle social des prémontrés au XIIᵉ siècle/(Warszawa,
1964).

[20] Christine Thouzellier, *Catharisme et Valdéisme en Languedoc à la fin du XIIᵉ
et au début du XIIIᵉ siècle* (Paris, 1962), deuxième édition (Louvain-Paris, 1969);
Kurt Victor Selge, *Die ersten Waldenser : Mit Edition des Liber Antiheresis des Durandus
von Osca*, Arbeiten zur Kirchengeschichte, 37, 2 vol. (Berlin, 1967); *Vaudois langue-
dociens et pauvres catholiques*, Cahiers de Fanjeaux, 2 (Toulouse, 1967); Christine
Thouzellier, *Hérésie et hérétiques : Vaudois, Cathares, Patarins, Albigeois*, Storia
e letteratura, 116 (Roma, 1969); *Quellen zur Geschichte der Waldenser*, édité par
Alexander Patschkovsky et Kurt-Victor Selge, Texte zur Kirchen- und Theologiegeschichte, 18 (Gütersloh, 1973); Albert Lecoy de la Marche, *Anecdotes historiques*,
légendes et apologues, tirés du recueil inédit d'Etienne de Bourbon, Société de l'histoire
de France, 185 (Paris, 1877), I, 292.

Il ne s'agissait là ni de problèmes dogmatiques, ni du droit des laïques de s'adonner à la prédication : l'interdiction générale admettait toujours la possibilité d'une exemption de la règle, pourvu que les laïques prédicateurs obéissent aux évêques et aux prêtres, et que 'sermo eorum sit sale sapientiae conditus' comme l'écrivait Bernard de Fontcaude dans son traité contre les vaudois [21].

La condamnation des pauvres de Lyon par le pape frappait aussi les *humiliati*. Parmi leurs erreurs communes Lucius III énuméra en premier lieu (1184) : 'omnes, qui vel prohibiti vel non missi, praeter auctoritatem ab apostolica sede vel ab episcopo loci susceptam, publice vel privatim praedicare praesumpserint... vinculo perpetui anathematis innodamus' [22].

La facilité avec laquelle les *humiliati* furent réincorporés dans l'Eglise sous Innocent III prouve clairement qu'il ne s'agissait pas là de questions dogmatiques. Les vaudois se trouvaient dans une situation plus difficile, car leur conflit avec l'Eglise venait de leurs idées erronées en matière de la foi.

Voici comment mon maître et professeur, le regretté Tadeusz Manteuffel a posé le problème :

> Au Moyen-Age, toute minorité idéologique risquait d'encourir l'anathème et d'être considérée d'emblée comme une hérésie. Tout dépendait, en fait, des relations établies par cette minorité avec les autorités de l'Eglise. Le refus de se soumettre aux décisions de ces autorités entraînait inévitablement l'arrêt de condamnation et la minorité récalcitrante devenait une hérésie. En revanche, une soumission complète aux pouvoirs ecclésiastiques garantissait une certaine tolérance pour les opinions de la minorité en question. C'est ainsi qu'il devient extrêmement ardu de tracer la limite exacte, dans bien des cas, entre l'orthodoxie et l'hétérodoxie. Il a fallu un temps, quelquefois très long, pour procéder à une différen-

---

[21] Migne, PL, 204, col. 812 : Et quoniam de laicis questio est, an verbum Dei seminare valeant in populis, distinguendum est : an sint catholici vel non. Nimirum, si sint catholici et honestas vitae eos commendet; si sermo eorum sit sale sapientiae conditus et iuxta capacitatem singulorum verbi mensuram dispensare noverint, secundum quantitatem profectus sui in scientia vel opere, ad nutum episcoporum vel presbyterorum, in quorum territorio fuerint, proximos exhortari, ut arbitror, poterunt, si tamen uxoribus alligati non fuerint, nec eos pondus terrenae sollicitudinis oppressit.

[22] Lev Platonovich Karsavin, *Očerki religioznoi žizni v Italii* XII-XIII vv. (Petersburg, 1912); Stanisław Bylina, *Wizje społeczne w herezjach średniowiecznych : humiliaci, begini, begardzi/* deutsch. Zusammenfas. : Die gesellschaftlichen Vorstellungen in den mittelalterlichen Häresien : Humiliaten, Beginen und Begharden/ (Wrocław, 1974).

ciation convenable des idées et pour définir l'essence même de la doctrine hérétique ... L'hérésie ne sait pas, du moins elle ne constitue pas toujours une doctrine hérétique par son essence, mais elle se forme ou plutôt elle est formée par des circonstances extérieures [23].

Il semble, en apparence, qu'il s'agissait au début d'une faute de conduite, donc d'un péché, et non pas d'une erreur en matière de foi. C'était le fil du raisonnement d'Alanus ab Insulis quand il constatait qu'un laïque, en préchant malgré l'interdiction, commet un péché mortel - mortaliter peccat - [24].

Bernard de Fontcaude fut d'un autre avis lorsqu'il rappela contre les vaudois les mots de Samuel : 'Quicumque etiam inobedientes sunt, infideles esse convincuntur' [25]. C'est la pensée de Grégoire VII : 'inobedientes Samuele prophete testante scelus incurrunt idolatrie, sine qua, videlicet obedientia, sicut beatus Gregorius in ultimo Moralium libro declarat, infidelis quisque convicitur, eciamsi fidelis esse videatur' [26]. Or, d'après Etienne de Bourbon 'hi ergo - Valdensis videlicet et sui - primo ex presumpcione et officii apostolici usurpacione ceciderunt in [1°] inobedienciam, deinde in [2°] contumaciam, deinde in [3°] excommunicionis sentenciam' [27]. La désobéissance était alors, selon Etienne, le choix - le jugement erroné de l'intelligence.

Or, on a lancé contre les adeptes de la *vita apostolica* la sanction prononcée jadis contre les partisans de Henri IV : 'Ereticum esse constat qui Romane ecclesie non concordat' [28].

[23] T. Manteuffel, *Naissance d'une hérésie*, dans *Hérésies et sociétés*, p. 100.

[24] Migne, PL, 210, col. 282.

[25] Migne, PL, 210, col. 797.

[26] *Registrum Gregorii VII*, édité par Erich Caspar in MGH, Epistolae, 2 (Berolini, 1920-23), p. 626.

[27] Lecoy, p. 292.

[28] *Registrum*, p. 504. Cf. p. ex. Anselme de Havelberg, *Dialogi*,PL, 188, col. 1226 : Certum est igitur et nulli, qui sani sit capitis, dubium, quod sicut una est Ecclesia, ita unius Ecclesiae unum caput est in terris, et hic est Romanus Pontifex, quem non solum auctoritas humani imperii, sed majestas divini judicii principaliter omnibus praeesse voluit, cuius quidem formam et institutionem maxime in ecclesiasticis sacramentis oportet omnes imitari, qui sub obedientia illius in fide Petri cupiunt salvari. Ita enim dicit beatus Ambrosius Mediolanensis archiepiscopus : Qui a Romana Ecclesia discordat, hunc procul dubio haereticum esse constat.

Giorgio CRACCO

PATARIA : *OPUS* E *NOMEN*
(TRA VERITÀ E AUTORITÀ) [1]

> dummodo nomen concordet operi,
> opus vero respondeat nomini
> (Arnolfo)

Invano gli studiosi hanno cercato di dare una spiegazione convincente del termine 'Pataria'. Né vale rifarsi ancora alla vecchia ipotesi del Muratori (Pattari = rigattieri, straccioni), che, all'analisi, risulta del tutto infondata. Il problema ora non è di tentare un'ennesima, e forzatamente precaria, spiegazione, bensì di esaminare il termine, al di là della sua matrice linguistica, come momento di un giudizio globale sul movimento milanese della seconda metà del secolo XI. L'indagine è tanto più allettante quanto più consente di cogliere, pur da un modesto angolo di visuale, il passaggio da una cultura 'teologica' a una cultura 'ecclesiologica'. Difatti il termine 'Pataria' nasce e si sfrangia in più significati quando, nel corso del più ampio processo di ristrutturazione del corpo ecclesiastico voluto dal papato di Roma, la giustificazione nella verità non può più prescindere dalla giustificazione nell'autorità, e a un concetto di eresia come traviamento dalle Scritture si affianca un concetto di eresia come disobbedienza alle gerarchie e all'*ordo Ecclesiae*.

I testi più interessanti per la storia del termine 'Pataria' si incontrano dopo la morte di Arialdo (avvenuta nel 1066) e il ritrovamento del suo corpo (circa un anno dopo), quando l'intensificarsi della guerriglia urbana per opera del laico Erlembaldo più fece avvertiti il clero locale e la gerarchia della pericolosità del movimento. In una lettera inviata da Alessandro II nel 1067 ai laici di Cremona per confortarli nella lotta contro gli eretici simoniaci e concubinari non si parla mai di Patarini (le fonti ecclesiastiche ufficiali del secolo XI evitano accuratamente il termine 'Pataria'), ma solo di *fideles*. E *fideles*, nel contesto della lettera, vuol dire uomini che operano secondo la *recta fides*, secondo la *veritas*, secondo quanto Dio, *inspirator omnium bonorum et bone memorie*

---

[1] Si dà qui il solo riassunto della relazione, che nel frattempo è stata pubblicata integralmente, con lo stesso titolo e con tutte le note giustificative, in *Rivista di Storia della Chiesa in Italia*, 18 (1974), pp. 357-387.

auctor, loro dettava. Ma la pur santa iniziativa dei fedeli doveva atte-
nersi a quanto i *sancti predecessores nostri* e quasi tutti i *conditores* di
sacri canoni avevano stabilito in materia di chierici simoniaci e forni-
catori. In altri termini, la fedeltà alla *veritas* comportava una fedeltà
conseguente all' *auctoritas*. Perciò la parola *fideles* assume, nella lettera
in questione, un valore più complesso, designando sia gli 'uomini di
Dio', sia, correlativamente, gli 'uomini del papa'.

Ma se i *fideles Dei* avessero trovato inaccettabile il comando del
papa? E' un caso che trapela da un altro testo, sempre del 1067, le
Constitutiones emesse da Mainardo e da Giovanni Minuto legati a Milano
per conto di Alessandro II, che rappresentano una stroncatura senza
via d'uscita per il movimento milanese. Chi aveva detto che l'*offensa
in Deum* di cui si macchiavano simoniaci e incontinenti configurasse
automaticamente il diritto-dovere, per i *fideles* di tutti gli ordini (anche
per i laici), di giudicare e punire, di erigersi a giudici e giustizieri? La
veritas, la *causa fidei* aveva già i suoi difensori autorizzati : le gerarchie
locali, o, in caso di impotenza o negligenza di queste, la gerarchia romana.
L'ossequio al *verbum Dei* viene, dunque, fatto coincidere con l'ossequio
alla gerarchia locale e centrale e al diritto canonico. E i membri del
movimento milanese non sono detti *fideles*, ma semmai rimproverati
di supporsi tali, ossia di aver giurato *ut per rectam fidem, ne haec mala*
(simonia e concubinato) *fierent, operam darent*. Appunto : la fedeltà a
Dio che non passasse per la Chiesa diventava una colpa : una colpa tanto
grave da far passare in secondo piano l'eresia dei simoniaci e degli incontinenti. Stava nascendo semmai (come sembra di capire dal tono delle
Constitutiones) una nuova eresia, possibile soltanto nel contesto autori-
tario e accentrato della Chiesa 'gregoriana' : l'eresia dei 'disobbedienti',
ossia di coloro che peccavano contro l'*auctoritas*, che si facevano rei
non già di una 'dottrina' aberrante, bensì di una 'ideologia', di un
'comportamento', di una 'spiritualità', che finivano con il dare scandalo
e con il turbare gravemente l'*ordo Ecclesiae*. Si noti : non che Arialdo
e compagni siano già dichiarati eretici, ma per la prima volta soggiac-
ciono alla diffida dell'*auctoritas*, sono guardati come turbatori di un
ordine costituito, come 'sovversivi'. Ne risente ben presto la terminologia :
come chiamare questi sovversivi?

'Patarini' si possono chiamare, a detta di Arnolfo, che scriveva quasi
certamente prima del 1075. E 'Patarini' nel senso di *perturbatores*.
La prima cosa che l'autore denuncia è la 'verticalità' del movimento
milanese, quel suo costituirsi a interprete e testimone unico ed esclusivo

del *verbum Dei*, quella veste di giudici e giustizieri infallibili che assu-
mevano i suoi capi e seguaci. Arnolfo non è contrario di per sé all'ispi-
razione divina ; apprezza anche la causa per cui combattevano Arialdo
e Landolfo Cotta ; ma non può tollerare le violenze e i disordini che
ne seguivano. I Patarini avevano scelto il modo più ingiusto e più
disonesto per servire una causa di per sé giusta e onesta : sovvertivano,
in nome della *veritas*, l'intero ordinamento ecclesiastico ; si permettevano
di giudicare altri uomini, quando solo Dio, che conosce i misteri del
cuore umano, può giudicare ; presumevano di vivere nella *veritas*,
mentre l'uomo, per sua natura, non può vivere che nell'*humilitas*. Ecco
in che senso Arialdo e compagni sono detti 'Patarini', cioè 'sovversivi'.

Fideles, dunque (nel duplice significato di uomini di Dio e di uomini
della Chiesa), o 'Patarini'? La terminologia si biforca e si contraddice
man mano che il dibattito sul movimento milanese entra nella sua fase
calda. Cade nel 1075 la *Vita Arialdi* di Andrea da Strumi, ossia l'apologia
del *leader* del movimento, scritta da chi nel movimento credeva e non
si rassegnava a vederlo declinare. Sia per la terminologia usata sua
per i contenuti questa *Vita* sembra una risposta ad Arnolfo, o almeno
(se Arnolfo scrisse dopo Andrea) alle critiche che Arnolfo poi fece sue.
Arnolfo aveva squalificato gli uomini della verità, privilegiando quelli
dell'umiltà. E Andrea da Strumi scrive la biografia di Arialdo *in veritate,
non pro humilitate sola*, e presenta Arialdo come colui che ha lottato
fino allo stremo, fino al martirio *in defensione veritatis*. La verità giu-
stificava l'opposizione ai preti *uxorati* (che in quanto tali cessavano
di essere *lucidi*, cioè di rispecchiare la verità); coinvolgeva nella stessa
opposizione anche i laici ('Dio non fa distinzione di persone'); rendeva
santa la battaglia contro i preti simoniaci, che erano responsabili di
una colpa *in Deo* : una colpa che obbligava *penaliter* non solo chi la con-
suma ma anche chi non fa di tutto per impedirla. Arialdo non disprezzava
affatto l'*ordo Ecclesiae* ; cercava, anzi, la copertura dell'*auctoritas*.
Non era sua colpa se, per ristabilire la *veritas*, doveva sradicare la Chiesa
dei simoniaci e dei concubinari. E' il rovesciamento della posizione di
Arnolfo : per Andrea da Strumi, Arialdo e compagni non sono affatto
'sovversivi' (il termine 'Patarini', infamante e denigratorio, mai viene
usato) ; sono solo e unicamente *fideles* : *fideles in defensione veritatis*.
Ma dopo il 1075 c'era ancora posto, a Milano e nella Chiesa, per i 'fedeli
della verità'?

L'alternativa terminologica 'Patarini' - *fideles* è risolta dagli eventi.
L'affermazione dell'ecclesiologia gregoriana, che significava identifi-

cazione di verità e autorità, lascia sempre meno spazio ai movimenti spontanei e carismatici; il confronto non è più tra carisma e istituzioni, bensì tra istituzioni tra loro contrapposte (papato e impero), oppure tra aspetti diversi della stessa istituzione. Così il termine *fideles* (nel senso di uomini che vivono secondo Dio) impallidisce e scompare (lo si trova *per incidens* solo in Bonizone); dilaga, per contro, presso gli avversari, ma anche presso gli amici del movimento milanese l'etichetta di 'Patarini'. Qui interessa rilevare che cosa significa 'Pataria', come *opus* e come *nomen*, all'interno dell'ordinamento ecclesiastico ormai consolidato.

In Bonizone da Sutri il movimento milanese appare come una creatura diletta della Chiesa di Roma. Se simonia e concubinato, oltre che essere un tradimento della *veritas*, sono anche un atto di disobbedienza nei confronti della *Romana Ecclesia*, la stessa Pataria, che quei vizi combatteva, è concepita come strumento utile al papato per ridurre a obbedienza tutti i disobbedienti a Roma. Per Bonizone, i disobbedienti a Roma, in questo caso, erano i chierici simoniaci e concubinari, i *capitanei* e i *varvassores* che li fiancheggiavano, coloro che rimproveravano ad Arialdo e seguaci di non battersi per l'autonomia della Chiesa Ambrosiana e di inchinarsi anzi servilmente a quella di Roma : *pauperes*, li chiamavano ; *racha*, li ingiuriavano, cioè *pannosi*, cioè 'Patarini' (*rachos enim grece, latine pannus dicitur*), ossia gente priva di nerbo, 'stracci di uomini'. I Patarini erano sì 'straccioni', ma non per mancanza di mezzi (in senso materiale), e neppure per 'contrapposizione alla venalità e alla bramosia di ricchezza dei loro avversari' (in senso spirituale), bensì per l'essersi ridotti a stracci nelle mani del papato rinunciando alla potenza e all' autonomia della Chiesa Ambrosiana. Tuttavia, soggiunge Bonizone, di questa povertà volontaria c'era da andar fieri : ecco perchè egli usa tranquillamente il pur spregiativo termine di 'Patarini'.

A Bonizone risponde Landolfo Seniore. Come dire che alla Chiesa di Roma risponde quella Ambrosiana. Ma in condizioni mutate : Milano, dopo il 1095, tornava al l'obbedienza romana ; il papato valorizzava le forze e la tradizione della Pataria : il che portava alla spaccatura dello stesso movimento. Ma Landolfo, che scrive la sua *Historia Mediolanensis* per riaffermare il primato della Chiesa dei preti, specie della Chiesa dei preti ambrosiani, non si fida, ed esplode in un atto d'accusa contro ogni forma di Pataria. Forse, squalificando la Pataria, intendeva squalificare anche il papato che ormai la proteggeva, e riproporre l'antinomia Milano-Roma. Per Landolfo, i Patarini uccidevano, con il loro comportamento, con le loro idee, sia la *veritas*, sia l'*auctoritas* ; giungevano addirittura a proporsi come unica Chiesa, cioè come 'anti-chiesa'. Landolfo, perciò, usa una terminologia che non si limita a denunciare il modo di difendere una causa di per sé giusta, come si trova in Arnolfo, e neppure a stigmatizzare gli avversari della Chiesa Ambrosiana (in oggettiva polemica con Bonizone), ma è anche tutta protesa a individuare l'esistenza di una Chiesa patarina in insanabile antitesi con la Chiesa tutta. Per il cronista, infatti, la *Patalia* non è altro che una finzione di *placitum Dei* : *sub obtentu placiti Dei, quod postea Patalia vocatum est*. E *placitum*, in Landolfo, non significa soltanto 'patto', bensì, soprattutto, 'giudizio', atto giudicante e deliberante tipico di un'autorità sovrana che pretende di parlare per conto e in nome di Dio. L'attacco frontale alla Pataria induce Landolfo a parlare scopertamente anche di eresia : i Patarini sarebbero ariani ; le loro concezioni deriverebbero da quelle dei Monfortini.

Il fatto che Landolfo parli di eresia indica che l'interpretazione del movimento milanese sia come *opus* sia come *nomen* entra in una nuova fase. Ciò che resta, nella pubblicistica, è il ricordo di una intransigenza morale che, man mano che cessa di fondarsi, e quindi di giustificarsi, nell' autorità, passa nel campo dell'*error*, nell'eresia. In avanzato secolo XII, il termine 'Patarino' diventa sinonimo di 'eretico'.

Gerard VERBEKE

PHILOSOPHY AND HERESY :
SOME CONFLICTS BETWEEN REASON AND FAITH [1]

According to Tertullian, philosophy is the ancestor of all heretics (*patriarchae haereticorum philosophi*) [2]. In his view there is a clandestine complicity between heresy and philosophy : 'ipsae denique haereses a philosophia subornantur'. Quite obviously Tertullian is referring to the influence exerted by the use of Greek philosophy upon the interpretation of the Christian message : in his view heresies are provoked by introducing Greek philosophical categories in order to explain the content of faith.

The same statement occurs in the *Philosophoumena* of Hippolytus [3], a work in which the author intends to confute all kinds of heresies. He agrees with Tertullian that all heresies ultimately originate from philosophy : each heretical sect derived its ideas and theories from some ancient Greek philosopher [4]. As a matter of fact, early Christian writers had to cope with the very delicate question, whether Greek philosophy and hellenic culture may supply some help with a

[1] The text of this contribution has been elaborated with the competent help of my associate Dr. W. Vanhamel (University of Louvain, K.U.Leuven).

[2] Tertullianus, *Adversus Hermogenem*, VIII, 3, edited by A. Kroymann, Corpus Christianorum, S.L., I (Turnholti, 1954), p. 404, 14-15 : haereticorum patriarchae philosophi. The same view is also vindicated in *De Praescriptione Hereticorum*, c. VII, 1-7, edited by R.F. Refoulé, Corpus Christianorum, S.L., I, p. 192, 1-193, 40 : e.g. VII, 3 (p. 192, 6-7) : Ipsae denique haereses a philosophia subornantur; VII, 5 (p. 192, 14-15) : eadem materia apud haereticos et philosophos volutatur, idem retractatus implicantur; VII, 6 (p. 192, 18-22) : Miserum Aristotelen! qui illis dialecticam instituit, ..., omnia retractantem ne quid omnino tractaverit; *De Anima*, III, 1; *Apol.* 47,9; *Adv. Marc.* I, 13; V, 19.

[3] *Philosophoumena* (*Refutatio omnium haeresium.* κατὰ πασῶν αἱρέσεων ἔλεγχος), edited by Paul Wendland, Die griechischen christlichen Schriftsteller der ersten drei Jahrhunderte, 26 (Leipzig, 1916).

[4] *Refutatio*, I, 8, (p.3, 18-21) : ἀλλ' ἔστιν αὐτοῖς τὰ δοξαζόμενα ἀρχὴν μὲν ἐκ τῆς Ἑλλήνων σοφίας λαβόντα, ἐκ δογμάτων φιλοσοφουμένων καὶ μυστηρίων ἐπικεχειρημένων καὶ ἀστρολόγων ῥεμβομένων, (...); V 2 (p. 77,5-9) ὅτι ἐκεῖνα δογματίζουσιν ἃ πρότερον οἱ Ἑλλήνων φιλόσοφοι ἐδογμάτισαν καὶ οἱ τὰ μυστικὰ παραδόντες ἀφ' ὧν τὰς ἀφορμὰς λαβόντες αἱρέσεις συνεστήσαντο. (...) ὅτι μὴ ἀπὸ τῶν ἁγίων γραφῶν τὸ δόγμα αὐτοῖς συνίσταται, ἀλλὰ ἀπὸ ἀστρολογικῆς.

view to a better understanding of the revealed truth. Isn't there a certain incompatibility between the message of the Bible as a special divine revelation and the teaching of prechristian philosophers who merely rely on the capacity of reason? The question arises whether a blending of prechristian philosophical categories and the revealed doctrine must not necessarily entail a distortion of the latter. Some authors wanting to preserve the divine message from any distortion, adopted a rather negative attitude towards the use of Greek philosophy for the purpose of interpreting the Christian doctrine : they strongly emphasize the gap between revealed truth and rational investigation.

A similar attitude may be noticed also during the Middle Ages : in 1177 or 78, Walter of St. Victor († 1180) wrote a treatise against the four labyrinths or minotaurs of France : *Contra quatuor Labyrinthos Franciae* [5]. The authors criticized in this work and therefore called 'labyrinths' of France, are among the most important representatives of Medieval philosophy and theology : Peter Abelard, Peter Lombard, Peter of Poitiers and Gilbert of la Porrée [6]. Since they were animated by the same Aristotelian spirit [7], they treated with 'scholastic levity' the mysteries of the Holy Trinity and the Incarnation of Christ, so as to vomit many heresies and to propagate a lot of erroneous doctrines [8].

---

[5] Le '*Contra quatuor labyrinthos Franciae*', edited by Palémon Glorieux, *Archives d'histoire doctrinale et littéraire du moyen âge*, 27 (1952), p. 187-335. Concerning the date of this work, see *o.c.*, p. 194-195.

[6] *Contra quatuor labyrinthos Franciae*, prologus, p. 201, 2-4 : quatuor labirinthos Francia, id est Abeilardum et alium Lumbardum, Petrum Pictaviensem episcopum et Gislebertum Porretam ...; IV, 8 (p. 274, 33-275, 1) : ... apostolica veritate devitans profanas vocum novitates et appositiones falsi nominis scientie quam quidam promittentes circa fidem naufragaverunt ... Ex his sunt sententie Abailardi et Porete, Lumbardi et Pictavini, prepositi scolarum Petri Comestoris. In the *Addimenta posteriora* of his work, Walther of St. Victor opposes the 'Verba hereticorum' (viz. : Peter Lombard, Peter of Poitiers, Gilbert of la Porrée and even John Damascene, the 'last of the Greet Fathers'!) to the 'verba catholicorum' (viz. : Ambrose, Augustine and Hilary of Poitiers) : Cf. *o.c.*, p. 317.

[7] *Contra quatuor labyrinthos Franciae*, prologus, p. 201, 2-4 : quatuor labirinthos Francie,... uno aristotilico spiritu afflatos; IV 7, p. 274, 15-21 : dialectici quorum Aristoteles princeps est, solent argumentationum retia tendere et vagam rethorice libertatem etiam syllogismorum spineta concludere ... Quid debet facere christianus nisi omnino fugere contentionem?

[8] *Contra quatuor labyrinthos Franciae*, prologus, p. 201, 2-6 : non dubitabit quatuor labirinthos Francie..., dum ineffabilia sancte Trinitatis et incarnationis scolastica levitate tractarent, multas hereses olim vomuisse et adhuc errores pullulare?

According to Walter of St. Victor, not only recent heretics, but all of them are generated by philosophers and dialecticians [9].

It is well known that the same negative viewpoint towards philosophy is assumed by Peter Damian (1007-1072), at least with respect to the education of a monk. In his works *De sancta simplicitate* [10] and *De divina omnipotentia* [11] he maintains that a monk should not know any philosophy, nor dedicate himself to the study of profane disciplines [12]. Human mind by itself is unable to grasp anything with certainty. Peter Damian shows very little confidence in the natural capacities of reason [13]. In his view philosophy is an invention of the devil [14]; the first professor of grammar was the devil who taught Adam to decline 'deus' in the plural (*Gen.* 3,5) [15]. In order to preserve its own rank, revealed truth has to keep philosophy at a subordinate level : it is only a servant or a slave of theology, since mere rational investigation by itself is unable to afford

---

[9] *Contra quatuor labyrinthos Franciae*, p. 197, 32-33 : quod novi immo omnes heretici a philosophis et dialecticis generantur; p. 270, 16-17 : tamen simul bibere non debemus calicem Christi et calicem demoniorum (pagan philosophy).

[10] *De sancta simplicitate scientiae inflanti anteponenda*, PL, 145, opusculum 45, col. 695-703.

[11] *De divina omnipotentia*, PL, 145, opusculum 36, col. 595-622; also edited by André Cantin, Sources-chrétiennes, 191 (Paris, 1972).

[12] *De sancta simplicitate*, PL, 145, col. 695 A : ante veri luminis aditum requisisti quam caecam philosophorum sapientiam disceres : ante ad eremum pervolasti, sequens vestigia piscatorum, quam liberalium artium non dicam studiis sed stultitiis insudares; col. 701 D-702 A : ita qui Deum et sanctos ejus sincero quaerit intuitu, non indiget peregrina luce ut veram conspiciat lucem; *De perfectione monachorum*, PL, 145, col. 306 : hi porro fastidientes eccclesiasticae disciplinae peritiam, et saecularibus studiis inhiantes, quid aliud quam in fidei thalamo conjugem relinquere castam et ad scenicas videntur descendere prostituas?

[13] *De perfectione monachorum*, PL, 145, col. 306 C : qui relictis spiritualibus studiis addiscere terrenae artis ineptias concupiscunt; *Sermo VI, de s. Eleuchadio*, PL, 144, 536 B : Idolatriae ritus velut a sapientibus institutus... Per hanc itaque vesanae sapientiae vanitatem poetae, philosophi, magi, siderum rimatores, omniumque disciplinarum liberalium instructi peritia, prodigiosa daemoniorum solebant adorare figmenta.

[14] *De sancta simplicitate*, PL, 145, col. 699 B-C : Et est sapientia de qua dicitur: 'non est haec sapientia desursum descendens, sed terrena, animalis, diabolica. (Joan. III)'.

[15] *De sancta simplicitate*, PL, 145, col. 695 C : Ecce, frater, vis grammaticam discere? disce Deum pluraliter declinare! Artifex enim doctor, dum artem noviter condit, ad colendas etiam plurimos deos inauditam mundo declinationis regulam introducit. Porro, qui vitiorum omnium catervas moliebatur inducere, cupiditatem scientiae quasi ducem exercitus posuit.

any efficient help towards a better understanding of faith [16]. It is impossible to scrutinize the divine nature by way of natural reasoning : what seems to be contradictory from our viewpoint, is not necessarily impossible for God [17] He is able to bring about v.g. that a past event did not happen : even the most basic principles of our natural reasoning are not valid any more when the divine nature is concerned. Consequently philosophical research is quite useless with respect to theological understanding, unbless it be totally subdued to the revealed doctrine. Some less known medieval authors, as Otloh of Saint-Emmeram [18] and Manegold of Luttenbach [19] profess the same doctrine : they could not allow faith to be submitted to dialectics, or in other words divine truth to be subordinate to the rules of human reasoning [20].

The discussion between Berengar of Tours and Lanfranc, who died archbishop of Canterbury, refers also to the same question whether philosophical theories may be used to interpret the content of faith. Berengar likes dialectics, he speaks the language of Aristotle and Porphyry, even when he deals with the mystery of the Eucharist [21]. In his view

[16] *De divina omnipotentia*, 7, 56-59 (Sources chrét., 191, p. 414) : quae tamen artis humanae peritia, si quando tractandis sacris eloquiis adhibetur, non debet ius magisterii sibimet arroganter arripere, sed velut ancilla dominae quodam famulatus obsequio subservire.

[17] *De divina omnipotentia*, 13, 21-23 (Sources chrét., 191, p. 448) : Haec porro impossibilitas (scil. : quae enim contraria sunt in uno eodemque subiecto congruere nequeunt) recte quidem dicitur si ad naturae referatur inopiam; absit autem ut ad maiestatem sit applicanda divinam.

[18] Otloh of Saint Emmeram, *Dialogus de tribus quaestionibus*, PL, 146, col. 60-134.

[19] Manegold of Luttenbach, *Opusculum contra Wolfensem Coloniensem*, PL, 155, col. 149-176.

[20] *Dial. de tribus Quaestionibus*, PL, 146, prologus, col. 60 : Dialecticos quosdam tam simplices inveni, ut omnia sacrae scripturae dicta iuxta dialecticae auctoritatem constringenda esse decernerent. (Col. 62 B) : major enim cura mihi est legendo, vel scribendo, sequi sanctorum dicta quam Platonis, vel Aristotelis ipsiusque etiam Boetii dogmata; c. XXII, (col. 89 A) : omnis namque septem liberalium artium scientia, quae nihil in rebus humanis praestantius est, per infideles dicitur primitus proleta. Hoc autem ... ideo divinae pietatis dispensatione factum esse credo ut pro scientiae tantae investigatione non opus esset fidelibus ... nimis laborare. *Opusculum contra Wolfensem*, c. 14, (PL, 155, col. 163 A) : in utraque (scil. : the mysteries of the Holy Trinity and the Incarnation of Christ) humanae inventionis argumenta deficiunt. Prima enim ... angelorum et hominum supergreditur intellectum, secunda totius philosophiae rationis evacuat firmamentum.

[21] Berengar of Tours, *De Sacra Coena adversus Lanfrancum*, edited by Willem Hermanus Beekenkamp, Nederlandsch archief voor kerkgeschiedenis : Kerkhistorische studiën, 2 (Hagae Comitis, 1941). According to Beekenkamp this work was written

the substance and accidents of bread and wine are unable to be separated :
when the accidents of bread and wine are still present, the substance
underlying these accidents must be there too [22]. Thus Berengar denies
the doctrine of transsubstantiation, and emerges into a symbolic spiritual-
istic conception of the Eucharist : bread and wine are a symbol (*figura*)
of the body of Christ and as such they may help to accomplish a spiritual
union with the glorified Lord in heaven [23]. Lanfranc takes Berengar to
task that instead of appealing to the sacred authorities, he relies on dialectical arguments [24]. However Lanfranc does not systematically reject
dialectics, he rather reproves an unwary use of them [25], as he blames
his pupil Anselm of Canterbury for writing theological works without
quoting the Holy Scripture [26]. And yet Anselm is not unaware of the

between 1063-1069 : *o.c.*, I, p. 10.The rationalism of Berengar is quite obvious in
the following text : *o.c.*, cap. XXIII, p. 47 : quamquam ratione agere in perceptione
veritatis incomparabiliter superius esse, quia in evidenti res est, sine vericordiae
cecitate nullus negaverit; ... maximi plane cordis est per omnia ad dialecticam confugere, quia confugere ad eam ad rationem est confugere, quo qui non confugit, cum
secundum rationem sit factus ad imaginem Dei, suum honorem reliquit.

[22] *De sacra coena*, c. XX, p. 42 : nisi caro haec individua proprium acciperet aliquid
per quod eam non lapidem, non panem sed carnem esse oculis corporis appareret,
nullo modo vel de nichilo vel de alio aliquo ut esset caro institui potuisset.

[23] Bread and wine are the body of Christ, not 'materialiter' (*De sacra coena*,
c. XXXIX, p. 120), 'corporaliter' (c. XLV, p. 157), or 'carnaliter' (c. XLIII, p. 146),
but 'spiritualiter' (c. XLV, p. 157). Cf. also *o.c.*, c. 37, p. 106 : quamvis panis et vinum
altaris post consecrationem sint corpus Christi et sanguis quantum ad spiritualitatem
vel rem sacramenti. In his work *Contra quatuor labyrinthos Franciae*, Walter of St.
Victor calls Abelard 'an other Berengar' because of his symbolic conception of the Eucharist : Hic (scil. Berengarius) enim hereticus asserebat in figura et sacramento totum
fiere ... (Abelardus) alterum se probat Berengarium. Nam sicut ille asserebat omnia
fieri in sacramento tantum, sic et hic (*o.c.*, p. 260, 33-35; 261, 15-17).

[24] Lanfranc, *Liber de corpore et sanguine Domini*, c. 7, (PL, 150, col. 416 D) : relictis
sacris auctoritatibus, ad dialecticum confugium facis. Et quidem de mysterio fidei
auditurus ac responsurus quae ad rem debeant pertinere, mallem audire ac respondere
sacras auctoritates quam dialecticas rationes.

[25] Lanfranc, *Epistola B. Pauli Apostoli ad Colossenses, cum interjectis B. Lanfranci
glossulis*, c. 2, PL, 150, col. 323 : non artem disputandi vituperat sed perversum dispu-
tantium usum; c. 7, col. 417A : Etsi quando materia disputandi talis est ut (per)
hujus artis regulas valeat enucleatius explicari, in quantum possum, per aequipollen-
tias propositionum tego artem, ne videar magis arte quam veritate sanctorumque
Patrum auctoritate confidere.

[26] Anselmus, *Epistolae* I, 68, *Epistola ad Lanfrancum* (PL, 158, col. 1139 A) : ubi ratio
defecit, divinis auctoritatibus accingenda, hoc et post paternam amabilemque vestram
admonitionem, et ante feci, quantum potui.

danger and warns against it : [27] although he has great confidence in reason, he at once stresses the priority of faith [28]. This is the meaning of the famous sentence : *'neque enim quaero intelligere ut credam, sed credo ut intelligam'* [29]. According to Anselm, revealed truth must be the starting point of all theological inquiry : faith is not based on rational investigation, but the understanding of revealed truth may be promoted with the help of philosophical categories [30].

The main reproach made by Bernard of Clairvaux and William of St. Thierry against Peter Abelard, William of Conches and Arnold of Brescia is related to the same basic question, the use of dialectics for the purpose to explain the content of faith [31]. Both, Bernard of

[27] *Epistola De Incarnatione Verbi*, c. 4 (edited by Franciscus Salesius Schmitt, II, p. 17, 22-18, 1) : (dialectici moderni), qui nihil esse credunt nisi quod imaginationibus comprehendere possunt. These dialecticians are like bats discussing with eagles about the sunbeams : *o.c.*, c.l, p. 8, 2-6 : qui, quoniam quod credunt intelligere non possunt, disputant contra eiusdem fidei a sanctis patribus confirmatam veritatem. Velut si vespertiliones et noctuae non nisi in nocte caelum videntes de meridianis solis radiis disceptent contra aquilas ipsum solem irreverberato visu intuentes.

[28] *Epistola De Incarnatione Verbi*, c.l, p. 7, 10-8, 1 : Unde fit ut dum ad illa quae prius fidei scalam exigunt, sicut scriptum est : 'nisi credideritis non intelligetis' praepostere per intellectum prius conantur ascendere : in multimodos errores per intellectus defectum cogantur descendere.; *o.c.*, c.6, p.21, 1-2 : posui ad respondendum pro fide nostra contra eos, qui nolentes credere quod non intelligunt derident credentes.

[29] *Proslogion*, c. 1, ed. F.S. Schmitt, I, p. 100, 18.

[30] *Epistola De Incarnatione Verbi*, c.l, ed. F.S. Schmitt, II, p. 7,1-2: semper eandem fidem indubitanter tenendo, amando et secundum illam vivendo humiliter, quantum potest quaerere rationem quomodo sit.

[31] Cf. Bernard of Clairvaux, *Epistolae* 188, 189, 190, 191, 193 (PL, 182, col. 351-359) William of St. Thierry, *Disputatio adversus Petrum Abaelardum* (PL, 180, col. 249-282); *Epistola 326, ad S. Bernardum* (PL, 182, col. 531-533); *De Erroribus Guillelmi de Conchis* (PL, 180, col. 333-340); In Bernard's view Arnold of Briscia, who was a popular preacher and who maintained a heresy of a different kind, was also influenced by the dialectical method of Abelard. *Epist.* 195 (PL, 182, col. 363 A) : adhaeserat Petro Abelardo : cujus omnes errores, ab Ecclesia jam deprehensos atque damnatos, cum illo etiam et prae illo defendere acriter et pertinaciter conabatur; *Epist.* 189 (PL, 182, col. 355 B) : Procedit Golias (=Abelardus) procero corpore, nobili illo suo bellico apparatu circummunitus antecedente quoque ipsum ejus armigero Arnuldo de Brescia. Both were condemned at the Council of Sens (1140) and the sentence has been ratified by Pope Innocent II : *Epistola Innocentii contra Abaelardum et Arnoldum de Briscia* (Mansi, 21, col. 565; PL, 179, *Epist.* 448, col. 517 B-C) : per praesentia scripta fraternitati vestrae mandamus quatenus Petrum Abaelardum et Arnaldum de Briscia, perversi dogmatis fabricatores, et Catholicae Fidei impugnatores, in religiosis locis, ubi vobis melius visum fuerit, separatim faciatis includi, et libros erroris eorum, ubicumque reperti fuerint, igne comburi.

Clairvaux and William of St. Thierry are firmly convinced that all heretical doctrines of Abelard originate from his philosophical theories ;
an excessive confidence in reason is the source of his heretical statements.
According to Bernard Abelard endeavours to empty the merit of Christian faith since he believes to be able to grasp the mystery of the divine
nature through human reason; [32] he is ready to supply a rational explanation of everything, even of those things which are beyond reason [33].
In Bernard's view it is quite unreasonable to try to transcend reason
through reason, as it is against faith to refuse to believe what could not
be attained through reason [34]. Instead of relying on the teaching of the
Church fathers, Abelard prefers to apply to philosophical doctrines and
so he introduces all kinds of new theories [35]. In a letter to Bernard William
of St. Thierry draws the attention to the same point : by the teaching
of Abelard Christian faith is seriously jeopardized : [36] dealing with Holy
Scripture Abelard behaves as he usually does in studying dialectics, he
constantly propagates new theories of his own invention, he wants to
control and to amend faith instead of accepting it and living in accor-
dance with it [37]. A list of particular doctrines put forward by Abelard
has been censured by the Council of Soissons (1121) and the Council

[32] Bernard of Clairvaux, *Epist.* 191, (PL, 182, 357 B) : totum quod Deus est, humana ratione arbitratur se posse comprehendere.

[33] *Epist.* 190 (PL, 182, col. 1055 A) : dum paratus est de omnibus reddere rationem,
etiam quae sunt supra rationem, et contra rationem praesumit et contra fidem.

[34] PL, 182, col. 1055 B : Quid enim magis contra rationem, quam ratione rationem
conari transcendere? Et quid magis contra fidem, quam credere nolle, quidquid non
possit ratione attingere?
This criticism apparently refers to Abelard's viewpoint that we ought to believe
not only because God has spoken to man, but because human reason is convinced. :
Introd. ad Theol,. 1.II, (PL, 178, col. 1050 D : nec quia Deus id dixerat creditur, sed
quia hoc sic esse convincitur, recipitur.

[35] *Epist.* 189 (PL, 182, col. 355 C) : In sugillationem doctorum Ecclesiae, magnis
effert laudibus philosophos; ad inventiones illorum et suas novitates catholicorum
Patrum doctrinae et fidei praefert.

[36] William of St. Thierry, *Epist. ad Bernardum* (PL, 182, col. 531 B) : nec de mini-
mis agitur, sed de fide sanctae Trinitatis, de persona Mediatoris, de Spiritu Sancto,
de gratia Dei, de sacramento communis redemptionis. Petrus enim Abaelardus iterum
nova docet, nova scribit ... Dico vobis, periculose siletis, tam vobis, quam Ecclesiae
Dei.

[37] PL, 182, col. 532 A : agens in Scriptura divina quod agere solebat in dialectica,
proprias adinventiones, annuas novitates; censor fidei, non discipulus, emendator,
non imitator.

of Sens (1140)[38]. The decision of this council was confirmed by a letter
of Pope Innocent II on July 16, 1140 : the author was convicted of heresy
and a perpetual silence was imposed upon him [39]. The main reason for
this severe sentence certainly was the attitude of Abelard towards faith :
he wants to rationalize the content of faith without any restriction. Dealing with a passage of Gregory the Great he states that we accept the
Christian message not because God has revealed it but because reason
is convinced of its truth [40]. Nevertheless Abelard strives to be faithful
to the Christian belief : as he writes in one of his letters (*Epis.* 17) he does
not want to be a philosopher opposing St. Paul nor an Aristotle separated from Christ [41].

According to some ancient and medieval authors heresy largely springs
from the use of philosophical concepts and theories in order to obtain
a better understanding of the revealed truth. Hence the question may be
asked regarding the period taken into consideration, whether philosophy is really the ancestor of all heresies? Without intending to vindi-
cate philosophy, it is quite obvious that some heresies at least have
little to do with any philosophical system : they rather spring from social
and historical situations, religious movements and r eformative tendencies inside the Christian community. In his work *Contra hereticos* [42]
Alan of Lille mainly deals with the Cathars and the Waldenses : these
latter too are charged with heresy, although they don't profess any
heretical doctrine; they are simply disobedient towards the Pope who
does not allow them to preach [43]. In the prologue of the treatise, Alan
draws a distinction between ancient and recent heretics : the former
tried to confute Christian faith with the help of rational arguments,

[38] Mansi, *Concilia*, 21, col. 568-569.
[39] Innocentius II, *Epist.* 447 (Mansi, 21, col. 565; PL, 179, col. 517 A) : universa
ipsius Petri dogmata, sanctorum canonum auctoritate, cum suo auctore damnavimus,
eique tanquam haeretico perpetuum silentium imposuimus; *Epist.* 448, (Mansi,
21, col. 565; PL, 179, col. 517 B-C).
[40] *Introductio ad Theologiam* (PL, 178, col. 1050 D) : nec quia Deus id dixerat
creditur, sed quia hoc sic esse convincitur, recipitur.
[41] *Epist.* XVII (PL, 178, col. 375 C) : Nolo sic esse philosophus, ut recalcitrem Paulo.
Non sic esse Aristoteles, ut secludet a Christo.
[42] *De Fide Catholica sive quadripertita magistri Alani editio contra haereticos,
Valdenses, Judaeos et paganos*, PL, 210, col. 305-430.
[43] PL, 210, col. 382 C-D : Isti Waldenses qui contra praeceptum domini papae
praedicant, imo contra totam Ecclesiam, huic sententiae (excommunicationis) sub-
jacent... Quibus etiam magis credendum est, idiotis, an sapientibus Ecclesiae uni-
versis?

whereas the latter don't rely on any human or divine reasoning, they simply fancy some monstruous theories quite arbitrarily[44]. Being laymen, these Waldenses are unable to preach and to disclose the authentic meaning of Holy Scripture [45].

Durand of Huesca, after he had been a Waldensian, repudiates heresy at the end of the summer 1207 [46]. Then he comes to Rome and together with his companions he professes his Christian belief before pope Innocent III : he is allowed to pursue community life, to practise complete poverty and to preach [47]. Before his conversion he already wrote a book against the Cathars : *Liber Antiheresis* [48]. In his work *Contra Manicheos*[49] written between 1220 and 1227 [50], he wants to proceed quite honestly, without relying on vague suspicions [51] ; arguing against the Cathars, he carefully analyses a treatise written by a representative of the sect and quotes textually many passages from it [52]. In his view the Cathars

---

[44] PL, 210, *Prologus*, 307 A-B : in hoc ab antiquis haereticis differunt quod illi humanis rationibus fidem nostram expugnare conati sunt; isti vero nulla ratione humana vel divina freti, ad voluntatem et voluptatem suam, monstruosa confingunt.

[45] PL, 210, col. 382 B-C : Praedicare autem laico non licet, et ei periculosum est, quia non intelligit quod dicit, nec Scripturas intelligit quas exponere praesumit.

[46] Antoine Dondaine, 'Durand de Huesca et la polémique anti-cathare', *Archivum Fratrum Praedicatorum*, 29 (1959), 228-276 (234).

[47] Innocentius III, *Regestorum sive Epistolarum libri*, XI, 196 (PL, 215, col. 1512 D-1513 B) : pauperes esse decrevimus... Consilia evangelica velut praecepta servare proposuimus, orationi juxta horas canonicas septies insistentes... Per idoneos et instructos in sacra pagina fratres, qui potentes sint in sana doctrina arguere gentem errantem et ad fidem modis omnibus trahere... See also Dondaine, *Durand*, p. 234 sq.

[48] Durand de Huesca, *Liber Antiheresis*, edited by Kurt-Victor Selge in *Die ersten Waldenser* : *Mit Edition des Liber Antiheresis des Durandus von Osca*, Arbeiten zur Kirchengeschichte, 37 (Berlin, 1967), II; Dondaine, *Durand*, p. 228-248; Christine Thouzellier, 'Controverses vaudoises-cathares à la fin du XIIe siècle d'après le livre II du Liber Antiheresis', *Archives d'histoire doctrinale et littéraire du moyen âge*, 35 (1960), p. 137-227.

[49] Chr. Thouzellier, *Une somme anti-cathare* : Le '*Liber contra Manicheos*' de *Durand de Huesca*, Spicilegium Sacrum Lovaniense, Etudes et documents, 32 (Louvain, 1964).

[50] Dondaine, *Durand*, p. 243; Thouzellier, *Liber contra Manicheos*, p. 35-38.

[51] *Liber contra Manicheos*, (ed. Thouzellier, p. 82, 8-11) : oblocuturus itaque demencie eorum alludendo sollerti sanctorum patrum energie, non deferam eos in aliquo suspective, sed in hiis tantum que disputando ab ore heresiarcharum animadverti vel in tractatibus eorum repperi notata nequiter et nefande. See also 119, 14-15; 210, 29-31; 256,11; 302,10; 304,4.

[52] *Liber contra Manicheos*, p. 82, 12-17 : compilationem igitur quandam ipsorum... quam habebam pre manibus, capitulatim interponere dignum duxi et post serio, prout

are not comparable to the Jews and the Saracens, who are not really heretics ; they did not abandon Christian faith, since they never believed the Incarnation of our Lord and the Sacraments of the Church [53], whereas the Cathars pretend to belong to the Christian community, although they distort the revealed truth [54]. In his exposé Durand particularly stresses the fundamental dualism of this heretical sect : in their meetings the Cathars teach their followers that the present material world is essentially evil, it was made and is still ruled by the devil [55]; hence there are two kingdoms, quite opposed to each other, the kingdom of God and the kingdom of the devil [56]. Since the present world belongs to the kingdom of the devil, they refuse to accept that our Lord came into it [57]. Arguing against them, Durand quotes many sentences from Holy Scripture proving quite clearly that the sensible world has been created by God [58], he also opposes the teaching of the Cathars concerning the origin of human soul : in their view the soul has been created before the making of the world and has been deceived by the devil, so as to become guilty of sin [59]. Regarding this last tenet however, Durand does not quote any passage from the compilation he constantly uses ; in this

sophia Patris qui habet clavem David michi dignabitur ostium aperire, fumum eorum teterrimum ventilabo.

[53] *Liber contra Manicheos*, p. 165, 7-9 : non enim Iudei moderni a fide discesserunt, quia numquam aliter fidem Christi habuerunt. Similiter possumus dicere de Agarenis (scil. : the Saracens); p. 236, 27-30 : qui discedunt a fide, profecto non Iudei ..., quia fidem incarnationis dominice neque sacramentorum sancte Ecclesie numquam veraciter crediderunt.

[54] *Liber contra Manicheos*, p. 237, 5-7 : que omnia moderni Cathari non solum diffitentur sed etiam horribili et intollerabili blasphemia naucipendunt. Unde patet quod ipsi proprie sunt qui discedunt a fide.

[55] *Liber contra Manicheos*, p. 115, 16-18 : Divine bonitati doctores impii derogando presentem mundum asserunt, id est quecumque possunt videri corporeis occulis, malignum, id est diabolicum creasse pariter et fecisse.

[56] *Liber contra Manicheos*, p. 135, 25-136, 2 : duo esse regna, unum diaboli et alterum Dei, intelligentes hunc mundum et omnia que videntur in eo regnum diaboli esse.

[57] *Liber contra Manicheos*, p. 160, 6-7 : in suo tractatu post premissa volentes ostendere Dei Filium non venisse in hunc mundum.

[58] *Liber contra Manicheos*, p. 115, 18-20 : quod (scil. doctrina Manicheorum), licet nulla testimonia Scripturarum insinent, sed dicant e contrario et affirment Deum omnipotentem hunc mundum fecisse.

[59] *Liber contra Manicheos*, p. 306, 5-9 : discimus modernos katharos credere animas salvandas in alio seculo peccasse et a principe tenebrarum ibi deceptas fuisse, ... dogmatizant omnes factas fuisse ante mundi constitutionem.

connection he mentions some doctrines concerning the human soul :
according to some other heretics it is a particle of the divine substance
or it is generated in the same way as the body ; the soul of the children
springs from that of the parents [60]. In his last chapter Durand deals
with the problem of predestination [61], which is also a digression from
the compilation of the Cathars he criticizes [62].

As far as the doctrines are concerned which are expounded in the compilation used by Durand of Huesca, one could hardly maintain that
they originate from any particular Greek philosophical system; they
rather show an amazing similarity to the basic features and conceptions
of ancient gnosticism, a similarity of which Durand is quite conscious.
According to the Gnostics too the world wherein we live, is essentially
evil, it is a gigantic prison governed by the law of necessity. There is a
gap between God and the world, God has nothing to do with this material cosmos : it was not created by Him, but by some lower power
that does not know God. Hence the Divinity is not only meta-cosmic,
but even anti-cosmic. As to man, he is composed of three elements,
flesh, soul and spirit ; flesh and soul originate from the cosmic powers,
whereas the spirit is a particle of the divine substance, emprisoned within
the soul. Being unaware of its true self, the spirit may be liberated through
the consciousness of its real nature, the knowledge of God and the knowledge of the world. In a view to the freeing of the soul and its return
to the divine substance, the Gnostics mostly preach a doctrine of abne-
gation ; some of them take the opposite stand and favour rather a kind
of libertinism [63]. This pessimistic dualism of the Gnostics was strongly
opposed by early Christian writers (Irenaeus of Lyon, Hippolytus of
Rome, Origen, Epiphanius of Salamis, Clement of Alexandria, Tertullian
of Carthago) [64], but also by Plotinus, who wrote a special treatise on

[60] *Liber contra Manicheos*, p. 306, 11-13 : alii heretici, qui discerunt animam partem
esse divine substancie vel nature, et alii qui dixerunt animas sicut corpora ex traduce
descendere vel oriri.

[61] *Liber contra Manicheos*, cap. XXI, p. 319, 13-336, 19.

[62] *Liber contra Manicheos*, p. 336, 14-15 : magnam digressionem fecimus in hiis
duobus capitulis ab hiis que scripta continentur in compilatione katharorum.

[63] Hans Jonas, *The Gnostic Religion* : *The Message of the Alien God and the Beginnings of Christianity*, Beacon Paperback, 18, second edition (Boston, 1963), p. 239-
254, 270-277; 'Gnosticism and Modern Nihilism', in *Social Research*, 19 (1952),
p. 430-452; 'The Soul in Gnosticism and Plotinus', in *Le Néoplatonisme* (Paris, 1971),
p. 45-53.

[64] Heinrick Dörrie, 'Divers aspects de la cosmologie de 70 av. J.C. à 20 ap. J.C.',
Revue de théologie et de philosophie, 6 (1972), p. 400-412.The author suggest a new

the subject : *Against those who say that the maker of the universe is evil and the universe is evil* (*Enn.* II, 9) [65]. According to Plotinus the cosmology of the Gnostics and their theory about the creation of the world is incompatible with Greek philosophy, especially with Plato's thought. The same statement applies to the medieval Cathars.

Another important document, written before 1214-15 [66], deals with the history of the cathar church in northern Italy : *De Heresi Catharorum in Lombardia* [67]. This writing is a valuable witness not only from an historical viewpoint, but also regarding the doctrine [68]. The author stresses the fact that the Cathars do not properly represent one religion with an organized hierarchical structure. They are divided into different sects, which profess some common conceptions, although they also are separated from each other through different doctrines. These sects are hostile towards each other and constantly fight against people who do not belong to the same group [69]. In some cases an agreement is made between sects, doctrinal differences are smoothed down or one sect is simply dominated and subdued by another [70]. Despite this division the Cathars of Lombardy have some spiritual kinship and religious links with members of similar communities in Bulgaria, Constantinople and France [71]. As far as the doctrine is concerned, the same pessimistic

interpretation of the pessimistic cosmology which was widespread about the beginning of the Christian era : in his view it probably developed in the suburbs of the great cities among the lower classes of the society. Apparently these poor people viewed the world and valuated it in a gloomy way because of the hardships of their social condition.

[65] Plotino, *Paideia antignostica*, introduzione e commento a cura di Vincenzo Cilento (Firenze, 1971). In fact the treatise Plotinus has written against the Gnostics not only includes *Enn.* II, 9, but also *Enn.* III, 8; V, 8 and V, 5.

[66] Antoine Dondaine, 'La hiérarchie cathare en Italie', *Archivum Fratrum Praedicatorum*, 19 (1949), p. 280-312 and 20 (1950), p. 234-324 (here 19, p. 290.)

[67] '*De Heresi Catharorum in Lombardia*', edited by Antoine Dondaine, *Archivum Fratrum Praedicatorum*, 19 (1949), p. 306-312.

[68] Dondaine, *La hiérarchie cathare en Italie*, p. 286.

[69] *De Heresi Catharorum in Lombardia*, p. 306, 4-12; p. 308, 38 and 309,7 : hec est unius partis hereticorum credencia; ... hec est dententia sive credencia alterius partis hereticorum.

[70] *De Heresi Catharorum in Lombardia*, p. 306, 22-23 : quidam vero de eius sapientibus, de hac divisione dolentes et ad unitatem eos reducere cupientes....

[71] *De Heresi Catharorum in Lombardia* tells the story of a man called Marcus, bishop of the Lombard Cathars, who formerly belonged to the Bulgarian sect and later moved to the community of Constantinople. His followers, during the time of his successor, wanting to get a Salomonian sentence about it, appealed to a bishop

dualism is professed as it is expounded by Durand of Huesca [72]; according to the author of *De Heresi Catharorum* it is a common opinion
of all Cathars that whatever is written in *Genesis* about the creation of
the world refers to the devil who is called God ; it was the devil also
who led the Jews out of Egypt and who sent the prophets to them [73].
Like the Gnostics the Cathars reject the Old Testament which is not
a part of the history of salvation : in their view the Old Testament
represents the kingdom of evil [74]. About 1250, John de Lugio, who
belongs to a group of Cathars, called 'Albanenses' wrote a treatise
against a more moderate sect of the same movement, the 'Garatenses'
or 'Concorenses' (Bishop Garathus founded the church of Concorezzo) [75].
This treatise bears a very significant title : *De duobus principiis* [76]. The
author maintains an outspoken dualistic doctrine against the more

of a French sect. : p. 306, 2 sq. : (quidem episcopus Marcus nomine), sub cuius regi-
mine omnes lombardi et Tussi et marchisianis regebantur, ... habebat ordinem suum
de bulgaria.... Relicto ordine bulgarie, suscepit... ordinem drugonthie. ... Quidam
episcopum ultra montes miserunt.

[72] *De Heresi Catharorum in Lombardia*, p. 309, 1-3 : qui habent ordinem suum
de drugonthia, credunt et predicant duos deos sive dominos sine principio et sine
fine, unum bonum et alterum malum penitus; p. 310, 9-11, 24-25 : qui habent ordinem suum de bulgaria, credunt et predicant tantum unum bonum deum omnipotentem sine principio, qui creavit angelos et IIIIor elementa; ... iste lucifer est ille deus
qui dicitur in generi creasse celum et terram et illa opera per VI dies fecisse.

[73] *De Heresi Catharorum in Lombardia*, p. 311, 12-16 : Communis omnium Catharorum opinio est, quod omnia que dicuntur in genesi ... sunt facta a diabolo, qui
ibi deus nominatur. Et similiter ille talis deus eduxit populum de egypto ... et misit
ad eos prophetas ...

[74] Raynier Sacconi explicitly states that John de Lugio accepts the whole Bible
(*Summa de Catharis*, ed. Dondaine, p. 75, 15-16) : iste Johannes recipit totam bibliam
sed putat eam scriptam fuisse in alio mundo), which is quite exceptional among the
Cathars. The opponents of John de Lugio, viz. 'the Concorrezenses' like almost all
the Cathars, reject the books of the Old Testament : *o.c.*, p. 76, 22-23 : reprobant totum
Vetus Testamentum, putantes quod diabolus fuit auctor eius.

[75] Antoine Dondaine, *Un traité néo-manichéen du XIIIe siècle : Le 'Liber de duobus
principiis'* (Roma, 1939), p. 17-18, 27-28. See also *Summa de Catharis* of Raynier
Sacconi (ed. Antoine Dondaine, Roma, 1939, p. 77, 24-26) : Item omnes ecclesiae
Catharorum se recipiunt ad invicem licet habeant diversas et contraries opiniones,
praeter Albanenses et Concorrezenses, qui se damnant ad invicem.

[76] First edited by Antoine Dondaine : *Un traité néo-manichéen du XIIIe siècle*
(Roma, 1939), p. 79-165; new edition and translation by Christine Thouzellier,
Livre des deux principes, Sources chrétiennes, 198 (Paris, 1973), 504 pp. The original
treatise *Liber de duobus principiis* of John de Lugio has not yet been discovered;
a summary of the work only is available : cf. Thouzellier, *o.c.*, p. 33.

moderate teaching of the Garatenses. Very few philosophical arguments
are put forward to support the doctrine about the two principles ;
he has no recourse to abstract metaphysical arguments concerning the
nature of finite and infinite, contingent and absolute. His main argument
is the experience we have of evil, which could not issue from God [77].
In his view the principle of evil is uncaused and eternal, it lies outside
the power of God [78], who consequently is not almighty [79]. Wathever
exists, is eternal like the two principles : creation does not mean an
increase of being, it only bestows a new way of being on things that
already existed [80]. The present world represents a temporary episode
wherein good and evil are blended together ; at the end of time a defini-
tive separation of the two will be effected [81]. John de Lugio does not
frequently refer to philosophical works, he quotes the *Physics* of Aristotle,
but the passage mentioned rather stems from Avencebrol [82]; he also
cites the *Liber de Causa Causarum*, which is the *Liber de Causis* [83];

[77] *Liber de duobus principiis*, c. 7 (ed. Thouzellier, p. 172, 34-174, 38) sic ipse deus...
esse penitus causa et principium omnis mali, quod apertissime est negandum; c.12,
190, 2-4 : oportet nos necessario confiteri quod aliud sit principium mali, quod contra
deum verum et creaturam illius nequissime operatur; c. 39, 296, 27-34 : sequitur ...
quod sit aliud principium mali, quod caput et causa est omnis iniquitatis,...; alioquin
ipse deus verus, qui fidelissimus est et iustitia summa et munditia pura, esset penitus
causa et principium omnis mali, et omnia adversa atque contraria ab ipso domino
penitus emanarent : quod vanissimum est et stultum opinari.

[78] *Liber de duobus principiis*, c.8 p. 174, 14-15 : ex illorum propria voluntate effecti
sunt demones atque mali; p. 332, 53-55 : est enim sine dubio principium malum a
quo hec eternitas sine sempiternitas et antiquitas proprie et principaliter derivantur.

[79] *Liber de duobus principiis*, c. 41, p. 302, 2-304, 5 : de omnipotentia autem domini
dei veri, qua nostri adversarii contra nos multociens gloriantur, affirmantes quod
non sit potestas vel potentia alia nisi sua, declarare disposui.

[80] *Liber de duobus principiis*, c. 26, p. 250, 29-31 : sic videtur manifeste, quod hec
nobilis creatio et factura bonorum a domino deo vero in eternum et in seculum seculi
est statuta; Raynier Sacconi, *Summa de Catharis* (ed. A. Dondaine, p. 73, 19-23) :
dicit itaque quod omnes creaturae sunt ab aeterno bonae creaturae cum deo bono
et malae cum malo deo, et quod creatores non praecedunt creaturas aeternitate sed
causa et quod creaturae ex deo sunt ab aeterno sicut splendor vel radii in sole qui
non praecedit radios suos tempore, sed tantum causa vel natura.

[81] Dondaine, *Un traité néo-manichéen du XIIIe siècle*, p. 24.

[82] *Liber de duobus principiis*, c. 63 (ed. Thouzellier, p. 398, 104-106) : sicut probat
Aristotiles in tertio Phisicorum. Thouzellier points out : Aristoteles, non inveni,
revera Avicebron, *Fons vitae*, III, 57, edited by Clemens Baeumker, *Beiträge zur
Geschichte d. Philos. d. Mittelalters*, I, 2-4 (Münster, 1892-95), p. 207-208. See also
A. Dondaine, *Un traité néo-manichéen*, p. 141, ad. 19, and p. 93, ad 3-11.

[83] *Liber de duobus principiis*, c.2, p. 166, 16-18 : et in libro De Causa causarum
scriptum est.

and he applies to some philosophical sentences which according to A. Dondaine could originate either from Al Kindi or Avencebrol. Hence the conclusion seems to be quite obvious : the fulcrum of the dualistic doctrine expounded by John de Lugio is not philosophical reasoning.

Concerning the doctrine of the Cathars, we also have some more evidence supplied by two inquisitors living in northern Italy : Raynier Sacconi who formerly belonged to the Cathar Church of Lombardy ; later on he became a convert and a dominican [84]. In 1250 he wrote a book intitled : *Summa de Catharis et pauperibus de Lugduno* [85] : he simply attempts to give a systematic exposé of the Cathar doctrine without discussion or confutation [86]. About 1260-70 another inquisitor, Anselm of Alexandria, a dominican also, wrote his *Tractatus de hereticis* [87], in which he incorporates the work of Sacconi [88].

Let us come back to our initial question : is philosophy the ancestor of those heretics I was dealing with, the Cathars and the Waldenses? In my opinion the answer to this question could only be negative. I know that scholars do not agree on the origin of Gnosticism : however recent research has stressed more and more the difference between Greek philosophy and Classical culture on one side and gnostic dualism : for that reason the explanation of Harnack, looking at Gnosticism as an extreme form of hellenized Christianity, has been more and more abandoned [89]. If Gnosticism does not spring from Greek philosophy, one

---

[84] Raynier Sacconi, *Summa de Catharis et Pauperibus de Lugduno*, ed. A. Dondaine (Roma, 1939), p. 66, 31 : in anno XVII quibus conversatus sum cum eis ...; Anselmus of Alexandria, *Tractatus de hereticis*, ed. A. Dondaine, *Arch. Fratrum Praedic.*, 20 (1950), p. 317, 25 : Summa fratris Raynerii condam de ordine predicatorum; p. 317, 29 : Anno domini M°CC°L compilatum est fideliter dictum fratrem R(aynerium) opus superius annotatum. See also A. Dondaine, *Un traité néo-manichéen du XIIIe siècle*, p. 7 : l'inquisiteur Raynier Sacconi, ancien ministre d'une des églises de Lombardie, puis converti au catholicisme et religieux dominicain.

[85] Edited by A. Dondaine in *Un traité néo-manichéen du XIIIe siècle*, p. 64-78.

[86] Dondaine, *Un traité néo-manichéen*, p. 76, 6-8 : ex eis compilavit (Johannes de Lugio) quoddam volumen magnum decem quaternorum cuius exemplarium habeo et perlegi et ex illo errores supradictos extraxi.

[87] Edited by A. Dondaine, *Arch. Fratrum Praedic.*, 20 (1950), p. 308-324. Concerning the date of this work, see : A. Dondaine, 'La hiérarchie cathare en Italie', *Arch. Fratrum Praedic.*, 20 (1950), p. 259.

[88] Dondaine, *La hiérarchie cathare en Italie*, p. 317, 25 sq.

[89] The interpretation of Adolf Harnack, *Lehrbuch der Dogmengeschichte*, I, fourth edition (Tübingen, 1909) has been assumed by several scholars : E. de Faye, P.C. Burkitt, R.P. Carey, A.D. Nock, A.J. Festugière and others. At the Colloquium

could hardly maintain that the Cathar and Waldensian movements originate from that source.

And yet in some other cases heretical doctrines are undeniably connected with certain philosophical systems and are the result of an attempt undertaken in order to interpret the revealed truth with the help of rational investigation. Already from the beginning of our era Christian writers had to face the question : which kind of philosophy was compatible with their faith and was fitting to be used in order to explain the content of their belief. During the first centuries Christian thinkers took a rather negative stand towards Aristotelian philosophy, because the Stagirite denies divine providence, the immortality of the soul and the creation of the world ; in his view the cosmos is eternal, it never came to be and will never pass away. The Christians were much more in favour of the Platonic system, since Plato accepts the immortality of the soul, the making of the world by the Demiurg, as it is described in the *Timaeus*; he also assumes a transcendent world of immaterial and unchangeable Ideas, which are the patterns of the sensible things. The Idea of Good is according to Plato the highest Form and probably coincides with the Divinity. The Christians generally thought this philosophy to be much more in agreement with the content of their own belief than any other system : for that reason they mostly introduced Platonic and Neo-Platonic categories for the purpose of explaining Christian faith. As to the Stoic philosophy, its moral doctrine as been very influential : even the Christians borrowed from the Stoics some important elements of their moral teaching as v.g. the doctrine of natural law. On the contrary Epicurean philosophy was generally reproved by the Christians, because of its doctrine on pleasure.

Not all attempts aiming at the interpretation of faith with the help of philosophy were harmonious and successful, without distorting the original meaning of the Christian message. In some cases these attempts were rather defective and failing, even when they were not censured by the Church authority. In his book *De natura hominis* Nemesius introduced the Platonic and Neo-Platonic doctrine on the pre-existence of the soul [90] ; he even did not reject the teaching of Iamblichus on the

of Messina however (April 13-18, 1966), S. Pétrement, the author of *Le dualisme chez Platon, les Gnostiques et les Manichéens* (Paris, 1947), was the only one who maintained the Christian origin of gnosticism.

[90] *De natura hominis*, II, p. 83-84 (ed. Christian Friederich Matthaei). Nemesius not only accepts the Platonic doctrine of reminiscence, which inevitably implies the

reincarnation of the soul among human beings [91]. Without being sentenced for heresy, Nemesius' interpretation could hardly be called a successful explanation of the content of faith. St. Augustine who at the beginning of his intellectual development, had accepted the Platonic theory of reminiscence, had abandoned it later because of its incompatibility with the Christian doctrine about original sin [92]. Faustus of Riez in order to stress the difference between God and the world maintained that God only is incorporeal : all other beings, even man, are completely corporeal [93]. As far as I am informed, Faustus has never been sentenced for heresy : and yet the question may be asked whether a materialistic anthropology is compatible with Christian faith.

Let us look more closely at some medieval heresies dealing with the relation between God and world. The main work of John Scot Eriugena, *De divisione naturae*, was condemned by Pope Honorius III, in 1225 (January 23) [94], that means about three hundred an fifty years after the death of the author. According to the Pope, the book of Scot is full of heretical perversity : all copies of the work had to be burnt. Nobody is allowed to keep even a part of it : if anybody owns this book or a part of it, he has to carry it to the bishop within fifteen days after he has been informed of the sentence, or else he will be excommunicated ; even more, excommunication may in some cases lead to condemnation for heresy, with all the consequences involved [95]. In his letter the Pope also refers

pre-existence of the soul, but he also opposes the psychological doctrine of Eunomius : in his view the soul could not be created when the body is generated, because of the Biblical text saying that the divine creation came to an end after six days. (*De natura hominis*, II, p. 108, ed. Matthaei).

[91] *De natura hominis*, II, p. 117 ssq. (ed. Matthaei).

[92] Cf. Etienne Gilson, *Introduction à l'étude de saint Augustin*, Etudes de philosophie médiévale, 11 (Paris, 1929), p. 94-95.

[93] Faustus of Riez, *Epistola* 3 (ed. August Engelbrecht, Corpus scriptorum Ecclesiasticorum Latinorum, vol. XXI, p. 174, 20-21) : quibus pro manifesto colligitur nihil esse incorporeum nisi solum deum; p. 180, 2-6 : equidem nobis ea, quae supra nos sunt, invisibilia sunt, sed omnia illi, sicut comprehensibilia, ita et corporea sunt, qui ex nihilo fecit omnia, ... ita et materia incorporavit et rebus omnibus, inter quas et anima censetur, ...; p. 180, 23 : unus ergo deus incorporeus, quia et inconprehensibilis et ubique diffusus.

[94] '*Epistola ad archiepiscopos et episcopos*' in *Chartularium Universitatis Parisiensis*, edited by Henri Denifle and A. [Emile] Chatelain (Paris, 1889), I, p. 106-107; Mansi, *Concilia*, 22, col. 811-812.

[95] ad loc. cit. : est quidem liber *perifisis* titulatur inventus, totus scatens vermibus heretice pravitatis ... mandamus, quatinus librum ipsum sollicite perquiratis et ubicumque ipsum vel partem ejus inveniri contingerit, ad nos, ... sine dilatione mittatis

to a previous Council [96]. Undoubtedly, Scot is a powerful and original thinker : through Pseudo-Dionysius, Maximus Confessor, Gregory of Nyssa and St. Augustine he came under the influence of Neo-Platonic philosophy, and endeavoured to build a synthesis of faith and rational thought [97]. In his view there is no opposition between faith and reason, however the former has a priority on the latter : faith first enters into the monument of Holy Scripture, then follows reason when the entrance has been already prepared [98]. Why was John Scot reproved as a heretic and why was the judgment passed only at the beginning of the 13th. century? Was he a pantheist? Some contemporary scholars have proved that he was not [99]: Scot very strongly emphasizes the divine transcendence [100]; God could not be directly grasped by a finite mind, which is

solempniter comburendum;... quicumque ipsorum habent vel habere possunt in toto vel in parte exemplaria dicti libri, ea vobis non differant resignare, in omnes qui ultra quindecim dies, ..., librum ipsum totum aut partem scienter retinere presumpserint excommunicationis sententiam proferendo..., quod si aliquo tempore convicti legitime fuerint hujusmodi sententiam incurrisse notam quoque pravitatis heretice non evadent.

[96] This is the opinion of Maïeul Cappuyns (*Jean Scot Erigène : Sa vie, son œuvre, sa pensée* (Louvain, 1933), p. 248, n.1). According to M. Th. d'Alverny the reference of Pope Honorius III to some provincial council of Sens, may easily designate whatever annual meeting of the bishops with their metropolitan between 1210 and 1215 (*Chartularium Universitatis Parisiensis*, I, p. 107 : a venerabili fratre nostro... archiepiscopo Senonensi et suffraganeis ejus, in provinciali concilio congregatis, justo est judicio reprobatus.) : 'Un fragment du procès des Amauriciens', *Archives d'histoire doctrinale et littéraire du moyen âge*, 18 (1951), 325-336 (p. 335, n. 3).

[97] *De Divisione naturae* I, 66, ed. I.P. Sheldon-Williams, Scriptores Latini Hiberniae, 7 (Dublin, 1968), p. 192, 33-194,2; vera enim auctoritas rectae rationi non obsistit, neque recta ratio verae auctoritati. Ambo siquidem ex uno fonte, divina videlicet sapientia, manare dubium non est; *Versio Operum S. Dionysii*, praef.. PL, 122, col. 1031 B; *Epistolae Karolini Aevi*, IV, ed. Ernst Dümmler, in Monumenta Germaniae Historica, Epistolarum, VI, second edition (Berolini, 1925), p. 158. : ducente Deo et rationis lumine; *De praedestinatione* I, 1, (PL, 122, col. 358A) : conficitur inde, veram esse philosophiam veram religionem, conversimque veram religionem esse veram philosophiam. Cf. Cappuyns, *Jean Scot Erigène*, p. 273-315.

[98] *De Divisione naturae* I, 71, ed. I.P. Sheldon-Williams, p. 204, 32 : per fidem quodam modo inchoat intelligi; *Homelia in Prologum S.Evangelii secundum Joannem*, PL, 122, col. 284D-285A : necessario praecedit fides in monumentum sanctae Scripturae, deinde sequens intrat intellectus, cui per fidem praeparatur aditus.

[99] E.g. : Germaine C. Capelle, *Amaury de Bène : Etude sur son panthéisme formel*, Bibliothèque thomiste, 16 (Kain-Paris, 1932), p. 51-60; E. Gilson, Préface, p. 6-7 : ceux qui soutiennent qu'Erigène est panthéiste ne prouvent qu'une chose, c'est qu'ils ne l'ont pas lu.

[100] *De Divisione naturae*, I, 3, ed. Sheldon-Williams, p. 38, 25-27 : Ipse nanque omnium essentia est, qui solus vere est, ut ait Dionysius Ariopagita. 'Esse enim', inquit,

able to know his existence only, not his nature [101]. Is it possible to frame
a definition of God? The only definition which may be attributed to
Him sounds as follows : He is that one who is more than being [102].
On the other hand Scot states God to be only one who truly is [103]. As
a matter of fact some expressions used by Scot may be interpreted in
a pantheistic way, and were actually understood that way by some authors
at the beginning of the 13th century. In Scot's view God is the 'essence'
(essentia or beingness) of everything [104], since He is beyond being ;
whatever is considered to be good, does not own its goodness by itself,
but only through participation in the supreme good, so whatever is
told to exist, does not possess being in itself but only through participation in the divine nature that truly is [105]. So there is a certain ambi-

'omnium est super esse divinitas'; I, 12 (p. 64, 35-66,2) : ita divina essentia, quae per
se subsistens omnem superat intellectum, in his quae a se et per se et in se (et ad se)
facta sunt recte dicitur creari, ut in eis... ab his, qui eam recto studio inquirunt cognos-
catur.

[101] *De Divisione naturae*, I, 3 (p. 38, 30-31) : ipse Deus in seipso ultra omnem
creaturam nullo intellectu comprehenditur; I, 45 (p. 138, 13-15) : Nam et causa
omnium, quae deus est, ex his quae ab ea condita sunt solummodo cognoscitur esse,
nullo vero creaturarum argumento possumus intelligere quid sit; I, 14 (p. 84, 13-14) :
illud autem esse quid sit nullo modo diffinit; I,8 (p. 50, 31-32) : non ergo ipsum deum
per se ipsum videbimus, ... (hoc enim omni creaturae impossibile est.). See also M.
Cappuyns, p. 330 : nous ne connaissons pas Dieu et le divin d'une connaissance
propre, mais seulement 'per translationem a creatura ad creatorem'.

[102] *De divisione naturae*, I, 45 (p. 138, 16-17) : ideo sola haec diffinito de deo praedica-
tur, quia est qui plus quam esse est. For that reason theology, according to Scotus, has
to adopt the 'via negativa' rather than the 'via positiva' : *o.c.* II, 1, ed. I.P. Sheldon-
Williams (Dublin, 1972), p. 4, 29-30 : verius per negationem de deo aliquid praedicare
possumus quam per affirmationem. Both methods however are brought to a marvel-
lous synthesis in the 'via eminentiae' : *o.c.*, I, 14 (ed. Sheldon-Williams, p. 84, 1-8) :
haec nomina quae adjectione 'super' vel 'plus quam' particularium de deo praedi-
cantur, ut est superessentialis. (...) Superessentialis est, affirmatio simul et abdicatio.
Cf. Cappuyns, p. 327 : cette négation qui accompagne l'affirmation et la purifie
n'est pas en effet une négation par défaut, mais par excellence.

[103] *De Divisione naturae*, V, 8 (PL 122, col. 876B) : Erit enim Deus omnia in omnibus, quando nihil erit nisi solus Deus.

[104] *De Divisione naturae*, I, 12 (ed. Sheldon-Williams, p. 64,5) : est (Deus) enim
omnium essentia.

[105] *De Divisione naturae*, I, 12 (p. 64, 6-9) : omne quod diciter bonum esse ex
participatione unius summi boni est bonum ita omne quod dicitur existere non in
se ipso existit, sed participatione vere existentis naturae existit; III, 9 (PL, 122, col.
644a) : Deus igitur praecedit omnia, quaecumque se participant, et quorum essentia
participatio ejus est.

guity in the language of Scot : being the principle of whatever exists, the divine nature does not belong to the level of being, it is beyond being ; on the other hand God alone truly is, since all finite beings are what they are through participation in the divine principle and for that very reason God is called the beingness of all beings.

During the first centuries of our era most of the heresies censured by the Church authority are related to the Holy Trinity and the person of Christ. Later on the interpretation of the Eucharist and the doctrine of predestination became of central importance. During the 12th and 13th centuries heresies deal with the relation of man to God and to the world : the consistency of man has been questioned by pantheism and monopsychism and it is the invaluable merit of some outstanding Christian thinkers of that time to have saved what may be called the Western and Christian conception of man, as a truly individual subject, the maker of his own destiny, the source of steady intellectual progress and the responsible principle of moral behaviour [106]. Scot was not a pantheist ; his work was doomed heretical and formally reproved, because the ambiguity of the exposé was thought to jeopardize the individual density of human existence.

Amaury of Bène was severly condemned at the Council of Paris in 1210 [107], some years after his death (he probably died in 1206) [108]: his body ought to be taken away from the cemetery and was to be thrown in unblest earth. A sentence of excommunication should be pronounced against him in all churches of the province. Ten clergymen, among whom was William of Poitiers, were degraded and handed over to secular Court ; four other clergymen were also degraded and put into jail for the rest of their lives [109]. The doctrine of Amaury was censured again in 1215 by Robert of Courçon, the legate of the Pope, in a letter he wrote

[106] See an article : 'L'unité de l'homme : saint Thomas contre Averroès', *Rev. Philos. Louvain*, 58 (1960), p. 220-249.

[107] *Chartularium Universitatis Parisiensis*, ed. Denifle-Chatelain, I, p. 70.

[108] M. Th. d'Alverny, *Un fragment du procès des Amauriciens*, p. 327 : Obligé de se rétracter, il (maître Amaury, originaire de Bène, paroisse du diocèse de Chartres) mourut peu après, sans doute vers 1206.

[109] *Chartularium Univ. Parisiensis*, I, p. 70 : corpus magistri Amaurici extrahatur a cimeterio et projiciatur in terram non benedictam, et idem excommunicetur per omnes ecclesias totius provincie. (Bernardus, Guillelmus de Arria, etc...., degradentur penitus seculari curie relinquendi. Urricus presbyter de Lauriaco et Petrus de S. Clodoaldo, ... etc.) degradentur perpetuo carceri mancipandi.

to the University of Paris [110], as it was reproved by Innocent III at the Lateran Council of the same year : the Council states that the teaching of Amaury is not only heretical, but foolish [111].

According to the information supplied by Thomas Aquinas and other sources, Amaury undeniably was a true pantheist [112]. In his view the distinction between God and the finite beings is only apparent and it will disappear at the end of time [113]. Translated into the philosophical language of Aquinas, Amaury teaches God to be the formal principle of everything [114] : thus He belongs to the substantial structure of all beings and constitutes their proper perfection [115]. Aquinas is quite aware of the immediate consequences of this doctrine ; he writes in his *Summa contra Gentiles* : if the divine being were the formal principle of everything, then inevitably all beings would be just one being [116]. In other words the individual subject would be suppressed as a subsistent being, and would be incorporated in the all embracing perfection of the Divinity [117]. As to the Ideas, which are the patterns of the finite beings,

[110] *Chartularium Univ. Parisiensis*, I, p. 79 : non legantur libri Aristotelis..., nec summe de eisdem, aut de doctrina magistri David de Dinant, aut Amalrici heretici, aut Mauricii hyspani.

[111] H. Denzinger, *Enchiridion Symbolorum* (Friburgi Brisgoviae, 1936), 21-23, n⁰ 433 (Mansi, *Concilia*, 22, col. 986) : Reprobamus etiam et condemnamus perversissimum dogma impii Almarici, cujus mentem sic pater mandacii excaecavit, ut eius doctrina non tam haeretica censenda sit quam insana.

[112] G.C. Capelle, *Amaury de Bène* (Paris, 1932), p. 25-50.

[113] Martini, *Chronicon Pontificum et Imperatorum*, ed. Pertz (Hannoverae, 1871), cited by Capelle, p. 105 : ideo finis omnium dicitum Deus, quia omnia reversura sunt in eum, ut in Deo immutabiliter quiescant, et unum individuum atque incommutabile in eo manebunt.

[114] S. Thomas of Aquin, *Summa Theologiae*, Iᵃ, q. 3, a.8., in corpore, (Editio Leonina, IV, p. 48a) : alii autem dixerunt Deum esse principium formale omnium rerum. Et haec dicitur fuisse opinio Almarianorum.

[115] S. Thomas of Aquin, *Summa contra Gentiles*, I, 26 (Editio Leonina,XIII, p. 82a) : Si igitur Deus sit omnium rerum esse formale..., sequetur quod esse cujuslibet rei fuerit ab aeterno. ... Si enim (Deus) est esse omnium, tunc est aliquid omnium, non autem super omnia.

[116] *Summa contra Gentiles*, I, 26 (Editio Leonina, XIII, p. 81b) : si igitur esse divinum esset formale esse omnium, oporteret omnia simpliciter esse unum. Cf. also the heretical doctrines, condemned at the Council of Paris in 1210 : (*Chartularium Universitatis Parisiensis*, I, p. 71) : Omnia unum, quia quicquid est, est Deus.

[117] *Contra Amaurianos*, edited by Clemens Baeumker, *Beiträge zur Geschichte der Philosophie des Mittelalters*, XXIV, Heft 5-6 (Münster, 1926), p. 8, 17-18 : Ergo, si omnia sunt ex eius essentia, et per ipsam : (ergo) *omnia sunt in eius essentia*.

they are from eternity present in the divine mind, they participate in the perfection and activity of the divine being ; on the other hand, since they are the patterns of the finite things they are also present in the created world : the Ideas both create and are created [118]. Moreover, in Amaury's view, creation is not the result of a free initiative : it is necessary : God is always covered with visible instruments, so that He may be grasped by creatures [119]. Besides there is a real identity between God and some finite beings, which are called 'spriritual men'. In them the Holy Spirit is embodied and reveals himself quite clearly [120]. Since the Divinity coincides with the formal perfection of everything, Amaury attributes little or no value to matter : in his view matter is non-being, it is unexisting [121].

According to G.C. Capelle the pantheism of Amaury does not spring from John Scot, although the author borrows some materials from the *De divisione naturae* and from the School of Chartres ; he also incorporates in his thought some hidden tendencies and aspirations of that time, especially the expectation of the Holy Spirit. As a matter of fact, Amaury takes over some expressions from Scot, without preserving their original meaning [122]. As a whole the doctrine of Amaury may be called an unsuccessful attempt at interpreting Christian faith with the help of Platonic and Neo-Platonic philosophy : these philosophical influences did not stem directly from Plato or Plotinus, they reached up to Amaury through Scot, Maximus Confessor and the School of Chartres. What is at issue is again the individual consistency of human existence. According to Nicholas of Cues the doctrine of Amaury was rightly condemned [123] ; in his view people with small intellectual capacity should

[118] Martini, *Chronicon*, p. 438 (Capelle, p. 105) : qui Amalericus asseruit ydeas, que sunt in mente divina, et creare et creari, cum secundum beatum Augustinum nichil nisi eternum atque incommutabile sit in mente divina.

[119] *Chartularium Univ. Parisiensis*, I, p. 71 : Deus visibilibus erat indutus instrumentis, quibus videri poterat a creaturis. Cf. Capelle, p. 30.

[120] Caesarius of Heisterbach, *Dialogus miraculorum*, c. XXII, (Capelle, p. 101-102): Unde concedebeant, quod unusquisque eorum esset Christus et Spiritus sanctus. ... Persona Spiritus sancti clare se manifestabit in quibus incarnabitur, et principaliter per septem viros loquetur.

[121] Capelle, *o.c.*, p. 36-37.

[122] Capelle, *o.c.*, p. 23, 68, 88.

[123] Nicholas of Cues, *Apologiae doctae ignorantiae*, edited by Raymond Klibansky (Leipzig, 1932), p. 29,1-5 : merito fuerunt condempnati (Begardi), prout etiam Almericus fuit per Innocentium Tertium condemnatus, in Concilio generali, de quo in capitulo 'Dampnamus de summa Trinitate'; qui non habuit sanum intellectum, quomodo Deus est omnia complicite.

be prevented from reading profound philosophical works : among others he mentions the books of Pseudo-Dionysius and the *De divisione naturae* of Scot [124]. The *Quaternuli* of David of Dinant [125] were also condemned at the Council of Paris in 1210 : all copies of the work were to be carried to the bishop of Paris before Christmas. If anyone is found after Christmas still owning the treatise of David, he will be guilty of heresy [126]. And yet the name of David does not occur in the documents of the Lateran Council of 1215 [127]. According to Albert the Great the error of David is a crucial one not only against faith, but also against philosophy [128] : relying on dialectical arguments based on the notions of *genus* and *differentia*, the author clings to a materialistic pantheism. In his view there is only one basic substance, ambracing all bodies and

---

[124] Nicholas, *Apologiae*, p. 29, 14-30 : Unde recte admonent omnes sancti, quod illis debilibus mentis oculis, lux intellectualis subtrahatur. Sunt autem illis nequaquam libri sancti Dionysii, Marii Victorini..., Iohannis Scotigenae Περὶφύσεως, Tomi David Dynanto,...

[125] Davidis de Dinando, *Quaternulorum Fragmenta*, primum edidit Marian Kurdziałek (Warsaw, 1963), LX - 109 pp.

[126] *The Condemnation at the Council of Paris in 1210* (*Chartularium Universitatis Parisiensis*, I, p. 70) : Quaternuli magistri David de Dinant infra natale episcopo Parisiensi afferantur et comburantur... Apud quem invenientur quaternuli magistri David a natali Domini in antea pro heretico habebitur.

The condemnation in 1215 by Robert of Courçon, the legate of the Pope, may be found in a letter he wrote to the University of Paris. (*Chart. Univ. Parisiensis*, I, p.78-79) : non legantur libri Aristotelis de methafisica et de naturali philosophia, nec summe de eisdem, aut de doctrina magistri David de Dinant, aut Amalrici heretici, aut Mauricii hyspani.

[127] Cf. Gabriel Théry, *Autour du décret de 1210*, I, *David de Dinant*, Bibliothèque thomiste, 6 (Kain-Paris, 1925), p. 10 : Cette sympathie (d'Innocent III pour David de Dinant) peut nous expliquer pourquoi en 1215, le concile de Latran condamne solennellement les doctrines d'Aumaury de Bène, mais ne prononce même pas le nom de David.

[128] Albertus Magnus, *Summa Theol.*, Iᵃ, tr. VI, q. 29, m.l, a,2 (ed. August Borgnet t. XXXI, p. 297) : ad errorem Alexandri et David de Dinanto et quorumdam aliorum, dicendum quod maximus est error, et contra fidem et contra philosophiam; *Summa Theol.*, Iᵃ, tr. IV, q. 20, (quaestio incidens,) (t. XXXI, p. 141) ; Iᵃ, tr. XII, q. 72, m.4, a2 (t. XXXIII p. 44) : error iste pessimus error est, et contra philosophiam, et contra Catholicam fidem; *Summa de Creat.*, II, q. 5, a2 (t. XXXV, p. 71) : et hujusmodi quae dicit, abhorret fides et ratio; *ibidem*, (p. 72) : secundum Catholicam Fidem et secundum omnium recte philosophantium attestationem dicimus, quod Deus et anima et hyle non sunt idem.

all souls, and this substance is God himself [129]. Bodies are made of a substance called matter (hyle), souls are made of a substance called reason or mind : God being the basic principle of everything is the reason of all souls and the matter of all bodies [130]. In this context Albert refers to the philosophy of Plato and Xenophanes who maintained the world to be sensible Divinity [131]. Accordingly in David's view, God, matter and mind are one single substance [132]. Aquinas also arrives at the same conclusion, all things are essentially one (*per essentiam unum*), [133] they are not a multiplicity of separate and independent substances, all of them constitute one single substance which coincides with God, who is at once matter and mind [134]. The *differentiae* belong to the level of sensible appearance [135].

---

[129] David of Dinant, *Quaternulorum Fragmenta*, (ed. M. Kurdziałek), p. 71, 2-4 : manifestum est igitur unam solam substanciam esse, non tantum omnium corporum, sed etiam animarum omnium, et eam nichil aliud esse, quam ipsum Deum. See also Albertus Magnus, *Summa de Creat.*, II P., q. 5, a2 (t. XXXV, p. 68).

[130] David of Dinant, *Quaternulorum Fragmenta*, p. 71, 4-7 : substancia vero, ex qua sunt omnia (corpora) dicitur yle; substancia vero ex qua sunt omnes anime, dicitur racio sive mens. Manifestum est ergo Deum esse racionem omnium animarum et yle omnium corporum. Cf. also Albertus Magnus, *Summa de Creat.*, II P., q.5, a2 (t. XXXV, p. 68); *Summa Theol.*, II P., tr. XII, q. 72, m.4,a2 (t. XXXIII, p. 42) : manifestum est igitur Deum esse substantiam omnium corporum et omnium animarum.

[131] Albertus Magnus, *Summa de Creat.*, II P., q. 5, a2 (t. XXXV, p. 68) : Et inducit ibidem Platonem et Xenophanem Philosophos, qui sunt hic consentientis : quia dicebant mundum nihil aliud esse quam Deum sensibilem. Cf. David of Dinant, p. 70, 24-28 : huic autem assentire videtur Plato, ubi dicit mundum esse (Deum) sensibilem... Si ergo mundus est ipse Deus preter se ipsum perceptibile sensui, ut Plato et Zeno et Socrates et multi dixerunt, yle igitur mundi est ipse Deus.

[132] David of Dinant, p. 71, 2-7; Albertus Magnus, *Summa Theol.*, II P., tr. XII, q. 72, m. 4, a2 (t. XXXIII, p. 42) : Patet igitur, quod Deus est et hyle et mens una sola substantia sunt.

[133] S. Thomas of Aquino, *II. Sent.*, d. 17, q.1, a.1 : (antiqui philosophi) ponebant enim omnia esse unum simpliciter..., et illos etiam antiquos philosophos secuti sunt quidam moderni : ut David de Dinando.... Consequitur esse omnia per essentiam unum.

[134] *ibidem* : (David de Dinando) divisit enim res in partes tres, in corpora, animas et substantias aeternas separatas; et primum autem indivisibile, ex quo constituuntur corpora, dixit 'yle'; primum autem indivisibile, ex quo constituuntur animae, dixit 'noym' vel mentem; primum autem indivisibile, in substantiis aeternis dixit 'Deum'; et haec tria esse unum et idem : ex quo iterum consequitur esse omnia per essentiam unum.

[135] *ibidem* : ponebant (antiqui philosophi et quidam moderni, ut David de Dinando) enim omnia esse unum simpliciter, et non differre, nisi forte secundum sensum vel aestimationem.

According to G. Théry, the doctrine of David is not the same as the pantheism represented by Amaury [136] : both have been censured by the same Council but their pantheistic view is clearly different ; neither the background, nor the argumentation and the conclusions are identical. The starting point of David's philosophical system seems to be Aristotle [137] and, according to Albert the Great, Alexander Aphrodisiensis, the famous commentator of the Stagirite [138]. He very often quotes Aristotle and when he asserts matter and mind to be identical, he mainly relies on the logic of Aristotle and his theory of change [139]. Dealing with this pantheistic doctrine, Albert always endeavours to dissociate David and Aristotle : in his view the whole error of David originates from misunderstanding the Aristotelian philosophy : materialism is not a necessary consequence of the Aristotelian thought [140]. Nor does David draw his interpretation of reality from the system of Scot [141]. When Albert firmly states that the doctrine of David is not only against faith, but also against reason and philosophy [142], it is because

[136] G. Théry, *Autour du Décret de 1210, I, David de Dinant : Etude sur son panthéisme matérialiste* (Kain-Paris, 1925), p. 52 : Amaury et David n'ont de commun... que leur mention dans le même texte et leur panthéisme ne se confond ni dans l'état d'esprit qui en est la base, ni dans ses conclusions.

[137] G. Théry, p. 81 : David de Dinant... a vécu dans une ambiance aristotélicienne, (et) a pris contact avec les écrits mêmes du Philosophe; p. 83 : Les Ecrits d'Aristote nous apparaissent donc comme la principale source d'inspiration du *De Tomis*.

[138] Albertus Magnus, S.T., I P., tr. VI, q.29, m.1, a2 (t. XXXI, p. 297); *Comm. I Phys.*, 1. I, tr. II, c. X (t. III, p. 38) : has autem opiniones sic explanat Alexander in quodam libello ... et David de Dinanto in libro *Atomorum* ; *Comm. I. Metaph.*, tr. IV, c. VII, ed. Bernard Geyer (Coloniae, 1960), t. XVI, 1, p. 56, 78-80 : Et haec opinio placuit Alexandro Peripatetico, et aliquid eius, quantum scivit, David de Dinanto ascivit. According to G. Théry (*o.c.*, p. 66, 72, 83) the relationship between David of Dinant and Alexander, as it is explained by Albert, is far from being historically proved. He rather points to the influence of some presocratic materialists whose doctrines David knew through the first book of the *Physics* and the *Metaphysics* of Aristotle.

[139] G. Théry, p. 81, 83.

[140] Albertus Magnus, S.T., II^a, tr. XII, q. 72, m. 4, a2 (T. XXXIII, p. 45) : omnis iste error provenit ex prava intelligentia dictorum Aristotelis.

David of Dinant did not thoroughly understand Alexander's commentary on Aristotle either : *Comm. I Metaph.*, tr. IV, c. VII, (ed. B. Geyer, t. XVI, 1, p. 56, 80) : perfecte et profunde non eam intellexit.

[141] G. Théry, p. 53 : aucun document n'établit une influence de Scot sur David et l'analyse des textes nous permet, au contraire, d'affirmer avec certitude qu'il n'y a entre ces philosophes aucun point de contact.

[142] Cf. *supra*, n. 128.

quite obviously the source of this error is philosophical reflection and dialectical reasoning [143].

At the end of this paper I want to draw some conclusions about the concept of heresy :

1. In many cases, not in all of them, heresy is a failed attempt at harmonizing Christianity and philosophy : many authors intended to interpret the revealed truth with the help of philosophical categories. In some cases they failed, because they were unable to preserve the original meaning of the Christian message.

2. Heresy and orthodoxy are correlative : to reprove some doctrine as heretical is never merely negative, it is at once to assume an attitude regarding the authentic meaning of the revealed truth. That means that orthodoxy is the result of a progressive historical disclosure : it has not been settled once for all. In the framework of this development heresy is one of the ways leading to the discovery of the true meaning of the Christian message.

3. Some heretical doctrines have been condemned by the Church authority. It would be a mistake to conclude from there that all other attempts at harmonizing Christianity and philosophy were successful and in agreement with the authentic meaning of the revealed truth. Some doctrines were not reproved because they were not influential.

4. Some medieval heresies show an outspoken kinship with gnostic trends in early Christianity ; their source could hardly be Greek philosophy, whatever their origin may be. Being characterized by a pessimistic dualism they are rather opposed to the general spirit of Greek thought.

5. Heresy is a doctrine which is thought to be incompatible with the revealed truth. However the notion of 'incompatibility' is very elastic : there are many degrees of incompatibility. In some cases it is quite obvious that a given doctrine is incompatible with Christian faith, in others it is rather controversial. Hence the concept of heresy is not univocal but analogical.

---

[143] Albertus Magnus, S.T., II^a, tr. XII, q. 72, m. 4, a2 (T. XXXIII, p. 45; cf. G. Théry, p. 113 : pour faire triompher dans la théologie catholique la philosophie aristotélicienne, une œuvre préalable s'impose : montrer que le matérialisme de David n'est point une conséquence nécessaire de l'aristotélisme... Les écrits du Philosophe sont la condamnation la plus formelle des doctrines de l'hérétique.

Jean Duvernoy

L'ACCEPTION : 'HAERETICUS' (*IRETGE*) = 'PARFAIT CATHARE' EN LANGUEDOC AU XIIIe SIÈCLE

Le mot 'hérétique' [1] a, en Languedoc au XIIIe siècle, un sens doublement étroit. Il désigne le cathare par rapport aux membres d'une autre confession (catholiques, vaudois, juifs, etc...). Il désigne le parfait cathare par opposition au simple croyant.

Non seulement le mot désigne le parfait cathare, mais il est le seul à le désigner, en règle générale du moins, du côté catholique. La vieille appellation d'"arien' (ou 'arrien') [2] et celle d'"albigeois', disparaissent. Les vocables en usage en Italie (patarin), en France (poplican, tisserand, bougre), en Flandre (piphle) ou en Allemagne (Ketter, devenu cathare par pédanterie), y sont inconnus.

Il va sans dire que les mots d'hérésie ou d'hérétique n'ont jamais perdu leur sens général, et qu'on les retrouve, de temps à autre, surtout chez les écrivains ecclésiastiques, dans un emploi correct.

Mais déjà avant 1200, Alain de Lille, en composant sa Somme, la divise en quatre parties : 'contre les hérétiques, contre les vaudois, contre les juifs, contre les payens', ce qui laisserait entendre que pour lui les vaudois n'étaient pas des hérétiques, si, en fait, il ne s'était pas simplement conformé à l'usage reçu dans le pays auquel son livre était destiné [3].

Pour Guillaume de Tudèle, l'auteur de la première partie de la Chanson de la Croisade, cette dernière est prêchée en France 'sobre'ls eretges e sobre'ls sabatatz'; c'est pour son malheur qu'Aimeri de Montréal 'vi los eretges e los ensabatatz'. De même, pour le continuateur de la Chanson, Simon de Montfort 'casses los eretges e'ls rotiers e'ls valdes' [4].

---

[1] Dans la langue vulgaire : heretge, herege, iretge, eretge, eretje.

[2] Yves Marie-Joseph Congar, '*Arriana haeresis* comme désignation du néo-manichéisme au XIIe siècle : Contribution à l'histoire d'une typification de l'hérésie au moyen âge', *Revue des sciences philosophiques et théologiques*, 43 (1959), p. 449-461.

[3] PL, 210, col. 308. L'ouvrage est dédié au seigneur de Montpellier.

[4] *La chanson de la croisade albigeoise*, éditée par Eugène Martin-Chabot, Les classiques de l'histoire de France au moyen âge, 13, 24, 25, 3 vol. (Paris, 1931-61), I, p. 25 et II, p. 71.

Même distinction chez Peire Cardenal : 'D'aqui eyson l'iretge e li essabatatz'[5].

Au mois d'octobre 1243, l'évêque d'Albi Durand forme dans sa ville une confrérie destinée entre autres à l'abaissement et à la poursuite de l'hérésie et du valdéisme : 'abaissament et encaussament d'eretguia et de Vaudezia et de tota mala error'[6], dans laquelle ne sera reçue aucune personne suspecte 'd'eretguia ni de vaudezia'.

Le formulaire des inquisiteurs Guillaume Raymond et Pierre Durand, de peu postérieur à novembre 1245, contient, à côté d'expressions normales, telles 'hereticos cuiuscumque secte', la distinction familière : 'super facto seu crimine heresis et Valdesie', 'si vidit hereticum vel Valdensem'[7].

Ce sens étroit peut s'expliquer aisément. On peut songer à une origine savante, le catharisme répondant au signalement donné par saint Paul, et étant l'hérésie par excellence, prédite par l'Ecriture [8].

Il est plus probable qu'il y a là simplement le reflet de son ancienneté et de sa prépondérance dans le Midi de la France. Les Vaudois, tard venus, et de statut équivoque [9], ont été des premiers à dénoncer par la plume et la parole l'hérésie cathare et à s'attaquer aux 'iretges'. Leur appliquer le mot aurait été particulièrement déplacé.

Cette distinction refléterait donc une habitude verbale locale.

* * *

Plus riche de contenu est l'acception spéciale qui réserve le terme d''hérétique' au parfait, le distinguant ainsi du 'croyant' et de celui qui se rend coupable des délits de bonne heure définis par l'Inquisition : fautoria, defensio, participatio, visio, adoratio. Il est, dans les procédures, reproché aux croyants d'avoir vu des 'hérétiques', de les avoir reçus, adorés, guidés, d'avoir cru que ce qu'ils disaient était vrai, mais jamais d'être hérétiques eux-mêmes [10].

[5] 'Un estribot farai', ed. René Lavaud (Toulouse, 1957), p. 208.

[6] Célestin Douais, *Documents pour servir à l'histoire de l'Inquisition dans le Languedoc*, Société de l'histoire de France, 299 et 300 (Paris, 1900), I, p. 88-89.

[7] E. Vacandard, *L'inquisition : Etude historique et critique sur le pouvoir coercitif de l'Eglise*, 3me édition (Paris, 1907), p. 315.

[8] I Tim. 4,2 : prohibentium nubere, abstinere a cibis....

[9] *Guillaume de Puylaurens et sa chronique*, éditée par J. Beyssier dans *Mélanges d'histoire du moyen âge*, 3-4, Bibliothèque de la fac. des lettres de l'univ. de Paris, 18 (Paris, 1904), p. 85-175 et 20 (Paris, 1905), p. 233-234, prologue (p. 119) : Valdenses contra alios acutissime disputabant, unde et in eorum odium aliquando (ad predicandum) admittebantur a sacerdotibus idiotis.

[10] Exemple de procès-verbal : Item il dit qu'il a cru que les hérétiques étaient

Il serait vain de recenser les passages où 'hereticus' a ce sens particulier. Il faudrait en effet citer l'entier corpus de l'Inquisition méridionale. Il suffit de relever que le baptême cathare, le 'consolamentum', a reçu le nom d''hérétication' : lui seul donne la qualité d'hérétique.

En dehors des documents judiciaires, on peut citer à nouveau le chroniqueur Guillaume de Puylaurens : 'les hérétiques se procuraient les plus larges maisons où prêcher publiquement leurs hérésies à leurs croyants'-'les hérétiques étaient tenus en tel respect qu'ils avaient des cimetières où ils enterraient publiquement ceux qu'ils avaient hérétiqués' [11].

Même emploi chez les troubadours : Peire Vidal ('l'eretge fals que no's senha') ou Peire Cardenal ('a)pellatz herege qui ne jura') [12]. Se signer ou jurer n'est pas interdit au simple croyant.

Bien qu'assez naturelle, en raison de la différence substantielle qui sépare le parfait du croyant dans tous les systèmes dualistes, la distinction s'énonce différemment en dehors du Midi.

L'Inquisition d'Aragon applique le mot 'hérétique' aux croyants dans un document qui concerne des fugitifs du comté de Foix, objet de procédures à Pamiers. Le rapprochement des deux rédactions est frappant, et le lecteur est dépaysé devant le texte de Lérida [13].

Rainier Sacconi, (Italie, 1250), emploie dans ce sens spécial 'catharus', et il se livre au dénombrement des 'cathari utriusque sexus' (parfaits et parfaites) de son temps. Ce sont ceux qui, lorsqu'ils n'appartiennent pas à la hiérarchie, portent simplement le nom de 'chrétiens' et 'chrétiennes'[14]. Or on sait que ce terme, usité de la Bosnie au Languedoc, n'appartient qu'à celui qui a reçu le baptême cathare, à l'exclusion du simple croyant.

On rencontre, par contre, un usage analogue à celui du Midi en Champagne. Aubry des Trois-Fontaines dit de Robert le Bougre qu'il 'ar-

---

bons et avaient une bonne foi et étaient véridiques et 'amis de Dieu', et il entendit dire aux hérétiques que Dieu n'avait pas fait les choses visibles et qu'il n'y avait pas de salut dans le mariage, et il l'a cru comme ils le disaient (Toulouse, bibl., ms. 609, f°1r° (1245).

[11] Loc. cit.

[12] Les poésies de Pierre Vidal, éditées par Joseph Anglade, Les classiques français du moyen âge, 11 (Paris, 1965), p. 147 ; Peire Cardenal, éd. Lavaud, p. 184.

[13] Le registre d'inquisition de Jacques Fournier, évêque de Pamiers (1318-1325) (Manuscrit nr. Vat. Latin 4030 de la Bibliothèque vaticane), édité par Jean Duvernoy, Bibliothèque méridionale, 2me série, 41, 3 vol. (Toulouse, 1965), II, p. 449 et ss. (1323).

[14] Summa de Catharis, publiée par Antoine Dondaine dans Un traité néo-manichéen du XIIIe siècle : Le Liber de duobus principiis (Roma, 1939), p. 68, 70.

rêtait les hérétiques d'après leur seule manière de parler et leurs seuls gestes' [15]. Il s'agit bien de parfaits, dont on sait par ailleurs qu'ils devaient multiplier les précautions verbales pour ne pas tomber involontairement dans le mensonge, et se reculaient pour ne pas être frôlés par les femmes, par exemple.

Il y a donc bien là un usage verbal constant, qui reflète une conscience commune. Elle n'est pas d'origine juridique. Parfaits et croyants repentis sont soumis aux mêmes pénitences; parfaits et croyants obstinés ou contumaces sont également abandonnés au bras séculier. Dans ce dernier cas, la sentence qualifie le laïc cathare d'hérétique [16]. On ira jusqu'à qualifier d'"hérétique parfaite' une croyante vaudoise qui refuse de jurer [17].

Il faut mentionner en passant que pour les cathares de l'époque, hérétique est synonyme de catholique, et, le cas échéant, d'apostat, lorsqu'on l'applique à une personne consolée qui veut se remettre à manger de la nourriture carnée [18].

Ainsi la notion d'hérésie est-elle beaucoup plus liée à un comportement qu'à une opinion. On peut aller plus loin, et dire qu'adhérer à l'hérésie, c'est embrasser un état ('status', 'ordo',) ou se rallier à ceux qui l'ont fait.

Aussi bien est-ce, pour le vulgaire, sous cette forme que sont apparues les choses. Dès le concile de Toulouse de 1119, les hérétiques sont présentés comme 'religionis speciem simulantes' [19], ils sont 'déguisés en religieux', mal d'ailleurs, quand il s'agit de cathares, qui allient la robe noire des moines basiliens à leur système pileux, inconnu de l'Occident, ou dans le cas des Vaudois, singularisés par leurs sandales.

La conversion de tels éléments, quand elle est possible, ne se conçoit guère que par le versement en bloc de la communauté dans une communauté analogue, mais soumise à l'Eglise, qu'il s'agisse de la fondation

---

[15] *E chronico Alberici monachi Trium Fontium*, dans Recueil des historiens des Gaules et de la France (=Bouquet), 21 (Paris, 1855), p. 618.

[16] E.g. Paris, Bibl. Nat., fonds Doat, t. XXI, f⁰ 145r⁰ : per diffinitivam sententiam esse hereticum condemnamus (il s'agit d'un chevalier contumace).

[17] *Registre de Jacques Fournier*, I, 519 : Confessio Huguete... heretice perfecte secte Valdensium seu Pauperum de Lugduno.

[18] *Registre de Jacques Fournier*, III, p. 269 : dimisistis viam Dei et reversus estis ad heresim, et estis factus yrregatz, pro eo quia comedistis carnes postquam fueratis receptus (vers 1305).

[19] Mansi, *Concilia*, 21, p. 226.

de Prouille, de l'organisation des Pauvres catholiques [20], ou de celle des 'Chrétiens', devenus les 'Frères', de Bosnie [21].

Il semble qu'on puisse à la rigueur faire abandonner aux hérétiques leurs idées, mais qu'il soit nécessaire de leur laisser leur règle.

**

Cette conception restrictive de l'hérésie et de l'hérétique sera, après la Croisade, à l'origine de graves malentendus entre la population méridionale et le magistère catholique, et particulièrement l'Inquisition.

Le jour de Pâques 1229 (15 avril), jour de l'entrée en vigueur du traité de Paris, les parfaits cathares quittent solennellement les localités pour se retirer dans des asiles clandestins ou, parfois, plus ou moins avoués, tels que Montségur, Dourne, ou Miramont. Les croyants les escortent en pleurant à leur départ [22]. Mais la 'terre est purgée' des hérétiques, qui sont 'exterminés', au sens juridique du terme.

Le pays croit, ou espère, que les conditions qu'on attend de lui depuis plus d'un siècle étant enfin réunies, la page est définitivement tournée; l'Eglise, de son côté, 'ne ferme pas son sein à celui qui revient', mais à condition qu'il ne soutienne pas, contre l'évidence, n'être jamais sorti.

Les consuls de Toulouse sont scandalisés par la prédication dominicaine, lorsqu'un Frère déclare qu''il reste des hérétiques dans la ville' [23]. Des troubles naissent lorsque l'Inquisition débute et s'attaque aux croyants. Un certain Jean Teisseyre, ou le tisserand, prend la population à témoin : 'Je ne suis pas hérétique, puisque j'ai une femme, que je couche avec elle, et que j'ai des enfants. Je mange de la viande, je mens et je jure : je suis un fidèle chrétien. Ne tolérez pas que l'on dise cela de moi, qui crois bien en Dieu, car ils pourraient en dire autant de vous... Beaucoup d'hérétiques incitaient le peuple à les lapider (les inquisiteurs)... parce qu'ils accusaient injustement d'hérésie des hommes honorables et mariés' [24].

[20] Cf. entre autres Herbert Grundmann, *Religiöse Bewegungen im Mittelalter...* réimpression (Darmstadt, 1961), p. 208 et ss., 100 et ss. :

[21] 'Confessio christianorum Bosnensium ann. 1203', Farlati, IV, 46; O.D. Mandić, *Bogomilska Crkva Bosanckih Krstjana* (Chicago, 1962), p. 435.

[22] *Pénitences de Pierre Sellan*, Paris, Bibl. Nat., fonds Doat, t. XXI, f° 199 r° : flevit in recessu hereticorum in die Pascha et associavit eos; f° 189 r° : conduxit hereticos in die Pasche; f° 201 v° : conduxit hereticos in die Pasche.

[23] 'Chronique de Guillaume Pellisson', publiée par Célestin Douais dans *Les sources de l'histoire de l'Inquisition* (Toulouse, 1881), p. 87.

[24] *Chronique de Guillaume Pellisson*, p. 93.

L'idée selon laquelle la compétence inquisitoriale ne s'étend qu'à des délits de comportement, à l'exclusion des délits d'opinion, est encore accréditée dans le comté de Foix au début du XIVᵉ siècle. La routine de l'Inquisition de Carcassonne aidant, l'opinion générale est qu'on ne peut condamner au Mur (prison) celui qui n'a pas 'vu' de parfaits, quelle que soit sa croyance avouée, et qu'il y a abus de la part de l'évêque à réprimer le simple fait de 'credentia' [25].

Pour l'opinion toulousaine après la paix, il n'y a plus d'hérétiques à Toulouse. Pour les Dominicains, les 'catholiques' sont en nombre infime. Si tendancieuses soient-elles, ces deux évaluations reflètent sensiblement la réalité. Que pense donc le reste de la population? D'après le toulousain Guillaume de Puylaurens, la 'masse' est bonne, mais il a suffi d'un peu de levain pour la troubler [26]. Cette masse n'a pas pu participer à vingt ans de guerre implacable sans s'être formé une opinion sur les causes officielles du conflit c'est-à-dire sur l'hérésie. Mais il convient auparavant de rechercher ce qu'en pensent les hérétiques eux-mêmes.

*
* *

Il ne saurait être question d'aborder ici la religiosité cathare autrement qu'en relation avec le thème étudié. Elle en apporte la confirmation et la justification à la fois.

Le parfait est l'expression même de l'hérésie. En fait, il l'incarne. Seul à être 'chrétien', puisque seul baptisé, ayant seul le droit de prier Dieu en lui adressant le Notre Père, seule intercession utile, il est porteur du 'Bien', (du 'Be' en occitan), qui n'est autre que le Saint-Esprit que le croyant adore lorsqu'il s'incline devant lui.

Ce 'Bien' a des vertus en quelque sorte magiques. Un chevalier cherche à voir des parfaits ; on ne peut lui en découvrir. Il se plaint : 'Tout est mort de ce qui était bon!' (1245) [27].

Sortant d'une hérétication, des croyants disent : 'C'est une chance pour ce brave homme, d'avoir été reçu par ces hommes de bien, et c'est une chance aussi pour nous d'y avoir assisté' (1241) [28]. Avant une héré-

---

[25] *Registre de Jacques Fournier*, II, p. 284 : multum mirabatur, quia multi qui sunt in muro de Alamannis erant inmurati et perdiderant bona sua, cum hereticos non vidissent, quod tamen non solebat fieri in Carcassona.

[26] *Op. cit.*, p. 159.

[27] Totum est mortuum quod bonum erat, Toulouse, ms. 609, fᵒ 237 vᵒ.

[28] Toulouse, ms. 609, fᵒ 144 rᵒ.

tication, on veut faire sortir un villageois dont on n'est pas sûr. Il s'exclame : 'Mais, monsieur, j'ai aussi besoin d'avoir ma part du Bien!' (vers 1303)[29].

Au XIVe siècle, la seule présence des parfaits porte bonheur : 'Depuis que les hérétiques ont été expulsés de Sabartès, il n'y a plus eu de beau temps dans le pays'[30]. - 'Depuis qu'ils ont été mis en fuite du pays de Sabartès, la terre n'avait plus produit autant que quand on leur permettait d'y rester, et depuis lors la terre n'avait plus rien fait de bon'[31].

On ne pouvait faire le mal le jour où l'on avait vu un parfait, et 'à ceux qui croyaient en eux, il n'arrivait jamais plus malheur ; ils avaient la richesse en abondance, et tout ce qu'ils faisaient tournait à leur avantage et bonheur'[32].

Un notaire de Soual (Tarn), disait en 1275 : 'La foudre et la tempête ne tombaient pas aussi souvent que maintenant, à l'époque où les hérétiques restaient dans le pays. Mais elles tombent plus souvent, maintenant que nous sommes avec les Mineurs et les Prêcheurs'[33].

Non seulement les hérétiques sont 'l'Église de Dieu', mais on va jusqu'à désigner chaque hérétique par le nom d"Eglise'. C'est ainsi qu'un berger se vante d'avoir donné ses vêtements à treize Eglises, c'est-à-dire à treize parfaits[34].

*
* *

Il est plus difficile de préciser la conception que l'on se faisait en Languedoc de l'hérésie dans les milieux ultras du parti catholique. Notre documentation la plus révélatrice des mentalités est en effet

[29] *Registre de Jacques Fournier*, I, p. 437 : Cor, senher, ta be m'auria obs ma part del Be!.

[30] *Registre de Jacques Fournier*, II, p. 335 et 353-354.

[31] *Registre de Jacques Fournier*, III, p. 307 : ex quo dicti boni homines fuerunt fugati de terra Savartesii, terra non fructificaverat ita bene sicut quando heretici permittebantur ibi stare, nec ex tunc terra Savartesii fecerat aliquod bonum. (Le Sabartès est la haute vallée de l'Ariège).

[32] *Registre de Geoffroy d'Ablis* (Paris, Bibl. Nat., ms. Lat. 4269), f⁰ 16 v⁰ (vers 1300) : illis qui volebant eis credere et dictis et factis eorum, nunquam veniebat aliquid infortunium, ymmo habundabant in diviciis, et omnia que faciebant erant sibi utilia et bona.

[33] Paris, Bibl. Nat., fonds Doat, XXV, f⁰ 216 v⁰ : fulgura et tempestates non solebant cadere ita frequenter sicut modo faciunt, tempore quo heretici manebant in terra ista, sed postquam sumus cum Minoribus et Predicatoribus cadunt frequentius quam solebant.

[34] *Registre de Geoffroy d'Ablis*, f⁰ 14 v⁰ dicebant quod ipsi (heretici) erant Ecclesia Dei. *Registre de Jacques Fournier*, II, p. 38 : ipse de rebus suis induerat XIII ecclesias, id est hereticos vestitos, quia dictus Petrus vocabat ecclesias hereticos vestitos.

de nature judiciaire. Or les gens qui ont à déposer devant l'Inquisition n'appartiennent évidemment pas en règle générale à ce parti. On ne peut guère noter que des invectives : 'diable', 'iretialha' (héréticaille) [35].

Une chose est certaine : les accusations systématiques contre les mœurs des cathares, qui ont abouti dans le nord de la France au sens très spécial de 'bougre', n'ont jamais pénétré en Languedoc [36].

Il faut plutôt noter, comme signe que l'hérésie n'est pas un phénomène subjectif et individuel d'opinion, le fait qu'elle est considérée comme une maladie : 'il n'y a pas de maladie aussi mauvaise que l'affaire des hérétiques, même la lèpre, car quand l'hérésie est dans une maison, c'est à peine si elle peut en sortir de quatre générations, ou même jamais' [37]. C'est là une maladie héréditaire. Il existe un 'genus hereticum', une hérédité hérétique que l'Inquisition retient dans l'appréciation de la culpabilité, et qui, bien que les incapacités civiles des descendants, peine accessoire de l'hérésie, n'aient jamais été sérieusement appliquées, entachent les familles auprès de l'opinion [38].

Le rapprochement avec la lèpre est d'ailleurs très poussé, car les deux calamités entraînent la ségrégation sociale. La disparition subite des gens, dans un village, est attribuée à ces deux causes indistinctement : 'les uns disaient qu'il était parti parce qu'il était lépreux, d'autres que c'était à cause de l'hérésie que sa femme et lui étaient partis' [39].

On va plus loin, et l'on traite globalement les cathares de 'lépreux et hérétiques' : 'Cette Rixende, lépreuse et hérétique, qui aurait dû être brûlée!' [40].

[35] *Registre de Jacques Fournier*, II, p. 367 : dyabolus erat et hereticus; t. III, p. 413 : credentes hereticorum omnes vituperabat, vocando eos 'iretialha'.

[36] De même, l''endura', le jeune rituel du 'consolé' qui ne peut pas dire le Pater, bien que mal vu de l'opinion, n'a jamais donné lieu à l'accusation de meurtre rituel, comme en Allemagne.

[37] *Registre de Jacques Fournier*, II, p. 110 : non erat aliqua infirmitas mala sicut factum hereticorum, etiam infirmitas lepre, quia postquam heresis erat in aliqua domo, vix de IIIIor generationibus poterat exire, vel etiam nunquam.

[38] *Registre de Jacques Fournier*, I, p. 192 : Interrogatus si dictus Guillelmus fuit de genere hereticali, dixit quod sic. (Il s'agit du bayle d'Ornolac (Ariège) dont la mère est morte au Mur de Carcassonne, ce qui ne l'a pas empêché d'accéder à ses fonctions).- Le bayle de Montaillou (Ariège), a lui-même comparu et avoué devant l'Inquisition avant sa nomination (ibid., II, p. 268).

[39] *Registre de Jacques Fournier*, II, p. 366. Cf. II, p. 200 : aliqui dicebant quod dictus Petrus fugerat propter debita, et aliqui propter lepram, et alii propter heresim.

[40] *Registre de Jacques Fournier*, II, p. 365 : leprosa et heretica, que debuisset esse combusta. (Il s'agit d'une croyante, et non d'une lépreuse).

Il n'est pas étonnant que les 'cagots', les parias descendants de lépreux, aient fini par se croire descendants des Albigeois, et que ceux de Navarre aient, en 1514, demandé au pape Léon X à être relevés de leur condition, qui provenait, disaient-ils, du fait qu'ils descendaient des armées du comte de Toulouse [41].

La notion d'hérétique a dû disparaître d'assez bonne heure de la conscience au profit de celle de 'hors-la-loi', et dans le dialecte ariégeois actuel, 'iretge', qui n'est plus compris, a le sens de 'sauvage' [42].

*
* *

Entre ces deux opinions extrêmes, règne cette masse, ce Marais assez tiède et indéterminé pour que de deux chroniqueurs qui furent aussi inquisiteurs, Guillaume Pellisson et Guillaume de Puylaurens, l'un ne la range pas au nombre des catholiques, et l'autre l'estime 'bonne en soi'.

Elle est caractérisée très nettement par le refus de prendre parti. On connaît bien la réponse du chevalier Pons Adhémar de Roudeille à Foulque, évêque de Toulouse, après les prédications de Diègue d'Osma et de saint Dominique (vers 1207-1208) : 'Nous n'aurions jamais pu croire que Rome avait des arguments aussi nombreux et aussi efficaces contre ces gens-là... - Pourquoi ne les chassez-vous pas, ne les expulsez-vous pas du pays, dit l'évêque? - Nous ne pouvons pas. Nous avons été élevés avec eux, nous avons des cousins parmi eux et nous les voyons vivre honorablement' [43].

Le même laxisme se retrouve un siècle après, alors que Croisade et Inquisition sont passées sur le pays. Un noble de Rabat (Ariège) déclare: 'Les hérétiques sont bien malheureux, s'ils ne sont pas sauvés, eux qui jeûnent et prient beaucoup, ne mangent pas de viande, ne couchent pas avec des femmes, et ne mentent pas' [44].

Le juge de Sabartès, châtelain de Tarascon, dit au comte de Foix (Roger-Bernard III, mort en 1302) 'qu'il verrait et entendrait volontiers des hérétiques, pour savoir ce qu'ils disaient et soutenaient; le comte

[41] Henri Marcel Fay, *Histoire de la lèpre en France : Lépreux et cagots du Sud-Ouest* (Paris, 1910), pp. 182-183. Cette assimilation se retrouve hors du Midi. Rabelais, employant sans doute une vieille locution, joue encore sur les mots : 'aucuns ladres, autres bougres, autres ladres et bougres ensemble' (Ancien Prologue du Quart livre de Pantagruel dans *Oeuvres complètes*, éditées par Jacques Boulenger, Bibliothèque de la Pleiade, 15, p. 375, cité par le professeur V. Topentcharov, *Bougres et cathares* (Paris, 1971), p. 13).

[42] A. Moulis, *L'Ariège et ses châteaux féodaux* (Verniolle, 1968), p. 15.

[43] Guillaume de Puylaurens, p. 127.

[44] *Registre de Jacques Fournier*, II, p. 59.

lui répondit de ne pas le faire, car si d'aventure il les voyait et les entendait, ces hérétiques lui mettraient un tel sophisme dans le cœur qu'il
n'en sortirait jamais' 45. Le même juge faisait volontiers de la théologie
à table, sur la création ou sur l'incarnation, notamment, en donnant les
argument contraires des hérétiques et des 'clercs', comme si ni lui-même,
ni ses convives, n'avaient appartenu à l'un de ces partis 46.

On ne se décide guère que sur la fin, et encore peut-on se demander si
l'on obéit plus à sa conviction qu'à la mode. Un noble de Castelnaudary
(Aude), Pons de Gibel, envoyé comme otage à Narbonne en 1226, est
sur sa fin. Il fait venir des 'hérétiques'. Il ne se remet pas entre leurs
mains, car 'ils ne sont pas de la religion des hérétiques du Toulousain'
(peut-être étaient-ce des Vaudois, plus accrédités en Narbonnaise qu'en
Lauragais). 'Il envoya chercher les moines de Boulbonne, et se donna
à eux' 47. Le cas n'est pas isolé. Un noble du Mas-Saintes-Puelles (Aude),
Guillaume de Malhorgues, est 'consolé' par des cathares sur sa fin.
S'étant rétabli, 'il reconnut qu'il lui était arrivé malheur d'avoir été
hérétiqué, il mangea de la viande, et se fit transporter à l'abbaye de Boulbonne, où il mourut et fut enterré' (vers 1237) 48.

Au tournant du XIVème siècle dans le haut pays de Foix, la tolérance
règne même dans les milieux populaires. Un villageois de Vaychis (Ariège)
dit : 'En Lombardie, on ne fait pas de mal aux hérétiques, aux Juifs
et aux Sarrazins ni à personne qui travaille convenablement. C'est
péché que faire du mal aux hérétiques, aux Juifs et aux Sarrazins, s'ils
travaillent convenablement et gagnent ce dont ils vivent' 49.

A côté de la tolérance, on rencontre d'ailleurs l'incrédulité la plus
nette, souvent alliée à la grossièreté verbale, qu'il s'agisse de l'eucharistie,
de la naissance du Christ, ou plus simplement de la nature de l'âme 50.
Sur bien des points, ces opinions franchement négatives sont éloignées

---

45 *Registre de Jacques Fournier*, II, p. 61.
46 *Registre de Jacques Fournier*, II, p. 54-55.
47 Toulouse, ms. 609, f° 251 r°.
48 Toulouse, ms. 609, f° 8 r°.
49 *Registre de Jacques Fournier*, II, p. 157.
50 *Registre de Jacques Fournier*, III, p. 464 : quod elevant capellani in missa simi-
latur pelalha de nap vel de rappa; II, p. 120 : Tu scis qualiter Deus factus fuit? Ego
dicam tibi : Deus factus fuit 'foten e coardan', et hoc dicens percutens unam manum
suam cum alia; II, p. 359 : aliam animam non habemus in ventre nisi panem; I, p. 264:
respicit homo, quando homo moritur, et nichil videt egredi de ore eius, nisi ventum.
Si ego viderem quod aliquid aliud egrederetur, ego crederem quod anima esset aliquid;
I, p. 260 : anima nostra non est aliud quam sanguis.

du catharisme aussi bien que de l'orthodoxie. Les intellectuels ne pensent pas différemment, et empruntent des arguments au rationalisme [51].

On ne peut donc être surpris que les clercs, l'Eglise, occupent une place similaire à celle des hérétiques, c'est-à-dire celle d'un clan étranger à la population. Il y a là, certes, un phénomène politique. Le pays, à l'époque de la Croisade, a été 'en guerre contre l'Eglise et le Roi'. Des Français et des clercs, ce sont les clercs que l'on hait le plus, car ce sont eux qui ont amené les Français dans le pays [52]. On souhaite contre eux 'l'extermination', au sens de bannissement : 'les clercs devraient être chassés, et si on s'entendait avec monseigneur le comte de Foix, on se garderait bien de laisser un clerc franchir le pas de Labarre' (un défilé en aval de Foix) [53].

A cet anticléricalisme, les motifs ne font pas défaut. Le clergé rural ne se distingue ni par sa foi (on trouve à l'époque de Jacques Fournier, parmi les curés, un cathare, un docète et un adversaire de la résurrection de la chair) ni par ses mœurs. La plupart des recteurs sont concubinaires, et dans le diocèse contigu d'Urgel, de l'autre côté des Pyrénées, les prêtres pratiquent, moyennant licence de leur évêque, une espèce de mariage civil [54].

L'intérêt s'en mêle aussi : Le père d'un prêtre souhaite que les prélats soient envoyés à Grenade ou outre-mer contre les Sarrasins, et 'qu'ils soient aussi zélés et courageux pour leur prendre leur pays et venger la mort du Christ qu'ils le sont à réclamer les dîmes et les prémices des carnalages' [55].

[51] *Registre de Geoffroy d'Ablis* (vers 1304), Paris, Bibl. Nat., ms. Lat. 4269, fo 50ro : ille clericus dixerat sibi pluries quod ipse et quasi omnes naturales Tholose et Parisius tenebant quod impossibile erat et etiam contra naturam quod de pane fieret corpus Christi, etiam per verba sancta.

[52] *Registre de Jacques Fournier*, III, p. 329 : Cum dominus Bernardus Saxeti bone memorie quondam Appamarium (episcopus) interrogasset eum quos ipse odiebat, clericos vel gallicos, responderat ei quod plus odiebat clericos, quia clerici introduxerant in partibus istis gallicos, et si clerici non fuissent, nunquam gallici venissent ad partes istas.

[53] *Registre de Jacques Fournier*, III, p. 331 (un cordonnier de la haute Ariège, en 1322).

[54] *Registre de Jacques Fournier*, I, p. 224 et ss.; III, 55; III, p. 7 et ss.; I, p. 252 : de modo quem tenent presbiteri in terra Palharesii quando habent concubinas et focorias... ipsas tenent palam et publice sicut laici suas uxores, et dicte uxores dotantur, et filii ipsorum... succedunt in hereditate paterna et materna... et quolibet anno vel quasi dant aliquid episcopo diocesano quod sic permittat eos stare.

[55] *Registre de Jacques Fournier*, II, p. 323.

Mais, dans l'ensemble, il s'agit avant tout d'un phénomène de mode et d'opinion. On chante, dans l'entourage de Bernard Saisset, évêque de Pamiers que Philippe le Bel accusa d'avoir intrigué pour libérer le Midi, la chanson de Peire Cardenal 'Clerges si fon pastor' [56] de même qu'avant la Croisade on disait : 'J'aimerais mieux être curé que faire ceci ou cela!' [57]

*
* *

De ces constatations, on pourrait être tenté de tirer la conclusion que le Languedoc a pris, à cette époque, une figure excentrique dans la chrétienté médiévale. Mais ce serait méconnaître, et la très belle religiosité qui se dégage de la poésie occitane, même et notamment chez les poètes anti-cléricaux, dont on n'a jamais pu prouver l'hérésie [58], et l'essor des ordres Mendiants qui s'est traduit par une architecture de premier ordre et la prolifération de couvents dans les localités les plus modestes.

Si l'état clérical, orthodoxe ou hétérodoxe, est l'affaire de quelques-uns, la foi est l'affaire de tous, et cette foi est entièrement orientée 'ad terminum' [59]. L'hérésie comme les réguliers offrent des recettes sûres de bonne mort. A l'hérétique, comme au clerc, qui entendent vivre leur foi de façon pratique ou sacramentelle dans la force de l'âge, et qui, de ce fait, sont distincts de la communauté, on demande d'être garants de cette promesse par une vie exemplaire.

Les contradictions se résolvent donc si l'on considère combien les traits dégagés : l'anticléricalisme de style, le nicolaïsme, et surtout la conception étroite de l'hérésie considérée comme le 'factum hereticorum', l'affaire de gens qui ont embrassé certain état condamné, rappellent l'époque révolue qui a précédé et immédiatement suivi le mouvement de réforme Grégorienne.

A une expression littéraire et une liberté de pensée en avance sur son temps, le Languedoc du treizième siècle a mêlé une conception de la religion archaïque, à laquelle les caractéristiques du catharisme ne sont probablement pas étrangères.

---

[56] *Registre de Jacques Fournier*, III, p. 319, 328-329.

[57] Guillaume de Puylaurens, p. 119.

[58] Cf. Lavaud, Peire Cardenal, p. 633.

[59] Cf. supra. On peut dire que le grand intérêt du catharisme est de procurer en quelque sorte le couvent à domicile : 'magnum erat quod homo posset salvare animam suam, credendo dictis hominibus, *moriendo in domo sua*' (*Registre de Jacques Fournier*, I, p. 237).

A la même époque en effet, le Valdéisme a évolué. Entre celui que l'on constate en Quercy avant la Croisade et au cours de la reconquête (1218-1229), où les Frères vaudois sont des anonymes étrangers à la population, et celui des communautés de paysans bourguignons de Gascogne un siècle plus tard, tout a changé [60].

A la différence du croyant cathare, le fidèle vaudois suit les dangereux préceptes de la secte. De même, béguins et béguines (en bas Languedoc) forment une communauté d'où la distinction entre 'hérétique' et sympathisant est entièrement bannie. Aussi bien laïcs vaudois et béguins non franciscains montent-ils sur le bûcher à côté du vaudois de 'statut' et du fratricelle, sort que ne connaît guère le croyant cathare qu'en cas de relapse, et malgré lui [61]. Vaudois et béguins atteindront l'aube des temps modernes. Le catharisme disparaît d'occident avec ses derniers 'hérétiques'.

[60] Cf. Jean Duvernoy, *Albigeois et Vaudois en Quercy*, Actes du XIXème congrès des Etudes régionales (Moissac, 1963), p. 110-121. Yves Dossat, *Les vaudois méridionaux d'après les documents de l'Inquisition*, Cahiers de Fanjeaux, 2 (1967), p. 207-226. *Le registre de Jacques Fournier*, I, p. 100-101, n. 36, d'après les Sentences de Toulouse éditées par Limborch.

[61] De 1318 à 1325, l'évêque de Pamiers Jacques Fournier abandonne cinq personnes au bras séculier. Quatre sont des vaudois. Il y a là un diacre (de la hiérarchie vaudoise), sa nourrice, un tonnelier et sa femme. Tous ont refusé de jurer. Or, explique le diacre, pour appartenir au 'status' vaudois, il faut être un homme, être instruit, et avoir fait, entre autres, vœu de célibat avant une véritable ordination. Le cinquième condamné est un paysan, à peine cathare, qui a abjuré sans difficulté, mais qui est relaps.

Mariano d'ALATRI

'ERESIE' PERSEGUITE DALL'INQUISIZIONE IN ITALIA NEL CORSO DEL DUECENTO

Con questa breve nota, lungi dal volermi cimentare in una disquisizione teorica sul concetto di eresia, intendo solo porre in rilievo alcuni contenuti emergenti dagli atti dell'inquisizione che fino ad oggi sono venuti alla luce o dei quali ho preso conoscenza in vista di una loro utilizzazione o pubblicazione[1]. Da essi risultano alcuni dati che ci aiutano a capire che cosa i giudici della fede perseguivano come eresia e, cosa ancora piú interessante, in che cosa precisamente consistesse, soggettivamente e oggettivamente, la 'eresia' degli imputati.

Gli eterodossi

Oggetto primo della *inquisitio* del giudice della fede è, anche in Italia, il catarismo, che nel Duecento è *l'haeresis* per antonomasia : infatti, negli atti inquisitoriali, i catari son detti correntemente *haeretici* senza altra specificazione[2]. Ma qui c'è da tener presente che, se sono relativamente numerosi i perfetti catari, ossia coloro che erano stati ereticati mediante il *consolamentum*, il cui nome ricorre negli atti dell'inquisizione, è invece estremamente esiguo il numero delle sentenze e, piú ancora, degli atti processuali istruiti contro di essi e giunti sino a noi. E' nondimeno provato che il giudice della fede — seguendo la procedura fissata nei manuali dell'ufficio[3] — cercava anzitutto di conoscere il contenuto della loro fede, affin di stabilire se si trattava, o no, di eresia.

[1] Saggi e ricerche sull'inquisizione sono elencati, cronologicamente, in Emil van der Vekené, *Bibliographie der Inquisition : Ein Versuch* (Hildesheim, 1963).

[2] Ilarino da Milano, *L'eresia di Ugo Speroni nella confutazione del maestro Vacario : Testo inedito del secolo XII con studio storico e dottrinale*, Studi e testi, 115 (Città del Vaticano, 1945), 32 : Alano di Lilla indirizza il libro primo del *De fide catholica*, intitolato *contra hereticos*, contro i catari, gli eretici per antonomasia. Nel corso del Duecento, in Linguadoca 'haereticus' (*iretge*) equivaleva a perfetto cataro, e cosí avveniva pure a Bologna nello scorcio del secolo : cf. Eugenio Dupré Theseider, 'L'eresia a Bologna nei tempi di Dante', in *Studi storici in onore di Gioacchino Volpe*, Biblioteca storica Sansoni, NS 31-32 (Firenze, 1958), 393.

[3] Raoul Manselli, 'Per la storia dell'eresia catara nella Firenze del tempo di Dante : Il processo contro Saraceno Paganelli', *Bullettino dell'Istituto Storico Italiano per il Medio Evo e Archivio Muratoriano*, 62 (1950), 123-138 (125-127).

Cito il caso di due catari fiorentini, Andrea e Pietro, catturati nel
1229 dall'abate Quirico di S. Miniato al Monte e condotti a Perugia,
dove, nella chiesa di Monteluce, alla presenza di Gregorio IX, fecero
una dettagliata abiura dei loro errori, dai quali risulta, chiarissima,
la loro appartenenza al catarismo dualistico [4].

La presenza del dualismo assoluto in Orvieto è denunziata dalla
confessione del pellicciaio Stradigotto da Siena, che nel corso della
inquisitio generalis degli anni 1268/69 riferí il contenuto delle prediche
ascoltate dalla bocca degli eretici [5]. Da esso non differisce la dottrina
di cui, in una pubblica *contio*, con la immediatezza di un comiziante,
si fa banditore, nel corso di un contraditorio con l'inquisitore, un ano-
nimo eretico della Campagna (l'odierna Cioceria), il cui ricordo ci è
giunto attraverso un *exemplum* [6]. Gli errori invece che, verso il 1250,
un eretico fiorentino confessa dinanzi all'inquisitore domenicano Ruggero Calcagni, riflettono alcuni aspetti dottrinali piú concreti del catarismo e non v'è in essi alcun accenno al dualismo assoluto [7].

A volte, attraverso l'inchiesta, l'inquisitore accerta persino l'appartenenza dell'imputato a una data chiesa catara, come nel caso di quel-
l'Albertino convocato dall'inquisitore a Ferrara nel 1273, il quale era
stato 'haereticus sectae de Bagnolo' [8], mentre dallo stesso processo
risulta che il famoso Armanno Pungilupo, prima di approdare al catarismo, 'fecerat vitam Pauperum de Lugduno, et tandem fuerat consolatus
in Secta Haereticorum di Bagnolo' [9].

Contrariamente a quanto a prima vista può sembrare, l'attenzione
dell'inquisitore, in questi interrogatori, non era rivolta ad accertare e,
meno ancora, ad approfondire la natura dell'eresia o il grado di colpe-
volezza soggettiva dell'imputato. A lui interessava soprattutto di verifi-
care, in base a dati esteriori quali l'ascolto di prediche, la pubblica

---

[4] Ilarino da Milano, 'Il dualismo cataro in Umbria al tempo di san Francesco
d'Assisi', in *Atti IV° convegno studi Umbri : Filosofia e cultura in Umbria tra Medioevo e
Renascimento* (Perugia, 1967), 175-216 (186-190).

[5] W. Cherubini, 'Movimenti patarinici in Orvieto', *Bollettino dell'Istituto Storico
Artistico Orvietano*, 15 (1959), 34 ; Ilariano da Milano, *Il dualismo cataro*, 209s.

[6] Mariano D'Alatri, *L'inquisizione francescana nell'Italia centrale nel secolo XIII*
(Roma, 1954), 51.

[7] G. Lami, *Lezioni di antichità toscane e spezialmente di Firenze* (Firenze, 1766),
II, 551s.

[8] Lodovico Antonio Muratori, *Antiquitates italicae Medii Aevi* (Mediolani, 1741),
V, col. 125 E.

[9] Muratori, *Antiquitates*, V, col. 126 A ed E.

professione di dottrine, atti cultuali e contatti sospetti, se v'era stata una manifesta adesione all'eresia, e di entrare in possesso del maggior numero possibile di elementi atti a metterlo sulle tracce di altri eventuali eretici o di loro aderenti. Insomma, l'inquisitore è un giudice, non un confessore e neppure un teologo [10]. Oggetto del suo intervento è il foro esterno.

Qualche volta, prima ancora che l'inquisitore si mettese sulle tracce degli infamati di eresia, questi venivano colpiti con gravi pene. Capita cosí con i 67 imputati, probabilmente credenti (com' è ovvio, il termine *credentes/credenti*, qui e in seguito, è preso in senso tecnico), che nel 1269 si erano rifugiati nel regno di Napoli e contro i quali, insieme al mandato di cattura, viene ordinato l'immediato sequestro dei beni. Non si conoscono altri casi del genere e, forse anche perché ignoriamo i precedenti e il seguito della vicenda, non riusciamo a spiegarci come si potesse condannare quale eretico chi ancora non era stato ascoltato [11].

E' superfluo fare un discorso a parte per quelle 'eresie' che, al pari del catarismo, il prof. Eugenio Dupré Theseider, in un suo brillante studio sugli atti dell'inquisizione bolognese di fine Duecento e inizio Trecento, dice 'tecniche'. Si tratta di eresie dal contenuto dottrinale manifestamente eterodosso, solidamente organizzate, con largo seguito di aderenti, dotate di grande forza di penetrazione in mezzo al popolo, proscritte in numerose bolle papali e ordinariamente caratterizzate nei manuali degli inquisitori. Esse erano presenti quasi esclusivamente nell'Italia settentrionale, e contro i loro aderenti l'istituto inquisitoriale applicò, di fatto, tutti i rigori del suo 'sacro arsenale' di leggi e pene. Negli atti incontriamo numerosi valdesi (son detti anche poveri di Lione[12]

[10] 'Non est disputandum cum hereticis, maxime in officio inquisitionis. Sed fides catholica sive articuli denunciandi, et queratur super hiis sine strepitu et litigio, ut, si credit, recipiatur secundum formam pretaxatam, si vero credere recusat, condempnetur' : cosí il testo d'una consultazione anonima riferita da Antoine Dondaine, 'Le manuel de l'inquisiteur (1230-1330)', *Archivum Fratrum Praedicatorum*, 17 (1947), 85-194 (93). Da notare che gli eretici italiani non sono cosí loquaci come i loro correligionari francesi e tedeschi : cf. Ignaz von Döllinger, *Beiträge zur Sektengeschichte des Mittelalters*, II, *Dokumente vornehmlich zur Geschichte der Valdesier und Katharer* (München, 1890), passim.

[11] D'Alatri, *L'inquisizione*, 53s. I can. 3 e 4 del concilio di Béziers (19 aprile 1246) tutelano i beni degli imputati col proibirne la confisca prima della sentenza legale : cf. Christine Thouzellier, 'La repressione dell'eresia e gli inizi dell'inquisizione', in *La cristianità romana* (1198-1274), a cura di M. D'Alatri (Torino, 1968), 437.

[12] Muratori, *Antiquitates*, V, col. 130 A; Gerolamo Biscaro, *Inquisitori ed eretici lombardi (1292-1318)* (Torino, 1921), 61s, 69-71, 77; D'Alatri, *L'inquisizione*, 127s.

e, contro uno di essi, Aliotto dell'Acconciato di Fucecchio, procede l'inquisitore francescano fra Caro d'Arezzo verso il 1290) [13], poveri lombardi, [14] apostolici e dolciniani [15], guglielmiti [16] e, finalmente, alcuni
sostenitori della liceità dell'usura [17].

I credenti

Ma la maggior parte degli atti inquisitoriali giunti sino a noi non
riguardano, come s'è già accennato, gli eretici consolati, bensí i *credentes* :
e tutto lascia pensare che questi simpatizzanti per l'eresia, di gran lunga
piú numerosi degli eretici consolati, in realtà comparissero anche piú
frequentemente dinanzi al giudice della fede. Essi costituivano la larga
frangia e la forza sociale dell'eresia, aderivano ai 'perfetti', prestavano
loro ossequio e assistenza, s'impegnavano a ricevere il *consolamentum*
in punto di morte (una volta preso l'impegno, c'era da temere che venis-
sero consolati anche dopo che l'avevano ritrattato [18]), e nel frattempo
ascoltavano la predicazione dei 'perfetti', partecipavano ai riti della
frazione del pane e alla recita comunitaria del Pater noster.

[13] D'Alatri, 'Archivio, offici e titolari dell'inquisizione toscana verso la fine
del Duecento', *Collectanea Franciscana*, 40 (1970), 169-190 (187).

[14] Biscaro, *Inquisitori*, p. 62.

[15] Gerolamo Biscaro, *Guglielma la Boema e i Guglielmiti* (Milano, 1930), 10;
G. Biscaro, *Inquisitori*, p. 79; Luchesius Spätling, *De apostolicis, pseudoapostolis,
apostolinis* (München, 1947); E. Dupré Theseider, *L'eresia*, 430-433, 441s; Eugenio
Anagnine, *Dolcino e il movimento ereticale all'inizio del Trecento*, Bibliotheca di Cultura, 69 (Firenze, 1964), 103-112.

[16] Biscaro, *Guglielma*, 15, 24, 26, 31.

[17] D'Alatri, *L'inquisizione*, 38, 93; ma cf. anche 48 nota 59; Dupré Theseider,
L'eresia, 390. Molto curiosamente, a numerosi eretici orvietani, condannati negli
anni 1268/69, viene proibito di prestare ad usura; qualora, poi, ne avessero già tratto
dei vantaggi, dovevano restituire i frutti maturati, come era previsto dalla bolla di
Alessandro IV, *Quod super nonnullis*, 1258 dic. 13 (cf. *Bullarium franciscanum*, II,
317) : '... quaestionem super usuris motam contra tales iudicialiter non debere audiri ab
inquisitoribus haeresis; nec decidi : nolentes quod per causas huiusmodi offendiculum
negotio Fidei praeparetur; eos tamen ad restitutionem usurarum, de quibus constiterit,
compellere poterunt; quibus in satisfactionem pro praedicto crimine huiusmodi
restitutionem in poenitentiam iniunxerunt'. Era una punizione vera e propria, e in
in tal modo si toglieva agli eretici un'occasione per influire sugli altri; ma, in pari
tempo, non equivaleva, questo atto, a giustificare, sia pure indirettamente, l'usura
esercitata dai cristiani ortodosi? Cf. D'Alatri, *L'inquisizione*, p. 72.

[18] Bernard Gui, *Manuel de l'inquisiteur*, a cura di Guillaume Mollat, Les classiques
de l'histoire de France au moyen-âge, 8-9 (Paris, 1964), I, 28s.; D'Alatri, *L'Inquisizione*, 59.

Dal momento che l'inquisizione trattava i *credentes* alla stregua degli eretici, è il caso di domandarci in che cosa poteva consistere la loro 'eresia'. Infatti, non solo agli estranei, ma anche ai simpatizzanti o *credentes* non ancora iniziati mediante il *consolamentum*, veniva tenuta gelosamente nascosta la dottrina dualistica che era alla base del catarismo. A volte non ne venivano messi al corrente neppure gli eretici consolati. Cosí, Pietro, uno degli eretici che fecero l'abiura in Perugia, si sentí in obbligo di specificare che molti articoli riferiti nell'atto di abiura egli non li aveva mai ascoltati per l'innanzi [19]. Bonpietro, finito sul rogo a Bologna sullo scorcio del Duecento, dichiarò che per lui le astruserie del crèdo cataro erano rimaste impenetrabili [20]. Ordinariamente gli eretici, nella loro predicazione propagandistica, si limitavano a ingerire nell'animo dei *credentes* dubbi circa la presenza reale di Cristo nell'eucarestia [21], magari insistendo sulla impossibilità che sacerdoti indegni potessero compiere sí grande mistero [22] e, molto piú frequentemente, impugnavano la liceità del matrimonio, del giuramento e della pena di morte inflitta ai delinquenti [23].

In alcuni casi, l'imputabilità di certi *credentes* diventa addirittura problematica, non solo per la mancata informazione o per la loro incapacità di comprendere le astruse dottrine che costituivano il fondo della eresia, soprattutto catara, ma anche per la impossibilità di un consenso consapevole a motivo della giovane età degli imputati. Cosí, nel 1289, Giovanni Perini si accusava davanti all'inquisitore francescano Bartolomeo da Siena che, 25 anni prima, essendo appena ottenne, aveva reso ossequio ai catari; [24] un'altra fiorentina, Giovanna, moglie di Marito di Cereto, confessa anch'ella di aver simpatizzato per l'eresia, mentr'era ancor fanciulla; [25] nel 1285, Bonaventura di S. Giorgio di Verona riferisce che Armanno Pungilupo, il famigerato eretico ferrarese venerato come santo subito dopo la morte, l'aveva indotto a fare la 'reverentia' a un eretico, e conclude : 'Quod et feci, nesciens quid facerem' [26]. Bonaventura non è detto 'credente', né dagli atti processuali risulta

---

[19] Ilarino da Milano, *Il dualismo cataro*, p. 189
[20] Dupré Theseider, *L'eresia*, 407s.
[21] Muratori, *Antiquitates*, V, col. 125 ACD.
[22] Dupré Theseider, *L'eresia*, p. 427.
[23] Dupré Theseider, *L'eresia*, 407s.
[24] D'Alatri, *L'inquisizione*, 89.
[25] D'Alatri, *L'inquisizione*, 83s.
[26] Muratori, *Antiquitates*, V, col. 122 D

che gli fosse imposta l'abiura; ma la cosa non andò cosí liscia a Bena-mata, moglie di Benvenuto Pepi, la quale, nonostante affermasse di aver creduto agli eretici soltanto a fior di labbra e non col cuore, fu con-dannata come eretica [27]. L'unico caso in cui un 'credente' potesse essere pienamente prosciolto per i contatti e gli impegni presi con gli eretici, era l'infermità mentale : ma questa bisognava provarla [28].

In questi e in altri casi che si potrebbero addurre, è superfluo rilevare che l'inquisizione perseguiva come eretico anche chi non aveva un'ade-guata conoscenza dei contenuti dottrinali dell'eresia, chi era incapace di intenderli e persino chi non aveva avuta alcuna intenzione di aderirvi interiormente.

Come si vede, gli atti dell'inquisizione forniscono dati per una valu-tazione di quella che era, o non era, l'eresia sia dal punto di vista ogget-tivo (contenuti del crèdo ereticale) sia da quello soggettivo (adeguata conoscenza ed ostinata adesione al medesimo crèdo). A proposito di quest'ultimo aspetto, dagli atti emergono dati che permettono di avviare un discorso circa la consapevolezza, o meno, che alcuni 'eretici' avevano riguardo alla propria identità. Alludiamo alla questione della buona fede ossia all'invincibile convinzione di essere nella verità : un elemento, questo, che non ha alcun peso sul giudizio del giudice della fede, ma che, credo, era determinante per chi, per la propria fede 'eterodossa', non temeva di affrontare una morte atroce. Cito un solo drammatico episo-dio : intorno all'anno 1269, una certa Spera, già damigella della marche-sa d'Este, stando in carcere a Verona in attesa di salire sul rogo, proruppe in questo lamento : 'Heu quam parum steti in ista poenitentia! Nam fueram facta bona christiana ab illo benedicto Armanno...!' [29]. Per l'infelice ragazza, ereticata dal ferrarese Armanno Pungilupo, l'eretica-zione catara era l'equivalente della professione che in quel tempo molti laici emettevano entrando nell'Ordine della Penitenza rinnovato da san Francesco!

Ciò ci induce a pensare che, nella maggior parte dei casi, la simpatia e perfino l'ingresso tra gli eretici non erano l'opzione consapevole per un crèdo ma piuttosto una ricerca, emotiva e confusa, di salvezza : un'opzione che, secondo gli individui, poteva essere fatalistica, im-pegnata oppure di comodo, protestataria e persino puntigliosa.

---

[27] D'Alatri, *L'inquisizione*, p. 74.
[28] D'Alatri, *L'inquisizione*, p. 37.
[29] Muratori, *Antiquitates*, V, col. 126 D.

I favoreggiatori

Piú fragili, spesso occasionali, e di svariatissimo genere, sono i vincoli che tanto sovente legavano agli eretici, piú che all'eresia, la variopinta schiera dei cosí detti favoreggiatori. Non di rado, è vero, la ricettazione e l'aiuto di ogni genere offerto agli eretici erano motivati da una marcata simpatia per la loro persona, se non proprio per la loro fede eterodossa. Infatti, non è raro il caso in cui i castelli di alcuni signori costituivano un porto sempre aperto e sicuro per gli eretici itineranti. Era di questi, per citare un esempio, Capello di Chia, un feudatario della Tuscia Romana infamato di eresia, contro cui fu organizzata una vera e propria crociata [30]. Ma altre volte il favore veniva accordato unicamente perché anche gli eretici erano impegnati nell'opposizione alla Chiesa Romana; oppure gli inquisitori ravvisavano gli estremi del favoreggiamento nella resistenza o nella tiepidezza con cui le autorità comunali inserivano le costituzioni antieretiche nel corpo degli statuti. E poi è tutt'altro che agevole e, non di rado, addirittura impossibile appurare fino a qual punto, in numerosissimi casi, sia in giuoco l'eresia oppure la politica. Quando un imputato viene condannato come *haereticus* oppure come *credens haereticorum*, sappiamo, almeno dal punto di vista formale, quel che c'è dietro quelle etichette; ma la cosa non è affatto chiara quando, soprattutto negli atti di vendita dei beni ereticali (e il piú delle volte si tratta solo di estratti) ricorrono le formule : *dampnatus propter haeresim, ob crimen haereseos*, oppure vi si legge che erano stati venduti i beni 'in inquisitionis officio per sententiam publicatis et confiscatis'. Qui la *haeresis*, per cui sono state inflitte multe e confische, potrebbe anche indicare (ed è tutt'altro che facile appurare la verità, se non si dispone di altre fonti storiche) che la condanna è avvenuta per favoreggiamento, spesso dovuto a motivi meramente politici.

E' certamente significativo il fatto che, nel 1304, a distanza di 45 anni dalla morte di Ezzelino da Romano (†1259), Benedetto XI fosse costretto ad ingiungere agli inquisitori veneti di non piú molestare, col pretesto dell'eresia, gli antichi fautori del tiranno : inutilmente, però [31]. Né è

---

[30] D'Alatri, *L'Inquisizione*, 44s.

[31] Benedetto XI, *Gravem dilectorum*, 1304 marzo 11 : gli inquisitori 'officium suum in illis partibus taliter studeant exercere, quod ad sedem apostolicam occasione processuum ab ipsis factorum clamor ulterius non ascendat'. Lo Sbaraglia (*Bullarium franciscanum*, V, p. 9 nota 6) ritiene che la bolla fosse indirizzata agli inquisitori domenicani, i quali erano subentrati ai francescani. Cf. anche Gerolamo Biscaro, 'Eretici ed inquisitori nella Marca Trevisana (1280-1308)', *Archivio Veneto*, 11 (1932),

meno sintomatico il fatto che Innocenzo IV, il vero organizzatore della inquisizione in Italia, riuscisse a rivolgere contro i fautori del defunto Federico II la legislazione antieretica che l'ancora giovane imperatore, sia pure sotto la spinta della curia romana, aveva promulgata contro gli eterodossi [32].

Basti quest'accenno per indicare quanto grande fosse il numero di coloro che potevano essere perseguiti come eretici, in un tempo in cui si era estremamente facili a dire *eretico* chiunque *come* eretico fosse stato condannato o anche soltanto imputato [33].

'Eresie inquisitoriali'

Man mano che ci si inoltra nella seconda metà del Duecento, si nota come gli inquisitori, per commissione della curia romana oppure di propria iniziativa, estendono la loro competenza a nuove figure di reato. Nel 1259 Alessandro IV, interpellato dagli inquisitori umbri a proposito della divinazione e del sortilegio, aveva limitato il loro intervento al solo caso in cui dette pratiche 'manifeste saperent haeresim', volendo che il 'negotium Fidei, quod summe privilegiatum existit, per occupationes alias non debeat impediri' [34]. Ma è sintomatico che la questione venisse proposta; ed anche se non sappiamo per quanto tempo la direttiva papale fu rispettata, è tuttavia accertato che nella prima metà del Trecento gli inquisitori perseguivano correntemente gli imputati per atti di divinazione e di sortilegio [35].

L'interpretazione erronea di un passo qualsiasi della sacra Scrittura veniva senz'altro bollata come eresia, e l'esegeta, non importa se ingenuo

---

148-180 (p. 175); Mariano D'Alatri, 'Due inchieste papali sugli inquisitori veneti (1302 e 1308)', *Collectanea Franciscana*, 39 (1969), 172-187 (177).

[32] Thouzellier, *La repressione*, 390s.

[33] Léon Garzend, *L'inquisition et l'hérésie*: *Distinction de l'hérésie théologique et de l'hérésie inquisitoriale à propos de l'affaire Galilée* (Paris, 1912), p. 99.

[34] Alessandro IV, *Quod super nonnulis*, 1258 dic. 13 : *Bullarium franciscanum*, II, 317.

[35] Mariano D'Alatri, 'L'inquisizione a Firenze negli anni 1344/46 da un'istruttoria contro Pietro da L'Aquila' in *Miscellanea Melchor de Pobladura*, a cura di Isidorus a Villapadierna, *Bibliotheca Seraphico-Capuccina*, 23-24 (Roma, 1964), I, 225-249 (233-235). Anche l'immoralità veniva perseguita non in quanto peccato (adulterio, bigamia ecc.), ma per il presunto errore mentale che ne costituiva il fondamento (concetto errato circa la natura del matrimonio). Le pene, però, erano piú leggere che nel caso in cui si fosse trattato di vera eresia : cf. Henry Kamen, *L'inquisizione spagnola* (Milano, 1966), 217-228.

oppure in mala fede, doveva rispondere dinanzi all'inquisitore. Cito il caso del sangimignanese Bonaccorso di Diotisalvi, che dal domenicano fra Ildino era stato accusato di aver detto in pubblico che un uomo coniugato può abbandonare la propria moglie, anche nolente, per entrare in un Ordine religioso. Il povero uomo fu assolto soltanto perché si scusò dicendo di avere mal compreso il passo di san Matteo e di essere incorso nell'errore per semplicità [36]. Maestro Roberto di Tarquinia, nel 1220, è dal vescovo Raniero citato e quindi scomunicato come eretico, perché — come risulta da un capitolo della citazione — 'pervertit auctoritatem apostoli ubi dicit : Raptus fuit ad tertium celum ecc.' Ma l'interpretazione di maestro Roberto, più che ereticale, è beffarda e decisamente oscena [37].

Non in forza di uno speciale incarico [38], ma in quanto inquisitori dell'eretica pravità, i titolari dell'ufficio della fede perseguivano i bestemmiatori. Per l'ambiente bolognese (ma la maggior parte degli imputati sono oriundi fiorentini) ne ricorda parecchi il Dupré Theseider nello studio già segnalato. In alcuni casi si tratta di volgari bestemmie, pronunziate nell'indignazione; altre denunciano un filone d'incredulità e di epicureismo; altre infine sono di sicura matrice eretica [39]. In ogni caso, difettava, in chi le proferiva, una esplicita, consapevole ed ostinata adesione a dottrine eterodosse. Per riscontrarvi l'eresia, bisogna dedurla o dall'affermazione blasfema o dalla vita poco esemplare del 'maldicente'.

In alcuni casi, il giudice della fede, sempre nella sua veste di 'inquisitor haereticae pravitatis', motiva in modo vago le pene da lui imposte, crediamo in difetto di una provata mancanza contro l'ortodossia. Così, sulla fine del Duecento, il domenicano fra Lanfranco impone una multa di 12 libbre ad Enrico de Calvo, 'qui multa commiserat et falso accusaverat quendam' [40], e, nel 1293, condanna Uberto di Valenza 'propter culpas suas et periuria' [41]. Il domenicano fra Manfredo da Parma multa diversi preti con motivazioni come questa : 'occasione

[36] D'Alatri, *L'inquisizione*, p. 60.

[37] Pietro Egidi, 'L'Archivio della cattedrale di Viterbo', *Bullettino dell'Istituto Storico Italiano*, 27 (1906), 116.

[38] Per citare qualche esempio, gli inquisotori furono incaricati di perseguire i truffatori che andavano predicando false indulgenze, di riconciliare e assolvere comuni, di procedere contro i cristiani che passavano all'ebraismo e contro gli ebrei che tornavano all'antica loro fede.

[39] Dupré Theseider, *L'eresia*. 426-430.

[40] Biscaro, *Inquisitori*, p. 62.

[41] Biscaro, *Inquisitori*, p. 60.

excessus sui' [42]. Altre volte, come nel caso dell'eretica Imilia, moglie del giudice Donazio di Mortara, viene invece specificato : 'propter culpas suas commissas in heresi'[43]. La condanna per lo spergiuro è abbastanza frequente e, a volte, comporta una distinta multa che va ad aggiungersi a quella imposta per l'eresia [44].

Segnalo infine alcuni casi, verificatisi anch'essi sullo scorcio del Duecento, nei quali gli inquisitori perseguono 'tanquam haereticos' o 'pro haereticis' alcuni gruppi di fedeli a motivo della loro insubordinazione all'autorità ecclesiastica, ma che in nessun modo si erano macchiati di delitti contro l'ortodossia. I fatti sono noti.

1) I Colonna, in conflitto con Bonifacio VIII, nella bolla *Nuper Iacobum* (9 luglio 1297) sono detti scismatici e blasfemi; il papa li vuole 'tanquam haereticos puniendos... secundum constitutiones a quondam Friderico olim Romanorum Imperatore editas contra haereticos, fautores, et receptatores eorum [...] necnon iuxta traditam vobis [inquisitoribus] formam ab Apostolica Sede exequendi Inquisitionis officium contra haereticos...' [45].

2) Un altro gruppo lo costituiscono 'nonnulli diversarum Religionum Apostatae, necnon et alii nullam de approbatis Religionibus professi, qui *Bizochi*, seu alio nomine se appellant' : contro di essi, che vanno 'dogmatizando palam diversos haereticae pravitatis errores', è inviato l'inquisitore francescano Matteo da Chieti, il quale deve agire 'tanquam contra haereticos', non escluso il ricorso al braccio secolare [46].

3) Finalmente, l'inquisitore francescano Angelo da Rieti, nel corso di un pubblico parlamento celebrato a Viterbo il 23 aprile 1286, minaccia di processare come eretico chiunque avesse osato opporsi alla ratifica della composizione o pace da lui stesso promossa tra il Comune di Viterbo e gli Orsini : 'haberet illum vel illos pro hereticis et impeditoribus officii inquisitionis, et quod procederet contra eum vel illos tanquam contra hereticos' [47]. Come di fatto avvenne, poiché fu aperto un processo per eresia contro 500 cittadini viterbesi, che solo nel 1304 videro accolta, da parte della curia romana, un'istanza di proscioglimento.

---

[42] Biscaro, *Inquisitori*, p. 88.

[43] Biscaro, *Inquisitori*, p. 60.

[44] D'Alatri, *Archivio, offici e titolari dell'inquisizione*, 186s.

[45] *Bullarium franciscanum*, IV, 440s.

[46] *Bullarium franscicanum*, IV, 435s.

[47] D'Alatri, 'Un mastodontico processo per eresia a Viterbo nello scorcio del Duecento', *Collectanea Franciscana*, 42 (1972), 299-308 (306).

Ora, si può osservare che le formule 'tanquam haereticos' e 'pro haereticis', avulse dal contesto, potrebbero essere interpretate : 'come se si trattasse di eretici', o se fossero eretici, il che significherebbe che, pur non trattandosi di eresia, il giudice della fede era autorizzato a adottare contro gli imputati la procedura in uso presso il tribunale della fede. Cosí intese, è superfluo rilevarlo, le predette formule in nessun modo denunzierebbero la presenza di un'eresia, non importa se reale oppure creduta e gabellata come tale. Ma se si tiene conto del contesto storico, non c'è dubbio che le espressioni 'tanquam haereticos' e 'pro haereticis' vadano intese : 'in quanto eretici, come eretici'.

Infatti, la bolla contro i pinzocheri si apre con un esordio circa la ortodossia : 'Incrementum catholicae Fidei'; [48] a riguardo dei Colonna, si può citare la difesa che, sotto l'aspetto legale, fece di essi il giudice bolognese Filippo q. d. Aldevrandini de Sala, il quale li dichiara ingiustamente scomunicati e condannati, 'quia non commiserant propter quod deberent vel possent excommunicari vel heretici pronuntiari' [49]. Infine, i Viterbesi, contro i quali fra Angelo e i suoi successori nell'ufficio aprono un processo per eresia, tengono a ribadire la loro provata ortodossia : 'quantumcumque homines essent catholici et fideles'; e Giovanni, camerario di Benedetto XI, nell'ordinare la revisione del processo, afferma di voler riportare l'ufficio dell'inquisizione al compito per cui era stato istituito, e cioè : 'ad extirpandam hereticam dampnatam nequitiam, non ad confundendam simplicium veritatem' [50].

Se ce ne fosse bisogno, una riprova dell'esattezza di questa interpretazione si potrebbe dedurre da due lettere che, negli anni 1300 e 1301, il card. Matteo d'Acquasparta indirizzava una agli inquisitori toscani e l'altra a fra Grimaldo da Prato, per autorizzarli a procedere contro alcuni chierici e laici che truffavano il popolo predicando false indulgenze. Ebbene, il legato nota esplicitamente, sia pure in forma dubitativa, che quantunque ciò esula, forse, dalla loro competenza [51], possono nondimeno procedere contro quei truffatori usando gli attrezzi del loro mestiere, vogliam dire la procedura inquisitoriale, non escluso il

---

[48] *Bullarium franciscanum*, IV, 435.
[49] Dupré Theseider, *L'eresia*, p. 424.
[50] D'Alatri, *Un mastodontico processo*, 307s.
[51] '...presentium tenore concedimus, commictimus et mandamus, quatenus, si forsitan se ad hec vestrum expresse officium non extendat, auctoritate nostra possitis...' : Livario Oliger, 'Alcuni documenti per la storia dell'inquisizione francescana', in *Toscana e nell'Umbria (1272-1324)*, *Studi Francescani*, 28 (1931), p. 195.

ricorso al braccio secolare [52]. Ma, altrimenti che nei casi sopra citati, nelle lettere di Matteo non si trova alcun accenno all'eresia, e tanto meno v'è l'invito a perseguire i predicatori delle indulgenze 'tanquam haereticos' o 'pro haereticis'.

Bisogna perciò prendere atto che sia le bolle bonifaciane, sia l'inquisitore frate Angelo intendessero parlare di eresia, anche se, d'altra parte, è chiaro che in nessun modo fosse in ballo l'alternativa tra ortodossia e eterodossia. A che genere di eresia, quindi, essi alludevano?

Il Dupré Theseider [53] parla di un'eresia perseguita dagli inquisitori, la quale può essere configurata come 'lesa maestà ecclesiastica', in quanto porta a un difetto di riverenza verso le 'somme chiavi' ed i suoi rappresentanti, il clero in genere e piú specialmente gli ordini mendicanti [54], soprattutto nei luoghi dove l'uno o l'altro di essi esercitava l'inquisizione.

Eresia, un termine vago

Ora, è innegabile che gran parte dell'attività svolta dall'inquisizione dugentesca in Italia è coinquinata dalla politica. Ma, anche quando l'inquisitore persegue — il piú delle volte, però, sarebbe piú esatto dire che è strumentalizzato per perseguire — traguardi politici, egli parte da presupposti religiosi. E, se si tien conto degli uomini e dell'ambiente, non era davvero difficile trovare motivi piú o meno validi per agire su terreno religioso, anche se con ciò — e, pensiamo, non senza motivo — il concetto di eresia diventava quasi necessariamente piú elastico, coinvolgendo sempre nove figure di reato. Cosí che non venivano perseguiti come eretici soltanto catari, valdesi, poveri lombardi, apostolici, dolciniani e guglielmiti col loro seguito di simpatizzanti e favoreggiatori, — ma anche bestemmiatori, spergiuri, increduli, usurai, trasgressori della morale sessuale, divinatori e, infine, la variopinta e numerosa schiera dei contestatori dell'autorità ecclesiastica a tutti i livelli e per i piú svariati motivi.

---

[52] '...invocato ad hoc, si opus fuerit, auxilio brachii secularis' : L. Oliger, *Alcuni documenti*, p. 195.

[53] Dupré Theseider, *L'eresia*, p. 396.

[54] Troviamo proteste di questo genere : è ingiusto che 'quicumque blasfemat fratribus excommunicatus est' : Dupré Theseider, *L'eresia*, p. 415; nel 1300 frate Lanfranco va a Vercelli 'occasione cuiusdam proposti S. Agathe qui dixerat verba que sonabant heresim contraria d. pape, et quia iniurabat fratribus nostris' : Biscaro, *Inquisitori*, p. 78.

Perciò, il concetto di 'eresia' che sorregge l'attività dell'inquisizione è diverso, e molto più ampio, di quello che ne fornisce la teologia, cosí che è necessario parlare di una 'eresia inquisitoriale'. Infatti, alcune delle 'eresie' perseguite dall'inquisizione difettano : 1) della *componente oggettiva* (negazione d'una verità rivelata, che la Chiesa propone a credere); 2) della *consapevolezza* del presunto eretico; e 3) della *ostinata adesione* del medesimo a una dottrina eterodossa. L'unico elemento sempre presente è l'insubordinazione all'autorità ecclesiastica, impersonata spesso da alcuni suoi rappresentanti più o meno qualificati. E ciò spiega, almeno in parte, il duro trattamento che gli inquisitori riservano ai contumaci, colpevoli, a loro dire, di rigettare il medico e la medicina!

Tutto questo, è ovvio, non facilita la comprensione o puntualizzazione del concetto di eresia, anche se etichettata con l'aggettivo di 'inquisitoriale'. Ma bisogna tener presente il fenomeno, che — e pure questo sembra ovvio — dovette in qualche modo essere il riflesso della indeterminatezza teologica del concetto, appunto, di eresia.

A questo proposito, mi sia consentito di citare una fonte estranea all'inquisizione, ma che mette a fuoco gli equivoci a cui il termine di eresia si prestava anche al di fuori di questa discutibile e discussa istituzione politico-ecclesiastica per la eliminazione d'eretici ed eresie.

Sul suo letto di morte, l'arcivescovo di Lincoln Roberto Grossatesta, rivolgendosi al frate domenicano Giovanni di S. Egidio che l'assisteva, avviava un importante discorso sull'eresia. Più che per la definizione da lui data 'Haeresis est sententia humano sensu electa, Scripturae Sacrae contraria, palam edocta, pertinaciter defensa'[55], il discorso è interessante per le applicazioni che il dottissimo e zelante vescovo ne deduce. Rinuncio a tradurre il brano, poiché sono certo che ne snerverei la forza argomentativa. Una volta enunziata la definizione, Roberto

> consequenter subjunxit, reprehendens praelatos maxime Romanos, qui consanguineis suis indignis, aetate et scientia insufficientibus, curam committunt animarum : 'Dare curam animarum parvulo, sententia est alicujus praelati, humano sensu electa propter carnem vel terrenitatem; et est contraria Scripturae Sanctae, quae prohibet fieri pastores, qui non sunt idonei ad arcendum lupos; et est palam edocta, quia manifeste portatur carta sigillata vel bullata; et est pertinaciter defensa, quia si quis voluerit contradicere, suspenditur, excommu-

[55] Matthaei Parisiensis, Monachi Sancti Albani, *Chronica Majora*, a cura di Henry Richards Luard, Rolls Series (London, 1964), V, 401.

municatur, et super eum praelium sanctificatur. Cui tota definitio haeretici convenit, haereticus est. Sed quisque fidelis tenetur opponere se haeretico quantum potest; qui ergo potest contradicere et non contradicit, peccat et videtur fautor esse, secundum illud Gregorii : "Non caret scrupulo societatis occultae, qui manifesto facinori desinit obviare". Sed fratres tam Minores quam Praedicatores maxime obligantur ad oppositionem contra talem, cum utrique habeant ex officio gratiam praedicandi; sunt ad illud officium per paupertatem liberiores, [et] non solum peccant, si ei non contradicunt, immo fautores ipsius existunt, sicut et Apostolus ad Romanos i. *non solum qui talia agunt, sed qui consentiunt, digni sunt morte.* Potest ergo concludi, quod tam Papa, nisi ab hoc vitio cesset, quam dicti fratres, nisi curiosos se exhibeant ad arcendum talem, digni sunt morte, scilicet perpetua'[56].

Come si vede, Roberto e persecutori degli eretici partono dallo stesso presupposto; adottano il medesimo metodo di argomentazione; l'uno e gli altri trovano nella sacra Scrittura testi per convincere di eresia gli aberranti e i loro fautori. La sola differenza consiste nel bersaglio : il Grossatesta punta il dito accusatore contro il papa, degno, se non si corregge, di 'morte ...perpetua' (la specificazione potrebbe essere polemica, contro la eliminazione fisica inflitta agli eretici : in Inghilterra non fu mai introdotta l'inquisizione medioevale); e, insieme al papa, eran degni di perire tutti i fedeli, e primi tra essi i frati minori e predicatori, qualora si fossero rassegnati a far la parte di cani muti!

Nel suo ragionamento, il vescovo non ammette distinzione tra peccato ed eresia, mostrandosi in tal modo piú radicale degli inquisitori, i quali, per citare un esempio, distinguevano tra usurai e difensori della liceità dell'usura.

Concludendo, mi sembra perfino superfluo rilevare come fosse facile — in mancanza di idee chiare circa l'eresia e sotto l'angoscioso assillo di salvaguardare ad ogni costo la retta fede — notare come eretico chiunque (un peccatore, un ingenuo, un debole oppure uno forse troppo prudente per cacciarsi nei guai), in un tempo nel quale la ortodossia era considerata il bene supremo per l'individuo e per la società, e in cui, senza di essa, si era, di diritto e di fatto, banditi da quella grande patria ideale che era ritenuta la *Christianitas*; e, circostanze permettendolo, si rimaneva privati di ogni diritto, non escluso quello alla vita, e nel modo piú atroce : col rogo.

[56] Matthaei Parisiensis, *Chronica Majora*, V, 400-402.

INDEX NOMINUM PROPRIORUM

Hic uno alphabeti ordine disposita sequuntur omnia antiquitatis et medii aevi nomina propria, tum virorum et mulierum, tum institutionum et librorum, quae in variis huius voluminis commentationibus allata sunt.

In orthographicis certas, quantum fieri poterat, secuti sumus rationes, innisi optimae notae libris, quales sunt indices *Thesauri linguae Latinae, Novi glossarii mediae latinitatis*, lexicorum a *Liddell & Scott* et a *Lampe* nuncupatorum, necnon glossarii quod *Mittellateinisches Wörterbuch* Germanice inscribitur. Ceterum quo maiori usui esset noster index, in ancipitibus remissiones adaugere non dubitavimus.

ABELARDUS (Magister Petrus) : 16, 17, 18, 26, 27, 37, 38, 40, 173, 176, 177, 178, 179.

ACCURSIUS FLORENTINUS : 44, 88, 95, 96.

ADELA, Flandriae Comitissa : 108.

ADEMARUS CABANNENSIS : 104.

AIMERICUS MONTIS REGALIS (de Montréal) : 198.

ALAIN DE LILLE : v. ALANUS DE INSULIS.

ALANUS ANGLICUS : 68, 69, 70.

ALANUS DE INSULIS : 110, 138, 166, 179, 180, 198, 211.
De fide catholica contra hereticos : 179, 180, 198, 211.
Summa de arte predicatoria : 110.

ALBANENSES (Cathari) : 184.

ALBERICUS TRIUM FONTIUM : 200.

ALBERTUS MAGNUS : 194, 195, 196.
Summa de creaturis : 194, 195.
Summa theologiae : 194-196.

ALBIGENSES : 131, 135, 141, 198-210 passim.

ALEXANDER II, papa : 29, 30, 167, 168.

ALEXANDER III, papa, v.et. ROLANDUS BANDINELLUS : 1, 36, 107, 114, 118, 119, 121, 122, 123, 130, 131, 141.

ALEXANDER IV, papa : 214, 218.

ALEXANDER APHRODISIENSIS : 196.

ALEXIOS I KOMNENOS, imperator Byzantinus : 153.

ALIOTTO DELL'ACCONSIATO DI FUCECCHIO : 214.

AL KINDI : 186.

AMALRICUS DE BÈNE : 191-196 passim.

AMAURY : v. AMALRICUS.

AMBROSIUS MEDIOLANENSIS : 13, 31, 32, 61, 173.

ANACLETUS, schismaticus : 36.

ANDREAS STRUMENSIS : 169.
Vita Arialdi : 169.

ANGELO DA RIETI OFM, inquisitor : 220-222.

ANSELMUS ALEXANDRINUS : 186.
Tractatus de hereticis : 186.

ANSELMUS CANTUARIENSIS : 176-177.
Epistola ad Lanfrancum : 176.
De incarnatione Verbi : 177.
Proslogium : 177.

ANSELMUS HAVELBERGENSIS : 12, 40, 41, 157, 166.
Dialogi : 41, 157, 166.

ANSELMUS LEODIENSIS, *Gesta* : 10.

ANSELMUS LUCENSIS (de Lucca) : 60, 62, 63, 85, 114, 115, 120.
Collectio canonum : 60, 114.
Liber contra Wibertum : 114.

Apokrifen Letopis (*Chronicon apocryphum*) : 155.

APOSTOLICI : 214, 222.

ARCADIUS, imperator : 85, 89, 91.

ARCHENFRED : 24.

AREFASTUS : 104.

ARIALDUS : 167-170 passim.

ARIANI : 34, 153, 198.

ARISTOTELES : 175, 179, 185, 187, 196.

ARIUS : 12, 13, 17.

ARMANNO PUNGILUPO : 212, 215, 216.
ARNALDISTAE : 124.
ARNO REICHERSBERGENSIS : 35, 39.
  Apologeticus contra Folcmarum : 39.
  Hexaemeron : 40.
  Scutum canonicorum : 35, 39.
ARNOLDUS-AMALRICH CISTERCIENSIS : 133.
ARNOLDUS DE BRIXIA : 17, 35, 36, 128, 177.
ARNULFUS MEDIOLANENSIS : 168, 169, 171.
ASSIZE OF CLARENDON : 11.
AUBRY DES TROIS-FONTAINES : V. ALBERICUS TRIUM FONTIUM.
AUGUSTINUS HIPPONENSIS : 9, 10, 12, 13, 16, 24, 26, 33, 51, 52, 112, 114-118 passim, 127, 133, 140, 143, 173, 188, 189.
  De civitate Dei : 9.
  De utilitate credendi : 9.
AVENCEBROL : 185, 186.
  Fons vitae : 185.
AVICENNA : 3.
AZO PORCIUS : 44, 86, 90, 93, 95, 96.
BARTHOLOMAEUS BRIXIENSIS : 44, 48.
BARTHOLOMAEUS SENENSIS OFM, Inquisitor : 215.
BASILEIOS, praedicator Bogomilus : 149, 153.
BASILIUS MAGNUS : 145.
  Hexaemeron : 145.
BEGGINI, BEGGINAE : 210.
BENEDICTUS XI, papa : 217.
BENEDICTUS NURSIUS : 15, 158.
  Regula : 158.
BERENGARIUS TURONENSIS : 175, 176.
  De sacra coena adversus Lanfrancum : 175, 176.
BERNARDUS DE BOTONE PARMENSIS : 44, 48, 55, 74, 86, 87, 140.
BERNARDUS CLARAEVALLENSIS : 12-26 passim, 27, 34, 35, 36, 38, 39, 109, 111, 118, 119, 126, 130, 177, 178.
  De consideratione : 15.
  De gradibus humilitatis : 14.
  Epistole : 16, 17, 22-25 passim, 177, 178.
  Parabole : 15.
  Sententie : 15, 16, 25.
  Sermones super Canticum : 13, 14, 18-24 passim.
  Sermones de temporibus : 12, 13.
  Vita S. Malachie : 14.
BERNARDUS CONSTANTIENSIS : 32.
  Liber canonum contra Heinricum IV : 32.
BERNARDUS DE FONTCAUDE : V. BERNARDUS FONTIS CALIDI.
BERNARDUS FONTIS CALIDI : 165, 166.
BERNARDUS PAPIENSIS : 49, 51, 53, 57, 82, 84, 138, 140.
BERNARDUS PARMENSIS : V. BERNARDUS DE BOTONE PARMENSIS.
BERNARDUS PRIM : 133, 136.
BERNARDUS SAISSET APAMIENSIS (de Pamiers) : 209.
BERNARDUS DE THIRON : 161.
BERNHARD DER SACHSE : V. BERNARDUS CONSTANTIENSIS.
BERNOLD DER SCHWABE : V. BERNOLDUS CONSTANTIENSIS.
BERNOLDUS CONSTANTIENSIS : 32, 120, 161.
  Chronicon : 161.
BÉROUL : 5.
  Tristan : 5.
BIZOCHI (secta haeretica) : 220.
BOGOMIL : 148, 149, 153, 154.
BOGOMILI : 144-156 passim.
BONIFATIUS VIII, papa : 100, 220.
BONIZO SUTRINUS (PLACENTINUS) : 32, 170, 171.
BORIL, rex Bulgariae : 150, 153.
BORIS, princeps Bulgariae : 144.
BRACTON : V. HENRICUS DE BRACTON.
BRUNO QUERFURTENSIS : 159.
  Vita quinque fratrum : 159.
BRUNO SIGNINUS (de Segni) : 100, 101.
BURCHARDUS WORMATIENSIS : 85.
CADALUS PARMENSIS, antipapa HONORIUS II : 36, 63.
CAELESTINUS I, papa : 84, 86.
CAESARIUS HEISTERBACENSIS : 193.
CAPELLO DI CHIA (haereticus) : 217.

Capitulum Angilramni : 60.
CARO D'AREZZO OFM, inquisitor : 214.
CAROLUS MAGNUS : 6.
CATHARI : 1, 2, 4, 11, 18-24 passim, 25, 27, 44, 83, 98, 101, 109, 122-125, 130, 144, 155, 179-187 passim, 198-224 passim.
Chronicon Laudunense : 107.
CLEMENS II, papa : 29.
CLEMENS III, antipapa : 101.
CLEMENS ALEXANDRINUS : 182.
CLEMENS DE OCHRIDA SEU LYCHNIDIENSIS : 146, 147.
CONCILIUM LATERANENSE III, a. 1179 : 9.
CONCORENSES (Cathari) idem ac GARATENSES.
CONRADUS SALISBURGENSIS : 27.
CONSTANTINUS CHRISOMALAS (Bogomilus) : 149.
CONSTANTINUS PRESLAVENSIS (Bulgaria) : 147.
CUNO RATISBONENSIS : 27.
CYPRIANUS CARTHAGINIENSIS : 63.
CYRILLUS (sanctus) : 146, 147.
DAMASUS I, papa : 54, 55.
DAMASUS (decretalista) : 49, 50.
DAVID DE DINANDO : 194, 195, 196.
Quaternuli : 194, 195.
De heresi Catharorum in Lombardia : 183, 184.
DEUSDEDIT, cardinalis : 62, 63.
Dialogus inter Cluniacensem monachum et Cisterciensem : 164.
DIEGO DE OSMA : 130, 134, 206.
DOLCINIANI : 214, 222.
DOMINICUS (sanctus) : 134, 206.
DONATISTAE : 89, 114, 115.
DONATUS : 114.
DURANDUS DE ALBI : 199.
DURANDUS DE HUESCA : 133, 180, 181, 182, 184.
Liber Antiheresis : 180.
Liber contra Manicheos : 180-182.
DURANDUS DE OSCA : v. DURANDUS DE HUESCA.
EBERHARDUS BAMBERGENSIS ep. : 37.
EKKEBERTUS SCHONAUGIENSIS : 2, 4.

Sermones contra Catharos : 2.
Elegantius in iure diuino seu Coloniensis : v. *Summa Coloniensis*.
EMMERICH II HUNGARIAE : 135.
EON DE STELLA : 1, 40.
EPICURII : 187.
EPIPHANIUS SALAMINUS ep. : 182.
ERLEMBALDUS MEDIOLANENSIS : 35, 167.
EUGENIUS III, papa : 15, 36.
EUGIBALDUS, eremita : 160, 162.
EUNOMIUS : 188.
EUSTATHIOS : 150.
EUTHYMIOS DE AKMONIA, monachus Byzantinus : 149-151.
EUTHYMIOS ZYGABENOS, theologus Byzantinus : 149, 150, 155.
Panoplia dogmatica : 149, 150, 154.
EVERWINUS STEINFELDENSIS : 18, 20.
EZZELINO DA ROMANO, haereticus : 217.
FACUNDUS HERMIANENSIS : 18.
Pro defensione trium capitulorum : 18.
FAUSTUS REIENSIS : 188.
FOLMARUS TRIEFENSTENIENSIS : 37-39.
FRANCISCUS ASSISIENSIS : 107, 108, 121, 216.
FRIDERICUS I BARBAROSSA : 83.
FRIDERICUS II, imperator : 73, 75, 76, 77, 79, 88, 97, 98, 137, 141, 218.
FULCO, ep. Tolosanus : 206.
GALTERIUS DE RAVENNA : 28.
GALTERIUS SANCTI VICTORIS : 173, 174, 176.
Contra quatuor Labyrinthos Francie : 173, 174, 176.
GARATENSES (Cathari) id. ac CONCORENSES : 184, 185.
GARATHUS CONCORENSIS, Episc. catharus : 184.
GAUFRIDUS D'ABLIS : 204, 208.
GAUFRIDUS AUTISSIODORENSIS : 24.
Vita S. Bernardi : 24.
GAUFRIDUS PARISIENSIS : 106.
GAUFRIDUS VINDOCINENSIS (de Vendôme) : 100.
GÉBOUIN DE TROYES : v. GEBUINUS AUGUSTOBONENSIS.
GEBUINUS AUGUSTOBONENSIS : 12.

GEOFFROY D'ABLIS : v. GAUFRIDUS D'ABLIS.

GEOFFROY D'AUXERRE : v. GAUFRIDUS AUTISSIODORENSIS.

GERARDUS CAMERACENSIS : 10.

GERHOHUS REICHERSBERGENSIS : 27-41 passim, 162.
De aedificio Dei : 29, 30.
De investigatione Antichristi : 36, 37.
De Simoniacis : 31, 34.
Dialogus : 30, 35, 39.
Liber contra duas haereses : 37, 38.
Tractatus et libelli : 31, 37.

GERMANUS patriarcha : 150.

GERVASIUS DOROBORNENSIS s. CANTUARIENSIS : 2.
Chronicon : 2.

Gesta Pontificum Cenomanensium : 2.

Gesta synodi Aurelianensis : 2, 10.

GILBERTUS PORRETANUS : 24, 26, 37, 38, 40, 173.

GIOVANNI, camerarius Benedicti XI : 221.

GIRALDUS SALESIUS (de Sales) : 161.

GNOSTICI : 182, 183, 184, 186, 197.

GOFFREDUS TRANENSIS : 44, 46, 48, 53, 70, 81, 84, 87, 89.
Summa in titulos decretalium : 44, 46.
Summa titulorum : 53.

GRATIANUS : 42-103 passim, 111-143 passim.
Concordia discordantium canonum : 42-143 passim.

GREGORIUS I MAGNUS, papa : 13, 16, 30, 61, 119, 179.

GREGORIUS IV, papa : 58.

GREGORIUS VII, papa : 29-32, 35, 58, 60-64, 78, 80, 105, 106, 108, 120, 160-162, 166.
Dictatus papae : 32, 61-63.

GREGORIUS IX, papa : 44, 73, 75-77, 79, 87, 99, 135, 137, 140, 142, 212.

GREGORIUS NYSSENUS : 189.

GRIMALDO DA PRATO : 221.

GUGLIELMITI : 214, 222.

GUIBERT DE NOGENT : v. GUIBERTUS NOVIGENTENSIS.

GUIBERTUS : v. et. WIBERTUS.

GUIBERTUS NOVIGENTENSIS : 2, 3, 8, 10, 36.
De vita sua : 2, 8.

GUIDO ARETINUS : 29.

GUIDO ASSISIENSIS episc. : 107.

GUIDO DE BAYSIO : 65, 69.
Rosarium : 65, 69.

GUILLAUME DE PUYLAURENS : v. GUILLELMUS DE PODIO LAURENTII.

GUILLELMUS CONCHENSIS : 3, 4, 5, 6, 10, 11, 177.
De philosophia mundi : 6.

GUILLELMUS DURANTI : 96, 99.

GUILLELMUS HIRSAUGIENSIS : 31, 32.

GUILLELMUS MONACHUS : v. GUILLELMUS CONCHENSIS.

GUILLELMUS NEUBRIGENSIS (GUILLELMUS PARVUS) : 1, 5, 10, 11.
Historia rerum Anglicarum : 1.
Vita Norberti : 1.

GUILLELMUS PELLISSON : 202, 206.
Chronique : 202.

GUILLELMUS PICTAVIENSIS : 191.

GUILLELMUS DE PODIO LAURENTII : 199, 200, 203, 206, 209.

GUILLELMUS RAYMUNDUS, inquisitor : 199.

GUILLELMUS DE SANCTO THEODORICO : 177, 178.
De erroribus Guillelmi de Conchis : 177.
Disputatio adversus Petrum Abelardum : 177.
Epistola ad S. Bernardum : 177, 178.

GUILLELMUS TUDELENSIS : 198.

GUNTHARIUS COLONIENSIS ep. : 59.

HADRIANUS IV, papa : 36, 37.

HAIMERICH : 111.

HENRICIANI : 23, 109.

HENRICUS II, rex Angliae : 1, 6.

HENRICUS IV, imperator : 32, 166.

HENRICUS ALBANENSIS : 123.

HENRICUS DE BRACTON : 7.

HENRICUS CENOMANENSIS : 162, 163, 164.

HENRICUS CLAREVALLENSIS : 2.
Epistulae : 2.

HENRICUS LAUSANENSIS : 1-5 passim, 23, 109.

HENRICUS REMENSIS : 122, 131.

HENRICUS DE SEGUSIA : v. HOSTIENSIS.

HIERONYMUS (sanctus) : 13, 16, 51, 52, 54, 63, 112, 124, 159.
Epistulae : 159.

HILARIUS PICTAVIENSIS : 13, 173.

HILDEBERTUS CENOMANENSIS : 1, 162.

HILDEBERTUS DE LAVARDIN, episc. Cenomanensis : v. HILD. CENOMANENSIS.

HIPPOLYTUS ROMANUS : 172, 182.
Refutatio omnium haeresium (Philoso-phoumena) : 172.

HIRSAU (monachi vagantes de) : 161.

HONORIUS II, antipapa : v. CADALUS PARMENSIS.

HONORIUS III, papa : 74, 75, 78, 188, 189.
Registrum : 188.

HONORIUS, imperator : 85, 89, 91.

HONORIUS AUGUSTODUNENSIS : 6.

HOSTIENSIS (Henricus de Segusia) : 44, 50, 55, 70, 74, 75, 77, 79, 82, 92, 93, 94, 95, 99, 141, 142.
Apparatus sive Lectura : 77.
Summa aurea : 44, 50, 55, 70, 93.

HRABANUS MAURUS : 4.
De universo : 4.

HUGO SANCTI VICTORIS : 22, 33, 111, 119.

HUGUCCIO DE PISA : v. UGUTIO PISANUS.

HUMBERTUS ep. SILVAE CANDIDAE : 120.
Adversus Simoniacos : 120.

HUMILIATI : 125, 131, 133, 164, 165.

HUMILIATI DE LUGDUNO : v. PAUPERES DE LUGDUNO.

IAMBLICHUS : 187.

IGNATIUS CONSTANTINOPOLITANUS, patriarcha : 81, 84.

ILDEFONSE DE SAINT-GILLES (comte) : 23.

INNOCENTIUS I, papa : 54, 55.

INNOCENTIUS II, papa : 17, 28, 36, 38, 40, 177, 179.
Epistola contra Abaelardum et Arnoldum de Briscia : 177, 179.

INNOCENTIUS III, papa : 57, 71, 72, 73, 75, 88, 89, 90, 92, 93, 94, 101, 102, 107, 126-141 passim, 165, 180, 192, 194.
De miseria humanae conditionis : 133.

INNOCENTIUS IV, papa (v. et. SINIBALDUS FLISCUS) : 44, 76-79 passim, 88, 96, 141, 218.

IRENAEUS LUGDUNENSIS : 182.

ISIDORUS HISPALENSIS : 2, 3, 5, 113, 159.
Origines sive Etymologiae : 2, 3, 5.
Regula monachorum : 160.

IVO CARNOTENSIS : 84, 85, 101, 120.
Panormia : 120.

JACOBUS DE FURNO (alias Fornerii) : 200-210 passim.
Registrum : 200-210 passim.

JACQUES FOURNIER : v. JACOBUS DE FURNO.

JOACHIM DE FLORE (vel Fiore) : 12.

JOHANNES ANDREAE : 100.

JOHANNES DAMASCENUS : 173.

JOHANNES EXARCHA (Bulgarus) : 145.
Schestodnev (= Liber sex dierum) : 145.

JOHANNES FAVENTINUS : 57.

JOHANNES GRATIANUS : v. GRATIANUS.

JOHANNES GUALBERTUS : 160, 161.

JOHANNES DE LUGIO : 184, 185, 186.
Liber de duobus principiis : 184, 185.

JOHANNES MINUTUS : 168.

JOHANNES DE ORVIETO : 2.

JOHANNES A S. AEGIDIO : 223.

JOHANNES A S. PAULO, cardinalis : 135.

JOHANNES SCOTUS ERIGENA : 188-196 passim.
De divina predestinatione : 189.
De divisione nature : 188-194 passim.
Homilia in prologum evangelii secundum Johannem : 189.
Versio operum s. Dionysii Areopagitae : 189.

JOHANNES TEUTONICUS : 44, 48, 54, 70, 71, 80, 84, 87, 93, 102, 120, 121, 137, 138, 139, 140, 142.

JOSEPHINI : 124.

JUSTINIANUS, imperator : 92, 95.

JUSTINUS MARTYR : 10.

KOSMA, presbyter Bulgarus : 145, 146, 148, 149, 150, 151.

Besedata (= *Sermones*) : 145, 149, 150, 151.
LANDULFUS COTTA : 169.
LANDULFUS MAIOR MEDIOLANENSIS : 170, 171.
Historia Mediolanensis : 170.
LANFRANCO, O.P., inquisitor : 219, 222.
LANFRANCUS CANTUARIENSIS : 175, 176.
In Pauli epistolas commentarii : 176.
LAURENTIUS HISPANUS : 49, 50, 51, 53, 69, 70, 86, 87, 93, 102.
LEO IV, papa : 59.
LEO IX, papa : 87, 120.
LEO X, papa : 206.
LIBERIUS, papa : 37.
Littera Bononiensis : 42.
LOTHARIUS SIGNINUS, cardinalis : v. INNOCENTIUS III papa.
LUCIUS II, papa : 2, 3.
LUCIUS III, papa : 83, 124, 125, 126, 129, 131, 165.
LUDOVICUS VII, rex : 2.
LUPOLDUS WORMATIENSIS : 73.
MAINARDUS : 168.
MANEGOLDUS LAUTENBACENSIS : 35, 175.
Contra Wolfelmum Coloniensem : 175.
MANFREDO DA PARMA, O.P., inquisitor : 219.
MANI : 2, 21.
MANICHAEI : 9, 10, 11, 21, 26, 89, 90, 113, 148, 150.
MARBODUS REDONENSIS : 162.
MARCUS, episc. Catharorum in Lombardia : 183.
MARINUS DE CARAMANICO : 97.
MATTEO DA CHIETI, O.F.M., inquisitor : 220.
MATTHAEUS D'ACQUASPARTA, cardinalis : 221, 222.
MATTHAEUS PARISIENSIS : 223, 224.
Chronica majora : 223, 224.
MAXIMUS CONFESSOR : 189, 193.
METHODIUS (sanctus) : 146, 147.
MICHAEL, imperator : 81.
MONETA CREMONENSIS : 107.
MONOPHYSITAE : 153, 154.
NEMESIUS : 187, 188.

De natura hominis : 187, 188.
NEO-PLATONICI : 187, 189, 193.
NESTORIANI : 153.
NESTORIUS : 17, 84.
NICOLAITAE : 29-34 passim, 101, 209.
NICOLAUS I, papa : 59, 81, 84, 86, 95.
NICOLAUS II, papa : 29, 30, 31, 62.
NICOLAUS DE CUSA : 193, 194.
Apologiae doctae ignorantiae : 193, 194.
NORBERTUS CENEBENSIS (de Gennep) : 163.
NOVATIANI : 27.
ORIGENES : 182.
OSTIENSIS : v. HOSTIENSIS.
OTLOHUS RATISBONENSIS : 175.
Dialogus de tribus quaestionibus : 175.
OTTO IV, imperator : 72, 73, 75.
OTTO FRISINGENSIS : 12, 40, 41.
Gesta Friderici I imperatoris : 40.
OTTO OSTIENSIS : 32.
PASCHALIS II, papa : 29.
PASSAGINI : 124.
PATARIA : 35, 105, 106, 124, 198.
PATARIA MEDIOLANENSIS : 62, 161, 167-171 passim.
PAUCAPALEA : 56.
PAUL DE ST. PÈRE : v. PAULUS CARNOTENSIS.
PAULICIANISMUS : 148.
PAULUS BERNRIEDENSIS : 35.
PAULUS CARNOTENSIS : 10, 104, 105.
PAUPERES CATHOLICI : 130, 131, 202.
PAUPERES DE LOMBARDIA : 214, 222.
PAUPERES DE LUGDUNO : 124, 125, 164, 165, 212, 213.
PEIRE CARDENAL : v. PETRUS CARDENAL.
PEIRE VIDAL : v. PETRUS VIDAL
PELAGIANI : 1.
PELAGIUS I, papa : 33.
PELAGIUS, haeresiarcha : 13, 17.
PETAR, monachus Bulgarus : 146.
PETROBRUSIANI : 109, 112.
PETRUS, rex Bulgariae : 144, 148, 153.
PETRUS ABELARDUS : v. ABELARDUS.
PETRUS AMBIANENSIS : 160.
PETRUS ATREBATENSIS : 125.
PETRUS DE BRUIS : 1, 2, 5, 23.

PETRUS CANTOR : 110, 131, 134.
PETRUS CARDENAL : 199, 200, 209.
PETRUS COMESTOR : 110.
PETRUS DAMIANI : 31, 56, 62-67, 72, 77, 101, 120, 174, 175.
  De divina omnipotentia : 174, 175.
  De sancta simplicitate : 174.
  Epistole : 32.
  Opuscula varia : 32.
  Sermo 6, de S. Eleuchadio : 174.
PETRUS DURANDUS, inquisitor : 199.
PETRUS LOMBARDUS : 33, 173.
PETRUS NOVIOMAGENSIS (de Castelnau) : 133.
PETRUS PICTAVIENSIS II : 173.
PETRUS A SANCTO CHRYSOGONO : 2.
PETRUS SELLAN : 202.
PETRUS VENERABILIS CLUNIACENSIS : 1-5 passim, 10, 23, 119.
  Adversus Petrobrusianos hereticos : 1, 4, 119.
PETRUS VIDAL : 200.
PETRUS VINDOBONENSIS : 37, 38, 40.
PHILIPP VON SCHWABEN, Herzog : 73.
PHOTINUS : 13.
PHUNDAGIAGITI : v. BOGOMILI.
PIPPINUS BREVIS, rex : 6.
PLACENTINUS MONTEPESSULANENSIS : 86, 90, 92.
PLACIDUS DE NONANTULA : 100.
PLATO : 183, 187, 188, 193, 195.
PLOTINUS : 182, 183, 193.
PONS ADHÉMAR DE ROUDEILLE, chevalier : 206.
PORPHYRIUS : 175.
PRISCILLIANISTAE : 90.
PSEUDO-DIONYSIUS : 189, 194.
PSEUDO-ISIDORUS : 101.
PUBLICANI : 1, 11.
QUIRICO DI S. MINIATO AL MONTE : 212.
RABELAIS : 206.
RADULFUS COGGESHALENSIS : 1.
  Chronicon Anglicanum : 1.
RADULFUS DE FONTFROID : 133.
RADULFUS GLABER : 104.
RAIMUNDUS DE PENAFORTE : 135.
RAIMUNDUS TOLOSENSIS, comes : 2, 3.

RAINERUS SACHONUS : 2, 11, 184, 185, 186, 200.
  Summa de Catharis et pauperibus de Lugduno : 2, 184, 186, 200.
RAINERUS DE VITERBO, cardinalis : 76, 77, 79.
RAMIRDUS CAMERACENSIS : 35, 106.
  Chronicon Sancti Andreae Castri Cameracensis : 106.
RICHARDUS ANGLICUS : 85.
ROBERT LE BOUGRE : 200.
ROBERTUS II, rex : 105.
ROBERTUS DE ARBRISELLO : 8, 161, 162.
ROBERTUS CURSONUS (seu Curtonus) : 134, 191, 194.
ROBERTUS GROSSATESTA : 223, 224.
ROLANDUS BANDINELLUS (papa Alexander III) : 118-123 passim, 127, 129.
  Stroma ex decretorum corpore : 118-123 passim.
ROMUALDUS (sanctus) : 159, 161.
ROTHARIUS, Lombardorum rex : 6.
RUFINUS BONONIENSIS : 56, 57, 82, 121, 123, 124.
RUGGERO CALCAGNI, O.P., inquisitor : 212.
RUPERT VON DEUTZ : v. RUPERTUS TUITIENSIS.
RUPERTUS TUITIENSIS : 30, 31.
SABELLIANI : 34, 153.
SEVERIANUS GAVALSKI (Gabaliensis) : 145.
  Schestodnevi (= *Libri sex dierum*) : 145.
SICARDUS CREMONENSIS : 49, 56, 57.
SIMEON, rex Bulgariae : 146.
SIMON DE BISIGNANO : 56, 57, 65, 69.
SIMON DE MONTFORT : 198.
SIMON TORNACENSIS : 33.
SIMONIA, SIMONIACI : 29-36 passim, 55-58 passim, 80, 100, 114, 119, 120, 121, 134, 162, 168, 169.
SINIBALDUS FLISCUS (Innocentius IV papa) : 141.
STEPHANUS, pseudo-papa : 84.
STEPHANUS, Angliae rex : 7.
STEPHANUS DE BOURBON : 164, 166.

STEPHANUS DE MURETO : 160.

STEPHANUS DE OBAZINE : 7.

STEPHANUS TORNACENSIS : 56, 57.

STOICI : 187.

SULPICIUS SEVERUS : 10.

Summa de Catharis : 2.

Summa Coloniensis : 53, 56, 57, 65.

Summa Monacensis : 56.

Synodus Atrebatensis : 10.

TANCHELINUS SEU TANCHELMUS : 1, 5, 119, 163.

TANCREDUS BONONIENSIS : 46, 47, 53, 55, 81-87 passim, 93, 137-140 passim.

TERTULLIANUS CARTHAGINIENSIS : 172, 182.

   Adversus Hermogenem : 172.

   De praescriptione haereticorum : 172.

THEODATUS AURELIANENSIS : 104.

THEODOSIUS II, imperator : 89.

THEUTGAUD TREVIRENSIS : 59.

THOMAS AQUINAS : 192, 195.

THOMAS DE MARLE : 8.

Tristan : 5.

UDO HILDESHEIMENSIS : 32.

UGUTIO PISANUS : 43, 48, 51, 56, 61, 65-70 passim, 80, 82, 86, 93, 101, 102, 126-129, 134.

URBANUS II, papa : 29, 30.

VALDENSES : v. WALDENSES.

VALDES : v. WALDES.

VICTOR IV, papa : 36.

VICTORINI : 110.

Vie de Saint Alexis : 158.

Vie de Saint Gilles : 158.

VINCENTIUS DONATISTA : 114.

VINCENTIUS HISPANUS : 93, 139, 140.

Vita apostolica : 28-30, 106, 130, 157-166 passim.

Vita s. Hugonis Lincolniensis : 3.

Vita s. Petri Parentinii : 2.

VITALIS DE SAVIGNY : 161.

WALDENSES : 44, 83, 101, 124, 125, 130, 132, 165, 166, 179, 180, 186, 187, 198-210 passim.

WALDES : 107, 108, 121, 124, 126, 136, 164.

WALTHERUS MAP : 110.

   De nugis curialium : 110.

WAZO LEODIENSIS : 10.

WERY GANDAVENSIS : 161.

WIBERTUS : v. et. GUIBERTUS.

WIBERTUS DE RAVENNA, antipapa : 36, 114.

XENOPHANES : 195.

YVES DE CHARTRES : v. IVO CARNOTENSIS.

ZIGABENOS : v. EUTHYMIOS ZYGABENOS.